# The
# Passionate People

What It Means To Be A Jew In America

## by Roger Kahn

A FAWCETT CREST BOOK
Fawcett Publications, Inc., Greenwich, Conn.
Member of American Book Publishers Council, Inc.

Library of Congress Catalog Card Number: 68-14812

Printing History
William Morrow edition published, May 17, 1968
First printing, January 1968
Second printing, March 1968
Third printing, June 1968

Alternate selection of the Mainstream Book Club, August 1968

An excerpt from this book has been published in
*The Saturday Evening Post.*

Grateful acknowledgment is made to:

New Directions Publishing Corporation for permission to translate
and reprint "Mauberley" II, from *Personae* by Ezra Pound.
Copyright 1928, 1954 by Ezra Pound.

Crown Publishers for permission to quote from *Fiddler on the
Roof* by Joseph Stein. Copyright © 1965 by Joseph Stein.

Acum Ltd., Tel-Aviv, for permission to quote from
*Shir Hachalutzim* by Joseph Papiernikov, first published in 1964
in a book of poems in Yiddish entitled *Von Zweiten Breshit.*

First Fawcett Crest printing, February 1970

Published by Fawcett World Library
67 West 44th Street, New York, N.Y. 10036
Printed in the United States of America

To Otto Friedrich

# *Contents*

### PART FOUR

### *Things Profane: A Mercantile Heritage*

### PART FIVE

### *Survivors*

### *An Acknowledgment*

### *Index*

# AUTHOR TO READER

THIS BOOK WAS SUGGESTED AT A LUNCHEON four years ago while an editor and I discussed a range of current topics. It seems to me now that I had wanted to write the book long before, but that may be illusion, wrought by artifice. The best of editors can make a writer take their inspiration as his own.

For months prior to the luncheon, I had been preparing an article for *The Saturday Evening Post* on lives stunted in a Negro ghetto. I remember Harlem with delight, compassion and despair. That day I was closest to the despair.

"Well," the editor said at length, "what do you feel like writing next, if anything?"

As I had wandered Harlem as a white man, I said, I would like to wander Germany as a Jew.

The reaction was terse and professional. "No," the editor said. "The story is not there. It's here."

Nineteen years after Hitler's death it seemed propitious, and more than that, essential, to begin a consideration of Jews in America. Their successes were immense, their freedom was expanding and yet, for many, the fires of the Holocaust burned alive. Soon afterwards, when I set forth again, it was not to wander Hitler's country, but my own.

I have read many forewords that explain precisely how the writer worked and what he suffered to create his books. I believe these pieces, but I seldom care. No one is forced to be a writer. Let me say only that I traveled and prodded and talked and listened and wrote, and have survived.

Technique is another matter I'd rather not discuss. Let all men take the last draft for the first. However, the major portion of this book describes individuals and it is inevitable, and possibly reasonable, for some to ask: Are all these people real?

The essays that follow are nonfictional. The account of the American Jewish Congress convention and a few individuals treated in separate sections are literally drawn from life. But is there actually an Auschwitz survivor named David Nazaretsky, a bottomless dancer named Marilyn Esther Wolf, a driving businessman named Morton Isaiah Applebaum or a desperate German woman named Herta Cohen? The answer is: not to my knowledge.

As I proceeded with research, it became evident that candor and exposure could vigorously be at odds. A man or woman who talked freely, even compulsively, often blanched at the thought of seeing frank words in print.

To set down lives as I truly saw them, I have created new identities for actual people. David and Marilyn and all the rest, specifically excepting Al Rosen, Shecky Green, Judge Harry D. Goldman and the Rev. Dr. Bob Wells, are such creations.

But are they real?

I hope the reader finds them so.

R. K.

# The
# Passionate People

# Part One

## Shadow on a Promised Land

IT IS NOT CANAAN, BUT FOR MANY IT WILL serve. No fierce protective Yahveh oversees and it is true that one is never entirely safe from the *goy*-Philistine, but for Jews —for the loud Babbitts and the agonizing rabbis, for the thin, lovely poets and the great-chested athletes, for the carnivorous makers of films and the pained, smug psychiatrists, for teachers, lawyers, hustlers, actors, doctors, politicians, strip-teasers, tailors, cellists, cabbies and non-representational painters; for raucous women made of brass and soft-eyed ladies in secret love with Byron, for the wild men of The Left and the liars of The Right, for religious fanatics and impassioned atheists, for most of these and most of the rest of that varied, vibrant polyglot labeled (but not defined) as "The Jews," America is the promised land.

Not America ultimately. Not America someday. Not even America soon. America now. This is the place, here, now, where millions of Jewish men and women are living with a freedom and a style beyond what their tormented grandparents knew how to dream. That is a fine thing, and deeply troubling. It is easier to contemplate a promised land than to live in it.

Rabbi Arnold Jacob Wolf, chubby, gentle and scholarly, leads Congregation Solel, a modern light-brick temple in the upper middle-class fastness of Highland Park, forty minutes north of Chicago when the Edens Expressway is clear. "I am," Rabbi Wolf says, with a brief deprecating smile, "a rabbi to Jews who have made it. The people here have the trappings of success." The smile vanishes. "Jews who make it in the United States are in trouble," the rabbi says. "The first six funerals at which I officiated were suicides. In some instances the wife followed the husband; a couple went. Extreme, yes, but if I told you it was unsettling, that would be understating."

Success, counted greatest by those who ne'er succeed, exacts vitiating demands of mind, body and spirit, and success is a basic fact of Jewish-American life. The average Jewish family (if there were one) has lived in the United States for

14

perhaps two generations. Success surrounds and infuses their lives. Success in business; success in educating children; success in entering the most hotly-sought endeavours. Jews are business owners, business managers, professionals, writers and artists. Few are laborers. Virtually none is a farmhand. The group that most closely matches them in standard indices of success has been in America many generations longer. Judged by income, education and occupation, American Jews resemble American Episcopalians.

Conditioned by the behavior of Christians in this century and before, one is inclined to think of Jews in terms of anti-Semitism. The thing lingers beyond all modern remedy like melanoma. It is true that today Jews are barred outright from a variety of American town and country clubs, and from schools, jobs, careers, resorts, homesites, graveyards and, in point of fact, from running as a major party candidate for President of the United States. But even here, in this vile outrageous area, the outlook betokens success. Cornell Medical School no longer admits having, and may no longer enforce, quotas limiting Jewish admissions. A Las Vegas used-car dealer who called himself Kelly the Kike is out of business. Ever since a New York Attorney General named Goldstein broke down the door, Jews with the money can winter at the Camelback Hotel near Phoenix, Arizona. A Jewish physicist, Dr. Jacob E. Goldman, is director of Scientific Laboratories for the Ford Motor Company of Detroit. The University Club of Rochester has accepted a few Jewish members. And still it stands.

None of this, as we shall see, is sufficient. Two decades after Adolf Hitler demonstrated its logical terminus, any anti-Semitism is a disgrace to America, to democracy, to humanity. In the imperfection of the American experience, in the imperfection of American success, one takes comfort in the fact that scores, perhaps hundreds, of anti-Jewish barriers that should never have been built, are coming down.

A recent study by a Jewish group examined the chances that a qualified Jew had to become president of an American college or university. They are not bright. There are only four Jewish college presidents in the United States, including two at Jewish-sponsored institutions. "But," one old Jewish warrior announces in exuberant cheer, "as long as they're studying college presidencies, that's marvelous. What was it, twenty or just fifteen years ago, that we couldn't afford to worry about the top. We had to knock ourselves out day and night, lobby, plead and threaten, to get some of these colleges to take Jews as *instructors*."

According to estimates and surveys, compiled and weighted under the direction of the American Jewish Committee, the Jewish population of the United States is approximately 5,660,000 people. The figure is inexact. Demography, the combination of skills that produced it, is the science of guesswork. But it is the best figure that we have or can expect to have. To fix the number of Jews by Federal census would probably be unconstitutional and would certainly be challenged. Although Jews are curious about themselves and devoted to self-study, they do not welcome inquiry by government. Too many governments for too many centuries have turned against them.

America, then, is a shade less than three per cent Jewish, which astonishes. The astonishing thing is that three per cent contributes so much to American commerce, intellectualism and vitality.

The greatest of American newspapers, *The New York Times,* has been a Jewish family property for almost eighty years. Jews run perhaps half the major book publishing houses: Random House, Simon & Schuster, New American Library, Alfred Knopf, Atheneum are a few that thrive under the leadership of Jews. The presidents of the three huge television networks, William Paley at C.B.S., Robert Sarnoff at N.B.C. and Leonard Goldenson of A.B.C. are Jews. So, probably, is the comedian, who once a year summons his courage and makes a joke about the shortcomings of the three huge television networks. He may even tell part of his joke in Yiddish. American comedy is overwhelmingly Jewish and a few dozen Yiddish words have moved directly from the stage into general use (although, as the novelist Wallace Markfield has cited "We have a long way to go till the millennium when men enter the world yelling 'Oi!' and leave it whimpering 'Gevalt!' ")

From the astonishing three per cent, comes a quarter of the undergraduate student body at Harvard. "Practically all" Jewish boys get at least some exposure to college. So many get advanced degrees that a Jewish dropout has been defined as an M.A.

The four preeminent American orchestras are conducted by Jews: Erich Leinsdorf at Boston, George Szell at Cleveland, Eugene Ormandy at Philadelphia and Leonard Bernstein, who is about to retire from the New York Philharmonic. A look at the rosters of these orchestras reveals string sections all but solidly Jewish clear back to the rear desk in the furthest corner of the second violins.

Bernard Malamud's best-selling novel, *The Fixer,* retold in carefully underdone prose a classic Czarist attempt to frame one Russian Jew with a sanguine libel. *The Fixer* won the 1966 National Book Award for fiction, which two years earlier had been bestowed on *Herzog,* Saul Bellow's extended account of an intellectual, ineffectual wandering American Jew. In a single and characteristic year, one careful researcher compiled a list of "books of Jewish interest published in America." Marginalia were discarded; the list totaled 258.

Where books lead, critics follow. Jewish critics proliferated so freely that one writer has made a most curious charge. He argues that Jewish novelists prosper because of the praise of Jewish critics. It is most curious because Jewish critics know no higher pleasure than coiling in wait for a Jewish writer to stumble by, except for the ecstasy of the critical strike.

"Painting in the classical sense," the Jewish artist Aaron Bohrod has observed in his vaulting studio beside Lake Monona near Madison, Wisconsin, "was never a traditional Jewish activity. The old rabbis took the Biblical prohibition— *thou shalt make no graven image*—as such a sweeping rule that they wouldn't let Jews paint anything at all. So except for religious artifacts, there is no traditional Jewish art." Freed of the old fundamentalism in America, Jews have sought to make up for centuries of lost painting. Distinguished contemporary canvases are splashed with rainbows of Jewish names: Auerbach-Levy, Levine, Schwartz, Soyer, Bohrod.

With shining pride, Jews describe themselves as people of the book. They challenge one to find in any other group so passionate and pervasive a dedication to culture. "Could you name me ten important Italian-American novelists?" asks a Jewish high school teacher from Brooklyn. "Or five? Or maybe you'd like to try ten Polish-American literary critics? We have our faults," he says, "but I submit that they do not lie in our approach to culture."

Not even professional anti-Semites charge the Jews of

America with being uncultured or ignorant. Indeed they follow quite another course. The trouble with Jews, they cry, is that Jews are too cultured, too intellectual, too smart.

## THE SUPERBAR MITZVAH

There are no poets in this enormous room; no poets, painters or novelists. The closest one comes to a literary critic is brushing the downy, thrice-braceleted arm of a full-busted lady whose defense of Sam Levinson's *Everything but Money* ("an important book as I happen to define the word important") was published in the letters column of a Sunday newspaper book supplement.

We are in the great banquet hall of Temple Beth-El (Place of God) standing beneath one of a matched pair of crystal chandeliers so delicate that each year Temple Beth-El administrators fly in two artisans from Switzerland to clean them. We are attending the Bar Mitzvah reception of Michael Farberman, aged thirteen, who lives in a homogeneous, heavily Jewish suburb of New York. Mike is a brown-haired, medium bright, freckled, pleasant and increasingly weary young man.

In the tradition of roughly seven centuries, boys are initiated into "the full practice of Jewish faith" at the age of thirteen by becoming Bar Mitzvah. The term mixes Aramaic (Bar) and Hebrew. It means Son of the Commandment. A Jewish boy who becomes Bar Mitzvah accepts the full responsibilities of following the commandments of his God.

Early this October Saturday, Michael, his younger sister Lanie, and his parents Max and Barbara Farberman drove to Temple Beth-El for the regular ten A.M. Sabbath service. Although Jews who interpret certain religious codes rigorously do not drive on a Sabbath, Rabbi Martin Blochman of Temple Beth-El has decreed that "the exigencies of transportation in the suburbs make Sabbath driving to Temple permissible. Frivolous driving, however, should be avoided as far as possible."

The Farbermans rode in their Oldsmobile Toronado, midnight blue, with four on the floor. Max Farberman is founder and president of The Fly-Ban Screen Door Company, a business he began fourteen years ago when the storm window company, for which he worked as a salesman, went bankrupt.

Designing most of the doors himself and selling all of them himself in the beginning, Max Farberman has built Fly-Ban into a corporation with a $930,000 annual gross. A poor boy once, raised without formal religious training, Mr. Farberman now donates $1,250 every year to Temple Beth-El. "I hope eventually to make it even more," he says, "the good Lord and the stock market willing."

The Temple is six years old. It was designed by a firm specializing in contemporary synagogue architecture and presents a busy front to the four-lane islanded parkway that runs close by. The basic material, buff brick, is supplemented with panels of stone, stained glass and wood. "Jewish baroque," one of the younger congregants calls it.

Inside, in the foyer, Max Farberman's name appears on a large bronze plaque that lists twenty-five leading contributors to the original building fund. Glass cases stand against the foyer walls. Two display religious objects, ranging from a massive bronze *menorah*, the nine branched candelabrum of "Chanukkah, the Festival of Light," to tiny wooden spice boxes used in a ritual that marks the end of the Sabbath. A discreet sign reminds: "All these objects available for purchase through the Temple Sisterhood, for benefit of Temple Fund." A third englassed case displays books. Here, above Herbert Gold's *Father* and *Molly Goldberg's Jewish Cookbook*, rests an aged, gold-lettered Haggadah—a book of instructions for the Passover meal. The illuminated manuscript is not for sale.

Michael and his family paused in the foyer for ten minutes this morning to greet relatives. Seventeen were there. They came from four separate suburbs and New York City itself and they represented six different congregations. As the adults shouted greetings to one another Michael stood silently against the case offering the bronze *menorah*. He felt partly confused and partly frightened.

Barbara, his mother, went from relative to relative, with embraces. "Darling," she cried. "Oh, Ben. It's simply marvelous! Nancy. How thrilling of you to come. It will make Michael very happy."

Aunt Nancy Farberman, sturdy but not plump, spotted Michael and charged. "Well, well, well," she called, "the Bar Mitzvah boy!"

Michael hunched his shoulders and cringed. Nancy pinched his right cheek and said, "So, my little Mike, whom I knew as a baby and wheeled in his carriage. So. You are a man. Huh? A *mensch*."

"Hope so, Aunt Nancy," Michael said, and began studying the bronze *menorah*.

As always, Rabbi Blochman opened the Sabbath service with prayers in English and in Hebrew that lead up to the ancient incantorial affirmation of monotheism. All the congregation joined the rabbi in chanting:

*Sh'ma Yisroel, Adonai Elohenu, Adonai Echad.*
*Hear, O Israel, The Lord our God, The Lord is One.*

Michael's Bar Mitzvah was a minor part of the Sabbath service but he had to sit on the platform alongside Rabbi Blochman's pulpit where everyone at temple could see him. His lips moved constantly. He was repeating over and over to himself the Hebrew words that he would have to say. The rabbi proceeded briskly. More prayers and singing. The *Amida:* a cycle of standing prayers. Then the rabbi read from the Torah: Genesis, Chapter twenty-two, verses one through eighteen. The passage included the story of the sacrifice of Isaac.

When the rabbi had almost concluded, he nodded at Michael, who marched to his place beside the pulpit. Michael inhaled hard twice, gulping air so close to the microphone that a gasping sound issued from eight concealed loudspeakers in the synagogue.

The whispering of congregants rushed up to Michael as a threat. Loudly, then, to still the sound; flatly in the accents of New York; fluttering, in the inconstant octaves of puberty, Michael spoke the great Jewish benediction:

*Baruch ata Adonai. Elohenu melech ha-olam asher . . .*
*Praised be thou, O Lord our God, King of the Universe . . .*
*who has given us the law of truth, and implanted within our*
*midst eternal life. Blessed art thou, O Lord, giver of The*
*Law.*

He had not silenced them with his Hebrew. The whispers still rose. Michael glumly turned to the pages from the *Haftorah,* The Books of the Prophets, which had been chosen in this service to complement the story of Isaac. Second Kings, chapter four, verses one through thirty-seven, tells of Elisha bringing a son back to life.

"*Eliahu ha-navi,*" Michael began. *Elisha the Prophet.* He read the rest in English. As Rabbi Blochman put it, Michael's eighteen months of Hebrew lessons "didn't take," and the rabbi thought it would be best for everyone if "young Mike" read the Haftorah in translation. The point, the essence of Bar Mitzvah, was for the boy to participate in the fullness of Jewish practice, whatever the language, the rabbi said. Jewish practice had meant not only Hebrew but at different times Portuguese, Spanish, even German. "So why not English?" Rabbi Blochman said.

Michael's voice was surer now, but staccato and still flat. He was concluding: *Then she went in and fell at his feet, and bowed herself to the ground, and took up her son, and went out.*

He grinned. He couldn't help himself. He had participated. It was over. He was Bar Mitzvah.

With practiced paternalism Rabbi Blochman clutched both of Michael's shoulders. Karl Wasserman, M.D., president of the Temple Beth-El Men's Club, strode to the pulpit and presented a large black Bible, embossed in gold letters, *Michael Eli Farberman.*

Michael, now a Bar Mitzvah, sat down and Rabbi Blochman began a sermon on "the art of growing old with grace and faith." To one of the women, whispering in a front pew, "It sounds like having an affair with a couple of aging Quakers."

All that was earlier. Now, in the temple ballroom, it is six o'clock and the gentle weather has held, and all of Michael's family is there, twenty-two persons, except for Aunt Paula who has phlebitis. The mixed clan of Farbermans and Steinbergs, a professional photographer named Katzman, five musicians including bandleader Buddy Arrow, eight waitresses in red and white blouses and skirts, four busboys in tuxedo pants, three cooks, two chefs, a salad man, the personal catering supervisor of Harry Aarons Kosher Katerers, Inc., two bartenders costumed to match the waitresses, Rabbi and Mrs. Stanley A. Blochman, 120 carefully chosen guests, are gathered in the enormous ballroom of Temple Beth-El to help Michael celebrate his own Bar Mitzvah. Michael feels better than he did in the morning. The worst of it, the Hebrew, is behind him.

Brown-haired, freckled Mike stands somewhat stiffly between his parents, contending with an army of mercenaries, arrayed in a reception line. He is proud of his new charcoal sports jacket and its silver-colored buttons. The line stretches farther than he can see.

The men, when they approach, clutch Michael's hand. The women hug him. With most of the handshakes Michael is given an envelope containing a check. Michael says thank you and grins and says thank you again. After a little while, he begins to have trouble remembering the names of the grown-ups, even of the grown-ups he likes. He places each envelope in a side pocket of the new charcoal jacket. Before a quarter of the line has passed, the pockets bulge. The jacket assumes a hippy, wealthy look.

Katzman the cameraman and his portable lights piece out faces in the greeting line without tolerance. The movie camera whirs. The hot lights blaze. Some of the guests are annoyed but one plump, florid man stares into the camera and winks. Then he taps his wife and orders, "Hey, Belle, I want you should look, too."

"Look? Me look?" says Belle. She is blonde as straw. She could be thirty-seven or fifty-five. "Why should I look, Sam?" Belle says. "You know I take a terrible picture."

Two bars are manned. The real one is doing a moderate business with pre-made martinis (four to one) and the caterer's private brand of eighty-proof Scotch, Clan Aarons, favored among the men. The women prefer sours, and blended whiskey and ginger ale.

Adjacent is a smaller bar, under a little sign reading: "The Bar's Bar." Lemonade, a purple punch and pink Shirley Temple cocktails are served to Michael's contemporaries, boys and girls.

The room fills quickly with prosperous, enthusiastic people, buzzing and boisterous. A crowd gathers around Michael's Uncle Sandy Farberman—"you know, like Koufax"—who is a vice-president of The Fly-Ban Screen Door Company and likes to tell jokes.

"So the Ambassador has to go on a secret mission to Geneva," Uncle Sandy is saying, "and on the way he gets lost in the Alps. It could happen, if he used the C.I.A. as guides." This is the prejoke joke. It demands a snicker.

"So a rescue party goes out to look for the Ambassador, calling, 'Goldberg, Goldberg, Goldberg, Red Cross!'"

"So finally near the top of the highest mountain in Switzerland they hear a faint answering holler." Uncle Sandy cups his hands to ready his mountain call. Then he softly cries his punch line: 'I g-a-a-ve at the office!'"

Uncle Sanford had meant to be a comedian. He played dates at small clubs on Ocean Avenue in Brooklyn and he spent a summer as an emcee in the Catskill Mountains, but in the end it hadn't worked out. The big break, as he puts it, never came. So he sold screen doors. What could he do? Was it so terrible? For tonight at least Uncle Sandy is an emcee again, at the Bar Mitzvah reception of his nephew, Michael —by the way, a nice kid he cherishes like his own two daughters.

Barbara Farberman, brunette, hard-eyed, wide-mouthed but pretty, has escaped from the receiving station. She breaks into the little circle and stands beside Sanford. "I think *now,* Sanford," Barbara says.

"Yeh, yeh, Babs," Uncle Sanford says. He drapes an arm around her, urging her toward him and looks deep into the hard mysterious eyes. "If you weren't my sister-in-law," he says.

Barbara leans toward him rigidly. His hand slides toward her bottom. "Please," Barbara says, sharply. "Now." She claps a hand on his, which is just below her waist. She spins away.

"Okay, okay, why not now?" Uncle Sanford says. He turns and walks to a microphone standing near the head table.

"Ladies and gentleman," Uncle Sanford says, "and I even include all *goyim* in that remark, ladies and gentlemen." An amplified voice is authority. The ballroom quiets. "I know there is still some Scotch not drunk but my hostess and yours, the beautiful Mrs. Barbara Farberman, has asked me to make the following announcement of great gustatorial— whatsa matter? You didn't know I went to college—impor- tance."

Uncle Sanford steps back from the microphone and bel- lows: "Places everybody! Places!" The guests surge toward where the food will be.

This is the critical moment for Barbara Farberman. Ar- ranging the seating plan was her ordeal, her Hebrew lesson. Actually, she wanted fifteen or twenty tables but her husband Max made her settle for twelve. "It'll go to fifteen hundred even that way," he told her. So, aside from the head table, she had twelve others to work with. Eleven really. One was taken up by children. "Considering our circle," she told Max, "eleven tables doesn't give me very much. It isn't as if we were only starting out. We happen to have a certain position in the community."

He was adamant. He could be a regular mule about money, as if they didn't have plenty, as if they were poor. So she had to work with only eleven tables. Well, that made correct groupings even more important.

Now take the doctors, for example. She liked the doctors and they were important men. Her own doctor, Doctor Moskowitz, was one of the biggest internists in the county. It was an actual treat for Barbara when the annual physical was over and she stood barefoot in the little white examining gown after the nurse had gone and Doctor Moskowitz had removed the plastic gloves and told her in a fatherly way that she had a wonderful body and she should take care of it. For marvelous men like Doctor Moskowitz you *had* to be thoughtful.

The doctors would want to sit together, but people liked to talk to doctors, so Barbara decided it would be best for the other guests if she spread the doctors out, and it might even be good for the doctors to sit apart, so they wouldn't spend the whole night talking medicine among themselves. Let them relax, Barbara thought. What is Bar Mitzvah for but to enjoy? She placed Doctor Moskowitz at Table Two, in the center, Doctor Schiffer, the pediatrician at Table Five right behind, and Doctor Kranzer—Jack Kranzer, who played golf with Max—at Table Four, close but to one side.

The seating was more difficult than selecting the invitations. For those she took the trouble to go to Cartier's in New York. You could make a mistake in Cartier's? Not likely. Not likely at all.

In the ballroom of Temple Beth-El, the guests find their table numbers printed inside the glossy programs supplied by Aarons Kosher Katerers. Barbara tries to see how things are working out. Doctor Moskowitz sits down before his wife. They must have had a fight. Why tonight? Why isn't she nicer to him? No, he's smiling; it is going to be all right. It would have been terrible if they'd picked tonight to fight.

The head table, placed on a raised platform, is reserved for Michael's immediate family and Rabbi and Mrs. Blochman. Almost all the other tables are full; the room is loud with creak of chairs, clang of silverware, and voices. Then Uncle Sanford barks a command into the microphone: "Everybody rise." Slowly, before a standing audience, the Farbermans themselves start toward the head table. Someone applauds. Someone else says, "Ssh!" The time for applause will come later.

Michael walks behind his father, head down. He has given his father all the envelopes. His pockets are empty now, but the new charcoal jacket and Michael's hair are rumpled beyond redemption.

Uncle Sanford still has the microphone. "As they used to tell them at the end of the last mile," he says, "Be-e-e-e-seated."

Rabbi Blochman remains standing and bows his head. The room is suddenly quiet. The Rabbi intones: *Baruch ata Adonai Elohenu melech ha-olam, hamotzee lechem min ha-aretz. Blessed art thou, O Lord our God, King of the Universe who bringest forth bread from the earth.*

Dinner begins with an appetizer of chopped chicken livers, scooped into balls and deposited within folds of lettuce. The dish is heavy, nourishing and, to most tastes, delicious. Chicken soup follows, steaming and fatty, with *knadloch,* a ball of *matzoh* dough, carefully allotted one to each guest.

At the Moskowitz table, an accountant says, "If we ate this every day, you'd be out of business, soon, huh Doctor?" It is an old Jewish fable that chicken soup cures all ills from a sore throat to athlete's foot. Moskowitz refuses to be amused. He does not like to hear medicine called a business. The socializers do that; they and the beatniks. "Call me at the office if you have questions," he snaps.

"Doctor works so hard," Mrs. Moskowitz announces.

"Well, I hope you make Internal Revenue very happy," says the accountant. He freezes his face into a smile.

At another table, Jerry Gaines, who owns The Big J, Television and Appliance Discounts, lifts the *knadloch* from the soup and examines it as it steams before his eyes. "This is like one of Grandma's," Jerry says. "Remember, Heshy? They were so rubbery, I hit 'em three sewers back on Crown Street." The distance between "sewers"—manhole covers— was used to measure batting power in stickball, a game of baseball with a broomstick that New York children played before automobiles commandeered their streets.

"They weren't rubbery," says Heshy Garson, president of Garson Wines and Spirits. (Jerry Gaines and Heshy Garson are brothers, but they could not agree on a successor to their

father's Gershenberger.) "Grandma's *knadloch* were tough.
They'd break the stick. You know what Grandma used for
dough? Portland Cement."

"Well, whatever it was, she musta vulcanized it," Jerry
says.

Rock Cornish Game Hen is the main dish. Aarons serves it
with *kasha* (groats) and *stuffed derma,* cow's entrails surrounding a heavy meal. The waitresses in their red and black
costumes are efficient. One or two are even cute. The meal is
going very smoothly. Nothing has been served cold. Everything is at least passable. The hen is outstanding. The ballroom is quieter now; at table after table, eating replaces active conversation.

Twenty minutes later, the catering consultant walks to the
microphone in front of Uncle Sanford's place at the head
table. He gets a confirming nod from Barbara Farberman and
proclaims—it is more a shout of triumph—"Ladies and gentlemen: Dessert!"

Busboys rush to their clearing. The ballroom lights dim. In
formation, the eight waitresses wearing red and black parade
from the Temple Beth-El kitchen bearing aloft and ablaze
Tarte aux Cerises, Flambée—flaming cherry tarts—the
specialité de la maison for Harry Aarons Kosher Katerers,
Inc. A ripple of applause, proper now, begins. Flames from
the cognac surrounding the tarts lick high in the half-dark
room. With the girls marching in perfect formation, it is a
spectacular. The applause grows. Even Doctor Moskowitz,
feeling better after the first three courses, joins in. "Barbara!"
he shouts, "Barbara!" He stands up at Table Two to catch
Mrs. Farberman's eye. "Barbara!" he calls. "Le flambée, c'est
magnifique."

"Merci, merci!" Barbara Farberman cries.

"Irving, sit down," says Mrs. Moskowitz.

As if cerises flambée were not enough, Harry Aarons Kosher Katerers, Inc., has brought forth from the earth at no
extra cost a mocha layer cake for the head table. It bears
thirteen candles. When the cake appears, with the lights still
dim, Uncle Sanford recaptures the microphone.

"The young people, and I don't mean you, Max, you alte-
you-know-what, will light the candles," he announces.
"Kindly approach, young people, as I call your names.

"Sharon Gold."

A pretty, round-bottomed brunette of twelve rises; the five-piece band, under Buddy Arrow, strikes up, "A Pretty Girl is Like a Melody." Sharon giggles and giggles, but manages to light a candle.

"Jonathan Feuer," Uncle Sanford says. "Come on up, Jack." The band breaks into "Boy o' Mine." One by one, Uncle Sanford's young people rise and light the white candles rimming the cake. The thirteenth and final candle, larger than the others, stands in the center by itself.

Uncle Sanford, who understands microphones, leans away to avoid feedback and overloading. Then, strongly, resonantly, he says: "And now, the man—and I don't mean boy —whose day this is. It's all yours, Mike. You're a grand little guy."

Michael Farberman, the forgotten, stands. Applause spurts, stops and spurts again. Michael's hair is no longer rumpled. For all the excitement, Barbara Farberman has seen to that. The dim light conceals two shiny chicken soup spots on Michael's lapels. His hands are trembling.

Uncle Sanford hands Michael a matchbook and says, into the microphone, "You're old enough to play with these now." Michael grins and lights a match, which promptly dies. He lights another, angling the match to feed the flame and moves it stiffly to the thirteenth candle in the center of the mocha cake. He does not burn himself. The candlewick catches. Buddy Arrow stamps his foot, the band breaks into "Sunrise, Sunset" from *Fiddler on the Roof.* Uncle Sanford clutches the microphone and croons in a hard, but on-key, baritone above the throbbing trumpet:

> *Is this the little girl I carried?*
> *Is this the little boy at play?*
> *I don't remember getting older.*
> *Whe-e-e-en did they?*

Around the room others join him in the song.

After coffee, Michael makes his speech. It is well past nine o'clock and Barbara Farberman has let him drink an entire cup of coffee. It is so late, she says; the boy has had to do so much; it is amazing that he can keep his eyes open at all, although, Barbara points out, he certainly has had plenty of preparation. Nobody can accuse her of letting Michael go to his Bar Mitzvah unprepared.

Writing the speech challenged Michael. He was frightened

until he came to realize that he would have a chance to explain some of his feelings to grown-ups. He wanted to do that so much that the fright became less dominant. There were a number of things that he felt he had to say but after several conversations at dinner, he understood that his mother felt that there were a number of things he *should* say. And they were not all the same. And Rabbi Blochman had further suggestions. And his own father simply said over and over: "It's your talk, Mike. Nobody else can make it for you. It's your talk."

Finally, tentatively, Michael told his dilemma to David Bar Oman, a blue-eyed Israeli engaged by Mrs. Farberman so that Michael could learn his Hebrew from someone who himself spoke it as a child.

"What are your disagreements?" Mr. Bar Oman wanted to know.

"Well, like, Mom says, I should be sure to mention her father, but I don't think I should because I never knew him."

"You have the right," Mr. Bar Oman said.

"But I don't want her to get sore at me," Michael said.

"It is your day, not hers," Mr. Bar Oman said. "Besides, if the speech is excellent, she won't be angry. She'll be proud."

"I don't know," Michael said.

"I'll help you with it," said Mr. Bar Oman, "at no charge."

Now tired, but excited by the day and fired by the memory of the hours with Mr. Bar Oman, who unfortunately was not invited, Michael rises to address the assemblage of well-fed, chattering adults. "Thanks," he says, above the buzzing, "are truly all that I have to offer to everyone here in this room."

"Closer, kid," says Uncle Sanford. "Move in on the mike."

"Mort!" a woman's voice shrills, louder than Michael's. "Quiet! The child is trying to speak."

"Is this okay, Uncle Sandy?" Michael says.

"A quarter-step in."

"Okay?" Michael says.

"Yeah," Uncle Sanford says.

"Shut up, Mort!" cries the shrill woman.

"Thanks," Michael says, "are truly all that I have to offer to everyone here in this room. . .

"I thank my parents for looking after me with love, even though I may have given them—Dad, anyway—a few gray hairs. I thank them for sending me to Hebrew school, even though on many days, I, like so many my age, protested I would rather play basketball . . ." Michael expands on the leitmotiv—the wisdom of parents—for a minute or so.

"I also thank," he says, "my younger sister Lanie for her love, even though I know that on many occasions, she has wished that she was my older sister." He grins quickly at Lanie. He waits for laughs. Mr. Bar Oman told him that the audience would break into laughter. It does not. There are not even chuckles. Lanie looks embarrassed.

Michael inhales and says, "I . . ."

"Closer," commands Uncle Sanford.

"Thanks," Michael says. "I especially want to thank my grandmother, Dora," Michael says. "I only wish the Lord had seen fit to spare my grandpa, Solomon Farberman, for this day, so that he could see me as I now am, Bar Mitzvah." Michael looks straight ahead so that his mother cannot catch his eye. He will only mention grandparents he has known.

"In the Torah this morning," he says, now glancing toward the notes Mr. Bar Oman helped prepare, "we read how the father of all our people was called on to sacrifice his own son. Although I am so fortunate in my life that I have not had to make great sacrifices—again, I thank my own father —I know that I am a Jew. Even as my fellow people did in Europe so recently, I would be willing to make any sacrifice that is necessary for my heritage. As I understand it, that heritage is one of peace and learning."

The buzzing is almost still. Not everyone is listening, but no one makes loud sounds any longer. The reference to the Holocaust brought quiet.

"In the Haftorah this morning," Michael says, "I read how the prophet Elijah revived a dead boy with the warmth of his body . . .

". . . So it is with Judaism. Tyrants come and try to destroy it, but the warmth of our heritage—peace and learning —and our belief in a firm but just God, will always revive the Jewish people, as it is doing everywhere today." Michael pauses. Mr. Bar Oman had worked hardest with him at this section. It was most important, Mr. Bar Oman said.

"I will always remember this day. I will always remember my Jewish heritage and my belief.

"I only hope," Michael Farberman says, concluding the first speech of his thirteen years, "that I am worthy of all these wonderful things that have come to me."

A few minutes later dancing begins. Buddy Arrow's band

plays on for hours; the band plays and the dancers dance
long after Michael Farberman, the Bar Mitzvah, has ridden
home in the midnight-blue Toronado and clambered safely to
the heights of sleep.

When one asks the parents and sponsors of a massive Bar
Mitzvah—an expenditure of twenty-five hundred dollars for a
first son is hardly rare—why they went to the trouble and expense, the answers tend toward repetition and shallowness. It
is a rude question, to be sure; a Jewish parent would be
wholly justified in saying, "Why I do what I do with my religion and my checkbook is nobody's business except, perhaps,
my rabbi's and my banker's." Almost nobody makes that
answer. Most Jews have an urgent, touching need to explain
and justify themselves. It is a response conditioned by centuries of persecution.

"You see," says Max Farberman, leaning wearily on a
glass case in the dim foyer of Temple Beth-El, after the band
has gone, "there are a couple of reasons at the least. We
wanted Mike to have a sense of tradition. What better way
than with Bar Mitzvah. Tell me, you should know, how many
centuries does that go back?"

"Most scholars trace it only to the Fourteenth Century."

Max looks disappointed. "You sure?" he says. "I thought it
was older than that."

Barbara Farberman's dark eyes flash. "I for one, happen to
be more concerned with the present than with the past," she
says. "Through this Bar Mitzvah, Michael was able to affirm
his Jewishness today, in a religious setting."

"It isn't so much a question of believing in God, like the
Catholics," Max says. "It's just nice to be here with family in
a religious place. You know what I mean? It's comfortable.
Nobody wants."

To many Jews, lavishness, hard to justify at best, can least
be justified when it is masked as religiosity. Scores of rabbis
gently remind congregants, "Frankly, ladies and gentlemen, I
would like to see less emphasis on the *Bar* [son of] and more
on the *Mitzvah* [commandment, or loosely, all the com-
mandments]." Lay critics can afford to be sharper.

"People in our circle," says the intense, fair-haired wife of
an English professor in the Far West, "simply let it be known
that we consider a big Bar Mitzvah very poor form. We are

activists; the message gets across, usually—but not every single time."

"She is thinking of one particular fellow, a surgeon," her husband says.

"What he did for his child was positively Lucullan," the woman says intensely.

"And what," the husband says, "could be more Jewish than that?"

More than one congregation has heard a proposal to ban Superbar Mitzvah receptions from the temple itself. (Some, but certainly a fewer number of these affairs would continue at country clubs and catering halls.) The money thus saved by parents might be donated to Jewish hospitals and community organizations, Israel, or various anti-poverty funds.

A Hebrew teacher in New York City indicts the Superbar Mitzvah solely as a threat to the Jewishness of the boys themselves. "This is a key event in a child's life," suggests the teacher, a tall aesthetic figure, who was once the victim of a Superbar Mitzvah himself. "It comes at a time when his body is changing and he is likely to be exceedingly sensitive. For many boys, it is *the* key event. They study for it, agonizing over Hebrew, sweating over their speeches. They believe that the day, when it comes, will be theirs. Then, for all the promise, it turns out to be just one more adult party, at which the kids are more or less in the way.

"The boys feel negative, exploited. 'Who needed this?' they say. 'It was all a fake.' I've heard young people denounce Jewishness, abandon it even, because they were so disturbed by their Bar Mitzvah, which was not, in my opinion, really Jewish at all."

Ultimately, the most powerful attack against the Superbar Mitzvah exposes its pretension of tradition. When Max, the amiable screendoor magnate, mentions Jewish tradition, he lifts a curtain on a caravan that rises and falls across millennia through Palestine and Babylon, Rome, Salonika and Spain, Turkey and Morocco and Brazil. There is not one tradition, but a hybrid. Sources are allied in some ways, variegated in others, mingling into headsplitting complexity. Understanding Jewish tradition is the stuff of scholarship. But one point is immediately apparent. Michael Farberman's catered, crowded, orchestrated Bar Mitzvah is not traditional at all. It is contemporary.

Two communities—broadly, Germany and Eastern Europe

—lineally feed American Jews. More than ninety-five per cent trace back to one or the other. The Kosher caterer's Rock Cornish game hen was unknown in the ghettoes of the Rhinelands and Sholom Aleichem assures us that in the muddy wooden *shtetls* of Czarist Russia, the only time a Jew ever got to eat a chicken was when one of them was sick.

According to Dr. Harold Weisberg, dean of the graduate faculty at Brandeis University, the Bar Mitzvah receptions, which offer mountains of meat "bring us close to an Old Testament problem: animal sacrifice." Earnestly then, after his small joke, Weisberg, like many other commentators, asserts that lavishness and conspicuous consumption are peculiarly American rather than peculiarly Jewish. Amid the $690, 295-square-inch color television sets and the $4,995 air-conditioned hardtops, on which American society seems unevenly to rest, it is not difficult to make that case. Americans have more things and want more things than any other people in the world.

Some Jews have embraced the American failing of materialism; a few are preeminent vulgarians. According to Weisberg, those Jews do not reaffirm their religion. They reject it. They do not serve their God. They worship something alien. In the United States, in prosperous times, they have discovered or rediscovered the Golden Calf.

The poor (although prosperous) Farbermans—taxpayers, supporters of the war in Vietnam, generous to both Jewish charities and the Community Chest—what have they shown with their complex Bar Mitzvah and their simple explanations?

Nothing that either of them understands.

Like most middle-class Americans, the Farbermans are practical people. They are good, even skillful, at contending with tangible situations. But the problem of affirming one's Jewishness in religious terms is an abstraction. At least, it starts that way. It proceeds from the set of abstractions that is Judaism itself.

In the beginning, the theology of the Jews was as mysterious as concepts of omnipotence and eternity. Over centuries it has been clarified and complicated by dialogues, philosophies, monographs. "Today," one rabbi suggests, "there can no longer be such a thing as a good, dumb Jew. He can only be one or the other. Good or dumb. Judaism is now too much to be understood by even the best-intended *schlemiel.*"

Max and Barbara Farberman want to affirm their Jewishness in religious terms. But neither studies the Torah in Hebrew. Neither is curious about the *Shulhan Aruch,* the basic code for everyday living prepared by a sixteenth century Turkish Jew named Joseph Karo. Neither approaches the dozens of volumes on Bible, ethics and morality called the Talmud.

Then why bother? Why bother with religious affirmation at all?

The answer to that question straddles a number of areas, and springs from a number of factors, some Jewish, some American, some both. But beyond question, the greatest single force is the fierce desire of Jews to be American at a time when every American from the beggars muttering "Gawd bless ya" for a dime, to the Presidents mouthing ghost-written prayers, is expected to be religious, as a condition of first-class citizenship.

No less an American than Dwight Eisenhower has insisted, "Our government makes no sense, unless it is founded in a deeply-felt religious faith." Significantly Eisenhower added, "And I don't care what it [the religious faith] is."


## THE HOLLYWOOD AGENT FINDS GOD

It is a private, naked time, 2:24 A.M. in California. Night has surged across the United States and now, 2:24—wait—2:25 in California, dawn is threatening New York.

Fuck it, Jack Schrager tells himself. Fuck New York. Jack Schrager is a Californian now. He wouldn't go back to the East Bronx if they gave it to him, urban renewal, spic rent money and all.

Jack Schrager lives above a canyon in Beverly Hills. He plays tennis twice a day, damn near all year round. He has a ranch house like no rancher ever saw. One kid at Southern Cal. The other? Well, he likes to play the guitar and hang wild on The Strip, and he even got himself arrested once, the Vietnik. But he'll straighten out. He only needs a little time and the right broad.

I got it here in my hip pocket, Jack Schrager tells himself. All of it. Everything. The big ball game. It is 2:28 A.M.

above the canyon in Beverly Hills and Jack Schrager is just the smallest bit, most expensively, high.

He gave up trying to fall asleep at 1:19, when Maggie the *shicksa*, wife number two, with all that long red hair, smiled mechanically across the big four-poster, rolled over bottoms up and went to sleep. Jack lifted the bedclothes and studied her pale buttocks. "My best part," she had told him almost shyly after the first time. It was goddamn all right, Jack Schrager thought, still studying. He'd never seen a can that perfect on a Jew broad. But who needed it? It was too goddamn late. The night was too goddamn creepy. He let the sheet fall back, reached for a paisley robe shipped from a New York tailor, and wrapping himself snugly started the long walk, down the carpeted hall toward the living room.

It stretched, modern and "western-style" and rich. At one end a fireplace, framed in rough, carefully-faced stone, stood dark. Jack Schrager turned the center knob in an electric control box, and flame sprang from a hidden pipe. In the fireplace larval rocks began to glow.

There was no noise, except the gas flame's hiss. Jack Schrager flicked a button on the control box and presently, in one side wall, an opaque panel came to life as Channel Two.

He watched the picture for a moment. Then he realized, Christ, it was one of his. He'd made the deal. That was part of the package of old bombers he'd sold the network eleven years ago. Got the dough for the new house and helped get the ex set up. This called for a small happening, Jack Schrager decided. He walked to the bar. What was that shaggy hewn stuff? Cottonwood, they had told him. He reached for a bottle of twelve-year-old Scotch and poured himself half an old-fashioned glassful. He thought briefly, and added a little more. Jack touched a simulated wooden button on the bartop and a simulated wooden slab in the front of the bar hinged open. Inside, a scoop brimmed with real ice, frozen into the initials J and S. Jack Schrager took a J. Just one. He wasn't up for ice. He walked back to the living room and when he saw the actress on the color TV screen, he tried to laugh. She was playing the part of a seventeenth-century English virgin. *Oh, Prithee, sir. Pray take your hand from mine.* Jack Schrager knew better. He had pritheed her to bed. No sweat. So had at least six other guys he knew from Hillcrest, none exactly a Sinatra with the broads.

"Here's to ya, lady," Jack Schrager said. "Prithee, prithee, yeah, yeah, yeah." He raised his glass and sank hard into the long, low western couch, spilling some twelve-year-old Scotch on the black fox fur upholstery.

"Goddamn," he said. He really laughed. He had suddenly remembered, time was important to him, 5:36 P.M., December 14, 1938, the day the big German workmen from the furniture company came to the cramped apartment on East 176th Street, and handed the old man a paper.

"Gentlemen, gentlemen," his father had said. "Patience, please. A little humanity."

The men had ignored him; silently they carried out two chairs, a rug and the couch covered in heavy brown cotton.

His father had cursed then. *"Drek, verstinkene drek."*

His mother had cried.

Jack Schrager drank all of his Scotch, poured himself another half a tumbler and now here he is, sitting, watching, waiting. For what? There isn't anything to wait for. He has what he wanted. He ought to go to sleep, but he is damn well not going to start with the sleep pills. Mixed with Scotch they kill you. Kilgallen found that, a smart broad like that died dumb. Well, Jack Schrager damn well wants to live. Goddamn, he has everything to live for.

In the beginning, he wanted to make fifty dollars a week. Then a hundred. Then, when he thought about getting kids through college, he decided that a hundred and fifty a week would cover him for life. He finished high school, took some college courses at night, drifted through five hustling years and suddenly there was a job selling films to television stations, on commission. Two years running, out of nowhere, nothing, he made more than seventy thousand dollars. Who figured? Who could figure? What a country, as long as you didn't buy your furniture on time.

All right, the broad was wrong. He knew it quick, or maybe in a couple of years. He didn't act on it. There was no time or maybe it simply didn't seem that damn important. But when the big money came, she couldn't handle it. Her ambition one day was to be a secretary in a lawyer's office. And the next damn day, when the big money started coming, she was "gawna swing." Some swinger. She could swing like she could sing, which was n.g. She ate and she drank and she got fat.

She had his kids. She was good at that, two fine boys that he was proud of, and she had even, for some cash, moved out to Glendale so that the split shouldn't be so wide. That was all right. She only held him up for what it cost. Eighty-eight hundred, including the down payment. Look, that divorce was no *mechayah*, no delight, but it was what it had to be, not only for him but for her sake, too. For her. What kinda life can it be living with a man who doesn't love you, and who never tries to make out?

On the screen, two men are dueling. Jack finishes his second Scotch. The men are dueling for Miss Prithee, with real foils.

"Hey," Jack shouts at the color picture tube. "Don't fight you guys. All you gotta do is ask. She'll take you both."

He smiles vastly and rises. Solemnly he pours a third drink.

The movie is terrible. "This the kinda thing," Jack mumbles, "makes you root for the Star Spangled Banner to come on."

He is not drunk. He handles liquor well. That is part of his job, as first vice-president of the talent agency. Keep drinking without getting drunk. The secret was never touch martinis. Feed the martinis to the broads.

He left the fat one. She was always getting drunk, drinking straight gin and swearing it was water and walking into walls. He kept his cash and slept around and when he met the *shicksa* with the wild red hair, he decided that money, now that he had it, wasn't what he wanted. All the time, he had wanted a beautiful woman, his own beautiful woman pledged to him. Well, now he had that, too. So? So what? *Nu?*

When was it, last Christmas, he flew his mother out. It was twenty-two degrees in New York that day. She saw the house and tried to play up to the redheaded *shicksa*. He sent them off to lunch together at Chasen's and they both told him they enjoyed it, but something was on Ma's mind. She kept trying to corner him alone.

"Jack," she said. "Jack. A minute please."

"Yeah, Ma. What is it?"

"Not here, Jackie. Alone."

"Ma. It wouldn't be polite."

"Please, Jackie."

They walked into the dressing room next to the bar and stood under the wild wallpaper of nymphs pursuing satyrs and Ma put both hands on his arms and she looked at him hard, just like sometimes she did when he was a kid and said, "Jackie, tell me. With all this, you are happy?"

"Nobody's happy, Ma."

"Nonsense."

"But I'm content."

"This is what you wanted, Jackie?"

"More than I wanted, Ma."

A sigh. Then, "Good, Jackie. Then I am happy for you."

Maybe he fooled his mother last Christmas. Anyway, she didn't bother him again. She stayed another few days. He had a fight with Maggie the *shicksa*. The two of them were bickering when the old lady left.

Jack sips his Scotch. On the screen Miss Prithee is coyly slipping into the arms of the bland, slow-witted actor who won the movie duel. Who could believe that? Jack Schrager thinks. Who could be fooled? But people were. Millions of people. Maybe he fooled his mother last Christmas, Jack Schrager thinks, but right now he does not want to fool himself.

He's lonely. He can't finger the reason. It's more than loneliness. He's discontent. Sad. In fact, he's miserable. He doesn't quite know why but if he weren't a grown man and tough, he'd start to cry.

This is what I wanted? Jack Schrager asks. It's gotta be. He looks around, at the signature Lautrec print, with its garish reds and greens; at the soft room light that flows from nowhere. Beyond the light he can dimly see the pool. In the Bronx, they would call it a lake. He thinks of Maggie. A piece like that, and all he'd have to do even now, even this late, is pat the pale bottom a couple of times and she'd roll over. What the hell else can there be? House. Woman. Dough. What the hell else?

He finishes Scotch number three. So how come, Jack Schrager asks himself, achieving all these things, I'm no happier than when I started out. A little less happy, maybe, to tell the truth. More things to bug me. Am I the same guy I was when I started out? Or have I changed? He throws the old-fashioned glass against the carefully roughened stone of the western-style fireplace and watches it shatter. Who was I then? he wants to know. Who the hell am I now?

His head drops forward. He shakes it back and forth. There is a tear. Goddamnit, there is a self-pitying tear or two in Jack Schrager's eyes. He doesn't care. He lets himself sink into a baritone sob.

When he looks up finally, the movie he sold is finished. A

High Episcopal minister is intoning the Channel Two closing prayer for May 27th. It is 3:06 A.M. in California, daylight in New York.

"As Christ sacrificed for us, so we must be willing to sacrifice for Him," the high-collared televised Episcopalian proclaims, "and make ourselves more holy in the name of the Father, Son and Holy Ghost. Amen."

"Goddamn, but he's right," Jack Schrager, the agent, says aloud. He stands up. "This Saturday," he announces to himself, "I'm going to synagogue."

It is not entirely fair to suggest that the current American religious revival has come about for all the wrong reasons. But it is not entirely unfair, either.

However deep and genuine its sources, American religion is packaged, advertised and sold. If it begins as a spirituality, it is converted into a commodity. However pure its origin, religious belief comes to be peddled by professional peddlers.

"God is not dead," a television announcer assures us, with crisp, nondenominational sincerity, while a camera pans across dune grass in the wind. "We have only to look for Him a little harder." One might believe the announcer except that we have heard the man before. An hour earlier he was hustling airline tickets to people who could not afford them. ("Come on. What are you waiting for? All you have to have is ten per cent down.") An hour from now he will hawk carcinogenic cigarettes, his earnest voice carrying over camera shots that suggest the good health of the outdoors; perhaps pictures of those same stalks of dune grass blowing in the identical, blasphemed wind.

In his slim, partisan volume, *Protestant, Catholic, Jew*, the philosopher and theologian Will Herberg recalls slogans posted in New York City subway cars:

> *Go to church—you'll feel better.*
> *Bring your troubles to church and leave them there.*

"On every ground," Herberg writes, "this type of religion is poles apart from the authentic Jewish Christian spirituality, which, while it knows of the 'peace that passeth understanding' as the gift of God, promotes 'a divine discontent with things as they are.'"

After the Saturday services at his synagogue, Jack Schrager feels better. He knew he would. The advertising men had made that promise; the rabbi himself had let it stand.

As Jack leaves, warmed by the California sun, looking forward to two sets of tennis, he holds hands with his redheaded wife. Maggie smiles. She feels vaguely better, too; even virtuous.

"You know," Jack Schrager says, "the way the rabbi talked about understanding the fullness of fellow men. That's a good point. I got to remember that one."

"Yes," Maggie says. She continues to smile at the sunlight. "Our minister, Dr. Ward, used to say the same thing back home."

"He couldn't have," Jack Schrager says. "This stuff is Jewish."

Maggie does not argue. They have reached the beige Continental. "Would you like me to do the driving?" she says. Jack Schrager nods and by the time Maggie has guided the big car out of the parking lot, Jack Schrager has decided to serve flat and hard to Marty Coleman's backhand. That should work better than messing around with a twist.

In these fervently ecumenical times, a number of theologians suggest that all religions are fusing in America. Startling though this idea is—don't we follow the separate but equal faiths of our fathers?—history seems to support it. Already America has fused much of what immigrants brought: dress and diet, language and culture, various outlooks on life. The concept of the United States as a melting pot has become banal but generally it is true; and the melting still goes on. With each generation, a man's tastes and life style tells less and less of where his forebears lived. One unexceptional individual prefers double-breasted English blazers, enjoys Fettucini Alfredo, delights in *Die Walküre* and thinks that his father-in-law is a *schnorer*. This reveals nothing of his antecedents. It merely suggests that he is an American.

Religion is unique. It is a faith, an identity, a hope, an over-whelming passion. But unique is not immune. American religions feel the forces of fusion and melding. They respond. According to proponents of the fusion theory, the major American religions have already responded; they have merged into the single official, but unestablished, religion of the

United States. The U.S. state religion lacks a formal name. Broadly it is the American Way of Life, under God.

That is the religion Mr. Eisenhower exalts when he argues that American government makes sense only to "the faithful." Mr. Eisenhower is not talking about catechisms, or about The Book of Common Prayer, or about the Kaddish. He is certainly not talking about rival interpretations of The Song of Songs. He is praising the American Way under God. The Pledge of Allegiance does the same thing. It has since 1954, when Congress amended it to include a religious reference.

The state religion is varied and commodious. There is almost limitless room under its vague canopy. Within, in comfort, one finds flourishing and growing, the sacred trinity of American life: Protestantism, Catholicism and Judaism. Each recognizes the others, and more than that. Recognizes, accepts, emulates, borrows, courts. The fusion has not passed the first stage, but even now rabbis adopt the Protestant practice of responsive reading and Catholic priests casually describe "our Jewish brethren, worshipping the same Lord," and ministers invite rabbis into their pulpits.

What we have, according to the fusion theory, are not three separate religions, running their heedless ways, the devil, or a fierce God, take the hindmost. Rather, we have three separate *denominations*. For all their distinctions, the denominations are primarily bound to do fealty to the American Way of Life under God.

The fusion theory is subject to sniping and outright assault. It is that political candidate's nightmare, a single approach, that draws equal fire from the Protestant, Catholic and Jewish Establishments. But if one dodges the ecclesiastical bombardment and accepts the fusion approach, the contemporary American religious revival assumes a theoretical unity that it long since has possessed in fact.

According to statistics compiled from a variety of sources, about half of the American people attend services on a regular weekly basis. Twenty-five years ago, the figure was thirty-six per cent. Although there are variations from group to group—Roman Catholics always seem to attend the most and Jews the least—the religious revival is national and universal. It is a phenomenon of all major American denominations; it is a phenomenon of the American Way of Life under God.

Perhaps the major wellspring is the American national awareness of the casual slaughters of our time. This is not something that bubbles up in everyday conversation, but its hold grasps deep and fast. Rabbis, priests and ministers hear of this awareness all the time. And no wonder. The preeminent massacres of human history, Hiroshima and Auschwitz, occurred within the lifetime of all mature Americans.

For vaporizing one hundred fifty thousand Japanese civilians, America was directly responsible. For murdering fifteen million Europeans, Americans bear the indirect but undiminished guilt of passivity. Guilt stands with fear and despair in the private places of the heart. *Such casual slaughters past, and what to come?*

The wrenching events behind, and imagined ones ahead, prompt self-examinations and questions. The former faiths are dead. The pillars are toppled; the old secular faiths are not believable any more.

Was one's old faith science? In the sacred service of science, men created the atomic bomb.

Was one's old faith a government of laws? In pure devotion to the laws of the government of Germany, men herded children into gas chambers for execution.

Destruction and evil deepen the human need to believe. Against his own record, man wants to be persuaded that he is a creature that builds, flawed perhaps, but far more good than bad. He wants to turn from slaughter with clean hands. He wants to be told, as all American religions tell, that human life has a high and holy purpose, if only one casts his burdens upon the Lord.

But religious belief is dynamic. It moves away from wellspring and ideologies. Jack Schrager is not thinking of atom bombs when he goes to synagogue. He does not think of concentration camps when he passes, unseeing, a plaque "in memory of the six million Jews." Jack Schrager is thinking about something nearer home. Himself.

In his own view, Jack Schrager is an American who happens to be Jewish. That is an imperfect identity, but it is the best that he has been able to find. In time of crisis, when he wonders who he is, Jack Schrager returns to the synagogue for reassurance, although to be an American who happens to be Jewish, one does not have to revere Abraham, or follow the laws of Moses or even, for that matter, believe in God.

## DAS LIED FON HALUTZIM

The only rabbi to rise this evening will make a secular speech, prolix and political. This wilderness of a dining room, blank, ominous and seemingly unplanned is partly, fractionally, filled by eight hundred Jews, most of them secular people. They are attending the biennial convention of an important, liberal, secular organization, the American Jewish Congress, in a hotel which litters the slope of one of the Catskill Mountains in New York State, with a compound of half-timbered buildings. Also seemingly unplanned. The eight hundred delegates meet tonight at Grossinger's Hotel without benedictions or *yarmulkes*.

For only ten dollars extra, above the "special convention-eers' rate" of $150 for a three-day weekend, the delegates are being served the Grossinger banquet menu: chilled cante-loupe, Spanish queen olives, California ripe olives, homemade plum tomatoes, potage Jackson, roast prime rib of beef au jus, stuffed derma, stringbeans almondine, chef's salad, mixed nuts, New England green apple pie, rainbow fruit ices, café noir (plus, on special request, pumpernickel, rye and salt-free bread with *pareve* oleomargarine). The hotel is proud of its banquet menu. It describes the menu as "famous 'round the world."

At one of the large, round tables, ranging before the twin-tiered dais, a lawyer is talking about the food. "One of the Rothschilds was here one time," the lawyer says, in a flat, unembellished New York accent. "This man has so many servants that his chef would not be caught dead in the kitchen." The white-clothed table is so large that this lawyer has to raise his voice.

"Now I'm serious," the New York lawyer says, loudly. "The food up here is supposed to be so special. Well, after a day or so someone asks this Rothschild what he thought. Was the food good enough for him? Was the food like the food at his estate? And mister, or Baron, Rothschild answers that it was not like the food on his estate at all. At his estate, the dogs ate better."

A bald, round-faced high school teacher from Boston laughs hardest. "One time," he says, "I read a magazine article about places like this. You know what they called it? *The*

*Derma Road.*" These are not simple people gathered in this vast and unplanned room, looking about, taking the measure of one another.

Last night, in a suite crowded with bodies, smoke, Scotch bottles, half-empty glasses and paper pails of ice, a newspaperman suddenly decided to recite Hamlet's soliloquy in Yiddish. Ice tinkled. Someone applauded. Someone else cried, "Oh, no!"

"Shh," said a hulking, big-faced man. "There's no call to be rude. There's no reason to hurt his feelings."

The newspaperman walked to the center of the coral, wall-to-wall carpet, holding a glass. His face was warped in concentration. The eyes were closed.

*Sein oder nicht sein*
*Dass iss die frage . . .*

"He's doing it," a black-haired man exclaimed. "Great. Isn't that great?"

"Great for whom," a heavy-bosomed girl said, irritably. "For Shakespeare, or for him?"

When the newspaperman finished, to light applause, the businessman who had rented the suite said that he had a complaint. The businessman had made a fortune in real estate; he was not scrofulous; and yet here at this free-thinking, semi-swinging, secular Jewish affair, he couldn't get a girl to dance, much less to bed.

"What am I doing wrong?" he wanted to know. The businessman had fashioned a towel into a turban and stood clothed in the costume of an Arab.

On an overflowing sofa a psychologist from St. Louis turned to a pretty dark-haired girl and said clearly, although not loud enough for her husband at the far end to overhear: "Believe me, all Jewish girls have sexual hang-ups. Like, what would you do if I grabbed your knee?"

The dark-haired girl stared impersonally at the psychologist. "Jewish men are hung up," she said. "Why do they always have to ask?"

Near a window, the heavy-bosomed girl turned to someone and said, "What kind of a Jew are you?"

"What do you mean what kind?"

"Well there are three kinds of Jews," the girl said. "There are religious Jews. You're not that."

"No."

"Then," the girl said, "there are gastroenterological Jews. They have to have *gefilte* fish in their belly to feel Jewish."

"Go ahead."

"Finally, there are cardiac Jews," the girl said. "That's what you are. That's what we all are. We've got a Jewish feeling right around the heart."

This is the convention of an organization that spent the 1930's in furious battle with anti-Semitism. At least three other major Jewish groups did the same. Now, as far as anyone can tell, there is barely enough anti-Semitism to go around for all the organizations pledged to fight it. But organizations do not willingly close up shop; they develop staffs, capital and lives of their own. When the original issues dim, they look for new ones.

The old Jewish "defense" groups are occupying themselves with civil rights generally, with the extremist right wing overall and with the broad vexing question of Jewish identification, which some suggest is the other side of the coin of anti-Semitism. As one professional Jewish organization worker has asked, "Isn't it only when mobs stop yelling 'kike' that real identification problems begin?"

That parenthetic question hangs; and these complex, predominantly secular, largely unpersecuted, Jewish people have driven long hours through spring rain to gather at this identifiably Jewish hotel.

"Why," a thin-nosed, gray-haired woman asks over nondescript prime ribs au jus in the wilderness of the dining room, "are we here? What are we doing in the Catskill Mountains, the Borscht Belt? Can anyone tell me that?"

"Where would you rather be, Molly?" a plump younger woman asks.

"Virtually anywhere. The Costa Brava. Paris. A first-class restaurant in New York."

"That isn't the question," says the gray-haired woman's husband. He is jowly, mustached, a prosperous New Yorker. "The question you should have asked, Molly," he says, "is what better place than this is there where an organization like ours can meet?"

"Harry, please," Molly says, a little sharply. "There are a dozen places that are better than this for conventions. Apparently someone at the top decided that this year we had to be super Jewish."

"I don't think that was the idea at all," the plump woman says. "The idea was to go to a very Jewish place, without being ashamed of the place or ashamed of being Jewish."

"Exactly," says Harry, the mustached New Yorker.

"Well, I don't see it that way at all," Molly says, retreating, throwing a hard look at her husband as she stabs her meat.

The day before, the convention program tried to provide a direct confrontation with identity. Leonard J. Fein, a sociologist at Massachusetts Institute of Technology, read a paper suggesting that the Jewish community must understand its own identity fully if it is to be safe from homogenization with the American community at large.

"Identity," Fein said, from the stage of the hotel's bare wooden theatre, "is a puzzlingly elusive variable. The images which people have of themselves are often transitory . . . but we need to know.

"We need to know . . . the characteristic forms of Jewish expression . . .

"We need to know, fundamentally what being Jewish means to those who call themselves Jews . . .

"Is being a Jew important? Is it costly? Is it pleasant? When is it relevant? And then, how do you go about doing it?"

That was yesterday. Now in the wilderness of the dining room, the waiters have started serving irrelevant desserts.

"Look!" cries a bright-eyed lady school teacher at a table near a side wall. "That waiter just gobbled up a piece of pie in two gulps!"

"What?"

"The waiter. He turned his back and shoved it down, the New England green apple pie." The teacher laughs easily. "Do you think the bosses here feed the help?"

"Ask Andy. He was with the N.L.R.B."

"Not tonight," Andy says. "Tonight I am with the Jewish community of the United States and with my wife and I would like another Scotch."

"I can't get over the menu," the teacher says, excited now. She laughs again. "Now what do you think would happen if we mated a Spanish Queen olive with a California ripe olive?"

"It would turn out to be a Sephardic olive," Andy says after a pause, "residing in Beverly Hills, but visiting friends once in a while near Tel Aviv."

At his table, Professor Leonard Fein is contending with a woman who wants him to answer the questions he raised in his paper. "You realize," Fein says, "such answers are not easy to supply."

"Professor Fein," says an elderly woman. "My grandson goes to Iowa. Is that a good place for a Jewish boy to go? Can he learn there?"

Fein bobs and weaves. He manages to continue eating. "But Professor," a woman says, "isn't Jewish identity really a matter of being comfortable with being Jewish?"

"To an extent," Fein says, sipping at coffee. "As a matter of fact, I remember walking across a lawn here earlier to sit for a minute and read. On the way I passed some people doing calisthenics to Yiddish cadence. *Ein zwei; ein zwei.* I felt just the slightest bit superior, until I sat down with my book. Then it struck me. They may well be more comfortable with Judaism than I."

Irving (Pat) Spiegel, curly, intense, sometimes poetic, sits in a distant corner at the press table. Spiegel is *The New York Times'* expert on Jewish news; he spends a major portion of his time pursuing Jewish conventions. He has opinions, not always fit to print.

"I have written something," Spiegel announces, "that I do not believe *The New York Times* will publish." He produces a mock dispatch about a real rabbi whose pomposity irritates him. "Put a head on this for me, someone," he says, and waves the story high. It reads (with names changed):

Special to *The New York Times*
Grossinger, New York, April 28—
    The Rev. Dr. Thomas Garber, Vicar of the Park Avenue "Hebrew" Congregation, in the midst of an oration on "Greek influence on Delancey Street," suddenly lost his balance and plunged into a snare drum in front of the lectern. The Congregation's orchestra of 130, who were playing Sousa's "Stars and Stripes Forever," had just reached a flute solo passage when Garber bounced off the drum's skin with a double roar.

"Pat!" someone says laughing. "Pat!"

"If I run for office," Spiegel says, "the ticket is no speeches, better desserts, government-supported Blue Mogen David; and butter with meat." He grins evilly. "Do I or do I not get the Jewish vote?"

Tonight there must be speeches. This is a convention. Thirty years ago, the speeches would have attacked Father Charles Coughlin and his Christian Front. Tonight the principal speaker is Michael Comay, Israeli Ambassador to the United Nations. Courteous applause follows his introduction. [The Israeli-Arab War.is yet to come.]

"I can remember," Michael Comay tells the expectant secular Jews, "when the world did not believe that Israel would last for eighteen minutes. And now we are eighteen years old." Mr. Comay is a dignified man, with a rough-cast face. He speaks without notes. He has been on his feet before.

"I remember," Comay says, "when the world thought that Israel would not survive its birth. I was there in the fighting when everyone waited for the Arab armies to drive us into the sea, and the days we fought, outnumbered and without water . . ."

A Philadelphia clothing executive sips lukewarm water, and says, "This fellow isn't the speaker Abba Eban is."

Mr. Comay turns to a recent Israeli foray. "There was nothing impulsive or indiscriminate about our action," he insists. "We may be criticized for crossing the frontier into Jordan, as we have been criticized before but no self-respecting sovereign state . . ."

An accountant from New York City considers his watch. "Just hope," he says, "that he spares us the pitch for Israeli bonds."

Michael Comay, South African Jew, courageous fighter, eminent Israeli, is telling successful, sophisticated American Jews things that they have heard before. His words, over the half-finished rainbow ices and the scraps of New England green apple pie, strike no fire. The secular delegates have braved spring rain, a *shtetl* of a hotel and this wilderness of a dining room to affirm their Jewishness in a secular way, but when Comay is finished they are frustrated. They have found no unity, no common sense of what it is to be a secular Jew.

Theodore Bikel, the entertainer, rises, holding a guitar. Thick-chested, black-haired Theo Bikel is a labor Zionist's son, born in Vienna. On the day of the Anschluss, twenty-eight years before, his father took Theo to a lawyer's office where the father supposed or hoped his son would be safe.

From a window of that office, Theo saw Adolf Hitler, riding down a street in angry triumph. The family fled Austria soon afterward.

Bikel carries the guitar, but he is not going to sing. "I will recite for you a poem," he says, the voice faintly accented by *Mittel-europe*. "It is a poem written by a man called Joseph Papiernikov, who fled Russia for Palestine many years ago. It is called *Das Lied fon Halutzim*—The Song of the Pioneers."

Bikel begins slowly, softly, but intensely. The Yiddish lines leap in dactyls as he recites.

> *Meer zennen, meer zennen, meer zennen, meer zennen—*
> > *Halutzim, peonairn,*
> *Oif felder, vas brennen,*
> *Oif felder, mit veestkite fon shsteppes farnommen—*
> *Vie shvelben mit freeling, die airshte gekommen—*
> > *Meer zennen!*

> *We are, we are, we are, we are—*
> > *Halutzim, pioneers,*
> *On fields, that burn,*
> *On fields of barren steppes—*
> *Like the swallows of spring, the first to arrive—*
> > *We are!*

Bikel stands very straight. The Yiddish dactyls are telling a story. He speaks louder now:

*We journey, we journey . . . not skimping on effort beneath the sun's fire . . . to find a warm home . . . we journey!*

Passion springs from him; the hall is silent.

*We are going, we are going . . . Halutzim, pioneers . . . sowing fields, singing with hope and life . . . though the soil does not lightly give in . . . Still we go!*

*We believe, we believe . . . a belief that uplifts us . . . we will cover the stony field with golden bloom . . . we believe!*

Now the big man throws out his arms and the strong baritone suddenly is as large as all the hall.

> *We are, we are, we are, we are—*
> > *Halutzim, pioneers,*
> *Who can and who will burn the bridge beneath—*

*And prove to the foe we are made of steel,*
*we are made of iron.*

   *We are!*

A wave of applause breaks. The right man saying the right poem has aroused the secular delegates. They remember now the Balfour declaration, the broken promises, the ancient libels. Jews cannot farm. Jews will not adventure. Jews cannot fight. Bikel's recitation, the passionate poem, have given lie to the libels.

No longer are the delegates comfortable middle-class Americans; internists, accountants and the proprietors of liquor stores. Instead, their velvet worlds forgotten, they have become border guards, tank commanders and *halutzim*, by poetic metamorphosis in the dining room of Grossinger's Hotel.

Identification, grave and earnest though it is to people who are lost, confused or variously unhappy, is also a loosely-structured intellectual game. The game begins with a question: Who am I? Discussion follows. People suggest answers. These prompt fresh questions and another round of discussion. The game spins on. It has no final ending. From the well-attended cradle to the plain pine coffin, Jewish identification is played over and over again.

"Does being Jewish mean a set of values?" a writer asks in a pamphlet issued by the "community-service" oriented National Council of Jewish Women, "and does it mean a particular outlook on God, man and the world? Or does it mean only having Jewish friends?" A housewife in Great Neck, New York considers these imperfect questions. "I don't know if there's any real difference between me and the Christian girls over in Brookville," she tells a neighbor, visiting beside the new steel sink. "But I am more comfortable with my own kind. Maybe that *is* what I mean by being Jewish."

"Oh, Lois," says the friend, "there simply must be more to it than that."

In the quest for Jewish identity in America, Dr. John Slawson, former Executive Vice-President of the American Jewish Committee, argues that "the Jewish tradition" speaks with "vigor and relevance" not only to Jews but "to all society." Slawson maintains that Jews have tried too hard to suppress "distinguishing Jewish characteristics," an error that contributes to "aloneness and uprootedness." But a Chicago businessman takes vigorous exception. "My kid was raised a Jew," the businessman says. "We filled his head full of tradition from the time he was two. So what happens? All he wants to do is go to Mississippi and help the *schvartzes* (Negroes), and he goes around bragging that he's an atheist. How do you figure that?"

The anti-Zionist American Council for Judaism distributes reprints of a discussion among three professors considering *What does Judaism offer the Modern American?* Here Dr. Jacob Petuchowski of Hebrew Union College asserts that if American Jews want a clearer sense of themselves, they must first wrest control of Jewish education away from Zionists. According to Petuchowski, "Zionist misuse of schools" has made Jewish young people believe "The Zionist has the real key that unlocks the treasures of Judaism." But the mere mention of the Council for Judaism drives an orthodox Detroit builder to roar with anger. "Zionism," the builder cries, in his lakeside home near Pontiac, "is the greatest thing ever for American Jews. When Israel won all those battles, the *goyim* found out once and for all that Jews could fight." He takes a deep breath. "Here," he says. "Have some more chocolate cake."

Crowds of sociologists and swarms of psychologists have published papers studying Jews as voters, as businessmen, as hoodlums, as citizens, as prostitutes, as fathers and as drinkers. Many authors look for an identifying unifying key. It is possible, after considering these reports, to conclude that Jews as opposed to non-Jews are slightly left of center, but moving right; prefer self-employment but are becoming increasingly interested in large corporations; commit proportionately fewer crimes of violence and contribute more generously to charities; dream of abandoning the urban brothel for a split level in Scarsdale, N.Y.; are intensely, almost desperately, devoted to their children, and do not drink as heavily as Christians, although they are getting there. It is equally possible to conclude from these studies that Jewish sociologists and psychologists are obsessed with studying Jews. The other conclusions may all be transient.

The game goes on in living rooms, at interdisciplinary conferences, in temples, on analysts' leather sofas, in restaurants, in mixed and all-Jewish country clubs. What does it mean to be a Jew? How does it feel? How should it feel? What in the world makes me Jewish?

In the world, there are twelve million possible answers, twelve million Jews being fortunate enough to survive into the final third of the twentieth century of the Christian era.

Is Sammy Davis, the Negro entertainer, really a Jew? What would happen if he tried to buy a house in an all-white Jewish neighborhood? Is Elizabeth Taylor Jewish? How can her children be defined? Did Mike Todd's family believe he had a Jewish wife?

Karl Marx's father converted to Christianity in 1824 when Marx was six years old. Was Karl Marx, the man, a Jew? Was Heine, the poet, who chose baptism as "a passport to culture?" Was Trotsky, the atheist, Jewish? Is Barry Goldwater? Was Jesus Christ?

Advanced logically, the difficult debates on Jewish identification lead on to further difficulty. After hearing the postulates, weighing scales of Jewish intensity, reading all the surveys from the field, one finally confronts a deeper issue. Identify with whom? Identify with what? Precisely who, exactly what, is a Jew?

Jews are not a race. They have neither common physical characteristics nor a common language. Probably more speak English than any other tongue. Jews are brown and white, tall and short, comfortable only in English or only in Yiddish or only in French, or only in Hebrew, or comfortable in all four. They pray to God eight times a day and passionately advocate atheism. "Jews?" someone has exclaimed in frustration. "There is no such thing as the Jews. They are members of a debating society that does not exist."

But most Jews, or most Jewish leaders, argue that the question of a meaningful definition is significant and relevant in the United States today. However, definition explodes beyond boundaries of time and place; it is a vital political issue in Israel.

Israel is sanctuary. That concept is as critical to the current Israeli republic as independence was to the young United States. Had a sanctuary such as Israel existed in the 1930's, hundred of thousands, perhaps millions, of the dead Jews of Europe, would live.

On July 27, 1950, the Knesset, Israel's parliament, formalized sanctuary, by passing its so-called Law of Return. Under this law, every Jew on earth who is not a criminal is endowed with a claim on Israeli citizenship. Any Jew who travels to Israel is at once free to immigrate without conforming to a quota. As soon as he enters, he can assume full Israeli citizenship without undergoing naturalization. The Law of Return is the enactment of one of the primary ideals of Zionism. It establishes Israel as a "Jewish national homeland." As pure law, of course, it is seriously flawed.

The Knesset, a political, not a philosophic body, chose not to attempt to define the word Jew. As a result the Law of Return specifically offered a promised land to a nonspecific or at least undefined group. Bad law makes hard cases, and incidents began almost at once. Was the Christian-born wife of a Jew eligible for citizenship? Were the children of mixed marriages? Were apostate Jews? The Knesset either did not know, or did not choose to say.

Almost seven years later, on July 18, 1957, David Ben-Gurion, then Prime Minister of Israel, elected to end the confusion with a concrete definition. In what he called his "credo," Mr. Ben-Gurion perhaps covered more ground than he intended.

Addressing an international Zionist organization, Ben-Gurion defined himself as "a Jew first and an Israeli afterward." A Jew, he said, was a member of "the Jewish people." That called for one more definition and Ben-Gurion was willing.

"There is a national unity of the Jews of the world," he said, "based upon a common destiny, a common heritage and"—here he began to court dispute— "common aspirations for the future." Did this mean that a Red Jewish factory manager in Leningrad and a capitalistic Jewish stock broker in Cleveland were working toward a common, somehow Jewish, end? From his primacy in Israel, Mr. Ben-Gurion stormed onward, adding mysticism and nationalism to his explanation.

"What has secured survival for the Jewish people," he argued, "is the Messianic vision of the prophets of [ancient] Israel, the vision of redemption for the Jewish people and for all humanity. The State of Israel is an instrument for the realization of this Messianic vision."

All Jews, Ben-Gurion asserted, owe loyalty to Messianic Israel. They owe it, no matter where they live or what they do or how they worship. "The Jewish people," he said, "all over the world is the State of Israel's foremost and most devoted ally."

Further, Jews beyond the borders of Israel, in Leningrad, Cleveland and everywhere else will always be confused about their identity. Confusion is a permanent but unifying condition of their existence. According to Ben-Gurion, they live in two worlds—Jewish and non-Jewish—and have no real roots in either. "It is only in Israel," he said, "that Jews are free as men and as Jews."

This speech, grained with truth, antagonistic to American constitutional theses, jingoist, arrogant, naïve and sincere, failed ultimately to satisfy even the orator himself. Within fifteen months, David Ben-Gurion confessed that for all his authority, for all his faith in Israel, he himself could not define a Jew.

Prompted by the citizenship problems of children from mixed marriages, Ben-Gurion wrote a long and careful letter on October 28, 1958, to *hachmei Israel*, "the wise men of the Jewish people." No such formal group exists. Ben-Gurion simply selected Jewish scholars around the world and asked them, quite humbly, for a lasting definition of a Jew.

A total of forty-three rabbis, essayists and scholars, including twelve Americans, responded to the request. Their answers compiled by bearded, Orthodox Baruch Litvin of Mt. Clemens, Michigan, have been edited by Dr. Sidney B. Hoenig of Yeshiva University, and published in a blue-bound volume, 420 pages long, called *Jewish Identity*. Considering replies from Le Grand Rabbin de France; the Chief Chaplain of the Israeli Army; Il Rabbino Capo, Livornio; the Chancellor of the Jewish Theological Seminary; Shmuel Y. Agnon, Nobel Prize winner; André Neher of the Université de Strasbourg; Moshe Silberg of the Israeli Supreme Court; Chaim Perelman of the Université Libre de Bruxelles; Harry A. Wolfson of Harvard; Joseph Soloveitchik, foremost American *Halachist*, and the rest, one is driven to only one position of certainty.

The *hachmei Israel*, the wise men of the Jewish people, do not agree on how to define a Jew.

According to the *Halachah*, the body of Jewish religious law, Jewishness is passed on through the mother, but not through the father. From an Orthodox Jewish viewpoint, the child in a mixed marriage always assumes the religion of the

mother. As some psychologists maintain, this indicates a ma-
triarchal society, consonant with the present emphasis on the
Jewish mother. But compassion lies here, as well. Under the
*Halachah,* the child of desertion or rape has always had full
status as a Jew.

In addition, the *Halachah* makes provision for converts. To
become a Jew, a female must submit to a ritual immersion
called *Tevilah.* According to Orthodox purists, the immersion
must be total, and the woman must be naked, stripped even
of rings. A male undergoes immersion and in addition must
be circumcised. The *Halachah* describes the Jew as a member
of a religious body, either inherited or willfully assumed.

Born a Jew, *Halachists* insist, always a Jew. One cannot
stop being Jewish by choice; personal choice is irrelevant to
Jewishness. The covenant between God and Abraham, renewed between God and Moses, is what binds Jews, according to the *Halachah.* The binding is eternal.

A Jew who joins the Roman Catholic Church sins, but so
does a Jew who simply neglects to pray. Neither condition al-
ters the individual's Jewishness. It makes him a bad Jew to be
sure. Good Jews may well despair for him. But his Jewishness is unaffected. In the interpretation of most theologians,
excommunication is unknown in the Jewish religion.

"You see," a bearded rabbi recently cried in the face of an
atheist, "being a Jew is something you're stuck with, like it or
not. You can't stop being a Jew, no matter to what lengths
you go. Only God could let you out, and He won't do it."

In the beginning, Jews were followers of Abraham. Speaking in the twelfth chapter of Genesis, God says to Abraham,
"I will make thee a great nation, and I will bless thee, and in
thee shall all the families of earth be blessed."

This is the covenant; from it springs the dogma of the
chosen people; from it emanates an essence of what it means
to be a Jew. *But not the only essence.*

*Not in America.*

*Not even in Israel.*

Oswald Rufeisen, born to an Orthodox Jewish family in
Poland, still is a Jew in *Halachic* terms. As a member of a
Carmelite Order near Haifa, Rufeisen calls himself Brother
Daniel, but he does not deny his Jewish mother. Several years
ago when he applied for Israeli citizenship under The Law of
Return, he described himself as "a Catholic of Jewish nation-
ality."

By four to one, the Israeli Supreme Court turned Rufeisen down. The majority did not challenge his birth or his sincerity. It conceded that on a strict religious basis, he might be called a Jew. But not on a foundation of legalities. The court decision praised Rufeisen as a lover of the Jewish people, and insisted that he remain "a lover from the outside, a distant brother."

Ultimately the Supreme Court of Israel would not define a Jew. Perhaps it could not. But it built toward a universal definition by ruling that secular facts must be applied.

"We don't say who a Jew is," says Will Maslow, executive director of the American Jewish Congress. "Practically, we accept for membership anyone who says he is Jewish and does not practice another religion. But we do not say that a Jew can be defined."

"Defiance of definition," the poet Karl Shapiro writes passionately, "is the central meaning of Jewish consciousness."

Yet this century has given us a definition and resolved questions of identity as well.

Those whom drunken Cossacks cursed as *Zhid* were free of abstract identification problems. The fullness of their Jewish heritage came home to them in the wail of pogrom.

And those who rode the slow cattle cars to Auschwitz must have known how brilliantly they had been defined. By fiat of an apostate Roman Catholic from Linz, a Jew was anyone who had three grandparents "wholly of the Jewish race." That is not a definition to please the *halachist,* the poet or the Jeffersonian democrat, but in this century, as almost every Jew in America understands and accepts and fears, it is the one that has mattered most.

# Part Two

## Gallery

BY RECENT COUNT, THERE WERE 212 SEPARATE but not equal, sometimes distinct, often overlapping, occasionally agreeing, frequently contending, communal, cultural, religious, secular, educational, social, welfare, Zionist and anti-Zionist Jewish organizations now functioning in the United States. Most Jews belong to none.

The American Jew, about whom it is dangerous to generalize, generally is not an organization man. Whether it is heritage, genes or coincidence, most American Jews seem to want to resolve their lives as independently as possible. Out of ancient instinct, or remembrance of recent cattle cars, they do not like to be herded. And they will not be. In a Jewish neighborhood, there is a plethora of leaders, and few followers. "Where I grew up," a businessman from the Brownsville section of Brooklyn recalls, "gambling was the number one sport. But we had a problem. Nobody wanted to place a bet. Every man considered himself a bookie."

On another level, American Jewish religion is a wonder of diversity. Judaism is fractioned into a minimum of three large divisions, within which subsections proliferate. From one extreme to another, American Judaism presents a theologic disparity easily as broad as that which separates Southern Baptist revivalists from Northern Unitarian intellectuals.

The secular variety of Jews is wider still. There is no American Jewish viewpoint on the war in Vietnam, or on the public postures of Stokely Carmichael, or on premarital sexual intercourse. Rather one finds scores, hundreds, of different points of view. There is, broadly, no American Jewish position on anything, except possibly anti-Semitism. Jews oppose it. However, they do not agree on how to fight back.

Surveys deceive. One learns from statistics that most Jews live in large urban-suburban centers; that Jews attend college at a rate significantly above the national average; that a high percentage of Jews work in "professional, technical and kindred occupations"; and that Jews typically earn more money than the prototype head of an American household. All these assertions are beyond challenge but they apply equally to other groups, such as White Russians and Japanese-Americans. Other sets of studies may be necessary to ascertain differences among Jews. Still the results will continue to be incomplete.

The disparity of Jewish life in America transcends the current methodology of surveys. Sitting beside the pool at Green Gables, a Jewish Country Club in Denver, watching children leap into the water, observing men stride from the eighteenth green, one knows that these people are not Philadelphians. They are westerners. One does not know this in a way that necessarily makes clinical sense. It is a feeling. The Jews of Green Gables in Denver are a different breed from the Jews of the Ashbourne Country Club of Cheltenham, Pennsylvania.

Talking to the Ropfogel family of Emporia, Kansas, one realizes that these are midwestern people. They are as alien to New York as a banking Lehman would be to the Flint Hills rolling south of Emporia. That does not make the Ropfogels either more or less Jewish than the Lehmans. It only makes them small-town, midwestern American Jews.

Multiply these examples ten thousand times. Vary the sum by changes of name and face, accent and eyes, skin tones and strength. Then, in a vague, imperfect way one can comprehend the overwhelming fact of Jewish life in America today. It is varied beyond any telling of variety.

For the most part, large Jewish organizations have a hard time accepting diversity. All organizations feel most comfortable with common, categorizable denominators. Indeed the so-called service organizations survive by appealing to specific and definable groups for funds. Sincerity and self-preservation mix as the large Jewish organizations issue press releases hailing a unity of outlook here, a common interest there and an increasing sense of Jewish commitment throughout the country.

The organizations are vocal and smooth; by contrast, the unorganized are mute. Reading Jewish news, as it is reported in newspapers and newsmagazines, one gets a sense of Jewish unity that does not exist beyond the printed page. Although no organization carries the antiorganizational banner of disunity, it unquestionably can be argued that with each generation, Jewish life in America is developing fewer common interests, more contending outlooks and a lesser commitment to things Jewish, whatever they may be.

There is a Jewish story that starts with a shipwreck and a Providential rescue on a desert island for twenty male survivors, of mixed faiths. The men take stock as rapidly as possible. They find plentiful food and water. The native women are amiable and pleasingly pale. After a month, the survivors decide to thank God and meet in three separate groups to plan their houses of worship.

Eight are Roman Catholics. They say a Hail, Mary, and build a church.

Nine are Protestants. They talk briefly and build two churches, one with a dirt floor for Fundamentalists.

The three Jews argue for a week before they can agree on what to do. Then they build four synagogues. Three cover specific branches of religious Judaism. The fourth gives them each a synagogue not to be caught dead in.

The Jewish inclination toward diversity ends only at a point of common concern.

Most major Jewish groups in the United States describe themselves as "defense organizations." They exist in order to defend Jews against anti-Semitism. B'nai B'rith (son of the Covenant), which dates from 1843, is "social and philanthropic"—in short, fraternal—but B'nai B'rith sponsors and underwrites the Anti-Defamation League, which "seeks to eliminate defamation of Jews."

The American Jewish Committee, founded in 1906, "seeks to prevent infraction of the civil and religious rights of Jews in any part of the world." Prosperous American Jews, of German descent, created the Committee following a Czarist pogrom in Bessarabia. To this day, the Committee retains a prosperous, conservative air; its current president, Morris B. Abram, is its first leader whose ancestry traces to Eastern Europe.

The American Jewish Congress, gathered earlier before Theo Bikel at Grossinger's, split from the Committee in the 1920's. By self-definition, the Congress "seeks to eliminate all forms of racial and religious bigotry; to defend separation of church and state, to promote the creative survival of the Jewish people; to help Israel develop in peace and freedom." Less affluent than the Committee, the Congress reflects the activism of the East European immigrants who followed German Jews to America. Its publication, *Congress Bi-Weekly*, is printed on rough paper and carries almost exclusively articles of Jewish interest. The American Jewish Committee publication, *Commentary*, is slick, secular and doggedly erudite.

The Jewish Labor Committee, to the left of the Congress and well left of the Committee, "seeks to combat anti-Semitism," and "aids Jewish and non-Jewish labor institutions overseas." Several leagues right of all the other organizations stands the American Council for Judaism, which "seeks to advance universal principles of a Judaism free of nationalism." Its commitment is to fight Zionism.

B'nai B'rith is by far the largest of the groups, claiming 400,000 members. According to spokesmen for other organizations, the figure is immodest; they suggest that B'nai B'rith officials count each individual in the families of its members in order to produce an impressive figure. "The real number," one charges, "is 150,000." Nevertheless, as a broad-based, multi-faced fraternal group, B'nai B'rith is inevitably larger than the defense organizations, which advocate specific programs and cannot, by their nature, meet simply for fun. The largest defense group, the American Jewish Committee, has no more than 30,000 members. Influence is quite another thing.

An unscientific, clinical examination of defense organizations is provided by the novelist, Paul Jacobs, in *Is Curly Jewish?* Mr. Jacobs postulates that the phrase, *Screw the Jews,* has been scrawled above a urinal in a saloon on Third Avenue in Manhattan. Offended, while urinating, a Jew calls four defense groups to complain.

In Mr. Jacobs' fantasy, a representative of the anti-Defamation League of B'nai B'rith dusts fingerprint powder above the urinal, photographs the graffiti and takes repeated pictures of the fingerprints. He then checks the pictures against A.D.L. files on the fingerprints of two million confessed American anti-Semites. Afterward, the A.D.L. runs the photograph in its bulletin, to show that anti-Semitism is increasing and that everyone should enroll in B'nai B'rith.

The man from the American Jewish Committee studies the men's room carefully; soon afterwards the Committee extends a grant to Columbia for a study of anti-Semitic wall-writing since Pompeii: At the same time, according to Mr. Jacobs, the Committee staff prepares a pamphlet proving that the martini was invented by a Jew. Ultimately, the American Jewish Committee informs its members that at its next annual meeting a distinguished medical authority will speak on Al-

coholism and Anti-Semitism: A Clinical View, to be followed
by a workshop discussion.

An official of the American Jewish Congress arrives at the
bar trailed by pickets bearing signs that demand, "Tear down
the Wall." Within the offices of the American Jewish Congress meanwhile, six lawyers are preparing a brief for the
U.S. Supreme Court, which demands a prohibition of the sale
of liquor to anyone making an anti-Semitic remark.

All the while, the Jewish Labor Committee has arranged a
series of weekend seminars for members of the bartenders
union, and prepared a resolution for the next annual meeting
of A.F.L.-C.I.O. The proposal orders union men not to re-
lieve themselves into anti-Jewish urinals.

Finally, the American Council for Judaism issues a statement. Its representative meets the press while flanked by two
Arabs, dispatched from the American Friends of the Middle
East. The Council spokesman denies that the Graffiti could
have been written "because there are no Jews, but only
Americans of Jewish descent." He then calls on the President,
the Secretary of State and the governors of the fifty states, to
condemn the efforts of Israel and the Zionists to identify Israel with American Jews.

Despite the Council, most American Jews devoutly admire
Israel. Although anti-Zionism has a strong history, particularly among Jews of German background, all but a small percentage of the Jews in the United States find themselves sup-
porting Israel, right or wrong, against her enemies. To most,
the feeling is visceral, profound, overwhelming, beyond fighting. It has produced acts of astonishing and impetuous generosity. The 5.6 million-man American Jewish community has
contributed more than a billion dollars to Israel in her lifetime. Discounting, as one should, a certain amount for high-
pressure fund raising, the figure remains barely believable. By
contrast, the West German government has paid Israel repar-
ations totaling only $860 million (although billions more
were awarded to individual Jewish victims of the Nazis,
many of whom have become Israelis). By further contrast,
the ethnic donations of other groups—Irish Americans to the
Irish Free State, Italian Americans to postwar Italy—are
dwarfed. When Israel battled four Arab countries in 1967,
the American Jewish response, in cash, concern and tears, as-
tonished even American Jews. As General Rabin's tanks

moved out, millions of American Jews suddenly discovered that they were Zionists.

What is it that concerns the Jews of America, in and out of their 3,100 synagogues (for the 64.9 per cent who attend services); after the B'nai B'rith discussions (for the eight per cent who may belong to B'nai B'rith); after the *Commentary* symposiums on Jewish identity, alienation, and religiosity (for the one per cent who subscribe to *Commentary*)? What concerns them after the round-table human relations, where-are-we-going, what-shall-we-be, how-do-we-know-who-we-are, are-we-really-Jews, if-we-are-what-makes-us-so, how-are-we-unique intergroup developmental conferences?

In the fine old phrase of Wordsworth, they are concerned with getting and spending; that and its results on cerebral cortex and coronary artery. As metropolitan middle-class Americans, they are afflicted with the worries of the American metropolitan middle class: yesterday's parking ticket, to-day's headache, and tonight's television commercial; the doctor who won't make house calls; the auto mechanic who overcharges; the pending real estate tax increase; fallout from China; male singers with long hair; World War III; the nursing home that acts insensitive to Grandma; the future of man; sex; and whether, now that we have put thirty dollars down on a new bedroom air-conditioner, this summer will really turn out to be as hot as last year's. The worries are ordinary. The kind of worrying is not.

Jews are people of terrible intensity. After two millennia of wandering and abuse, concern stabs them more deeply than it stabs other Americans. They feel more; perhaps Jewish sensors are more exquisitely refined. That would help explain why the white civil rights workers murdered in Mississippi "happened" to be Jews, why that vast apparatus of putative concern, psychiatry, is largely a Jewish monopoly; why Jewish community campaigns have drawn more than 2.5 billion dollars in contributions during the last two decades; and why that instrument of infinite concern, the violin, is played brilliantly by men named Milstein and Stern and matchlessly by Jascha Heifetz.

Does intensity wholly explain? C. P. Snow, considering Jewish achievement, suggests, "the Jews, who have not been lucky in much, have obviously been lucky in the genes.

"Where," the English author asks, "has this wonderful gene pool come from?

"No one has been able to give me an answer that seems remotely satisfactory."

The concept of a remarkable primal gene pool satisfies by itself; it answers any number of questions at once. All the gifted, vibrant, intellectual Jews in America are explained away by referring to genes within the loins of Abraham, Sarah and other Palestinian nomads dead three thousand years ago.

Millennia intervene. Jews have intermarried and been joined by converts and been persecuted. It is not difficult for the environmentalist to refute Snow with a counter theory. He simply suggests that two thousand years of Christian anti-Semitism have created a climate in which Jews have had to excel if they wished to survive.

Various behavioral distinctions appear to differentiate Jews from others. The psychiatrist, Karl Menninger, has observed that the Irish throw bricks and the Italians throw knives, but that quarreling Jews hurl words. Jews do not very often start barroom fist fights or play middle linebacker in the National Football League, or assault and batter policemen. In the sentence of one New York City detective, "When it's a violent crime, we pretty generally rule out the Jews." Across centuries, physical violence has become synonymous with Jewish disaster, with pogroms. For more than 2,000 years, in all that desperate reach from Joshua until the Israeli War of Independence, Jews had to exist without experiencing the gutjoy that comes with winning a battle.

Their traditions turned away from the physical and education became a passionate concern. More than any other immigrant group, Jews stormed the battlements of the American educational system which, notably on college and graduate levels, responded by erecting higher battlements to bar them. Once the phenomenal number of Jews in college was attributed to an ethnic Jewish thirst for knowledge; now with more and more Jewish collegians reportedly emulating the Christian and his gentleman's 'C,' its sources are understood to be more complex. Jews proceed from a background which emphasizes learning; they also live in a society where everyone who wants to be successful is expected to submit to education by degrees.

Social justice concerns Jews in a complex variety of Jewish ways. It is true that some Jews are the merchants of Harlem, selling *shlock* goods at exorbitant prices and charging usurious rates for time payments. As liquor store owners they purvey firewater to the wild young men of Watts; Jews are slumlords and exploiters of the underprivileged. But, in the angry words of Nelson Glueck, the archeologist who is president of Hebrew Union College, "For every Jew who owns an apartment in a Negro ghetto and extracts every miserable penny from shoving a dozen people into a room, I warrant that you would find a hundred Jews who think that this is a despicable performance. I'm not trying to deny a fact," Dr. Glueck says. "It exists. It's ugly. It's unforgivable. I'm ashamed of it. But not to the point of saying it is characteristic of the Jew of the United States. I think it's not. More characteristic is their willingness to battle for the rights of human beings."

As underdogs, Jews have distilled an essential emotional underdogism. The Jew—a substantial majority of American Jews—intuitively sympathizes with the persecuted Negro. Emotionally, the Jew identifies and sees part of himself in the Negro victim. Frequently he sees things that are not there. Later, when the real Negro turns out to be a different individual from the imagined pseudo Jew, when he turns out to have a different and unJewish set of responses, his Jewish sympathizer is disappointed. His emotional underdogism has not built to a philosophy. Still emotional, he is outraged. "Why don't they take care of their own orphans," he demands, "and build their own hospitals the way we do."

But the chief difficulty, the growing disaffection between Jews and Negroes in the United States, rises most sharply on the Jewish side when underdogism is overwhelmed by stronger factors, such as fear of violence. To most Jews, a rioting Negro does not look like an underdog. He is a law-breaker, a hoodlum, a threat. In America Jews do not yet feel as secure from threats as a detached interpreter might think.

Despite full faith in Thomas Jefferson and the Constitution, despite the careful studies suggesting a decline in anti-Semitism, and despite the obvious flowering of Jewish success, survival remains *the* mortal concern of the Jews of America. In the flow of history, it could hardly be different.

All men respond to self-preservation, but the Jewish survival cry resounds through a darker horn. It rings from antiquity through York, 1185; Spain, 1492; Recife, 1654, and all the sanguine massacres of modern times, renewed by each fresh attempt at extermination. The Jews' determination to survive as Jews is one of the unique developments in man. Without question it dominates enormous areas of the Jewish experience in America, perhaps (and irrelevantly) the only great Western country which has never been the scene of a pogrom.

Survival troubles American Jews when their children marry Christians. Will their grandchildren be lost to the heritage?

Survival disturbs a Jewish dentist whose son is failing physics. "You are dragging us back toward the ghetto!" the dentist roars.

Survival stirs in a Jewish writer, married briefly to a titled Anglican, who looks at their wrinkled newborn daughter and announces, "I see five thousand years of suffering in her face."

Survival moves, ubiquitous and polymorphic, within a prosaic Jew intent on building a business for his son and within an ethereal Jew passing on to his daughter precepts of intellectual humanism.

Survival is why almost every American Jew responds instantly when he is asked, "Do you think that *it* can happen here?" Shock of recognition tears at the face. The mouth drops. An answer begins. "It" commands at once into Jewish minds the image of the slaughter of the Jews of America. The image is strained, implausible, irrational and, for all that, no less real.

## THE SPEECH OF A FOOL

American Jews are not cotton-pickers or clam-rakers. They are disinclined to sweep factories, collect garbage or serve as men's-room attendants. In what is surely an expression of their urge to survive, they aspire higher, strive harder, want more and relax less than the general unclassified American. Jews have waited a long time for the American opportunity. They want urgently, desperately, to 'succeed. They pursue power, position, money, independence, respect. In the American society, the supertypical way for a Jew to achieve all five at once is to embark on the practice of medicine.

Approximately ten per cent of 277,575 physicians in the United States are Jews. Although that is more than triple the percentage of Jews in the total population, the figure by itself does not say very much. It does not describe thousands of others Jews, driven toward medicine, who are not able to become doctors. It does not hint at the historic anti-Semitism of medical schools. It does not suggest the nature of the Jewish struggle to enter a field whose leaders decided, as business improved, that they wanted no more than a fractional minimum of Jews sharing the spoils.

A variety of investigations after World War II brought attention to the quota system as it was practiced by scores of medical colleges. One common rationale had been to accept Jews in proportion to their numbers in the population, or roughly three per cent. Using this guide medical school officers were able to ignore the significantly higher percentage of Jews among their applicants, a practice which some still strive to defend. They also ceased to judge men and women on merit, which is indefensible.

The investigations led to a relaxation of quotas, sometimes voluntarily and sometimes, as in New York State, under the blackjack of an anti-discrimination law. The situation has improved for Jews who want to become physicians, but inside medicine today they often find their place narrowly retricted.

Certain hospitals deny Jews staff privileges. Others grant Jews rights without authority. Except at Jewish hospitals and a number of superior nonsectarian institutions, the evidence argues powerfully that Jews are *de facto* barred from becoming chiefs of service.

While the Jewish physician takes care of his patients, his Christian colleagues seem to prefer, without him, to take care of the large issues of U.S. medical policy, from fighting the socializers on up, or down. The Jewish M.D. is on the inside of a putatively desirable field. But within he still finds himself an outsider.

Dr. S. A. Wilson, M.D., as he likes to be called, attending internist at Harrison Hackbart Memorial Hospital, lives in a huge, expensive, amorphous home, constructed of redwood and glass on the highest hill in a university town in the Carolinas. Outside, through the rear living room windows of triply thermal glass, the second highest hill rises, beyond a valley. When seasons change, the outlook is breathtaking. "I only wish," complains Sam Wilson, a short, powerful, knobby man, "that my patients would give me time to enjoy it once in a while."

"People simply have no respect for a physician's privacy any more," says Carol Wilson, white-haired, handsome, in a deep red hostess gown. "They say he's grumpy, but I don't know how poor Sam puts up with all the—pardon me—shit, as well as he does."

"If I didn't grump," Dr. Wilson says, "they'd be knocking at my front door all night long. And it's never the really sick ones that bother you. The psychs are the ones. The psychs kill you."

Sam Wilson's M.D. was a long time in the winning. Under the black moods that strike more frequently as he approaches sixty, he says it is the only damn thing he ever really won. Sam Wilson wishes he were a surgeon, but years ago, when he had the staying power for extra years of residency, the way was barred to Jews. He flirts with the idea of retiring from practice. He has money. His son, Clem, teaches English to freshmen in Boulder. But retirement would mean the official end of Dr. S. A. Wilson, M.D. He would become S. A. Wilson retired M.D. He would almost be plain Samson Wilson. And that, after all these years, would not be bearable. Whatever else he has not done (and Lord, he knows better than anyone how deeply he has failed), Sam Wilson has become a Doctor of Medicine. At fifty-seven, he can no longer sign his name to a golf card without appending the letters of his triumph, M.D.

He is not the only doctor in the town. The university teems with doctors of philosophy expert in the humanities and in what Wilson regards as the lesser sciences. He is not even the only M.D. But he is certain that he is the best. When challenged, S. A. Wilson, M.D. believes that he can make a diagnosis, save a life, or lose it after the right fight, more consistently than any other physician in the community. He knows it. He suspects the Christian doctors know it. But it is not something they discuss.

"Hey, Sammy," Crandall Peppinoe, a sandy-haired surgeon bellowed at him down the line one day when the hospital cafeteria served hamsteaks. "I catch yew eatin' any uh this, I'm goan call yuh rabbi, hee-yuh?" That was what the Christian doctors discussed with S. A. Wilson, M.D. Rotten bigot's jokes.

Except for the time Peppinoe's button-nosed wife contracted mononucleosis and they were scared to death that it might be leukemia. That night after he examined her and they waited for the blood tests Peppinoe called him Sam, not Sammy, and his wife blinked frightened eyes and called him doctor. Afterwards, Peppinoe sent a bottle of bourbon with a note, "To the Doc, from his real good friends." No one made kosher jokes at Doctor Wilson when in trouble.

Dr. S. A. Wilson, M.D. moved to the university town years before, after New York soured. He had never enjoyed New York City; it was simply his entranceway into the world, the place where his father imported fruits and made money and his mother fawned.

Samson was the oldest son, and Hannah Doktorman Wilson began her son's piano lessons when he was five. By seven he could play a Chopin Mazurka. He started the violin at nine. Unfortunately, by the time he had reached the third position, even the violin teacher suggested that the boy limit himself to the piano. There was a problem of imprecise pitch, on top of uncertain rhythmic sense. Sam had to abandon serious pianism before he was fifteen.

But he performed splendidly at Townsend Harris, a public high school for superior students where the full syllabus was crammed into three exciting years. He won the chemistry medal, and as a sophomore at Columbia he decided that he would be a chemist, specializing in ketones.

"Sam, Sam," said his father. "Why do you have to break your mother's heart again?"

"Again?"

"The first time was when it turned out you were not Josef Hofmann."

In the spacious living room, nine floors above West End Avenue in New York City, they laughed. "You could be a fine chemist," the father said. "Of that I do not have the slightest doubt. But finer still is something else. You could be a doctor. That would make everybody proud."

As if on cue, Hannah Wilson entered the living room. "You would have a profession everywhere in the world, Samson," she said. "Do you know what that means? And everywhere you would be a respected member of the community."

Their persistence did not flag, and the obsessive concern for his personal future embarrassed Sam. The day on which he finally agreed to accede, to abandon chemistry for medicine, was largely devoted to making an altruistic speech. He had quietly joined a campus Socialists' club, and that afternoon delivered a heady talk. "Until the tools of production are placed directly into the hands of workers," Sam Wilson told a small audience, including a reporter from the student newspaper, "there can be no true democracy in the United States."

At home that night he mentioned medicine casually. After Marx, Hippocrates was an anti-climax. Sam was surprised at the way his father jumped up and shook his hand. His mother's round face twisted and she began to weep enormous tears, crying, "It's happiness, Samson, nothing but happiness." The brown mascara ran on her downy cheeks.

When Columbia, Cornell and N.Y.U. medical schools rejected her son, Hannah Dokterman Wilson cried again. So, in great privacy, did Sam. What did they want? He had a B-plus average, brought down from A-minus only by his weakness in foreign languages. He was a C student in German and French. But the science marks were a straight, consistent A. Glumly he enrolled at N.Y.U.'s graduate school to take a Master's in the chemistry of ketones.

That autumn his father spoke ferociously. "I have been making certain inquiries," Isaiah Wilson told his son. "I am not a man devoid of influence, as you may realize."

"About what?" Sam said. "Inquiries about what?"

"And it turns out," the father said, "that the person who kept you out of medical school was you yourself."

"What?"

"A certain speech you made, the speech of a fool. It was reported in the campus newspaper. It got for you some attention."

"I made a lot of speeches, Dad," Sam said.

"You know to what I refer. I have found out that the medical schools in the city would not automatically reject a Jewish boy who gets C's in French and German. They do reject a Jewish boy with C's who shows dangerous radical leanings."

"Oh, Jesus Christ," Sam said.

"Don't use profane language at me," Isaiah Wilson said. "I do not blame them. Your best hope, now, I am informed, is to reapply after you have gotten the Master's to a few schools —I have their names here—outside of the city where your fame has not spread." If Isaiah Wilson were not a cultivated man, he would have spat.

The medical school that finally accepted Sam, two years

after his graduation from Columbia, was located in the midwest. From that time, Sam never wanted to live in New York City again. New York was the place of his humiliation.

He found the Carolina university town on a vacation drive with Carol, a rabbi's daughter who had a small dowry, important in their early years together. It was the prettiest place either of them had seen. "Why not practice here," Carol said.

"Why not?" knobby Sam Wilson said, agreeing.

He has gone from middle years to the brink of age in the Carolinas, becoming squatter and more ugly and more grumpy with each season. They only tolerate me when they need me, Dr. S. A. Wilson, M.D., thinks. They only put up with me when a child contracts croup or a professor sags with hepatitis or a wife writhes into labor on a weekend when Hank McGranery, the O.B., is out of town. It is a point of honor with Dr. Wilson to bark at all his patients.

"What are you bothering me for?" he shouts at a French instructor's thin, nervous wife, when her daughter's 102° turns out to be an indeterminable and insignificant virus. "There are no other symptoms. Why couldn't you let it wait until morning? You're an intelligent woman, aren't you? Answer me. Well?"

He grumbles either way. "You should have called me at least a day sooner," he berates a mathematician. "That rasp in your wife's chest is called pneumonia. She's very sick, and maybe she'll get sicker. If you pray, I suggest you say one tonight for antibiotics."

Dr. S. A. Wilson, M.D. loves the practice of medicine, in which he is uncomfortable, more than he loves the people he treats, particularly those people, who looking at him see not the disappointed arhythmic pianist, the denied chemist, but only a squat, bald-headed knobby man, who is going to hurt them or charge them ten dollars or both. "People," Wilson says repetitively, aimlessly, "do not respect a doctor any more."

In the university town, the Ph.D.'s practice an inverse snobbery. In the presence of Dr. S. A. Wilson, M.D., they pointedly refer to one another as "mister." It is as if "doctor," having been taken over by physicians, is no longer a respectable title for a man of learning. Wilson was bitterly hurt when he deduced the implication. (Did he deduce it, he wonders, or is it something he imagines?) But privately, in those recesses of his mind which he has not been able to seal he concedes that these snobbish, intellectual patients may have something there.

He has seen things in the practice of medicine which do no honor to the art of healing. He has seen greed, incompetence, sadism, sexual aggression disguised as medical practice. But he will not speak out. It is not for him. He can never speak out; he cannot forget what happened to him because he had spoken out, made the speech of a fool when he was at Columbia.

He has too much now. He cannot afford large risks. He has his practice and his hospital affiliation and his handsome, conservative wife. But if he could speak out, Dr. S. A. Wilson, M.D., would tell them a thing or two worth hearing.

"Medicine," Sam Wilson wants to say, "is to help people. That"—and sometimes he believes this now—"is why I became a doctor.

"I see two kinds of people dominating American medicine," Sam Wilson wants to say. "There are the incompetents and the fascists. Take McGranery, a Catholic, right? A decent guy sure. But a slow-moving, slow-thinking man. He has killed kids. He's damaged women. Not out of malice. McGranery just doesn't know; and what we say is, it's lucky he's in O.B. where everything works out most of the time anyway. Nonsense! He's an incompetent. I wouldn't let him take a wart off Carol. Then there are fascists. By fascist I mean someone who does not give a stinking damn for the fate of other human beings. You find the fascists running the medical schools and the hospitals. They care about systems and figures and birth rates and death rates and methodology, but what do they care about that little colored kid, dying in a shack, crying in pain?

"We doctors have to do something," Sam Wilson wants to tell them. "Not the money-grubbing lawyers or the no-good newspapermen or the ignorant laymen. The best of them don't know. Doctors are supposed to be special people, like rabbis, and it's up to us to change the way things are. Medicine means money, so that's what we get, young people who want to be rich. Bright? Sure. Gifted? Sometimes. But the motivation is all wrong. Medicine is a moneygrubbers' business now, just like importing exotic fruit. We've got to stop that; we have to start getting the best young people, like my own boy, who went off to teach Keats and Shelley instead of practicing medicine.

"I know how we can do it," Sam Wilson wants to announce. "I don't need any fat Madison Avenue sharpies or any A.M.A. weasels to tell me either.

"We make it a law. Laws are the foundation. This law says that no doctor in the country is allowed to earn more than twenty thousand dollars a year. That's plenty. Nobody starves. And nobody gets rich. You want to make money, go import fruit. Go work on Madison Avenue. You want to practice medicine. Haaa! Good. Wonderful. Then be a doctor for less than twenty thousand a year."

If only he could know the precise hour of his death, Sam Wilson thinks that he could really make the speech. If only he knew when his heart, which worries him, was about to enter its final spasm, the anvil falling on his chest, then he would do it. Twenty-four hours before his death he would stand up in Union Square, New York City, or wherever they make great speeches these days, and the things he would tell them, they would not soon forget. Not soon or ever.

But Dr. S. A. Wilson, M.D. does not know when he will die, and too much is at stake in his life to let his tongue wag loose. He is a doctor with an important affiliation at Hackbart Memorial Hospital.

When an intimate, Mel Brannum, who owns the Carolinas Motel, complains that a specialist missed a diagnosis and overcharged, Dr. Wilson simply says that medicine, like anything else, is imperfect.

"Then why don't you try to set it straight," says Brannum, a Unitarian and an activist.

"Why should Sam look for trouble?" Carol Wilson says.

"I would," says Dr. Wilson, "if my nose was shaped different. It's tough enough for me now as it is."

"What the hell is that supposed to mean?" Mel Brannum says fiercely.

Dr. Sam Wilson, the outsider in Christian-American medicine, has exposed himself more than he intended. "You wouldn't know, Mel," he says, shifting into his grump, erecting his profession as a shield. "The problems that exist in medicine today are nothing that a layman could possibly understand."

## THE HORN IN THE CELLAR CLOSET

Why music so charms Jews is sheerest mystery. Their legacy of chants, if sometimes touching, is unexceptional. There is no Beethoven, no Brahms in the Jewish past. Not one of the great eighteenth- and nineteenth-century composers was a Jew. Felix Mendelssohn-Bartholdy came from a Jewish family, but worked hard all his life at being Lutheran; besides, his creations are not of the highest rank.

Yet in the twentieth century, as if from nothing, out of thin air, a Jewish armada has conquered musical performance. Jewish names comprise the aristocracy of performers: Heifetz and Horowitz; Elman and Rubinstein; Piatigorsky and Koussevitsky; Bernstein and Stern, Fleisher, Glazer, Gomberg, Graffman, Roisman, Rosen, Schneider.

One understands the violin. It sings of the Wailing Wall. But piano, flute and oboe? Clarinet, double-bass and tuba? Timpani and tunable bells? Playing these instruments, with their chirps, roars, grunts, snorts, idiosyncrasies and songs, Jews dominate serious musical performance in America.

The reason is elusive. Music is art and yields its secrets hard. Musicians themselves joke: "When they put together the Israel Philharmonic they found they had twenty-seven first violins."

A bitter story one Jewish musician tells describes a future in which Negroes have become the ruling class, and Jews are menials. "Why," asks one Negro, dining at a pleasant restaurant, "can't the waiter bring the food, without doing a jig right up to the table?"

"You know how it is with these Jews," the other Negro says. "They've got this natural sense of rhythm."

They have rather, a natural drive, which sometimes channels itself against reason into an unfailingly demanding craft, whose rewards are illusory and uncertain. As a physician, Sam Wilson has been able to avoid economic stress. To a great degree he is his own master. As a moderately successful musician, Wilson would not have been able to finance his hilltop home and he would have had to work how and when he was ordered. It would have been different only if he were one of the top few dozen instrumentalists in the world.

For every soloist, one finds hundreds and hundreds of orchestral players having, as one complains, "someone shake a stick in my face for my whole life." Orchestral wages are not generous. Gifted musicians have to seek pupils to remain solvent. They must teach scales and their renown is minute, limited to children, a few friends and a handful of compulsive program readers.

For every orchestral player, laboring through his repetitive routine, there are thousands of other musicians who do not play at all. The life distressed them. The discipline broke them. They were not good enough.

Something in the American Jewish spirit rises to meet the agony and challenge of playing great music. That is a point in which American Jews take pride. "Hey, Bud," bellows the Texan, in the story, after his chauffeur has gotten lost on the lower East Side. "How do you get to Carnegie Hall from here?"

An ancient bearded man considers briefly. Then in answer he calls out the Eleventh Commandment. "Practice," the old Jew says, "Practice. Practice."

Harry Wolf, small, chubby, brown-haired with sensitively curved lips, is refusing to play Brahms' *Second* on his phonograph in the cellar. "Brahms is popular for only one reason," Harry Wolf says. He sucks a cigarette and raises his left hand to prevent interruption. "Brahms is popular," Harry says, "because his stuff fits just right on both sides of a long-playing record. Figure it out. His symphonies take about forty minutes, give a little time for the interpretation, either way."

Harry Wolf strides up und down the damp concrete floor. He calls the cellar a playroom. In one corner, his daughter, dark-haired and fourteen, curls prettily before a softly-playing TV.

"How's *Gunsmoke* tonight, Trudy?" Harry says, striding toward the girl. He wheels before she answers. She does not look up. Her father strides away.

"Out here," Harry Wolf says, "we like Western shows. I guess they don't care for them so much back in New York. Out here we have no time for phony sophistication." Harry hurls his cigarette to the floor and grinds it out. "But we got air to breathe," Harry says, "and unpolluted water, and tomorrow when the sun comes up, I'm going to show you the mountain in my backyard."

One wall of the cellar is papered with tan whooping cowboys, who ride broncos against a background of bland blue. Laundry droops on a drying rack nearby. There is almost no furniture in the playroom-cellar. Harry barely breaks even as the proprietor of Wolfcubs: Harry Wolf's Western Dog Breeding Centers & Kennels. Gwyneth Wolf supports the family. She is secretary to the president of The Great Divide Insurance Company. Slight and delicate at thirty-seven, Gwyn Merritt Wolf earns $115 a week.

"What I like to do," Harry twangs carefully in the cellar, "is go up into the Punchub Range and camp. Take a packhorse. Ever make a packhorse trip? The nights are cold, pardner, believe you me." Harry lights a cigarette and starts to pace again. "Somebody left an old school-bus near a little mountain lake," he says. "It's not much, but it's dry. Ever sleep in an old schoolbus on the side of a mountain? Living. Not what you got back East with the smoke and the soot. Real Western living." Harry is wearing dungarees and a plaid, open-collared shirt. His belly bulges slightly. "I know," he says, "I know. I smoke too much. Smoke too much and don't screw enough." He laughs and leans against the wall paper and tugs the dungarees away from his crotch. His chunky body is outlined, like the tiny patterned cowboys, against the backdrop of bland blue. "This daughter of mine is really going to be something," he says. "You ought to come around again when she's grown up."

No one meeting Harry Wolf in the bare cellar of his small undistinguished house would imagine even for an instant that he was once a personal good luck charm to the famous conductor Hannes Mannstein. "Vulfie, Vulfie," Mannstein would cry. "Verefer I haf orchestra you play. Always, Vulfie, you bring me luck. *Nicht wahr?*"

Harry was born in the Bronx. He grew up in a home crowded with delicate china and glass-fronted fruitwood cabinets that were heirlooms. His father Carl, who believed that the death of Jude the Obscure was the culmination of art, could not hold a position as a theatrical press agent, a newspaperman or an assistant manager in a hotel, although he held a degree from the Missouri School of Journalism. When the Depression came, Carl Wolf sat home day after day, reading the Eleventh Edition of the *Encylopaedia Britannica*.

Harry's mother Sylvia had studied art. She was a water colorist. Now she found a job selling corsets in a department store in midtown Manhattan. After work Sylvia ranted at her husband. She developed a spastic gall bladder. Carl responded by losing control of his left leg. There was no medical explanation for the condition, but he could no longer be expected to look for a job. In the schoolbus on the mountain Harry awakened one cold night to the memory of his mother screaming. "I studied the human body to paint, not to fit *yentas* into corsets! Not so I could work in a store!" She spun and clutched her middle, coughing thin rapid coughs, then wailing. His father limped away. "If it only wasn't for this damn leg," he said. Then he sat down at the Sohmer upright and played Mozart's *Turkish March* badly, chanting a monotonic accompaniment.

Harry was their hope and their faith. They were descended from Germans and not entirely Jewish. On each side, Harry had one Christian great-grandmother. But his parents did not deny their Jewishness. They took pride in their German *kultur,* to which they believed their Jewishness added an equal culture, a more ancient tradition and a crowning level of sensitivity. They were arrogant people in failure, Nietzschean heroes and Chosen People both.

When Harry was three, his father blankly struck the C-major chord and Harry walked to the piano and picked out the three notes. His parents were so excited they called the pediatrician. He promptly came to marvel, and the Wolfs knew. They had a musician, right there on Eden Avenue in the Bronx. Through aimless angry years, in a too-small apartment where there was never enough money and which friends who were teachers seemed always to avoid, Harry's musical destiny sustained the family. His parents were Jews who had no religion, except their son.

Harry could play almost any instrument he tried. He wanted to quit the piano when he was eleven. He preferred the guitar. Both parents were furious. "The guitar is simply not a serious instrument," Carl Wolf announced. "I hereby forbid you to play it." Harry practiced at the home of a friend but the other boy boasted too much of Harry's skill and his father overheard and hunted down the instrument and had it brought to the Eden Avenue apartment. There, while Harry pleaded, but would not weep, Carl Wolf gimpily stamped the guitar to death.

Harry's piano exercises continued joylessly. He joined the band at De Witt Clinton High School, and brasses thrilled him. It was the growl he felt; something of himself was in that bite. The piano, no matter how you touched it, resisted you. It had a voice of its own. Harry played trumpet, cornet, trombone, whatever was needed. A few weeks after he first picked up the French horn, he was trying a simple hunting call when Mr. Margolies, the bandleader, became very excited and told Harry to see him later for a conference.

"I think it must be something in your lip formation," Mr. Margolies said.

"The horn is a respectable instrument, isn't it?" Harry said.

"Brahms certainly thought so; you know the golden sound that opens the last movement of his *First*." Mr. Margolies began to hum the theme.

"I mean, not like the trombone or the trumpet."

Mr. Margolies finished humming. "A lordly instrument," he said. "Not only Brahms but that louse Wagner thought so, too." He began to hum the sword theme from *The Ring*.

"Well my parents . . ." Harry stopped. Mr. Margolies had reached the sword's crescendo. "My parents," Harry said, finally, "want me to concentrate on the piano."

"You are a wind musician," Mr. Margolies said. "You have more natural ability on the horn than anybody that's been in Clinton for the past ten years. You tell your parents that. You tell your parents I want you to study *horn* at Juilliard." He hummed four notes from Brahms. "Pianist?" Mr. Margolies said. "Even I am a pianist. Pianists, *feh*."

Sylvia Wolf bought a horn for Harry's fifteenth birthday. Harry lived in a courtyard room, which had never been tidy. When the horn came, Harry cleaned his den fanatically. "He wants it to be a fit place for a horn," his father said. Harry went in and closed the door and began to try the Brahms theme. He soaked the embrouchure over and over again. He played until his lips were sore and Mr. Sirota from next door rang the doorbell and complained.

"Stop the horn, son," Harry's father said, loudly. "You see, for a small apartment, a piano is more suitable."

After Harry won a partial scholarship to Juilliard, his parents agreed that the horn was the perfect instrument for him; more than that, he must, without question, become the finest hornist on earth. "Harry," his father, Carl, told him. "Here is something important for you to remember. You are a Wolf." The father's limp had disappeared and he was working as a bartender, as the only member of the bartenders union with a degree from the Missouri School of Journalism.

"Because you are a Wolf," his father said, "you will find that the world is going to expect a lot of you. You are carrying a high family tradition."

"It would be wonderful, darling," Sylvia Wolf told her son, "if you played not only with the orchestra, but solos. Mozart has written concerti for the horn, you know."

"Of course he knows," the father said. "And so has Strauss."

There was not much time for music after Harry graduated from Julliard in the spring of 1941. He found a job as a spare horn in a summer concert series and auditioned for a number of permanent orchestras. Two promised him the first opening that developed, but for weeks and then months there was no work.

The Metropolitan Opera Orchestra hired Harry on November 28th, and on December 9th he enlisted in the Air Corps. He refused to play in the Air Corps band. He had inherited a strain of jingoism from his father. He enjoyed making a brief speech to anyone who would listen. "There'll be a whole lifetime for me to blow my own horn," he said, "as long as this country stays free. If it doesn't, then even the horn won't matter. What do you think they do with hornists in Dachau?"

He became a ball turret gunner. He was a fine marksman and outwardly tranquil under fire. He did not panic. Sometimes he wondered to himself if it was just that he was trying to show everybody, as if everybody cared, that here was one Jew with guts. He flew forty-three missions in B-24s and the worst danger came on the day the European war ended and a rookie pilot, only six missions old, tried to see how close he could bring the left wing-tip to the Mediterranean Sea without actually touching the water. Harry was not afraid only because he was drunk.

Something had happened to his throat. Back home he could not play his horn properly. A doctor suggested that tissues had been dried out in the upper altitudes and the best cure was six months away from airplanes. Harry bought a 1940 Nash and drove across the country slowly, spending his Air Corps savings as he went. On the way back East, in Indianapolis, he heard Hannes Mannstein needed men. Harry auditioned with a borrowed horn. Mannstein looked quizzical.

"I'm better than this," Harry said. "I got some throat trouble in the Air Corps. I'm just getting over it."

"In the Air Corps band?"

"I was a gunner."

*"Also."*

Harry never knew whether Mannstein hired him for the Indianapolis Symphony because he heard genuine promise or because he approved of Jewish boys who had fired on Messerschmitts.

He traveled with Mannstein. After three years in Indianapolis, they moved to a larger city and then to a metropolis, where Harry became spare horn in the great orchestra Mannstein built. He recorded most of the Beethoven symphonies; Brahms, whom he ceased to like; Strauss and Mahler of whom he became fond. He studied horn-playing voraciously. He talked about nothing else on the night that he and Gwyn fell in love.

"There are only three horn sounds in the world," Harry told her. "Three basic sounds. The rest of us are merely apostles to them." He put a Dennis Brain recording on the phonograph in his small apartment that he had carefully cleaned. He intended to take Gwyn to bed that night for the first time.

"Brain," he said to Gwyn, "is silver." They listened to the graceful, airy sound.

"Now," Harry said, "I think you're ready for the bronze." He played a recording by the first hornist of the Vienna Philharmonic. "You hear that darker tone," he said. "You hear how different it is from Brain's." They listened and he drew her toward him. She wanted to be a poetess. She had come to the city for "pace" from a small, flat town in North Dakota. Harry found himself excited by the panting breaths drawn by this dark, delicate Christian-atheist girl.

"Finally," Harry said, drawing away from Gwyn, trying to measure her excitement, "you have earned the right to hear the gold. I don't play this recording for everybody. It's a rare old seventy-eight. The man who plays on it, Bruno Jaenicke, is the greatest hornist who ever lived."

The record crackled and hissed. It had been played frequently. But the sound underneath was golden and Harry was moved and forgot his seduction briefly and then remembering it again, but perhaps honestly, too, he said to Gwyn, tears in his eyes, "I would give ten years of my life if I could make that sound myself."

In love, Gwyn blinked behind her discreet spectacles. "I'm sure you play the horn as well as that," she said.

"Yeah," Harry said. "Yeah." Abruptly, the Air Corps came roaring back into him. He was the gunner who shot down Nazi Messerschmitts. "Let me tell you something, young lady." He stood up. "You can bet your round rosy bottom that I cannot play a horn as well as that, now or ever in my whole fucking life. My fucking parents, that was all they ever wanted of me. Make it in music; make them the big deals on the block. You're not a Jew. You don't know what it is to be raised by people like that, who don't give a damn for you, just for what you can do, who don't really give a damn for their own son." He was a brave man but his tears were spilling. "If once," he said, "if only one damn time, they had said that it was all right for me to be a failure; if once they let me be not great, just so-so, mediocre. But that isn't how Jewish parents are."

He shrugged and regained control. "I can't play it that fucking good at all, Gwyn honey," Harry said, and he fetched his horn and he sat on the floor and he played it for Gwyn as long as he could, and it was lovely and she cried for him, but it was not Bruno Jaenicke; and too tired to mount, he fell back to the floor and they slept, Harry and Gwyn, beside the horn.

Three months after the marriage, Harry walked up to Hannes Mannstein and resigned. The old man blinked, touched the back of Harry's neck and said, *"Leb wohl,"* nothing more.

Pacing in the playroom, without books or music, Harry Wolf talked about the Bronx. "The only way I go back there," he says, "is in my pickup, dog-delivery truck. It's a little banged up, but on the side in big letters, it says *Wolf-cubs*. Well, my mother says I better not dare show up in the old neighborhood driving a dirty truck, so I've worked it out. I haven't been back to the Bronx in seven years."

He puffs his cigarette and strides to his daughter and pats her neck and walks to a closet. He reaches high and takes down the horn. He shakes it and dirt falls to the concrete floor.

"That dirt," Harry Wolf says, "is from the time I tried to grow roses in it. They died. The best thing for this horn is to be a potty for some baby. Let me know if you have a big-assed kid."

The outside of the horn still shines as though someone, Harry or Gwyn, has polished it.

"The dog business is going to pick up, isn't it, Trudy?" Harry says.

"Yes it is going to, Daddy."

"Tell us why."

"Because it pays to be a bitch," Trudy says, and giggles.

"Gwyn's working late tonight," Harry says, starting to march soldierly on the concrete, "but when she gets here she'll be glad to see you. You know about those *shicksas*. She'll make you a helluva drink."

He opens the closet door and strains his frame to reach the shelf and slides the horn from sight. "Now what the hell do you want to listen to music for anyway?" Harry says, closing the door.

## STREAM OF CONSCIOUSNESS

Harriet Fromkin, M.D., practicing psychotherapist, conscious intellectual and unsuccessful poetess, has decided to permit herself an evening drink. Vanessa, the housekeeper, has borne a Scotch sour, carrying the glass on a small, etched silver tea tray. "We use J.&B. That is the Scotch to drink, am I correct?" Harriet Fromkin asks, hazarding coyness. She will have no more than one. She seldom does. "After two drinks I get fuzzy," Dr. Fromkin says, "and I cannot stand to be that way. *Ever.*"

She is a brown-haired woman of fifty, with crow's-feet radiating from the corners of dark eyes that are still lustrous. She has carefully preserved a figure, inclined toward dumpiness at best. Even in the trim purple suit, her waist is short and her bust is overfull. But the soft eyes of Harriet Fromkin beguile.

"Now," announced Dr. Fromkin brusquely, after a quick disinterested sip of her Scotch sour, "if you are looking into Jewish involvement in psychiatry, the best place to start is at the source. Among the founders, the people closest to Freud, only Carl Jung was not a Jew. I read a paper years ago that began: 'If we had no further illustration than the character of Freud, we should have a basis for suspecting some connection between the Jew and psychological genius.'

"And we have vastly more illustrations than that. What is the saying? 'Half the analysts in America, and ninety per cent of the good ones, are Jews.'"

Dr Fromkin strokes her brown hair three times. "History doesn't tell us enough and numbers tell us nothing. I am aware of those considerations. I also accept, unlike some of my colleagues, the limits of the behavioral sciences. So I will concede that I am theorizing, and when I theorize I reserve the professional right to make an honest error and the womanly right to reverse my theories tomorrow."

She sips quickly again, makes a wry face and settles into the wing chair, crossing her ankles, but keeping her knees close together. "Psychiatry offers the title of doctor, the income of medicine and the humanism of the arts. Jews are interested in all three, and something beyond. Jews are obsessed by people. Good people, bad people, happy people, fornicating people. In medicine we say the surgeon deals in things. A gall bladder is a thing. The internist deals with disease; the strep throat. But the psychiatrist deals with people. The psychiatrist confronts people on the most intimate professional basis of them all. He turns them inside out."

Harriet Fromkin shudders slightly. "That excites me even as I say it to you," she says. "Perhaps I say too much. Perhaps all I have the right to tell you is much less: that I would not be nearly so happy nor so contained a woman if I were struggling in a garret somewhere with only my attempts at poetry to sustain me, or—the other side of the coin—having to work till exhaustion day after day painting red throats, injecting penicillin and prescribing for menstrual cramps."

The rectangular room in which Dr. Harriet Fromkin sits, 180 feet above Park Avenue, is furnished in ovals and soft shades. The coffee tables show measured curves of fruitwood. Sofa and conversation pieces and the wing chair on which she sits and its ottoman, are all patterned in rusts and orange. The wallpaper, scenes from a *bois,* is green. Everywhere crystal hangs in tear-shaped pendants. This is the living room where Dr. Harriet Fromkin played the ebony baby grand for hours while her two children practiced stringed instruments. That is where she rejoiced when she and they finally played a simple movement of an early Beethoven trio and finished at the same, or approximate, time.

"I think," Dr. Fromkin says, raising her ankles to the ottoman, "that there is a renaissance quality to the practice of psychiatry. I have artists for patients. One has to understand art to treat an artist. Isn't the field of psychiatry really the field of all human knowledge? That is why I use the term renaissance, and that, too, is why Jews are so interested in it. Jews are the renaissance people of modern times."

She lights a cigarette hastily. The last point is impetuous, not previously considered. She rushes ahead. "But I am tired of conscious Jews and conscious Jewishness," she says. "Aren't you? You certainly must be. Although since my divorce I have been a far more conscious Jewess myself. Jewess. I loathe the word. Jewess. Negress. There is something inherently degrading in each."

She excuses herself and pads from the room to see if Vanessa has left. She is wearing large furry slippers. Her bottom is flat. The books on her rosewood shelves display a European intellect. Mann and Rilke; Kafka and Stendhal; the great Russians. There are few English novels. Dr. Harriet Fromkin prefers Proust to Dickens, and Brecht to Eugene O'Neill.

When she returns, she is carrying a small Scotch and soda. Her hand is white and lined and freckled. "I hope the proportions are right," Dr. Fromkin says. "You'll tell me if they're not. Don't be timid. A timid man seldom gets what he wants."

When she finds her place in the chair, she picks up her narrative precisely in a throaty voice, which occasionally rises to nasality. "You've heard of Cromwell, New York? There is no reason why you should."

Harriet C. Fromkin was born in Cromwell, New York, a railroad town sixty miles from New York City. Her father, Emmanuel Cohen, the village druggist, was reasonably well-accepted in the community. "We were not very Jewish," Dr. Fromkin says. "When my grandfather, Isaac, lived with us, there was some observance, out of respect for his wishes. But when I was still very young, he had to be put into a home for the Hebrew aged, and after that there was no religion in our home."

Wrapped in her own story, Dr. Harriet Fromkin has forgotten her Scotch sour, which sits, warming. She crosses and uncrosses her legs, holding her torso erect. "But we were Jews, oh yes," she says. "The Klan burned a cross on a nearby mountain and the Irish trainmen, for whom Papa made medicines, called him Sheeney Cohen behind his back."

At first, Harriet intended to become a teacher. Her father thought that was right for an intelligent young girl. Not until she was fifteen did Harriet recognize what Emmanuel Cohen refused to see. Jews were not employed as teachers by the Cromwell schools.

Shocked, Harriet went to her class advisor, Catherine Brickel, and asked if she had any chance to become a teacher.

Miss Brickel looked past Harriet, vacantly. "In Kansas," she said, "I've never heard of any problems for Jewish people. Have you considered attending college where I did?"

Although her father wanted "Cornell or at least Syracuse," Harriet Cohen insisted on following the path of Catherine Brickel; she enrolled at the University of Kansas in Lawrence. There pedagogy led into psychology and psychology led to medicine, which to Harriet was a bridge into the greater world of psychiatry.

In the Park Avenue living room, beside her warming drink, Dr. Fromkin says that she cannot recapture the exhilaration that came with her exposure to Freud. "It was like drawing back a curtain," she says, "behind which was myself. I was eighteen or nineteen years old. And I was born."

Harriet Cohen was an intense physician, prim and naïve. Once, as an interne, she was instructed to catheterize a young Negro and while she was working, handling the man's penis, it grew hard. At once Harriet puffed into a rage. "Now really," she told the man. "I can't help you if you're going to behave like that. You are going to have to learn not to do that. I won't stand for it!" The erection angered her, as a lewd advance.

Dr. Martin A. Fromkin, whom she married, was assertive but seldom erect. Now, as Harriet begins to talk about her former husband, she reaches for the warm sour and sips hard. "Martin's aggressiveness," she says, "paralleled an aspect of my grandfather. I shared a room with my grandfather when I was two. At the time we met, I was too rigid and too cautious to have allowed anyone, except Freud himself, to sweep me off my feet. Martin, who liked to talk more than touch, came as close as was possible."

The marriage lasted for nineteen years but in her living room Dr. Harriet Fromkin insists that it always was doomed. "I could have saved it," she says. "If I had been willing to sublimate my intellectuality, curb my ideas and hold my tongue, I would be married today. I have always been able to sublimate my sexuality, thanks in part to my training. But I will not sublimate my intellect. Why should I? Can you think of any reason why I should? And there I was, married to a psychiatrist-to-be, who said that Mozart was boring and that Paul Klee drew lines. After a long time fighting it, I grasped the alternatives. Either I could give up my identity or my marriage. I chose to remain the woman you see. A third Scotch? Are you sure you'll be all right? Martin drank Bourbon. He was bigger than you."

Dr. Fromkin pads off and returns quickly. Now, besides the drink, she is holding a framed photograph of her children. They stare, long-faced, dark-eyed, sensitive. Both are at college.

"I have never really gotten away from being the rather proper, smalltown Jewish virgin," says Dr. Harriet Fromkin, alone at fifty. "My professional life has been a conflict, as the lives of so many psychiatrists must be. Here I am, after all, a girl who was not allowed to date boys until her senior year in high school, working in a field which demands tolerance of the wildest sexual behavior.

She rises and begins to walk back and forth in front of her comfortable chair. "My divorce is my failure," she says. "I berate myself. In my home, my mother and father couldn't get along. But divorce was unthinkable. It was immoral. I think of that and sometimes guilt seizes me and almost makes me cry.

"There is a poem I have written. May I recite it?

> I am heaved off
> By a blank, heedless, unwearying sun, heaved off.
> And if I seem to blaze,
> My brief coronial fire
> Will die when I die
> Or before."

The poem is important to Harriet Fromkin. When she has finished reciting, she returns to the chair, shakes her head and retreats behind elaborate spectacles.

"You see my point," she says. "You see, Judaism has heaved off Harriet Fromkin. I sit here successful, and I have taught my children to respect others, and books, and a love of music. But all of that, compared to the tradition my Grandpa passed to me, is ephemera. The debris, however lovely, of strange lands.

"Grandpa Isaac is the important one, not me. Judaism has

survived because of dirty, bearded, Orthodox men like Grandpa. They carry the tradition and they raise someone like Papa, who then raises someone like me.

"I don't know if my grandfather was literate in English—certainly as you and I understand the term, he was not. He was a peddler. But this strange and unwashed itinerant, who walked all the way from New York City to Cromwell, more than sixty miles on foot, and scratched out a living, was the one that started something. Not my father and certainly not myself.

"In this little bearded man were the traditions. I have only had to refine them. Morality. Hard work. Reverence for learning. Drive. Respect for other human beings. Compassion.

"I want a relevance equal to my grandfather's. My grandfather—who did not know what the word relevance means."

She looks as though she is about to weep. "Listen," Dr. Fromkin says to her visitor, a Jewish man of forty. "I've wanted to ask you something all night. Are you married, or divorced or what?"

## SCHMUYEL GREENFELD, THE MORMON

Humor, like any art, resists definition, and when Americans casually talk about Jewish humor in the United States, they compound complexity by discussing two things at once. There are Jewish jokes, which are not necessarily jokes told by Jews. Then there are Jewish comedians. A Jewish comedian may rely heavily on Jewish humor, or lightly, or not at all.

Only in the narrowest sense can Jewish jokes be said to be jokes about Jews. Above low insult humor (and above the vulgarities offered as wit by anti-Semites) Jewish jokes broadly are jokes about people seen through sad, ironic, tolerant Jewish eyes. One finds sources in the sad, tolerant wisdom of the Talmud, although the Holocaust has lately added bitterness. Usually, the jokes remind us that man is flawed and weak and mortal and God can be grim, but it is best to try to view both kindly. They are what they are, and anyway, they will not change. So when two Jews meet at a public bath one remarks tolerantly, "I see a year has passed," and Sholom Aleichem's Tevye observes that with the help of God he has starved three times a day, and Harry Golden points out during Barry Goldwater's campaign that he always knew the first Jewish President would be an Episcopalian. Irony lightly tempered by bitterness.

The Jewish comedian, as various as Jack Benny, Lenny Bruce, Jerry Lewis and Mort Sahl, towers in contemporary humor. His drive towards success coincides with the paramount demand of show business, where without drive the certain end is obscurity. Comedy uniquely gratifies his needs. In the spotlight, before a laughing audience, the Jewish comedian is accepted. He can feel all the warmth in the room. But his humor is also a camouflage, hiding that which he wishes to hide, transforming, concealing, protecting.

He has played this lounge more nights than he can remember. Across more years, when the children were sick, through the life and death of his marriage, hung over, aching, joyful, until now by acclamation it is his room. He works bravura performances in his own way. Ed Sullivan gave him six minutes. A TV series bound him to a stock role. A New York nightclub signed him for a seventeen-minute spot. "Seventeen minutes," he says, "is how long I need to clear my throat." But here, in this so-called lounge—a cramped, small-staged showbar in a Las Vegas hotel—Shecky Greene, the Jewish entertainer, is at home.

There is no cover in the Starlight Lounge and gentlemen need not wear neckties. An odd lot of faces assembles. A fat giggly woman from Oklahoma sips a pink drink, blinks owl eyes and grows more giggly. A great-chinned man from Midland, Texas, loud about oil leases and poontang, drinks Jack Daniels topped with soda, vacantly. The weekend couple, matching a Y.M.C.A. room clerk with a bill-collecting lady from the telephone company, suffers a bit of passion and hold hands. Young bucks from Biloxi, money from who knows where, proclaim the search "fowah a amateur in this town"; and the blonde-wigged cocktail waitress wiggles her broad tail.

This is Shecky's room, but these are not Shecky's friends. They are his audience, these and the others. He may talk to them briefly later, a sentence thrown over his shoulder from the crap table, or from a booth where he eats whitefish, flown specially from a Jewish caterer in Chicago. But they are clients, no more. There is nothing personal between Shecky and these people once his curtain has fallen.

On stage he offers all. Mostly he is a comedian. That is how he is billed. He sings, and acts and mimics and philosophizes, but he calls himself a comic. "What else?" he seems to say. "A chubby Hamlet?" He comes out of Chicago where he might have been a cantor, but he has too much drive and too much sense of madness and too much adrenalin to have lingered in the synagogue. He needs an hour and a half on stage twice a night.

He does not seem to know how good he is. He can make an audience laugh or cry, starting at the stroke of midnight and again at two A.M. seven nights a week, but he is embarrassed to make adults weep. He stands in the spotlight, backed by four musicians, finding humor in the fierce wrenchings of his own life, pretending that he and his life are not really serious.

He sings a little before the curtain rises. The room rattles with talk and clattering ice. The sound from behind the curtain quiets people. When the curtain rises the audience is ready; they see a stocky, dark-haired man in a tuxedo.

At first he seems devoid of grace. He is heavy-bodied and beginning to develop jowls. But he moves quickly, agilely. Football lineman move that way when they are in shape. He sings a romantic song and then, impatient with it, stops and begins to talk about a German who has been head waiter in the lounge. "I don't know where he was in the war," Shecky says, "but when you asked for a table, he'd go: Table? *Achtung, schweinhund!*" Shecky cracks an imaginary Nazi whip through smoky air.

He is a democratic fellow, Shecky tells the audience. He doesn't want anyone to think that he cares what a person is. "It doesn't matter," Shecky says. "This is America. If I was Poe-lásh, I'd say I was Poe-lásh. If I was Ít-lee-yan, I'd tell you I was Ít-lee-yan. If I was German, I wouldn't say, because my parents are Jewish."

Howl. The audience explodes. There are some professionals on hand tonight. Groucho Marx is there. Marx gazes dourly at Shecky Greene.

"Wait a minute," Shecky shouts. "The band didn't laugh. What's going on here with my band!" He turns and faces the pianist, his own hands poised like a conductor's. "All right,"

Shecky says. "I want a guffaw." He beats time and the pianist laughs in tempo. Shecky moves to the drummer. "You," he says. "A *yuk*." At Shecky's downbeat, the drummer conforms. Soon Shecky leads the band in a four-voiced laugh, almost with counter-point.

"Look," Shecky says, turning back to the audience, picking up the thread. "It doesn't matter what you are. In the war, on an aircraft carrier I bunked next to a guy six-foot-six. He looks me over and he wants to know, *Hey what kinda name is this, Schmuyel Greenfeld? What are you?*

"I say to him, *What are you?*" Shecky stared up at an imaginary giant.

"Mormon," the giant says.

"All right," Shecky says to the audience, "so for four years I was Schmuyel Greenfeld, the Mormon. There was nothing wrong with that. Except how would you like to have to give ten per cent of everything you got to a bunch of farmers you never even saw?"

He is working hard. He holds a drink in his hand and says "Dean Martin" and spills the drink on his fly. It is really tea. He starts to talk about his life. His wife was an Indian, he says. "Not an Indian Indian," he says. "An American Indian, with tepee and feathers. Wild.

"You know something," he says. "When they lock you up as a drunk here, there's no bail. You can't get out. Murderers they let out. That's true. Not drunks. Let's face it. When I drink, I go wild. So they lock me up and then I can't get bail. I say to the sheriff, *Let me out. I promise you I'll commit a murder.* No good. No bail."

Suddenly, Shecky is singing an air from *Butterfly*. Herb Dell, the pianist, fingers a Puccini background and Shecky by himself plays all the parts. He sings and narrates. Pinkerton dazzles Cho Cho San. She sings her rapture. Pinkerton sails away. He was not serious. How could she know?

The perspiring comic, with tea-stained trousers, bursts full-voiced into *Un Bel Di*. Nobody laughs. People are moved. Shecky hurtles on. Butterfly has a son. Shecky falls to his knees, holding Butterfly's child. He hums a lullaby. His large fleshy face is tender.

Pinkerton will not come back. The chubby man who plays Butterfly in a crowded Las Vegas showbar, blindfolds the child and reaches for a dagger.

*Amore, addio, addio!*
*Piccolo amor!*

*Harikiri.*

And Shecky Greene springs to his feet to imitate Harry Belafonte.

"Mr. Shecky Greene." In front of the small stage Groucho Marx is standing.

"What is it?" Shecky cries. "What is it?"

"There's no need to shout," Groucho Marx says.

"Give him a mike," someone calls.

"It's my room," Shecky says.

"It's your room," Groucho says, "and you can have it."

Shecky is uncertain. Groucho is an intimidating man. With a half grin, Shecky hands down the microphone.

"I want to say something serious," Groucho says. "I normally go to bed at midnight. It's very late for me. I want to say that this man Shecky Greene, comedian, singer, actor, whatever you want to call him is one of the most extraordinary talents I have ever seen." Marx returns the microphone and sits down, looking somber.

The room is silent, startled. Then everyone applauds. It is a remarkable tribute. Shecky's pianist begins to weep. "I feel like cryin' myself," Shecky says, "when I think of what I signed for."

Afterwards, Shecky goes out for a snack, shaking his head, trying to act as though he was not moved. "What do you make of that?" he says across a table. "What do you make of what Groucho Marx did?"

"Marvelous," someone says.

"What does it mean?" Shecky says. "It's one forty-five. At two I've gotta give another show."

It is 2:11. Groucho Marx had gone to bed. Shecky is bouncing on stage again before fresh, demanding faces. Marx's accolade belongs to the past. "Van Gogh," Shecky is saying, "was a very great painter, but the world did not recognize him and so he was frustrated. And the greater his work, the more he was frustrated. He knew he was a genius. He knew.

"And finally this great painter, unable to stand the frustration, took a knife and cut off his ear.

"And now people knew. Now in this odd world at last they understood.

"And they ran to this man, who had cut off his own ear, and they said, *Van Gogh, Van Gogh. You were right. You are a genius!*

"And Van Gogh said, *Huh? . . .*"

His former wife is bringing the children in a day or two. A Jewish holiday is coming. Shecky will not go to temple, but he has a holiday sense. He will not perform at twelve or two.

"I miss the kids," he says. He is eating the whitefish from Chicago. "I'm not a Jewish comic," he says. "I don't use much Jewish stuff."

As if the approach of Schmuyel the sometime Mormon could be anything but the work of a man who understands with exquisite Jewish consciousness how fate sports with mortals and how mortals, to survive, defend themselves with laughter.

## MELAMMED TO THE SCHVARTZES

To suggest that *all* Jews pursue, like furies, the difficult and the demanding is to embrace the paranoia of the anti-Semite. It is also incorrect.

Although evidence insists that the Jews of America are superior, ambitious and creative in many directions, neither ambition nor drive is common to them all. Not every Jew possesses or even approaches the intensity of Sam Wilson, M.D., of the young musician Harry Wolf, of Dr. Harriet Fromkin or of Shecky Greene. Thousands are moderately content to spend their lives more placidly, as civil servants, shopkeepers or teachers.

Jews become teachers quite as naturally as Irishmen become corner cops, and usually for more noble reasons. In a tradition common to almost every Jewish community on earth, the teacher, the *melammed,* is accorded enormous respect. The fluttery virgin schoolmarm of the American Western and the fatuous principal of television series, although created in part by Jewish hack writers, are totally alien to the main of Jewish thought. Traditionally, the Jewish teacher embodies learning, symbolizes discipline and projects virtue. He is the inheritor and caretaker of knowledge, among people who revere knowledge next to the Almighty.

In the days after World War I, as more and more American Jews qualified as professors, American colleges began systematically to bar them. "Is there no way I can get a professorship at a decent university?" a Jewish scholar asks, in a story told by the late Heywood Broun.

"Why, certainly you may," another Jew points out. "Just have Felix Warburg endow a chair for you."

University bigotry, however, proved to be an enormous benefit to the largest city in the country. In New York thousands of Jewish men and women, possessed of every requirement for college teaching save acceptable ethnicity, made a generally satisfactory compromise by becoming teachers in the public schools. Salaries were good, security and leisure were certain and the work was stimulating. The Jewish students of New York were an earnest dedicated group and in classroom interplay often inspired both pupil and teacher. Public school scholarship of the highest order quickly developed. Townsend Harris High School, Bronx High School of Science and later the High School of Music and Art—with overwhelmingly Jewish student bodies and faculties—were, at the least, a scholastic match for Andover or Lawrenceville.

Today, the times and the New York City school system are vastly altered. Colleges have shed bigotry sufficiently to employ Jewish professors, capturing most of the leading scholars and, in the city itself, lagging salary scales, the middle-class exodus to the suburbs and the constant integration uproar have downgraded academic standards. To an extent, the very nature of teaching, the *melammed*'s work itself has been transformed. "Sometimes," says short, gentle, bald Bernard Rogovin, "I don't know if I'm an educator or a *gauleiter*."

Bernard Rogovin, thirty-seven, is an experienced teacher of history and speech at a junior high school in a gray, impoverished wasteland of Negro Brooklyn. "It's funny," he says. "My uncle had an auto parts store right near the school. My cousin grew up down the block. But the store front is empty now and all the Jews have left the neighborhood. What I'll show you at the school will be a shocker. It shocks me and I've been going there every day for seven years."

The junior high, five stories tall, is named General Terhune Slocum. It is red brick and gray granite, massive, undistinguished, defaced by chalk obscenities. The slum from which it rises stands bleak with wood frame houses covered in a tarpaper that has been patterned to pass as brick. Tight steel grills guard the 110 windows of General Terhune Slocum Junior High. They were not installed to protect pupils from rock-throwing vandals. Instead, the grills are there to protect passersby, Mr. Rogovin explains, from the children within who hurl inkwells and sometimes window poles fifty feet above the sidewalk. "These are a different kind of kid," Mr. Rogovin says.

At high noon, Mr. Rogovin will begin his fifty-minute recess to eat lunch. That would be a good time to meet, he proposes. "When you get to the school, ask at the office, if you get confused," he says. "Joe Cohen will know where I am."

"Is Joe Cohen a teacher or a pupil?"

"What? Are you kidding?" Mr. Rogovin says, excitedly. "There aren't any Jewish pupils at General Slocum. It is all Negro and Puerto Rican. All. Absolutely one hundred per cent."

Just before noon, a tall, sallow man stands before the office. "Joe Cohen?"

"Who wants to know?"

"I have an appointment with Mr. Rogovin."

"Anybody could say that," the tall man says, unsmiling.

A blonde woman opens the office door. "Are you the one Mr. Rogovin is expecting?" she says.

"Oh," Joe Cohen says. "Sorry. I'm a couple payments behind in my car and I didn't know who the hell sent you. These repossess guys'll lie and cheat. Mr. Rogovin will be here in a minute when classes break."

A bell and a cry proclaim the period's end. As the bell rings the hall fills with running, shouting children. Mr. Rogovin and two women teachers, white faces, amid the black and tan, are ignored. Mr. Rogovin waves meekly and points toward the office. There, he suggests eating upstairs for lunch in the teacher's room. "If you can make four flights," he says. "On the way, I can show you some of the stuff the kids do."

Paintings and sketches cover the walls of a ground floor corridor. One in green and black and red shows a Negro hanging from a twisted tree, perhaps a cyprus. It was done by an honor student to illustrate the book *Strange Fruit*. Others show Negro children. There are two badly drawn portraits of John F. Kennedy. The best work, a black and white sketch of a rearing stallion, was done by a clerk in the principal's office.

The teachers' room at Slocum Junior High School com-

mands a three-sided view five stories up. Below, the wasteland stretches drab and filthy. Some of the roofs are littered.
On one, two men are drinking from a bottle.

"You see," says Mr. Rogovin, in the teachers' room, sitting
at the head of a long table. "It is not true that all our teachers are Jews. This gentleman is Mr. Carlton Jackson."

Mr. Rogovin grins. Mr. Carlton Jackson nods.

A half-dozen teachers have gathered at the table, eating
dry sandwiches provided by an automatic vendor. "I'm having the damndest time with my twelfth graders," a hawk-
nosed woman says. "I'm trying to give them iambic pentame-
ter and their accents interfere."

"To them, *you* have uh accent, Miz Pinkus," Carlton Jackson says.

"Well, I mean," Mrs. Jacqueline Pinkus says, reddening.

"Everybody has some kind of accent, Jackie," Mr. Rogovin says, "Because everybody comes from somewhere. I'm a
Brooklyn kid, from Toid Avenyuh meeself."

Carl Jackson silently leaves the table and walks to a huge
chair, covered in parched black leather. Settling into it he begins to read *Pinktoes* by Chester Himes. Carl Jackson came
to General Slocum Junior High from a normal school in
South Carolina. His drawl troubles a few of his colleagues
and himself. He has heard them speculate about his intelligence, and he has told none of them that his own speech
makes him almost weep; it is as if God implanted a piece of
wood down the center of his tongue.

Mr. Rogovin takes his lunches in the bright, tense teachers'
room regularly. He believes that he is needed there. He could
eat in a cafeteria, five minutes away from the school, but the
teachers' room is where he has eaten for seven years. Eight
years ago he taught in an elementary school. Before that he
sold insurance. Before that he was an infantryman in Korea.
His wife Dorothea thought he should teach, when they were
married in 1953. She was going to substitute in English herself.

Mr. Rogovin walks away from the table in the teachers'
room and drops into a straight-backed chair, a long way off
from Carl Jackson. "I can tell you why I got into this," he
says. "My dad was in business. He had a grocery. They didn't
push me or anything, my folks, but I just didn't want to be in
business. I found out I wanted to do something more important than sell. I mean, even insurance, you tell yourself you're

more than a salesman. You're an advisor. That way you make yourself feel significant. But a few months of that was enough. Too much.

"The thing was I wasn't much of a student. I couldn't pass a math course if my Aunt Bertha was the teacher. The other thing was I didn't give a damn for some of the fancy fields, like law. I started Brooklyn College at night, and I goofed around. They make you go at night, if your grades are rotten, to prove that you're sincere. I was sincere, but it took me forever to find out I was. It took a while to get the damn degree and then the education courses, but I finally made it, and I'm a pretty good teacher. No genius, but I carry more than my load."

Mr. Rogovin teaches at General Slocum under Principal Dr. Horace Lewis Goldfarb, who is sixty-two and has recovered from a stroke. Dr. Goldfarb, forgetful and remote, does not want to retire. He enjoys the idea of being a junior high school principal. His children are grown. Harry Krantzer, Dr. Goldfarb's assistant, is a big athletic man, who has told Mr. Rogovin that he is the best teacher in the school. But he has reprimanded Mr. Rogovin for "intemperance" and for "trying to do too much too damn fast." Harry Krantzer intends to become a principal himself.

On an average, seven girls leave General Terhune Slocum Junior High School each year to become mothers. Two years ago, Mr. Rogovin, hearing moans, burst into an empty classroom and marched toward the coat closet where a Puerto Rican boy was making noise. Under him a Negro girl, her hair dyed red, giggled softly. She stared coldly at Mr. Rogovin and pulled the boy's head toward her throat. "Doan you mess us up, teach," she said, "and when I gits through with him, I goan give you a chance."

Mr. Rogovin announced a suspension on the spot but Dr. Goldfarb reinstated the two children. Under pressure from a civil rights group, Dr. Goldfarb had agreed to allow no more than one suspension per month. He would not, he said, stomach white teachers persecuting Negro pupils under any circumstance. Dr. Goldfarb believed that the monthly suspension should be husbanded "until we really need it." For the last two-and-a-half years at General Terhune Slocum, none had really been needed. The redheaded girl soon took to rolling her eyes at Mr. Rogovin when they passed in the hall and calling, "Hey, how 'bout it now, teach baby!"

Instead of suspensions, Dr. Goldfarb arranged for a vacant classroom to be set aside for the most difficult children every day. There, after being banished from their regular group, they were to be taught a new program, called Cooperative Citizenship: Living Together as Friends. When Mr. Rogovin was in charge of Cooperative Citizenship he read a simple civics textbook on the various systems of government. When Carl Jackson had C.C., he simply glowered. Mr. Jackson would be taking over C.C. more and more. Dr. Goldfarb felt he got results and besides, working there distressed Mr. Rogovin. Somehow these semi-literate children had invented another name for Cooperative Citizenship. "C.C.," they said, "stands for concentration camp. We goan to the J.C.C." The "J," Mr. Rogovin knew, stood for Jew.

Drunkenness, often on kosher wine, was a more serious problem than pregnancy at General Slocum Junior High and hopelessness was the most serious problem of all. When Mr. Rogovin began at Slocum he despaired for children whose mother—and grand-mother and great-grandmother—lived on welfare checks and whose father was transient or unknown. With Harry Krantzer's help, he prepared new programs as rapidly as he could. He introduced a history of Negroes in America. He pleaded with Dr. Goldfarb, who ducked, but let him go on to the District Superintendent, in whose office Mr. Rogovin raised his voice and was granted enough money to buy texts on Negro history and the poetry of Langston Hughes. His wife had introduced him to Hughes and to Countee Cullen. Mr. Rogovin was deeply moved for reasons he could not define, when he read Cullen's:

> I marvel at a curious thing.
> To make a poet black and bid him sing.

But it was beyond the arts and beyond the art of reaching. That was what Mr. Rogovin learned day by day in the failure of his seven years at Slocum. He worked and plotted and related to these strange, pathetic kids and threw out everything, or tried to, that he had been taught as a middle-class Jewish boy, listening to middle-class Jewish teachers. But how could he relate to fatherless girls who smiled through intercourse in classroom closets before their breasts were fully formed?

At the end of the day, a chilly winter Thursday, Mr. Rogovin comes home to talk to Dorothea. Asher, his own boy, thirteen, appears in the small living room of the fourth-floor apartment, and vanishes to do his homework, the way Bernie himself had vanished afternoons almost thirty years before. Not everything has changed, at least not in the fourth-floor apartment, 4-B, in this aging dark brick apartment house in a neighborhood in transition, where teachers can afford to live.

Paintings of still lifes, with sterile wax apples, hang on the living room walls. Bernie has started to paint summers, now that he no longer can work in camps. He finds that when July comes, he is too spent to assume another job. He needs the vacation to re-assemble himself.

The years have exacted other tolls. Once he fought and felt strong, but since the failure—and every cry in a hallway at Slocum is a failure to Mr. Rogovin—he has been drained. Dorothea is a handsome, dark-haired woman, but now she wears her hair in a bun. For a long time now, the bun has stayed tight. Bernie is the one who has been tired. A sharpness has come to Dorothea. He blames himself.

"Decent day, dear?" she says from the brown couch in the living room, not really asking. "Make me a healthy rob roy."

Bernie walks to a lightwood cabinet that serves as the bar. "Jackie Pinkus insulted Carl Jackson at lunch," he says, beginning to mix the drink.

"Bernie," Dorothea says, "you are getting to sound more and more like a CORE Jew. You're looking at everything the wrong way. You know what a CORE Jew is, do you not?"

He carefully adds a dash of vermouth to a small glassful of Scotch. "It was out of stupidity," he says. "She blundered about accents."

"CORE Jews see a Negro-hater in every woodpile," Dorothea says.

"I don't like that talk," Bernie says. "CORE Jew may sound okay to you, but I knew Southern guys in the Army, and it sounds like niggerlover to me. Where the hell is the ice?"

He walks into the kitchen and gets her ice and pours himself a glass of milk and thinks that it is time to tell her and he knows that it will be a long time, maybe never, before she grasps the totality of his failure, of his own—Freud forgive him—castration.

"Dorothea," he says, handing her the drink. She leans forward on the couch, a compact, handsome, frustrated woman. Her legs curl gracefully beneath her. She nods.

"I'm going to transfer out of Slocum. I'm going to Flatbush."

"Oh, Bern."

"I can't stand it any more," Bernie says. "What am I doing knocking the life out of myself, busting my balls teaching these kids who don't want to learn."

"Good, Bern," Dorothea says. "Sit here by me."

"Today," he says unmoving, "is when it happened."

"What was it? Another closet scene."

"No," Bernie says, "No, nothing like that. Nothing at all. It's just that I was an alien. I mean I felt like one all day. In my own town, in my own school, in my own profession, I'm an alien, and I don't want to be an alien any more. I want to teach where I belong, with Jewish kids."

Dorothea laughs.

"Very goddamn funny," Mr. Rogovin says, fiercely.

"I'm sorry," she says, "but I was only thinking how hard you fought my father so Asher wouldn't have to be Bar Mitzvahed."

"Jews are my people," Mr. Rogovin says, "although I happen not to believe in God."

Ash stands in the hallway, frowning. "Can I go down to Gold's for a soda, Dad?" he asks.

"You done with your homework?"

"Almost."

"Then get back in your room and finish it!" Mr. Rogovin shouts. "You get no soda till you're all done. What do you think I want to raise? An idiot?"

## MAIN STREET

The dark, alien slum to which the pursuit of teaching led Mr. Rogovin dismays Harry Goldenrammer in his native reach of the great prairie. "No, no, no," Harry shouts. "Don't tell me any more. I don't know how anybody can stand it in New York."

Harry is one of the 8,895 Jews living in Nebraska. He is one of the thousand beyond the urban centers of Omaha and Lincoln. In the flat, sprawling community of Somerset (alt. 1,171; pop. 6,438) all the Jews are named Goldenrammer. They are the families of Harry Goldenrammer and his brother Arthur. But since Arthur married Ann Goodhue,

Harry Goldenrammer tells friends at the Commerce Club, after a Saturday Scotch, "I got the only full-blooded Jewish kids in town."

The remark draws a laugh, but no one is certain if it is true. The Goldenrammers, who occasionally drive to Omaha for religious services, are the only practicing Jews in Somerset, but there are a half-dozen families that were Jewish once but changed their minds. The Winters, who came from Massachusetts, are Congregationalists, which would have surprised the first of them to come west, Aaron Gershovinder. The Fishers are Presbyterians. The Meyers are Christian Scientists. The Millfields are Methodists. Herbert Millfield, First Vice-President of Somerset National Bank, is fair and thin-lipped but carries before him a replica of the large curving nose that adorned the face of his grandmother, Sarah. People at Somerset National still remember Herb Millfield's reaction when a Jewish traveling salesman approached his desk and tried to cash a check.

"So," the salesman said, considering Herb's nose, "you don't know me. So. What does it matter? Our kind should stick together, especially out here."

Herb, a short, proper man who seldom swore, stood up and ordered Hank, the guard: "Throw this Jew the hell out of my bank."

Afterward, when the story circulated, Herb Millfield called on Harry Goldenrammer to apologize. "I didn't mean your kind of Jew," he said.

Harry stared down at Millfield. "I ought to throw you the hell out of here," Harry said.

Somerset is generally unprejudiced. It has been fortunate in having both a liberal newspaper and a heterogeneous population, combining Scandinavians, Germans and Anglo-Saxons in numbers that forced each group to recognize the other. The earliest Jews to arrive were peddlers, walking or riding a cart, selling pots, pans, razors, looking for a place where a man could make a living with a store. The first wave of Jewish peddlers to reach Somerset came from Germany. Fishers and Meyers were among them, and Herb Millfield's forebears, who were then Millfelds. There were others, Hirsh and Loeb and Goldtree, whose names vanished without trace, through intermarriage and the exercise of choice.

Somerset was democratic, if essentially conservative. It accepted the essentially conservative German Jews when they came as one more variety of Somersetter. In turn, the Jews embraced Somerset and its ways. Few people were shocked when Abraham Fisher joined the First Presbyterian Church in 1891. From the beginning, in Somerset, no one was a Jew who didn't want to be.

By 1923, the year of Harry Goldenrammer's birth, democracy had destroyed the Jewish community. By Somerset's own definition, the Goldenrammers were the only remaining Jews.

"I'll be damned if I'll change," Sol Goldenrammer, Harry's father, announced, "even though I may be damned if I don't." Sol, who wavered between agnosticism and Reform Judaism, ran the better of Somerset's clothing stores, and made enough money to buy a sturdy, square brick house on a gentle rise to the north of town. There, Rose Levenger Goldenrammer, who had come west from the German-Jewish community of St. Louis, devoted her life to establishing a suitable Jewish home. Religion was moderately important. Culture was transcendent. Rose owned the earliest Steinway Grand to reach the county.

Harry was not the first-born. The oldest boy, whose brain was damaged by the obstetrical forceps of a general practitioner, was kept on the attic floor of the family's red brick home. That was his world, where he could harm nothing, or be harmed. He learned to articulate his name the summer before he died. "Drrr-vid, Drrr-vid," he said, the tongue driving against the roof of his mouth. Pneumonia killed David Goldenrammer at nine.

"This little town," Harry says, striding ebulliently down Hacker Street toward Main, "is a pretty damn good place to be if you're a Jew." Harry swings his arms when he walks, and his gangling joints hang loosely. "What do you need?" Harry asks. "Drugs without a prescription? No sweat. The druggist, Larry Nearing, he'll give you whatever you want if I ask. Ronnie Merritt, the doc, he'll make a night house call any time I ask, and I can get your car fixed for a fair price at Shearing's. Not because I'm a Jew or I'm not a Jew. Because this is my town. I mean something here. These people are my friends. Isn't that the way it ought to be?"

Harry likes to walk down Hacker toward Main, alongside the two-story buildings, yellow-fronted, busy, past Ramsdell's Shoes and Jobey's Hardware, toward the big corner store that bears his family name. Harry says over and over hello and hey-hiya to passersby. His flat voice is loud. His face, unlined although his hair is turning gray, has innocent, uncommitted features. Watching him stride up Hacker Street toward Main, no one could be sure that Harry is a Jew. The issue would not enter many minds.

As a child in Somerset, Harry never knew anti-Semitism. "Hey," he says, passing Lundgren's Radio-TV-Stereo, "we never had any of that here." Gerald Winrod, the Kansas proponent of fascism, won a few followers in Somerset, but they were nothing more substantial than handymen, drifters, and one grocery clerk. Father Coughlin's radio sermons alarmed some of the important men in town. Listening to Coughlin's fanatic preaching on Bolshevik Jews, they began to worry about a Popish Plot to capture the United States.

Sol Goldenrammer was deeply respected as an honest merchant. "Harry," he told his son, "a Jew in business has to be twice as honest as the other fellow. Never forget that. They're looking for you to cheat. They're always expecting something. You know what to do about that, Harry? You've got to forget this stuff. You hear that honesty is the best policy. For a Jew, honesty is the *only* policy."

Goldenrammer Drygoods, begun with a wagonload of levis spread over wormy tables, twice moved to larger stores. Finally Sol commandeered a busy corner of Hacker and Main. The source of his success was unmysterious. He worked harder than his competitor and offered better values. His obsession with honesty persisted. Sol Goldenrammer replaced merchandise even when he knew he was being cheated.

At Hacker and Main Harry ambles loose-gaited into the store. "Hey, Art!" Harry shouts. "This is Artie. Meet Art."

"Hiya," says Art, who is smaller than Harry and whose face is pointed. "You looking for an overpriced suit?" Art says. "We got plenty."

"Helluva store," Harry says. "Best store in the state outside of Omaha. Art's always kidding around."

In 1938, when blunt descriptions of Nazi Germany began appearing in the liberal *Somerset Appeal*, Dr. Dowell, the Methodist Minister, called on Sol at the store and said, with studied formality, that he would appreciate the chance to say a few words.

"You want a suit special?" Sol said.

It was after school. Harry was wrapping a package. "You

can hear these words, too, young man," Dr. Dowell said. He was plump, with burning blue eyes.

"Yes, sir," Harry said.

"A group of people at our congregation have been discussing conditions in the world," Dr. Dowell said.

"Yes," Sol said. Sol put one hand on Harry's left shoulder, and set his squat robust frame.

"We are appalled by the rise of Nazism," Dr. Dowell said, "which we regard as terribly anti-Christian."

Sol smiled hard. He stayed rigid. "Well, if you don't mind," he said to Dr. Dowell, "I have always regarded the Nazis as anti-Jewish."

"We realize, Mr. Goldenrammer, that we must consider the possibility, however hateful, of Nazism arriving here, in America, in Nebraska, in the streets of Somerset."

"I think not," Sol said softly, almost sullen.

"We *hope* not, Mr. Goldenrammer, but have you considered what it would mean if our hopes are misguided? Have you considered your family? Have you thought what the Nazis would do to your boy here?"

In a tone Harry had never heard from his father before, Sol said, "I have considered that more deeply than you, sir."

"I am here to invite your conversion to Methodism," Dr. Dowell said. "It is a demanding, but rewarding, religion, as I know it. We will welcome you and your family into our church. And further, should the Nazis come to Somerset, you and the boy here would surely be spared."

Striding out of Goldenrammer's Drygoods, in Somerset, it does not trouble Harry that Hitler probably would have rejected Dowell's conception of a Methodist, as he would certainly have rejected the Somerset conception of a Jew. Smiling in the prairie sunshine, Harry remembers his friends.

Sol sent his son to the University of Missouri, which pleased Rose and which taught Harry that he was a Jew. He had to join a Jewish fraternity in which he felt uncomfortable; the Eastern Jews seemed frightening and strange.

Afterwards, Harry was a good infantry corporal, who suffered through the Battle of the Bulge. He saw dead American soldiers there, bodies piled like cordwood, faces frozen, screaming or begging in the silence. The dead Americans stirred Harry more than the pedicular European Jews he observed at Bergen-Belsen. "I didn't know people who looked like those concentration camp Jewish guys," he says, turning off Main Street, to Norris, "but those dead soldiers. You never saw anything like it. Regular guys like you and me."

When the war ended, Sol was dead of cardiac arrest and Rose was dying of breast cancer. Harry reviewed the economy of Somerset and invested part of his inheritance in the principal liquor distributorship. Arthur had become a serious jazz pianist, and was about to marry Judge Goodhue's daughter, Ann. When Arthur faltered, and assessed his talent, he realized that he faced a life of playing dance tunes in wooden buildings erected by the Veterans of Foreign Wars. After that Harry assigned his brother all of Goldenrammer's Drygoods. The store was mildly profitable and endlessly annoying.

Liquor, joined with his good sense and integrity, made Harry a successful man. He courted a German Jewish girl, whom he had met at Missouri, and the wedding would have pleased his mother. Sheila, the bride, was gentle and chubby. Women were not deeply significant to Harry's life. He wanted simply a St. Louis girl as comfortable as his mother. Soon after the wedding, Harry put his liquor money into oil leases and after that he became rich. "Cuh-mon intuh my office," affluent Harry Goldenrammer says on Norris Street, in Somerset, Nebraska, "and I'll pour you a little of my booze."

The office, a flight up in a stone building, is paneled in an imitation hardwood. A tiny bar, made of a wood-grained plastic, stands in one corner. "I only peddle decent stuff," Harry says. "How about a couple of Chivas Regals?

"Want to ruin my profits with soda?" Harry says. "No. Goddamn good. Hey, it's got to look pretty dull to you, huh? And all the broads along Hacker are ugly. It isn't New York." He hurls down his drink and pours himself another. "You want to tell me," he says, "that all the broads are homely here in Somerset."

He opens his mouth and draws his left index finger across his teeth. "But I love it here," he says. "This town was good to my Ma and my Dad. It's been wonderful to me. I mean, really wonderful. So what am I running down the girls to you for?"

Harry sips his Chivas. "Say, you like poker?" he asks. "We got some fine poker games every Saturday and alternate Wednesday nights. We hold them at the Commerce Club. You know Clyde McCoy has played there? We're not small. That's the man, man, who plays *Sugar Blues*.

"I win at poker," Harry says. "I don't know why, except I got that kind of mind. Jewmind. I know what you're thinking. I went to Missouri. They had some funny ideas there, the Jews and gentiles both. But it ain't that way in Somerset and that's why it breaks my damn heart to have to leave."

He slams his hand against the leatherbound green blotter on his massive desk. "I didn't mean to say that. Damn. I didn't mean to tell you," Harry says. He looks at the framed American flag on one wall. "But, damn," he says, "you won't be around and you can keep something to yourself." He pauses, looks at the flag again and says slowly, "I am going to move to Omaha. Selling the house. I'm keeping the business but I'll be living in Omaha three months from now."

He finishes his drink. "Look," Harry says, "I'll still come back here to play cards, but I got these three daughters. Rosa, Carolina, Laura and I wanted a son, but the girls mean a lot to me.

"Now this is going to sound real square to you. Real square. But I'm a Jew and damnit that's important.

"I want Jewish grandsons.

"I want my daughters to marry Jewish guys. That's why I'm leaving Somerset. I got no choice.

"How they gonna find a Jewboy to marry 'round here?"

## BIRCHVILLE

Whether Harry Goldenrammer really has to move to Omaha, whether his explanation for the move is basic and complete, are considerations that may invite doubt. But beyond Somerset, Nebraska, in a number of localities in the United States, Jews feel alien for an inescapable external reason. They are deliberately made to feel that way. However bland the euphemism, however intricate the rationale, the essential message of certain American communities is, "We don't want Jews."

Politically such areas tend to belong to the right wing. The mentality that would solve American economic and social problems by repealing the Sixteenth Amendment and impeaching the Chief Justice is congenial to oversimplification. And anti-Semitism, with its single indictment of a pluralistic group, before it does anything else, oversimplifies.

Ideas do not boil in the brain of Miriam Fleischaker, a thick-waisted woman of forty-one, whose walk suggests a peasant background. She is not contemplative. She does not speculate on the decisions which propelled her to move to this sloping, troubled California street. She is impatient with high dreams, false eyelashes and introspection. "I live here in Orange County," Miriam says, "because my husband's plant is nearby and it's convenient. There is nothing more complicated to it than that."

Except for two complications which Miriam discusses only reluctantly: The Fleischackers are the only Jews in the 1200 block of San Luis Rey. And a half-dozen of their neighbors are members of the John Birch Society.

"This dentist across the street," Miriam says at length, screwing up her round face in distaste, "is the head of one of the biggest Birch chapters anywhere. As far as I know, Dr. Reade has only two interests—the Right Wing and pornographic movies. He runs the movies in his basement all the time." Miriam raises her full black brows for emphasis and indictment. Her morality is wholly conventional. "Kathy Reade," she says, "is really very nice. She's gone out of her way to be kind to my kids. But after I found out about Dr. Reade, I moved the family to another dentist."

Miriam, in tan skirt and flowered blouse, sits on a brown sectional sofa, in a large, square living room, with one wall of brick, two walls of wood and one of glass. Immediately beyond the glass wall a cement walk and a cyclone fence, bounding a swimming pool, crowd in too closely. There is no sense of space. "We have the creature comforts here," Miriam says. "There's no ignoring that. They're important to us. They were important even to my father, and he was an idealist."

Morris Kolodny, Miriam's father, was also a tailor. He arrived in the United States in 1911, savored the Lower East Side of Manhattan briefly, gambled that America extended farther and although his friends called him reckless, pushed on to Los Angeles. There he opened Morris' Cleaning & Pressing near Brooklyn Avenue in Boyle Heights. Miriam grew up in an undistinguished gray frame house near what Morris called "the store."

She was a pleasant, chunky girl, bright but not brilliant, plagued first by acne and later by a mustache that she variously bleached, tweezed and shaved. She was intent on finding a man and making a better home. After high school, Miriam Kolodny had to work for seven years while Dave Fleischacker from Boyle Heights took his degrees in electrical engineering at U.C.L.A. and earned an instructorship there. She was a file clerk and then a secretary in a small real estate company, waiting patiently and lending Dave money before they were married. After the wedding, they moved into a small house on Citrus in Los Angeles, which Morris the tailor helped them buy.

Dave Fleischacker was tall, bespectacled, buck-toothed and perennially preoccupied. He seemed pleased with Miriam's sense of home, cooking and comfort. Dave wanted three children and when Miriam produced Barry and Douglas within three years, Dave decided that he had to earn more money. He was specializing in advanced computer circuitry, and after he scouted industrial prospects, a company called Potento-Tronics offered him fifteen thousand dollars to join their research staff near the city of Santa Ana in Orange County.

The increment was significant and the people at Potento-Tronics all but insisted that the Fleischackers move from Los Angeles. Studies had convinced them, they said, that commutation destroyed the critical sense of teamwork. The personnel director gave Dave the name of a real estate agent in Orange County who could find something suitable, "say in the thirty thousand dollar range." Dave scratched his sandy hair, and was awarded one thousand dollars as an outright relocation fee.

The agent showed the Fleischackers three houses. "We're real proud of our educational systems in Orange County," he told Miriam. The Fleischackers chose the middle-priced one, on San Luis Rey, at $31,250. Its exterior was stucco-like, and dyed pale blue. Within, it was roomy. It came with forest green wall-to-wall carpeting at no extra charge.

Sitting on the brown couch that blends with her green carpet, Miriam says she cannot remember when she first realized that hers was the only Jewish family on the block. She became pregnant almost as soon as they moved and there was that excitement, plus the furnishing, finding the sectional, and showing her father the fine big house and seeing about financing so they could build the pool. The awareness came gradually, allied to other realizations.

There were no Jewish obstetricians nearby. Miriam would have to be delivered by a Christian. There was nothing wrong with that, so long as he was not Catholic. Dave even joked about her being afraid of rough *goy* hands. But after the jokes, the condition was still there. Then, she could not find a temple within miles. They would have to drive clear to Anaheim for services. They had not worshipped often in Los Angeles but suddenly, in this cold suburban scene, going to temple became important.

Miriam had a hard time with the pregnancy that produced Laurie. Dave's hours at Potento-Tronics were always long and sometimes they included weekends. Pregnant Miriam saw her husband less and less. She worried about this pregnancy. Something would go wrong this time, she believed. Twice, without telling her Christian obstetrician, she returned to the old Jewish doctor in Los Angeles to make certain that she, and the Christian obstetrician, were all right.

Soon after Laurie was born, normally, easily, Miriam decided that her feeling of isolation in Orange County was not imagined. "Do you realize," she said to Dave early one evening, "that in the fourteen months we've lived on this block, not one person has invited us in for a drink?"

They were sitting in their kitchen, a big square room with bronze-tinted appliances, a stainless steel sink, and coils of fluorescent light.

"Nonsense," Dave said. "They drop in on you to borrow something and you borrow from them. Besides, didn't that dame next door take the baby all day when Dougie broke his wrist?"

"I'm talking about social situations," Miriam said.

"And you don't drink much, anyway," Dave said.

"I get the feeling," Miriam said, "that everybody on this block socializes with everybody else, except nobody socializes with the Jewish Fleischackers."

"You know what," Dave said, standing up. "That sort of thinking is what causes anti-Semitism. I got a good job. The kids got a decent school. Why do you want to look for trouble?"

"I don't understand how you can say that," Miriam said. "I don't understand how an intelligent person like you can say that anti-Semitism is caused by Jews."

Dave mumbled and called Barry and challenged him to a wrestling match, beginning with David pinned flat by the boy on the forest green carpet in the living room. Walking past, Miriam said loudly, "And what makes you think the schools are any good?"

Timidly at first, and by herself, Miriam had attended meetings of the P.T.A. Almost at once, she decided that something was wrong, terribly wrong. In the spotless, air-conditioned assembly hall of the Frederick Futter School, where the P.T.A. met bi-monthly, a resolution was introduced to prohibit classroom discussion of the United Nations. Miriam was startled that it was Dr. Hartstein, her detached Christian obstetrician, who introduced this thing quite passionately. She was amazed when speaker after speaker, lawyers, salesmen, housewives rose to repeat the identical phrase: "The United Nations is too controversial for young people."

A man kept calling, "There is nothing controversial about peace." He was not recognized and the anti-U.N. resolution passed with a great "aye" of victory.

Although the coldness sometimes seemed to be elusive—the neighbors did smile and the teacher did say that Barry was a prize student—at other times it was entirely real. One morning Miriam's home-delivered *Santa Ana Register* published a letter attacking "the Jew Trotsky." On a Saturday, when she took the boys to Knott's Berry Farm near Anaheim, to see recreations of the Old West, she found the bookshop there littered with right wing documents and aggressive Christ militant pamphlets. Driving past the marquee erected on the grounds of the Central Baptist Church of Orange County, she saw an advertisement for the Rev. Dr. Bob Wells' sermon on "The Sins of the Jews."

Loy Snider, who owned a chain of gas stations, introduced Miriam to the enlightened minority of the region. She met Loy at a P.T.A. meeting after he had introduced a proposal for theoretical support of integrated schools. The resolution was attacked and tabled.

Miriam introduced herself afterward and Snider, a huge, jowly black-haired man explained that he was trying to organize "a citizens' Anti-John Birch Society."

"We would be for that," Miriam said, "although my husband may not want to get involved."

The moderate group met informally and irregularly at one another's homes. It consisted of Snider, an executive from a food packaging company, a few engineers, a woman M.D., several professors from the University of California at Irvine, and Miriam, recording secretary and activist.

Miriam learned about Orange County from Loy Snider. Its settlers included old wealthy California conservative families and later a core of German farmers. Loy's own father was Hannoverian. With time, Orange County grew prosperous and inbred. There were no Negroes. After World War II, as Southern California boomed, the old stronghold was threatened. Newcomers, suburbanites and even Jews were invading. The County responded by moving farther right.

All that his group, as Snider envisioned it, could do, was observe right wing activity and try to organize enclaves of resistance. "We can't beat the Birch bastards back," Snider said. "Not just yet. Not here. But we can let 'em know that we are here too. At least that'll get us started."

Soon after Miriam joined the anti-Birchers, the *Santa Ana Register* published an advertisement from Central Baptist Church soliciting attendance at the Rev. Dr. Bob Wells' forthcoming sermon. According to the ad, the sermon was entitled: "Can the Vatican Get the Jews off the Hook, Re the Murder of Jesus Christ?"

Miriam decided that she would have to go. "I want to hear this," she said. "I want to know what all this is. I owe it to my kids."

"It could get unpleasant," Loy Snider said. "You may need company, and I can't make it there myself. We've got some family problems."

"Maybe Dave will go with me," Miriam said.

Dave went bowling. Miriam drove alone to Central Baptist Church. Central Baptist was a complex of buildings, with school and offices. The church itself was bigger than Miriam had expected. Although she was early for Dr. Wells' sermon, the pews were almost full. She was fortunate to notice one open place well down the center aisle. The congregants graciously crowded together to give her room.

Miriam was relieved when the Rev. Dr. Wells stepped into the pulpit. He had a square, open, almost youthful face, although he might well be past fifty. He did not look antagonistic. He wore eye glasses and he seemed to peek out at the audience of his congregants.

Wells began the sermon slowly, talking about the New Testament and what it said about the killing of Christ. His voice was flat. The cavernous church made Miriam uncomfortable. Otherwise, she might have become bored. But suddenly, quite without warning, the flatness erupted into rolling peaks of anger. Wells was quoting. He shouted from the Book of Acts:

"The Apostle Peter points his finger at the men of Israel
. . . *all* the house of Israel. *All* the house of Israel is involved
and *all* the house of Israel are called to face up to the fact
that the one whom they have crucified has been made both
Lord and Christ."

Alarm jerked Miriam erect in her pew. "He's talkin' to *all*
of Israel," the minister said, "referring to *all* of Israel, placing
the blame on all of Israel, that the nation of Israel was guilty
of taking the life, of killing the Prince of Peace."

As the Rev. Dr. Wells explained it, ecumenism was a Jewish-Catholic scheme, based on expediency. The news media
were part of the plot. They were helping the Catholics expediently to forgive the Jews for Christ-killing, a culpa which
suited mysterious Judeo-Papist ends. But who appointed the
Catholics to rewrite history? That was what Dr. Wells really
wanted to know.

According to Wells, Pontius Pilate was a benevolent bystander. "When finally," Wells preached, "Pilate was not willing to go through with it and he said *I'm not going to do it.
I'm going to wash my hands on the whole affair,* and called
for a basin of water and washed his hands and turned Jesus
over to them and said *See ye to it,* then they did not apologize. They did not hesitate. *They did not say No! You do it!*
They were very happy to accept the responsibility and they
said *His blood be on us and our children.*"

Miriam sat back. She wanted to leave. But her face, with
its large brows and curving nose made her afraid to be noticed.

"My friends," said Dr. Wells congenially, "it was not a
gentile who said that. It was a crowd of *Jews* who said that.

"The gentiles did not place the blame upon the Jews. The
Jews placed the blame upon themselves. In those days they
were not trying to get out from under the condemnation of
this. In those days, they did not shy away from it. In those
days they did not say *Please do not charge us with the guilt
of this man's murder.*

"They did not say, *Please do not charge all of us. Do not
hold our whole nation responsible.* These were the leaders of
the nation who made the decisions and the leaders of the nation said, *So be it. We don't mind. You turn him over to us.
That's all right. His blood be on us.*

"And not only that. They went farther, and said, *And on
our children.* And later on, when Peter stood there on the

day of Pentecost and looked that same crowd in the face and pointed his finger in their direction and said, *You are the bloody red-handed murderers of the Son of God,* he was just simply reminding them of a responsibility they themselves had officially accepted . . . *Let his blood be upon us and our children!*"

Miriam was angry. The word "children" stirred her. She wanted to stand up and shake her square fist in this ranting man's face but as quickly as he had appeared, the ranting man was gone.

"Now, my friends," Dr. Wells spoke in the peaceable voice and manner he affected. "I want to pause here for just a moment." He was almost smiling, Miriam thought. He seemed to be looking at her. "I don't want you to get the wrong impression. I don't want you to get the impression that I am saying that the Jewish people are so very, very bad and that we are so very, very good. Nothing of the kind.

"I am just trying to produce the facts of the record. The Jewish people did this and a lot of people say they did it because they were Jews!

"That isn't true. Not any more than when a gentile goes out and cuts somebody's throat, he does it because he's a gentile.

"The Jews did it because they were sinners!

"THEY DID IT BECAUSE THEY WERE SINNERS, not because they were Jews."

Dr. Wells, Miriam noticed through substantial fright, played on his congregants. He went from bland to brash, soft to loud, mellow to guttural. It was all practiced, she began to think, the way a band practices. Looking up at Dr. Wells, a phrase entered Miriam's mind. A band of hate.

He wanted to discuss the present, Dr. Wells said, and why in the present Jews still suffer because they murdered Christ. "I have never talked with a responsible leader," he preached, "who said to me, *Dr. Wells, we as a people made a tragic and a cruel mistake. It was a terrible thing that we did. Jesus did not deserve to be killed. He should not have been put upon the cross. We have confessed before Almighty God and asked His forgiveness.*"

Miriam trembled with impotence. Jews do not confess. Jews atone. Don't you understand anything? That was what she wanted to cry. She looked about. The people in the pews were old and young. The faces, although none was the same, might have been faces at the P.T.A. Damnit, Miriam wanted to shout, why are you listening to this man? She was trembling and silent, except for her breath, which came in gasps.

"On page one hundred and twenty of the book called *A Jew in Love*," Wells preached, "I read, *One of the finest things ever done by the mob was the crucifixion of Christ.*"

He paused. Miriam still was silent.

"Now," Wells said, "my Jewish friends, and there are some of them here tonight—" My God, Miriam thought, is he really staring at me? "—my Jewish friends," Wells preached, "how do you expect us, who love the Lord Jesus Christ, to feel toward that?

"This is a representative statement," Wells said, raising his voice, "because there are many others who have made similar statements. *One of the finest things ever done by a mob was the crucifixion of Christ.*" He was quoting a minor book by a professional hostile, a newspaperman gone Hollywood, that late, self-hating, commercializer of Hemingway novels, Ben Hecht.

"A representative statement," Wells repeated. Where was Maimonides, Miriam thought, or Herman Wouk?

"*Intellectually,*" Wells quoted Hecht, "*it was a splendid gesture. But trust the mob to bungle. If I had been in charge of executing Christ, I'd have handled it differently. You see what I'd have done was have him shipped to Rome and have him fed to the lions. They never could have made a saviour out of mincemeat.*"

The Rev. Dr. Bob Wells paused. Faces blazed up at Miriam as she walked out of the Central Baptist Church of Orange County.

Behind, Wells was asking if this was what the Jew really thought of his saviour. Behind, too, was the clatter of her heels. All the faces played on her own, as spotlights, and she was old and frightened, with acne scars and thick brows and downy cheeks and a body that was too thick and she had come here really only to inquire and, walking up the aisle, away from Dr. Wells, she thought, My God, what could happen to herself and her children and to Dave—even uncommitted Dave—if this man were allowed to go on, and she had to go home and talk to her children and tell her husband about this evil upon which she had stumbled.

She woke Dave from a sound sleep in the big round bed that lately they had purchased. "Whuh, whuh?" Dave said.

She tried to tell him.

"It'll blow over," Dave said. "Fuh God's sake, Miriam, what time is it?"

"I don't know."

"Well, fuh God's sake, if it's so late you don't know, don't bother me."

Dave pulled the blanket toward his ear and went to sleep and Miriam walked into the bathroom, where now two sinks stood side by side, and turned on both nozzles of the shower, and for the first time since the final labor pains with Barry thirteen years before, she yielded to agony, threw back her close-cropped head and roared out tears.

## A JEWISH EDUCATION

The combative Jew coincides with no stereotype. Brawling, ferocious Jews, pugnacious Jewish athletes, are not found in the cliché. They exist, a select minority, only in reality.

The roster of American sport is not rich in Jewish names. A half-dozen Jews among the five hundred major league baseball players are all one finds at any given time. Still fewer play professional football. During periods of affluence almost no Jews become boxers.

In the great majority of Jewish homes, children are not encouraged to pursue sport as a career. Sports suggest frivolity and Jews even in America are far from frivolous. Athletics run, or seem to run, counter to traditions of the Book.

Additionally, American sports has harbored gruff, violent, shallow anti-Semitism. Scores of Jews, breaking with tradition, entering sports, soon discovered that discretion was a major part of athletic survival. James Hymie Solomon, a second baseman for the Yankees in the early 1930's, played as Jimmy Reese. Some years earlier a major league pitcher named Harry Cohen performed as Klondike Harry Kane. In the first words uttered by Francis X. Farrell, the "Alibi Ike" of Ring Lardner's remarkable short story, one finds a traditional ballplayer's attitude. "What are you calling me Ike for?" Farrell complains. "I ain't no Yid."

There has, of late, been a certain mellowing; Ike and his teammates have been dead decades. "But the game," says one

Jewish New Yorker who recently pitched in the American League, "is partly needling, and as long as it is, you're gonna jab people where it hurts.

"You know a better way," the pitcher asks, "to sting a Jewish ballplayer than to call him a long-nosed son of a bitch?"

Big, and nicely groomed, and tough, he walks past an electronic device that clatters market reports in a brokerage office in Cleveland. "Hello," he says. "How are you? Good to see you again. Let's go in here." (*Fairchild Camera up two-and-an-eighth.*)

He indicates an anteroom and leads the way with strong, easy strides. "Well," he says, "what's all this? I'm glad we could get together. I hope I can help." He pulls out chairs and sits behind a metal desk. Pipe and tobacco pouch appear. The big hands strike a match. He puffs and looks across the desk, a graying, friendly, and confronting man.

At forty-two, Al Rosen, a successful securities salesman for Bache & Company, has talked through more interviews than he remembers. When he played third base for the Cleveland Indians he was direct and opinionated and reporters often sought him out. Now, five years after the last base hit, he is not going to speak about batting or fielding or even about the prospects of Fairchild Camera. He is going to talk about what it has meant, through a life spent mostly in the elemental world of athletes, to be a Jew.

"Feel," Al Rosen says. "To me a Jew is feel." His voice is full and powerful. "The wanderings," he says, "and the searchings and the longings are in your background, and they make you feel compassion and they drive you to search for something good."

He puffs the pipe. "Compassion is fundamental," he says. "When I think of Vietnam and the inhumanities in that war and in all wars generally, even if it is one illiterate African chopping off another illiterate African's head, I get an inner sense of horror. I get a kind of outrage at the wrongness of it. I have to believe I feel this way because I am a Jew and I have a heritage that calls up horror and sadness at people hurting other people."

His face, broad and handsome, is dominated by a rugged nose that has been broken several times. He has lost some fights but, one suspects, Albert Leonard Rosen has won many more than he has lost. He is not afraid.

His grandfather, a Polish immigrant, ran a department store in Spartanburg, on the coast of South Carolina, but soon after Al was born, the grandfather died, the store went bad and the family had to move. The Rosens settled in Miami, Florida, moving into a neighborhood without other Jews. Rosen's father left the family when his son was eight.

"My mother had to work," Rosen says, in the anteroom at Bache, "and my grandmother took care of the house. I was a big kid, matured early, and I was working myself by the time I was eleven.

"I think of Jewish learning, sometimes. You know, with Papa standing there, a ruler in his hand, saying *Read, read mein kind*. It wasn't that way in my house, even when my father was there. Nobody made me read. The only reason I read when I was a kid was that I had to read in public school."

He cannot recall the first time he heard "Jewboy." The word was a part of his childhood. It was important for some of the others to call him a name. It let them show one another how brave they were. *Lookit the Jewboy. Go home an' eat yuh matzos, sheeney. Come on, let's get the lousy kike.*

"What is it?" Al Rosen asks, after forty-two years. "Is it because your nose is a little bigger, or your hair is a little curlier, or you don't go to Sunday school on Sunday morning or you're not in regular school on Yom Kippur? What is it?"

As he grew bigger and rougher, in Miami, Al Rosen began to spend time in a boxers' gym. He watched professionals, studying, and after a while sparring, with them. His Jewish education was measured in hooks and jabs and crosses and dropping a right hand larrup over somebody else's low left.

"I wanted to learn how to end things," Rosen says. "That was important. I wasn't starting trouble in those days, but when it came to me, I wanted to end it, and damn quick."

With his young athlete's body and the big heavy fists, and the intelligence and the courage and the drive, he learned what he wanted. He ended some fights others started, with furious speed. After that he heard "Jewboy" less frequently. It was easier, some of the others realized, to accept the Jew than to challenge him. And not only easier; less painful as well.

He went out for football at a Miami high school and after one early practice, six or seven boys piled into the coaches' car. "Rosen," the coach said, "what are you doing out for football?"

"I love to play the game," Rosen said.

"Rosen," the coach said. "You're different from most Jews. Most Jewboys are afraid of contact."

He could always hit a baseball hard and often. Hitting was a gift within himself. By the time he was twelve or so, he was good enough to consider trying out with men's teams, playing the kind of softball where a beefy pitcher forty-five feet away whips rising fastballs out of a windmill windup. He had to earn his way all by himself. There were no Jewish softball teams where he could gently learn. If he wanted to play, he would have to play among men, who hadn't known Jews, or didn't want to know Jews, or who figured that if this big, young Jewboy was gonna play with them, he better have it, and have it all. He did. In his early teens, he traveled around the state of Florida on a fast-pitch softball circuit. He was a shortstop, but what he liked most was swinging the bat.

After two years in high school, he went to Florida Military School, a prep at St. Petersburg, on an athletic scholarship. His mother was tremendously proud. He lettered in baseball, basketball, football, boxing and made the dean's list. "Some of my best friends there," he says, deadpan, "were gentiles."

It was a long time ago, before the Holocaust, and in the office, his pipe on the table, Al Rosen says that he was a big-mouthed kid. "Like most Jewish kids who grew up in a neighborhood where you had to fight," he says, "I was very aggressive and I had this chip on my shoulder and I was looking for someone to knock it off, and look, I had my share of guys who knocked it off and who I couldn't take. But I was ready, ready for any of them. Maybe if I'd grown up in a Jewish neighborhood I would have been a different guy. I think being the way I was, comes out of that environment. When you start out by having to fight all the time for your pride and self-respect, how are you gonna know when to stop?"

He was in the Army and had some college but he wanted to be a ballplayer and when he was struggling up through the minor leagues, there were times when he wished his name was something other than Rosen. Anything other than Rosen. Smith. Jones. Abernathy. Just not Jewish. Fighting his way up, being Jewish was just one more damn handicap, on top of all the other things that made it so damn tough to make the majors.

He was a tenacious, dogged hitter, who stood close to the plate, challenging the pitcher. In his first full year as a Cleveland regular, he hit thirty-seven home runs. In order to intimidate him, pitchers threw fast balls at Rosen's ribs and head and arms. The theory is simple, and as old as baseball. A man consumed by self-preservation will not be able to concentrate on getting a hit. Rosen went down under fast balls time after time, diving for the safety of the dirt. When he got up, he stood in just as close, just as defiantly.

It hurt to be struck by a baseball, traveling ninety miles an hour, but Rosen would be damned if he'd let a pitcher see him writhe. The worst pain came when the ball struck the funny bone in his left elbow. That happened twice. Each time he clenched his teeth and fought the pain and pretended it was minor. In his tweedy jacket, with his pipe, in the anteroom at Bache, Al Rosen says, "There's not a guy living who ever saw me rub."

He thinks back fifteen years. "Throwing at me had nothing to do with my being Jewish. They did it because I could hurt 'em with my bat. I heard some things but I didn't hear 'Jew bastard' when I was playing in the majors as much as some people seem to want to think." The old Cleveland Indians, Al Rosen's team, were, in a baseball context, sophisticated, *bon vivants,* possessed of a strong team and party sense. They were not beer-drinking ball-players. For the Indians, it was martinis, vintage wine with dinner, and stingers afterward. They were a splendid team. The New York Yankees dominated the American League and baseball in that era and the only team that ever beat the Yankees was the Cleveland Indians. They did it twice.

Once, when Rosen was a rookie sitting in a Boston bar, he overheard someone talking about the big-nosed Jewboy. He had no chance to defend himself. Before he could move, Joe Gordon, a veteran Cleveland infielder, got up without a word and punched the offender's mouth. Gordon, not Jewish, was a strong, well-coordinated man, who hit hard.

Rosen won respect from his colleagues and from players on other teams by hard, combative, courageous ballplaying. Once, when he was crouched at third base in Fenway Park, the Boston ball park, a huge, mediocre catcher began to call him names. Third base was close to the Boston dugout, and Rosen heard the names quite clearly. They were the old names, from his Florida youth.

"Time," Rosen said to an umpire. Then he started toward the dugout, where he was going to have to take on a bigger man and, team loyalty being what it is, perhaps some of the other Boston players as well. Suddenly two Boston stars, Bobby Doerr and Johnny Pesky, grabbed the catcher and convoyed him out of the dugout and down a runway. They were not protecting him. There in the runway, Doerr and Pesky shouted their contempt for a man who would cry racial epithets at as fine a professional as Rosen.

By the polished standards of the major leagues, Rosen's fielding at third base was only average. But he worked hard at scooping ground balls, getting throws off quickly, and charging bunts and within a few years he grew proud of his skills. On one occasion a runner slid into third, and Rosen picked off a throw and slapped him with a tag.

The umpire spread his arms wide. The man was safe.

"No," Rosen yelled. "No, dammit. I had him. You blew it."

The umpire walked in a semicircle toward George Strickland, the Cleveland shortstop. Quietly, gentile to gentile, the umpire said, "I'll get that Jew bastard one of these days."

"I'm going to tell him you said that," Strickland said.

"You wouldn't do that," the umpire said.

"I'm telling him," Strickland said, "and after he takes a belt at you, if he misses, I'm going to get you myself."

These were the passionate words of friendship. No one assaulted the umpire. All that ultimately occurred was that the umpire told some other umpires that Strickland of Cleveland was a Bolshevik, a troublemaker.

Rosen was a winning ballplayer, intolerant of losing and as demanding of others as of himself. Once when the Indians were about to play the Yankees, a star lay on a white table in the trainer's room, complaining of a sore muscle. "I just can't make it today," the star said.

"The big man," Rosen said, "takes off against Washington. The big man puts up with pain to play the Yankees."

The man on the table cursed briefly.

"Look at Mantle," Rosen said. "He plays on a worse leg than yours every day."

There was more profanity.

"I've been kidding you," Rosen said, withdrawing into formality, "and it's obvious that you're not kidding me. I think it best that you not say anything further to me and I won't say anything further to you."

Rosen wheeled and was at the door of the trainer's room when he heard, "You yellow son of a bitch."

He turned. The other Cleveland player was standing up, fists cocked. Rosen strode through punches and knocked the other ball-player down. It took two men to pull him away.

Rosen fought for a lot of reasons, but he had learned to fight because he was a Jew. When he was established and a star, nationally famous, he was unhappy with his name once more. He wanted one even more Jewish than his own, perhaps Rosenthal or Rosenstein. He wanted to make sure that there was no mistake about what he was.

An accident shortened his years in baseball. He was playing first base and a runner screened his view just before a hard drive crumpled the index finger of his right hand. He did not stay out of the lineup long enough. When he returned, pitchers threw inside fastballs so that whenever bat and ball connected, the finger was jarred. The injury failed to heal but in the All Star game of 1955, with his right index finger stiff and useless, Rosen hit successive home runs. That autumn he had to retire. He now has fifty per cent use of the finger.

Rosen's second career has provided security and a chance to think life over, to reach conclusions in quiet times. He and his wife are exposing their children to religious Judaism. Rosen wants them to have facts, legend, belief, history before them. Then hopes they will decide for themselves whether they are religious. He is a suburbanite now, with country club membership. He is addicted to tennis, but he remembers the violent years.

"A big thing about fighting," Rosen says, "is how much do you have to lose. Ten guys can terrorize a thousand. Look at the motorcycle crowd. They have nothing so they can afford to fight." He relights his pipe with the big hands in the anteroom. "I suppose the same was true of many of the early Nazis. They had nothing to lose."

He has thought often of the Holocaust. Certain pictures of Jews being led to death choke him with emotion. He carries the burden of being a Jew proudly. He is stronger than most, more resolute, and more courageous. Talking to him in the anteroom, one suspects that even now, as parent, businessman and tennis player, he would react to an anti-Semitic remark by shedding the tweed jacket, along with the courteous broker's manner, and punch hard, to end it fast, the way he used to in Miami, Florida, so that whoever started this, and whoever was observing, would remember next time they were inclined to pick on a Jew.

But that is only the second deepest consideration of his life so far. "When I was up there in the majors," Al Rosen says, "I always knew how I wanted it to be about me.

"I wanted it to be, *Here comes one Jewish kid that every Jew in the world can be proud of.*"

The big, graying, broken-nosed man relights his pipe and intensity makes the strong hands tremble.

## TORAH IN WAYNE COUNTY, NEW YORK

According to one professional estimate, approximately seventeen per cent of the lawyers in the United States are Jews. The figure, roughly six times the percentage of Jews in the population at large, is phenomenal.

In the Manhattan Yellow Pages, the number of Jews past the bar is illustrated still more impressively, if hyperbolically. No fewer than eighty lawyers named Cohen, from Aaron to William J., purchased mentions in the 1967 New York classified telephone book, along with fourteen lawyers named Cohn, from Allen C. to Sol, and five named Kohn, from Harold Storch to William S. The full listing of attorneys, beginning with Irving Aaron of Madison Avenue and ending with Philip Zwirn of West 136th Street, provides a splendid *aperçu* of American-Jewish names: Abramowitz and Zucker; Bernstein and Weinberg; Cantor and Thaler; Diamond, Safirstein and Rubin; Greenberg and Rothstein; Balaban, Epstein, Levine, Marcus, Pinkus, Schein, Scheinberg; Scheinfeld; Scheinman; and Schenck: The most famous of Jewish trial lawyers, Louis Nizer, is so successful that he can afford to go unlisted.

There is nothing mysterious or portentous in the troops of Jewish attorneys practicing in Manhattan and beyond. Jews choose law easily out of Jewish tradition and, just as relevant, attempts to exclude them from the American bar have been neither as persistent nor as successful as discriminatory efforts in other professions. Christian physicians, working with Christian deans, once were able almost to cut Jews off from medical schools. Christian engineering firms refused to hire Jews with such unanimity in the 1920's and 1930's that it was common to find Jewish electrical engineers selling haberdashery. But in hard times and good, there has never been a period when qualified American Jews were unable to find acceptance at law schools. They have been barred from some, but never all. Further, good Jewish lawyers have generally been able to make a living. A number of individual law firms, many with otherwise unassailable claims to distinction, have *de facto* refused to hire Jews. As one affluent Jewish lawyer has remarked in New York City, "But all we've ever asked anywhere is half a chance. We've been granted that, and more, in the legal field."

The Hebrew word, Torah, which means Pentateuch, also means law. By itself, this testifies to the importance law carried among the ancient Jews. They awarded law the word—almost a title—that described the holiest of their scriptures. In dispersion, after the destruction of the Second Temple, this sacrosanct respect was reinforced.

Codes of law are most vitally significant to the weak and to minorities. The others can look after themselves. Since the dispersion of 70 A.D., Jews have been a minority in every nation where they lived, except for the brevity of Israel. In England and France and Russia and Spain, Jews were not always well served by the law. Frequently it was turned against them to tragic effect. But coming out of the Torah tradition, and living as a minority, Jews have looked to the law, however imperfect, however evilly administered, as their surest shield. In America, where, as Thomas Jefferson wrote in a letter occasioned by the opening of a Manhattan synagogue, "law protects . . . by putting all on equal footing," Jewish reliance on law was finally confirmed.

It is entirely natural to find, in a country conceived in Jeffersonian ethos, that the inheritors of Torah flock to practice law. This is not to invest every Jewish negligence practitioner, collection specialist, and stock arranger with the wisdom of Abraham or the dignity of Jefferson. One professor of law remarks that "you'll find plenty of Jews, along with plenty of non-Jews, laboring in these sewers of the profession. Perhaps Jewish representation at the bottom is a little out of proportion; so is Jewish representation at the top. I am not simply talking about Abe Fortas on the Supreme Court, or Paul Freund teaching at Harvard, either."

The best of Jews in law tempers compassion with a sense of social order. The Honorable Harry D. Goldman of Rochester, New York, Associate Justice of the New York State Appellate Division, is a short, round-faced man whose looks are reminiscent of the late (half-Jewish) mayor of New York, Fiorello H. LaGuardia, and whose compassionate good sense asserts itself slowly.

Judge Goldman is a cautious man and a Republican. Thomas Dewey appointed him to the bench two decades ago when it was said, in law offices and at political clubs, "You can't make a Jew a judge in upstate New York. They'll never stand for it." Since his appointment, Harry Goldman has been invited to join a number of private clubs in Rochester. "I am still," he says, gently, "the same man that I was before I reached the bench, before some of these clubs would consider me."

Goldman was raised on a farm near Rome, New York, among easy, rolling hills. "To support us," he says, "my father was a peddler. He was a commercial traveler, like Barry Goldwater." The Judge makes a wry face. He is not that kind of Republican.

"I, being the youngest," Goldman says, "could afford to go to Harvard very easily. My brother Manny, being older, had to go to work. There wasn't that much money left when his time came. My father did what he could. Before he died, he was able to buy a cemetery for the town. It wasn't much; maybe twenty thousand dollars paid over twenty years. But he did it and, you see, I took lessons there. Concern for others."

Harry Goldman smokes a pipe. He sits in his high office that looks down on the Genesee River, hurrying in little waterfalls, through Rochester. He recalls the *pushkies*, little metal boxes with coin slots that his mother placed in the kitchen of the farm. "One for a Yeshiva in Palestine," he says, "and one for a consumptive hospital in Denver and one for HIAS" (the Hebrew Immigrant Aid Society). He has been stern behind the massive oak desk. Now his face softens. "On Friday night," he says, "when she lit the candles and when we had a penny, which was not every Friday night, she would pick me up and I would drop my penny in the *pushky*." The judge's eyes are looking far away. "And sometimes," he says, "the solicitors would come around. They were very high-class solicitors. They never kept more than seventy-five per cent of the take."

Now, Goldman is past president of the Rochester Jewish Welfare Board, a trustee of two Roman Catholic Hospitals and a major benefactor of an orphanage in Leghorn, Italy. On the huge desk an Italian priest's letter of thanks sits in a frame.

"Making money isn't difficult," Goldman says. "I speak as one who has made a reasonable amount. But making money does not automatically make one charitable.

"Some Jews may be obsessed with the sort of image they present, but a Jew is unwise to live as an ambassador to the *goys*. When, as happens in Rochester, the Community Chest gets twenty per cent of its gifts from Jews, that earns your spurs. Each man builds his heaven, and my heaven is here."

Charity is intense and ultimately private for Judge Harry Goldman. It flows, like his choice of the law, out of Jewish tradition. "Well, they gave me a dinner," he says, "and they presented me that bronze plaque you can see there on the wall." He points impatiently. "Joe Wilson [the president of Xerox] and Bill Vaughan [the president of Eastman Kodak] have that plaque, too. When I got up to thank them at the dinner, first I said things like, *Behind every successful man stands a disbelieving mother-in-law.* Levity. But then I was serious. Pearl Buck has written, *What we do, we do for secret reasons of our own.* I told them the secret reason for the charitable things that I have done. *I've done them to enhance the happiness of Harry D. Goldman.*"

Two of his sons are lawyers; the third works for Kodak. His high station and his high office are a world of space and meaning, above his boyhood as a part-time peddler's son. "We have been opening doors," Judge Goldman says. "I was the first Jew on the Appellate Division. You understand the system in New York State? The Appellate Division is higher than the Supreme Court. Don't demand perfect consistency in legal terminology. My initial appointment was to the Supreme Court. I remember a colleague, Jewish, who had been waiting a long time to become a Supreme Court judge. When the opening came, I told him, take it. No, he said. We will fight for it without jeopardizing our friendship. When I won, he told me sorrowfully that he would be seventy years old when my term was up. He was appointed before very much longer. Right now I'm on the Appellate Division and two Supreme Court judges in the county are Jews and no one protests. No one says any more, *They won't stand a Jewish judge.*"

The small justice is imposing behind the enormous desk. He begins to talk toward a philosophy. "I thought," Judge Goldman says, "the greatest love was what I felt for my wife, but now I have corrected myself. I have told her, it is for my grandson." He grins, but does not show a picture. "If I don't talk to my grandson every other day, I die."

The judge's voice deepens. "What do you care about apartheid?" he says. "If you care for your grandson, you care. What do you care about children in India dying at two months, people starving in the streets of Pakistan? They're hearing about us, that we have toilets and running water. If you care for your grandchildren, you'd better care.

"I could live out my ten years," Harry Goldman says, "and die in peace here, but in Wendell Willkie's phrase it is one world, and if it is getting larger, it is also getting smaller. We had better care about one world for our grandchildren."

The Negroes in Rochester have rioted. "We reap the whirlwind," Goldman says, quoting Hosea. "We get what we deserve. You cannot keep a dog chained to a stake and starving for ten years and then be surprised that when he is released he bites the first man he sees."

Before his promotion to the Appellate bench, Judge Goldman once rode the circuit into Wayne County, apple country south of Rochester where hills bow and bend against wide sky. In Wayne, farmers hire unscreened migrant Negro pickers in auto-loads, a half-dozen at a time, to procure help at the cheapest possible rates. One picker, handsome, black and somber, was denuding an apple tree of fruit when the farmer who had hired him appeared and silently reached to touch his penis.

Quickly the Negro spun on his ladder and, with his picking knife, cut off the homosexual farmer's head, in a single, prodigious outraged swipe.

When Goldman came to the circuit court, the sheriff reported the details and said, "Do you want to talk to this nigger?"

Judge Goldman said, "Don't use that language in my presence."

"Well," said the sheriff, "do you want to see this Negro?"

"Yes," said the Judge, "and keep him manacled."

The prisoner entered and Judge Goldman said, "Do you have an attorney?"

"Huh?" said the Negro picker, whose name was Isaac.

"A lawyer," Judge Goldman said.

"What's that?" Isaac said.

"Someone to help you," Judge Goldman said.

"Yeah, I want someone to help me," Isaac said.

Isaac liked the judge. He came from a tiny village in Georgia and one night in a fight he had killed another Negro with his knife. He was sorry and so was everybody else. That was all. Nobody cared much but Isaac and the dead man's people.

When Judge Goldman was next in the rural courthouse, he asked Isaac, "How are you being treated?"

"I's cold, Jidge," Isaac said. "I's awful cold."

"Sheriff," Judge Goldman said. "Is there heat in this man's cell?"

"Sure, there is," the sheriff said. " 'Course, I'll go down there and check it anyway."

Isaac, lean, and manacled, approached the bench with enormous eyes. "Jidge," he whispered. "Jidge."

Harry Goldman nodded for him to continue.

"Jidge," Isaac said. "They is a car goan down to Georgia soon. Wouldn't it be all right if I gits on it, Jidge? Nobody would know. I won't tell nobody. Nobody would know but you and me."

Goldman tells the story softly in his judge's office, five floors above the hurrying Genesee. The memory of wide-eyed Isaac moves him.

"What can you do, weep?" snaps Harry D. Goldman, inheritor of Torah, guardian of American law. "Society has got to be protected. Law cannot be perverted by emotion.

"I gave him thirty years to life."

In the semi-serious self-mockery certain Jews habitually affect, someone has defined the Jew in America as "Irving Everyman." The postulate pleases some. It is to their taste. It coincides with the remark of a rabbi who insists, "The Jew in America is like everybody else, except more so."

What fine, perilous structures can be built on uncertain

foundations. Once one accepts the rabbi's first few words, everything else rises securely in place. But is it correct to accept any generalization?

It is true that the Jew in America is various. He is rich man and mendicant, rabbi and atheist, Zionist and pursuer of the Soviet anti-Zionist line. Trying to describe his personality, one calls forth a dignified, cajoling, dedicated, self-involved, hypersexual, anti-libidinous, base idealist, who is sensitive, tearful, smiling and gross.

When one crosses the American continent in a jet airplane, one compresses perhaps a lifetime's journey into five hours. The view stirs questions: what has the blinding desert of midday to do with the wheatfields of morning, or the city and the sea of afternoon?

Pluralism, like variety, is an imperfect word, but pluralism, like variety, drives close to the center of the American experience. Comprehension and acceptance of pluralism, like variety, comes hard. Out of laziness, or insularity, or ignorance, or obsessive concern with themselves—and all the combinations and variations on these themes—some Americans say:

*The Jews are smart.*
*The Jews don't want to fight a war.*
*The Jews can't wait to go and fight for Israel.*
*The Jews have money.*
*The Jews are good husbands.*
*The Jews shun Christians.*
*The Jews control banks.*
*The Jews are revolutionaries.*
*The Jews are the deadly, vulgar architects of the middle class.*
*The Jews are gifted.*
*The Jews are dull.*

Of course. And no.

Individual Jews fit almost any single statement that can be conceived. The variance possible within five-and-a-half million persons exceeds the individual imagination. But together, unanimously, or even very consistently, the Jews of America do not say, think, want, control or shun anything at all.

That is a deep meaning of pluralism, and the pluralism of Jews in America is more various even than the terrain. Ultimately, this pluralistic variety which may seem abstract and unsettling, is actually something quite concrete.

In the sense that millions and tens of millions of Americans use the term, in this country in this time, there is no such thing as The Jews.

# Part Three

<hr style="border-top: 3px double;" />

## *Things Sacred:*

## *A Variety of Services*

ONE DICTIONARY DEFINES JUDAISM AS "THE RE-ligious rites and doctrines of the Jews," a definition which is unassailable within its own terms. Jewish rites and religious doctrines do constitute Judaism, and nobody is going to argue about that. Not much more that can be said about Judaism is safe from intense dispute.

The doctrinal foundations of Judaism are monotheism and the twenty-four Books of the Jewish Bible, from which the Christian Old Testament has been taken. The Hebrews were the first people able to sustain monotheism in the ancient world. Primarily through the Bible, Judaism now attempts to teach the fatherhood of a God, who is one, and the brother-hood of man. But Biblical conceptions of fatherhood, broth-erhood, man and God Himself, vary from book to book and sometimes from chapter to chapter. The Bible all but de-mands interpretation. If there is a richer source for theologic disagreement than rival interpretations of what the Bible *really* means, it does not come easily to mind.

The Talmud, a work of interpretive scholarship, dating from the Sixth Century, is longer than the *Encyclopaedia Bri-tannica*. It brings together a thousand years of discussions of Jewish law, pointed stories told by and about rabbis, and di-dactic expositions on a variety of topics from the nature of God to the time before Creation. The study of the Talmud, the interpreting of Talmudic interpretations, is a formidable lifework for a Jewish scholar. If he is gifted, his own reinter-pretations become in turn the subject of superinterpretations. The process, technically the dialogue and *responsa* (an appli-cation of general laws to specific situations) has been going on for centuries and continues. It accumulates rebuttal on top of dissent on top of opinion. Understandably, advanced Jewish theology today is vastly too complex for ready comprehen-sion.

Similarly the rites of Judaism accumulated over the centu-ries, although concessions to changing times have led to dras-tic modification. Modern Jews do not, for example, practice animal sacrifice because the ancient Hebrews did. But at an extreme, contemporary Jewish rites may include donning a special prayer shawl, binding phylacteries to the left arm and head, putting on a skullcap, praying at least three times a day, following rigid, complex dietary laws, which come directly from Chapter Eleven of Leviticus; devoting Saturday, the Sabbath, entirely to rest, feasting, study and prayer, and setting aside, in all, a quarter of each year for the observance of religious holidays. To be a totally observant Jew leaves time for little else, even in a lifetime of eighty years.

Throughout historic Jewish wanderings, in Babylon and Spain, Poland and Germany, Turkey and Russia, Judaism has withstood and adjusted to a bewildering variety of cultures. Some of the Talmud reflects Babylonian society. The *Kol Nidre*, a sacred chant of Yom Kippur, the great Day of Atonement, supposedly takes its melody from a medieval German air. The fur-trimmed hats worn by the men of devout Hassidic Jewish sects trace to Eastern Europe in the eighteenth century. Judaism has always had to withstand and to adjust; it is now withstanding and adjusting to the troubled freedom of contemporary America.

Like every other religion transplanted from Europe, American Judaism has not remained what it was. European great-grandparents would not recognize many of the temples or the practices of their American great-grandchildren. Some traditionalists condemn America's "holy-roller Judeo-Protestantism," but all except a tiny fraction of religious Jews concede that significant changes had to be made. In a confined European ghetto, a rabbi could demand that Jews follow literally the stricture against riding on a Sabbath. The same rule applied by a rabbi in Stamford, Connecticut would guarantee him an empty synagogue. The suburban Jew cannot practically be denied a Sabbath chariot.

Deep questions, raised by change, burn toward the heart of Jewish theology developing in the United States. The fundamental point sundering American Judaism is its own relevant theologic source. Can the source be said to be the Torah, the Pentateuch, with its exacting laws, pillars of fire and harsh, demanding Yahveh? Or does Judaism as it is practiced in the United States really derive from the Nevi'im, the gentler Books of the Prophets, which are pervasively concerned with social justice, ethics and mercy?

Is it still possible in an egalitarian society for Jews to assert that they are a chosen people, and if it is, for what have they been chosen? Or is the concept of being chosen an aspect of Jewish fundamentalism that must properly be discarded in modern times?

Is Messianism—the belief that a personal Messiah of the House of David will appear and bring salvation to all mankind—viable? Or will there be no real Messiah but rather the coming of Messianic times when "nation shall not lift up sword against nation, neither shall they learn war any more?"

Is it necessary for the American Jew to wear the traditional skullcap, the *yarmulke*, in temple, or can he show respect for God as well by sitting bareheaded? In other words, may he look like other Americans, while praying, or must he continue to display symbolic physical evidence of his Judaism to remain a good Jew?

Such questions do not yield up their answers easily, finally, or, perhaps, at all. The answers forthcoming in the United States have been reached imperfectly by fractioning. American Judaism is no longer a single unitary religion. Instead it is a collection of three enormous subgroups, within which there is further segmentation. The answers to all these questions vary with (and to a smaller extent within) each group.

The major forms of contemporary American Judaism are called Orthodox, Reform, and Conservative. It is difficult to outline each precisely because, in addition to overlapping and duplication, each is eager not only to describe itself but to describe the other two as well. There is a hot, if usually discreet, rivalry among the three large Jewish groups. Probably it is simplest for the uninitiate to think of them as denominations within Judaism and to recognize that Jewish interdenominational relations can be just as good and just as horrible as interdenominational relations within Protestantism.

## THE FAITHFUL REMNANT

The oldest of Jewish denominations is Orthodoxy. The term, Hebraic neither in sound nor origin, was first applied in 1807, when Napoleon was freeing Jews from the ghettos of Europe. It described Jews "who accepted the fullness of Jewish law and tradition."

Orthodox Jews take the Torah as absolute divine revelation. They do not see it as the work of God-inspired men. To an Orthodox Jew, the Torah is a direct creation of God's hand. It is to be believed and obeyed literally, book, chapter and verse. As even a casual rereading of Leviticus or Deuteronomy indicates, Orthodoxy is immensely difficult to follow in contemporary America.

Orthodox Jews are also expected to observe a lengthy code set down in 1567 by Joseph Karo, a refugee from the Inquisition who lived in Turkey. Karo's *Shulchan Aruch* (or *The Prepared Table*) was a compilation of the existing rules for Jewish piety. It demands in its first words that the Jew rise and prepare for the service of his Maker, and then proceeds to the prayers, rites, taboos and rules which so dominate the life of the Orthodox Jew.

Within the general grouping of Orthodoxy, one finds an unusual, appealing collection of mystics called Hassidim. Although the Hassidim, like the majority of Orthodox Jews, trace their traditions through thousands of years of accepted rabbinic teaching, they also in a sense proceed from heresy. Their founder, an eighteenth-century Polish Jew called Israel Bal Shem Tob (Master of the Good Name) was accused of being the principal Jewish heretic of his time.

The Besht, as the Bal Shem Tob was acronymically entitled, appeared when East European Judaism was profoundly depressed. Successive promising Messiahs had proved false. The most promising of all, Shabtai Zvi, had actually converted to Islam. Within the *shtetls*, poverty was universal. The great rabbis insisted on learning so as to split an ordinary man's skull. In this climate, the Besht preached, through homilies and parables, against the sterility of learning for its own sake. He spoke of a God diffused in "holy sparks" throughout the universe, a God in all men and in all things. Not only formal prayer, but every human action, said the Besht, was an act of worship. Whatever joined a man to God, be it prayer, dancing, singing, meditation or drinking wine, should be praised. Opposition to the Besht was profound, somber and intransigent, but his movement grew. One recaptures a sense of its vitality from a prayer supposedly spoken on a Yom Kippur morning, in the vanished Polish village of Berditshev, where, instead of beginning his day with self-castigation, one Levi Isaac is said to have walked out the door of his hut, looked up at the sky, all but shaken his fist, and deeply chanted:

Good morning to you, Lord of the world!

I, Levi Isaac, son of Sarah of Berditshev, am coming to you in a legal matter concerning your people of Israel.

What do you want of Israel?

It is always: Command the children of Israel!

It is always: Speak unto the children of Israel!

Merciful Father! How many peoples are there in the world?

Persians, Babylonians, Edomites!

The Russians—what do they say?

Our emperor is the emperor!

The Germans—what do they say?

Our kingdom is the kingdom!

The English—what do they say?

Our kingdom is the kingdom!

But I, Levi Isaac, son of Sarah of Berditshev, say:

"*Yisgadal v-yiskadash shmai rabbo!*"—[*Magnified and sanctified be the great name.*]

And I, Levi Isaac, son of Sarah of Berditshev, say:

I shall not go hence, nor budge from my place

until there be a finish

until there be an end of exile—

"*Yisgadal v-yiskadash shmai rabbo!*"

With such hearty defiance, Hassidism swept Eastern Europe. One finds the old mystical independence enduring among American Hassidic Jews today. Where other Jews define rabbis as educated laymen, the Hassidim follow *rebbes* —holy men—who can work great deeds because more "sparks of God" are diffused within them than within others. One studies to become a rabbi. The title of *rebbe* is usually inherited.

"What is ahead for you people?" someone recently asked a Hassid, whose *rebbe* is in his sixties and without heirs. "What will happen when your *rebbe* dies?"

The Hassid said quickly, "We think only of the present." He stroked his beard, sized up the questioner and decided to continue. "Beside," he said, "before our *rebbe* dies, the Meshiach [Messiah] will come."

According to a 1964 study, there are 204,815 male worshippers affiliated with 1,607 Orthodox Jewish synagogues in the United States. Almost half can be found in New York

State; virtually all live in large urban centers. There are only 1,800 Orthodox Jews in all of Texas; there are 90 in the state of Mississippi. How many there are altogether, is a demographer's guess. By what does one multiply 204,815? The Orthodox generally shun birth control, suggesting a large figure, but there are many old Orthodox Jews whose children have drifted into Conservative Judaism, suggesting a small one. Using a compromise of 3.3 Jews per Orthodox family, there were in the United States at the end of 1964, 673,755 Orthodox Jews. There may be more in the Soviet Union; there are about the same number in Israel.

The Orthodox are generally regarded as the right wing of American Judiasm, a designation they themselves reject. "I prefer," says Dr. Leo Jung, senior rabbi of the Orthodox Jewish Centre in Manhattan, "that we call our form 'Judaism' and use modifiers for those forms that deviate." Perhaps the preeminent American Orthodox scholar, Rabbi Joseph Soloveitchik of Roxbury, Massachusetts, devotes himself entirely to study of the *Halacha,* Jewish law, and to teaching his strict interpretation of the *Halacha* to others. When David Ben-Gurion asked for a definition of a Jew, Rabbi Soloveitchik responded politely but somewhat patronizingly. Citing the rigid *Halachik* position—a Jew is either the child of a Jewish mother or a convert—he wrote Ben-Gurion that "these are basic [and] we need not present quotations or sources to substantiate our opinion. Such would be superfluous."

Orthodox Jews tend toward the arrogance of the devout. Their very devotion forbids the concession of error. With such total dedication to a creed, one is bound up to certitude. If the creed is wrong, the man himself is destroyed.

The one area in which it is possible to prompt admissions of uncertainty from Orthodox Jews, is, curiously, their fundamental ability to survive in America. "We recognize," one rabbi says, "that we have a real problem; taking a religion that matured in the ghettos of Eastern Europe, that grew in poverty and hardship, and keeping it alive in this overly relaxed and overly affluent society. The one way we believe we can preserve it is with our [parochial] schools."

Orthodox Jews currently support a system of about four hundred private Jewish elementary and high schools, in addition to Yeshiva University, an Orthodox institution which runs on an annual budget of almost forty million dollars. The Orthodox emphasis on parochial education is so universal and so consistent that one cannot find a single Orthodox spokesman who will publicly oppose federal and state assistance to schools affiliated with religious groups. Government aid to schools is now an article of the Orthodox faith.

"We came to be interested in Federal aid for the same reason many others did," says Rabbi Joseph Kaminetsky, director of *Torah Umesorah,* the Association of Jewish Parochial Schools, "to help children. Before 1960, we didn't want to become involved because we have many violent opponents— the Jews who say we're building ghettos—and we didn't want to make trouble for ourselves. Then in 1960, things changed. A private school was no longer looked on as a second-rate school.

"Why," asks the Orthodox Rabbi Kaminetsky, "should my child be persecuted when I want to save him from this mad lewd world, just because liberals have a church-state bogey? The public school is non-God-centered. I believe in God-centered education."

Somewhat less intense, Rabbi Norman Lamm, of the Jewish Centre in Manhattan, says that he supports Federal aid to Catholic schools as strongly as he supports aid for Jewish schools, with all help extended "preferably through indirect techniques.

"England," Rabbi Lamm adds, "is a democracy which has proven itself at least the equal of America, but which has no church-state separation."

"Why," Rabbi Israel Klavan of *Torah Umesorah* asks a luncheon companion, "are you opposed to Federal aid to our schools?"

"Principle."

"Isn't it also," Rabbi Klavan says, "that you are afraid that Federal aid to parochial schools will result in a vast increase in the power of the Roman Catholic Church, through their schools?"

"I suppose that's part of it."

"Hah!" cries Rabbi Klavan, his trap sprung. "Then fight it on that level. Fight it on the level of preventing a Catholic take-over. But don't fight government aid to the schools."

From a variety of Orthodox leaders come clear and reasonably consistent positions of their body on other matters. They reject ecumenism "because it supposes a common commitment and Jews and Christians do not have that commitment. Christ supervenes." They demand wholehearted and complete devotion to the Torah and the *Shulchan Aruch* from all Orthodox Jews, "however inconvenient that may be." They believe that any man can speak directly with God, roughly as Moses did, without the need for clerical or saintly intermediaries. They scoff when other Jews express concern at losing numbers through intermarriage. "A sorry thing, but trival," one says. "Faithless Jews have always passed from our midst. Through our schools a faithful remnant will remain."

The Orthodox, the most disciplined of Jews, have influence and effect beyond their numbers. Although many are clean-shaven, and almost all wear modern dress, that is not the image the Orthodox suggest. Known by their most tradition-alistic members, the Orthodox seem to stand unanimously for positive old values. It is positive to wear a beard and a *yarmulke;* it is negative to shave the beard and to go bareheaded. It is positive to boast of a deep and private understanding with a very real God. It is negative to talk of the search for the meaning of a God who cannot be imagined. It is positive to walk down the street, in beard and cloak, proclaiming, albeit silently, "I am an Orthodox Jew. I follow the old faith. I would follow it to the very ovens of Auschwitz." It is negative, by contrast, to walk down the street beardless and in a business suit, looking for all the world like a *goy.*

## THE FIRST SERVICE

It is the fourteenth day of the Hebrew month of Adar, a cold, late, February twilight in New York City, and two men are going forth to behold a *Purim.* "This is going to be a unique experience," one of them predicts. He is a chubby rabbinical student at a Conservative Jewish seminary, and he is excited. "I promise you, there is nothing like a *Purim* with the Hassidim of Brooklyn." The other, an older man, is more subdued.

*Purim* commemorates events that are told in the Book of Esther. According to the story, ancient Jews living in Persia were threatened with murder because one of them, the proud, dignified Mordecai, would not do reverence to Prince Haman. Ultimately, the pleas and prayers and tears of the Jewish Queen Esther moved the Persian King Ahasuerus to spare the

Jews and use the gallows to hang, instead, the hangman Haman. The theology is minor, but *Purim* has become a significant event in American Jewish life, particularly so after Hitler. On the day when Julius Streicher, the most desperately anti-Semitic of all the Nazi war criminals, stood upon a gallows near Nuremberg, waiting for the trap door to be sprung, his final words were: *"Purim, 1946."*

The rabbinical student is agitated on the drive to Brooklyn. He talks ceaselessly. "We are going to see real Jews," he says, as the car rolls south past Hudson River docks. "There is going to be something real. Real Hassidic life. Real Hassidic dancing. Real Hassidic chants. Have you ever heard a real Hassidic chant?"

"Paul Robeson sings one on a record I have," says the older man, who is driving.

"Who?"

"Paul Robeson."

"Who's he?" the rabbinical student wants to know. His world is narrow. When he finds out who Robeson is, he says, "No one who is not a Jew could sing a Hassidic chant right. Don't tell me Robeson can. You ever heard Cantor Moshe Koussevitsky?"

The world headquarters of the Lubavitcher Hassidic Movement is located in an indistinguished four-story building at 770 Eastern Parkway, a broad street, with malls and benches, that was typically middle-class Jewish two decades ago. There is nothing middle-class or typical about 770 Eastern Parkway any longer.

It is a cold night, but on the street, weaving in the wind, Hassidic men, bearded, wearing long black coats and black fedoras, talk to one another in Yiddish. Most of the black-cloaked bodies are gathered in front of 770; about the building bodies ebb and flow.

A little sign, hand-lettered in black, is hung on the hump-backed trunk of a fifteen-year-old car parked on Eastern Parkway. "Warning," the sign reads. "Keep your distance. Driver may be intoxicated."

The men have been drinking; they have all been drinking. *Purim* is a triumphant festival. The hangman himself is hanged. The Hassidim cheer it in and out with glasses of wine, or slivovitz, or sweet and potent brandy. They drink long and hard, even as agnostic Jews, even as *goyim*.

The synagogue, once a three- or four-family apartment

house, is overflowing into the street. The boys and men are everywhere. The women are segregated, subdued and silent in the street, shunted onto a higher floor to pray inside. One simply does not notice women at a Hassidic service.

The two strangers who have come to visit proceed toward the crowd at the synagogue. Steps lead down into the hall of worship. Here men push out roughly. Others push in. All are bearded. All wear long curls, the *payus,* that many Orthodox Jews call a mark of devotion to God.

Out of the cold, caught in the sweat of bodies, the Conservative rabbinic student is less manic. For all his talk, he is alien to this kind of Judaism. His companion is silent. Bodies, cloaked in black, surge, and suddenly the two find themselves driven down the steps and inside the Hassidic synagogue. Before them a tableau is spread.

Worshipping men are standing in rows that rise from a sort of pit at the center of a large room. Row after row of men stand solemnly. The visitors, uncomfortable, curious, follow the worshippers' eyes. The eyes are aimed into the pit. Small children tug at fathers, saying in Yiddish that they want to see. The faces of the little boys are not the faces of children at all; they are the faces of men, but smaller. One sees faces of that sort in medieval art.

But the eyes. The eyes stare into the pit where old men, the elders of the Lubavitchers, sit at a table, their black costumes set off against white tableclothes as in the beards, too, of these pale and aging men, white and black are set against each other. At the center, where all the glances meet, one finds a handsome man, with soft eyes wide apart. Above a tidy beard, his face is warm. Menachem Mendel Schneerson, the Lubavitcher *rebbe,* is in repose. From time to time he stirs and speaks quietly into a small microphone. It is not all medieval. His Yiddish fills the room, carried through two enormous rectangular speaker enclosures.

The *rebbe* is warning his flock about tactics. He says that a lesson of *Purim* was that Jews should not use tactics, but should have faith in God. That is his message. Simple. Direct. The only faith is an absolute faith in God. He speaks quickly, and the rabbinical student is embarrassed because he cannot understand what the Lubavitcher *rebbe* is saying. The *rebbe* is multilingual; his flock is most comfortable with Yiddish.

On the *rebbe* talks, persuasively, not commandingly; then

he is through. He lifts a small glass of wine to his lips and nods to his flock with a soft look.

A sound, part sob, part shout, is born. The *rebbe* has favored everyone with his nod. He sips; everyone sips. The stiff tension that accompanied the sermon is gone.

Someone begins a chant. *Daa, daa, da-da-Da. Daa, daa, da-da-Da.* The tune is vague; the notes all close together, but the rhythm is strong and persistent. *Daa, daa, Da-Da-DA. Daa, daa, Da-Da-DA.* The Hassidim stamp feet with the final *DA*. Around the room, bearded heads bob in time; and more than heads, bodies move. A thin young man, with scraggly sideburns of red, bounces up and down in little paroxysms; an older man, huge and black-bearded, moves only slightly, glancing far away. The small boys catch the excitement. Suddenly the ceiling shakes. The women upstairs have heard the chanting. The Hassidic women are dancing, too.

Wine flows. The *rebbe* himself sips and nods. The shout grows louder. All in honor of Haman, the Hangman, himself hanged perhaps twenty-five hundred years ago.

"Come on," says the rabbinical student. "Enough already. There are simpler Hassidic places." The visitors leave the shaking Lubavitcher synagogue and drive down empty Brooklyn streets toward Williamsburg. Beyond the chanting the Adar night has grown still colder.

In one Williamsburg synagogue the men wear hats whose enormous brims are trimmed with fur. In another, there are no rows, no seats, only a few religious artifacts, bare floor, and a large box, standing in the center like a stage. Bearded Hassidim in black cloaks stand on the box. The *rebbe* is in the center. There is no loudspeaker system here. Nothing contemporary. Some menace seems to stir in the men who notice the visitors, the two curiosity seekers. But perhaps it is not menace but the visitors' own concern. The rabbi's preachings do not carry past the bodies of the men near him. This is how synagogues were in Poland long ago.

The visitors, in conventional clothing and conservative haircuts, stand near the entranceway, the escape. A youth approaches, with friends trailing. The boys' sideburns are long, but their beards have not yet grown.

The young Hassid considers the visitors. One is wearing a finely-tailored coat of midnight blue. He is obviously a man of means.

"*Bist a Yid?*" the young Hassid asks. Are you a Jew? The

Hassid talks a streak of Yiddish. He holds out his right fist, showing a cylinder of quarters. It takes time to comprehend what the young Hassid wants. He is begging. The well-dressed visitor remembers that in Havana once he saw a Jewish beggar, and gave him a few pesos. But that was in another country.

Here, on this cold *Purim* night, something in the man rebels against a healthy Jewish boy begging alms in free America. He shakes his head.

Another torrent of Yiddish assaults the man in the finely-tailored coat. He shakes his head again. His companion falls back. The young Hassid embraces the man, pleading. He tries to kiss the man on the mouth.

One of the elders from the synagogue grabs the young Hassid and leads him to one side. Then the elder, ominous, black-robed and bearded, approaches the clean-shaven middle-class visitors and says ebulliently in Yiddish, "You're not from the neighborhood?" With absurdity, menace disappears. The elder explains that he told the boys that this was no way for them to treat strangers. The conversation ends. There is nothing more for the curious to see.

Leaving, the man in the finely-tailored coat passes the boy who was begging. The boy looks at the man with desperate eyes that have a hardness, too, and in the end, for whatever reason, it is the man, and not the Hassidic boy, who looks away.

## THE REFORMER'S LOT

One of the earliest recorded Reform Jewish sermons in the United States was preached in 1841 by a South Carolina rabbi named Gustav Poznanski. "This country," Rabbi Poznanski told congregants at Beth Elohim in Charleston, "is our Palestine; this city our Jerusalem; this house of God our Temple." To immutable followers of Orthodoxy, Rabbi Poznanski was guilty of heresy thrice, or once a phrase. To many Orthodox Jews today, Reform remains heresy, all the more distasteful because it appears to be a success.

Reform is the Judaism of change. It rose in Germany during the early nineteenth century when the ghetto walls came down and Jews wanted to assume freer ways with their new life. German Jews, arriving after the European disturbances of 1848, spread Reform throughout the United States. Estimates suggest that there are about a million American Reform Jews but, Albert Vorspan, director of programs for the Reform Union of American Hebrew Congregations, candidly says: "I disbelieve every figure I see." (For years the Reform and Conservative movements reported almost exactly the same number of members, apparently because their public relations divisions were watching one another.)

Reform services generally dispense with Hebrew. They are conducted mainly in English. Reform Jews are not required to follow the *Shulchan Aruch*. They are spared the prayer shawls, the phylacteries, the *yarmulkes*. Where Orthodox Jews attend "synagogues," Reform Jews are likely to go to "temples." Reform Jews have even been willing to risk the wrath of Yahveh by abandoning the dietary laws He set down so carefully in Leviticus. The Reform Jew is a man who has tasted a ham sandwich and survived.

To Reform theologians, the essence of modern Judaism lies far from a literal interpretation of the Torah. They speak of "respecting" the Torah, of recognizing its "literary, symbolic and historic qualities." But as one rabbi points out, "We would have to worry about anyone over the age of thirteen who seriously believed that the world was saved by Noah's Ark."

Reform Jews are taught to emphasize the ethical teachings of the Biblical prophets. Charity, justice, mercy, and brotherhood are pillars of Reform, whose theologians would meld Jewish tradition with the present world. "Have we not all one father?" asked the prophet Malachi. "Hath not one God created us? Why then doth every one of you despise his brother, violating the covenant of his father?"

"Now there you have it," says one Reform rabbi, cheerfully. "Malachi might be talking at the United Nations today."

The oldest rabbinical seminary in the world is the Reform Hebrew Union College, which was founded in Cincinnati by Rabbi Isaac Mayer Wise in 1875. (It is the oldest since the European Holocaust.) As an aging ideology of change, American Reform Judaism suffers from a certain duality. It is the most deeply established and probably the wealthiest variety of American Judaism. As such, it is inclined toward conservative positions. But it is dedicated to the unconservative doctrine of a changing religion in a changing world. One can find both the most liberal and the most reactionary of Jews alike bearing the banner of Reform.

Some time ago, Reform members in Mississippi held a meeting called "Jews for Segregation." In the 1950's, a pamphlet, using Biblical and Talmudic quotations, presented, in Bible Belt style, "The Jewish View of Segregation." Although many southern rabbis denounced the pamphlet, its authors considered themselves members of Reform. But in current America, Reform Jews are a force generally urging the country left, if one takes Lyndon Johnson as a centrist. Rabbi Jacob Weinstein, president of the Reform Central Conference of American Rabbis—nine hundred strong—was invited by a pacifist clerical group, the Fellowship of Reconciliation, to visit South Vietnam. Asked as an individual, he felt that he should seek approval of the Central Conference. He got it, but by less than three-to-two.

As liberal Reform leaders see matters, Jews are now in "the post-revival" period. The religious, or church-going, revival, roughly from the end of World War II through the presidency of Dwight Eisenhower, involved Jews as well as Christians; church and synagogue membership both increased by as much as twenty per cent. Now, Jews as well as Christians are concerned about depth. To at least one Reform rabbi, "the revival was, now that we can analyze it, disappointing, not to say, empty. It was chiefly a search for easy answers and comfortable religious concomitant to suburbia."

Reform leaders admit to more self-criticism than one finds in the other branches of Judaism. They see themselves as offering a comparative abstraction—ethics—in an era when people want assurances. They gauge their impact as limited. They accept the idea that the temple is not the hub of modern Jewish life and do not feel that it necessarily should be, but they are concerned that their appeal to young Jews, particularly young Jewish intellectuals, has not been stronger. The leaders are reasonable, aspiring men, and rationalists. "We feel," one says, "that a rabbi, ideally, is someone with academic superiority and an interest in the humanities. We do not believe that he must have 'a call.' "

## THE SECOND SERVICE

Rosh Hashanah, the first and second days of the Hebrew month of *Tishri,* falls early in the American autumn. This is the Jewish New Year, traditionally a time for reflection and renewal.

The Reform services at the Leo Baeck Temple, west of Los Angeles, on Sepulveda Boulevard, have been highly praised for their integrity. But here, on Rosh Hashanah, there will be no medievalism, nor any naked passion. Instead the promise is for an excellent sermon, delivered by a bright young rabbi, to a responsive upper middle-class audience. The rabbi is so popular that he will have to hold two services this evening, one at 6:30 and one at 8:30, so that all of his congregants can be accommodated.

Leo Baeck Temple is a stone monolith, dwarfed by steep Western hills at dusk. Half an hour before the first service, the parking lot is already starting to fill. The cars are big, Cadillacs and Oldsmobiles, Continentals and Chryslers, but there is a Volkswagen or two among them. People climb from the cars, and the men begin groping for blue tickets. Admission on Rosh Hashanah is by ticket only. There is a limited number of seats and no standing room.

In his office, Leonard I. Beerman, smoothfaced and dark, the chief rabbi of Leo Baeck Temple, says that he would like to discuss his work at length but, unfortunately, at this particular period of the year there is not time. All the high holidays, Rabbi Beerman explains, do not mean that a rabbi's other work stops. People still die and must be eulogized. People still marry. The rabbi sighs. Besides, he observes, what he could say would not really be different from what a number of other Reform rabbis could say as well.

The interior of Leo Baeck Temple is carpeted in soft maroon. The seats, covered in blue, stretch in pews. Prayer books fit in neat holders before each seat. Above, there is a vastness of stone, all stone; untinted, neutral stone. The people are well and quietly dressed; the men in dark suits, the women in dark dresses. There is no rush to get to seats, precounted and presold. The men are bareheaded. In a way it is as startling to see Jewish men assembled without *yarmulkes* in temple as it is to see bearded Jewish men on a street.

Services at Leo Baeck Temple are conducted with the assistance of organist and choir. The choir is integrated. Negro and Oriental faces star among the choristers. One need not be a Jew to raise one's voice at Leo Baeck.

Rabbi Beerman has a high forehead over small tidy features. His voice is quiet and intense. "This is a New Year. Do you really believe that? Do you know what a New Year means?" Rabbi Beerman throws questions out at the audience, the congregants. "A new beginning," he says. "Another opportunity to endow with sanctity this transient, fragile experience we call life." Briefly, listening, one thinks of the televised lectures of Leonard Bernstein.

Questions. As a modern man, practicing a modern permissive faith, Rabbi Beerman is surrounded, so it seems to him, by questions. "Our men," he says, "caught up in their work, their professions, wondering about the fundamental worth of what they do. Our women, with their special bourgeois mystique. It is not enough for them to be women. . . . Life and its purpose evoke confusion. Where are we going? What do we really want? Who are we? None of us is free of these questions. And this is what burdens the rabbis as the summer approaches its ending and the Rosh Hashanah is about to appear."

Abruptly, the sermon is not about congregants. It is about rabbis. The lot of rabbis is one uncertainty of which Leonard Beerman speaks with authority. "For us rabbis," he says, "it is all like the story of a certain Hassid, Rabbi Hanoch. What Rabbi Hanoch told was of a man whose stupidity was such that he could not find his clothing in the morning. Finally, the man decided to make notes on a slip of paper, listing where he put things as he undressed. The next morning, reading the slip of paper, he found his clothing quickly. But when he was fully dressed, he asked, 'That's all very well, but now where am I myself? Where in the world am I?' The man looked and looked, but never found himself."

"That," Rabbi Beerman says in the elegant stone temple in West Los Angeles, "is precisely how it is with us rabbis. Summer is ending in confusion. Violence in the streets. The far-off places to which we send our young men. Out of sight and for too many, out of mind. Things fall apart. And we rabbis are expected to make sense of it all, to create order, like so many gods."

The man who stands before the Reform Jews of Leo

Baeck Temple is not Authority, as the Lubavitcher *rebbe,* nor even a man of very much confidence. He is a mixture of uncertainties and confusions and scholarship, but, one suspects, he may not be quite so tentative as he appears.

"Buried under everything we are," Rabbi Beerman says, in the regal plural, "man, Jew, rabbi, buried beneath the accumulation of memory, lust, greed, love, kindness, there lurks something out of which we have oozed. There lies the secret that will explain it all.

"There is a way that is illumined by reason, governed by compassion and tenderness. Out of tradition come leaping familiar words: It hath been told thee, O man, what is good and what doth the Lord require of thee: to do justly, to love mercy and to walk humbly. What is hateful unto thee do not do unto thy fellow man. Love thy neighbor as thyself. . . . Who is a strong man? He who converts an enemy into a friend. These words speak for all the redeeming moments of grandeur in the life of man."

The rabbi has been quoting the Bible and certain books of Jewish law, but earlier, when he said things fell apart, he was quoting William Butler Yeats. Now, in his pulpit at summer's end, he seeks to become two people: himself the rabbi and something he calls, with an Elizabethan flourish, "the antic," and anti-rabbi. Rabbi Beerman tells the congregants that in some corner of the mind the grinning antic sits.

" 'It is all prattle,' " the antic says, to Rabbi Beerman, " 'A playing with words. It is a lie that you perpetrate. Redeeming moments of grandeur! Fancy talk you rabbis give us. I shall tell you of redeeming moments of grandeur! I shall tell you of horror and wrath, etched into the past and burned into the present by man's barbarism, arrogance and stupidity. I shall tell you of cool detachment and moral sterility and the enormities they make possible.' "

The rabbi in his pulpit cannot resolve the public argument within himself. "As the old moon wanes and the new moon you will see in the heavens tonight, the moon of Tishri, is about to be born, the argument continues. The Rosh Hashanah comes once again to trade blows with the rabbi."

Rabbi Beerman pauses for a moment's breath. "I shall leave the celebration of America to those who are paid to make us laugh and keep us happy," he says in the temple close to Hollywood. "You and I may worry about the number of calories in a martini, but most of the world's people suffer from malnutrition. While we drive our children *me-shugga*, [crazy] pushing and manipulating to see to it that they get into appropriate colleges, there are seven hundred million illiterates. Most of the world has a per capita income two thousand per cent less than ours.

"What has that got to do with us and with Rosh Hasha-nah?" Rabbi Beerman asks himself. He is assuming a duality again. "What do you know, rabbi, about the economic system? Have you ever had to meet a payroll? Must you forever engage in this stupid, useless moralization? You live very well. Must you, of all people, be reminded that you are a Jew? Never have our people had it so good. Of course, there are poor, and there are Negroes. Aren't we working on these problems? What we need is less of this moralizing, and more spiritual advice. We are descendants of a noble heritage. Can't you make us feel proud?"

To begin to answer the questions that he has posed for himself, Rabbi Beerman cites a professor. It is a part of Jews of whatever denomination to demand scholarship from their rabbis. Leonard Beerman does not disappoint. Professor Herbert Marcuse, Beerman cites, has suggested that an individual's "encounter with life" is governed by the society in which he lives. "What we can know," the rabbi says, "is that in a thing-ridden society such as our own we find ourselves in things that sate our lives, our homes, our automobiles, our boats. It is a good way of life. But as Professor Marcuse contends, it inevitably produces the experience of frustration.

"We cannot escape," Rabbi Beerman argues. "A return to poverty and simplicity will not provide the answer. So what does all this mean? It means, very simply, that it is difficult to be human. . . .

"The distinctive quality of our faith has been its will to righteousness. So long as man has not achieved his humanity, so long as the Messianic expectancy has not been fulfilled, the world is in distress, and it needs to be mended, to be made whole and holy.

"It is at such a time that the New Year comes to remind us that our world and its people, you and I, need desperately to be mended. Our world needs Jews. It needs troubled people, men and women who care, men and women who are not ashamed to be sensitive . . . our world needs men and women who have the courage to be afraid of all the forces which have removed their own humanity."

Afterward, Rabbi Beerman stands at the end of a receiving line, shaking hands and greeting congregants, elegantly and gracefully. His pleasantries are easy. He may be saving himself. It was a long sermon, and this is only intermission. In just a few moments, he is going to have to go over all the same ground, the same pained questioning of the world and of himself, the same quotations from Micah and from Hillel and from Yeats, the same carefully tentative conclusions; he is going to have to do it all over again for the 8:30 audience, almost as though everything were staged, almost as though he were a performer, playing, with slickness and sureness and a certain smugness, his indisputably sincere role.

## THE EISENHOWER JEWS

Conservative Judaism, which claims 1.2 million members, holds a vague sway over the formless middleground of Jews in America. "Somewhere with the complex phenomenon of Conservative Judaism," observes Professor Joseph L. Blau of Columbia in *Modern Varieties of Judaism,* "any person who wishes to identify himself with the Jewish people can find a position blending tradition and innovation in precisely the proportions acceptable to him."

The Conservative movement arose late in the nineteenth century, in both Europe and America, out of opposition to the freedoms of Reform. It was not a reaction against Orthodoxy. It was a movement back toward Orthodoxy by people, many of whom felt that "what the Reform really want is to be like the Christians." But it did not go back all the way. Conservative Judaism is centrist, straddling a multitude of positions, not always comfortably. If somehow Dwight Eisenhower found himself forced to become a Jew, he would immediately embrace Conservatism.

The Conservative Jews make sweeping concessions to modernity. Most drive on the Sabbath. A majority ignores dietary laws. But "wherever possible," they try to retain elements of Jewish religious ritual. In a Conservative house of worship, which may be called either a temple or a synagogue, the Torah is usually stressed. Breaking with Orthodox practice, men and women sit together, but the men are likely to be wearing prayer shawls and *yarmulkes*. The service, in English, will include as much Hebrew as the rabbi thinks his congregants can endure.

Although Conservative Judaism, blending rather than innovating, fails to excite theologians, it unquestionably fills a significant need. Reform was the religion of German Jews, who prospered in America before the great waves of East European Jewish immigration began to break in the 1880's. The East European Jews carried with them a *shtetl* Orthodoxy that clashed with the fabric of American life. The Conservative Movement satisfies hundreds of thousands of descendants of these Orthodox Jews. Within their Conservative congregations, they feel and look indisputably Jewish under white-fringed prayer shawls. But at home or in business, their routines are no more disrupted from normal patterns of American life than if they were free-thinking followers of Reform.

Simply because it is so broad-based and so centrist, Conservative Judaism is not consistent enough for precise definition. No less a figure than Dr. Louis Finkelstein, president of the Conservative Jewish Theological Seminary, acknowledges fluctuations in his own belief. Doctor Finkelstein says he follows Jewish law and practice much more literally now than he did twenty-five years ago when he was just as good a Conservative Jew. "A good many of us live by *Halacha*," he says. "But then there are many others who live by only part of it."

Curiously, this essentially vague and ineloquent movement has as its most respected spokesman one of the most eloquent of religious Jews. He is Abraham Joshua Heschel, a white-bearded professor at the Jewish Theological Seminary. Professor Heschel, who has written on the Bible, on rabbinics, on mysticism, is a leader of clergymen opposed to the war in Vietnam. In addition, he played a major role in the interfaith discussions that preceded the recent Vatican Declaration on Jews. But he also embodies traditionalism: One former seminarian insists in a burst of exuberance, "Professor Heschel is Mister Jew!"

Heschel's family was Eastern European and Hassidic, but he studied for his doctorate in Berlin. He narrowly escaped Hitler and came to the United States in 1940, after which he began teaching at the Reform Hebrew Union College in Cincinnati. Although he left the Reform Seminary for the Conservative, he will not define himself with a label. "I am a person," Professor Heschel says, "who tries to be a Jew." He is not happy with the way Jewish religious life is categorized in

America, "but by now I'm afraid the denominations are here to stay."

American Judaism, he feels, is young, mobile and lacking both tradition and the old European dedication. There was, "particularly in the Reform movement, self-conscious patriotism. Many people seemed to be afraid that following dietary laws was un-American." Professor Heschel feels that this has diminished, but there still remains an "enormous lack of Jewish knowledge" among the Jews of America. European Jewry was "saturated" with learning. Jewish education in America, he says, must now "combine reverence for learning with the learning of reverence."

He inspires the young men he teaches. One former student remembers going to Heschel with a problem several years ago. The student had been attending Columbia and was about to enroll in the Jewish Seminary. Leaving a university for a seminary depressed him; he thought he would find his new place narrow and parochial.

Professor Heschel heard the young man kindly. Then he said, "You know, in the final analysis, Moses was a very parochial man."

## THE THIRD SERVICE

No holiday in all the Jewish calendar is as important as Yom Kippur, the Tenth of *Tishri*. Yom Kippur is the day of fasting and atonement when the religious Jew faces his God, admits his sins and prays for forgiveness. The ritual is remote from the Roman Catholic confession. The Jew on Yom Kippur prays for forgiveness by God for sins against God. He gains no absolution from his sins against men. That can come only through making amends to the people he has wronged and winning their forgiveness. Yom Kippur is a time to stand stripped of pretense, rank, position and title, and place absolute trust in the mercies of the God of Abraham and Isaac, and of Job, if one is a Conservative Jew.

Yom Kippur Eve rises warm and cloudless about Temple Beth Sholom, Place of Peace, Conservative, in Las Vegas, Nevada. The temple is a red brick building adjoining an empty lot on a residential street called East Oakey Boulevard. It has been a hot summer in Las Vegas, the days reaching 110 degrees, so that night, advancing with a rush of desert blackness, is a benediction. At twilight, outside Temple Beth Sholom, Las Vegas homes stretch briefly toward the East. After that comes desert, dun-colored hills, and a deep, dark sky.

The evening begins unpleasantly with a man standing at the temple door, demanding tickets. Prices range up to one hundred dollars, and all the tickets have been sold. The man at the gate is hostile, wary of crashers.

"Is there some way I can get in?" asks a musician. He is trim, white-haired and crew-cut.

"You got a ticket?" says the gate guard.

"I'll buy one for whatever you say."

"Sold out," the gateman says, and turns to take the tickets of a family group approaching from the other side.

The musician waits. "Look," he says to the gateman. "I don't put much stock in religion normally, but this one holiday, I got to observe. For my father."

"Sorry," the gateman says.

"The money is no sweat," the musician says.

"Look," says the gateman, "I'll see if I can find somebody to help you. Meanwhile, don't block the entranceway, will ya? People are trying to get in."

"I got to get in myself," the musician says, and minutes later, after restating his reverence for his father a dozen times, he is allowed to purchase a ticket for fifteen dollars.

In a small foyer, outside the place of worship, prayer books are stacked on tables, along with *yarmulkes.* In addition, on this holy night, there are *tallises,* white, silken prayer shawls that are worn over one's clothing. Proceeding inside, one hears whispered greetings. This is Mr. Banks from one hotel. This is Mr. Entratter from another. This is Mr. Hank Greenspun, the estimable publisher of the *Las Vegas Sun.*

It is hotter in the temple than it should be. It is almost as hot as day. Slowly one realizes what has happened. The air-conditioning system at Temple Beth Sholom, Conservative, is refusing to work on Yom Kippur Eve. It has broken down. In the rows of benches, up and down the temple, men, women, and children are using their prayer books as fans.

The pulpit is not imposing. There is an interracial choir, but it is small. This Yom Kippur service begins with a layman, striding to center stage. He carries a cello. The buzz of congregants subsides. The cellist launches into the *Kol Nidre,* the sacred Jewish chant for Yom Kippur.

The cello resounds dark and elegiac; *Kol Nidre* is a medieval melody and stabbing. There is nothing grand, Beethovian, about it. It is simply a haunting, plaintive, tearing theme with a few simple elaborations and restatements. The cellist, who earns his living in a Las Vegas hotel orchestra, plays with a slight excess of vibrato. One longs briefly for Piatigorsky's grand tone and then, more sensibly, listens pleasurably to this fine sound. Temple Beth Sholom is a synagogue, not a concert hall.

Afterwards, there is a sort of repeat. A cantor chants *Kol Nidre,* and shortly, it is time for the sermon. Rabbi Aaron S. Gold of Temple Beth Sholom is not immediately imposing. He does not possess the charisma of the Lubavitcher *rebbe;* he is not a contemporary existentialist, like Leonard Beerman. He is physically small. His manner is earnest. The group that has come to hear him this Yom Kippur is an odd mixture: alienated entertainers, professional gamblers, the children of racketeers, show-business hangers-on, and that broad Jewish middle class of jewelers and doctors, lawyers and clothing salesmen, school teachers and bail bondsmen. But because the temple is in Las Vegas, the mixture is topped, likely as not, with some outright hoodlums.

The concept of sin, Rabbi Gold earnestly tells his congregants in the Nevada desert, has gone out of style. We blame everyone but ourselves. He is reading from longhand notes. "Johnny," the rabbi says, "failed in school because his mother didn't give him enough affection—that's why he grew up to be a killer. Jane is a poor wife because her father never admired her. She lies and feigns illness. Bill cheats in business because he was weaned early, forcefully toilet-trained." The rabbi is disturbed, in an orthodox rabbinical manner, at permissiveness flowing from knowledge and misunderstanding of sociology and psychology. On this Yom Kippur he is upset at Jewish sins of permission.

" 'To be conscious of no sin, is the greatest sin of all,' say our sages," Rabbi Gold tells his mixed group in Las Vegas. "At some point in life, we must stop blaming others and begin blaming ourselves. We can't escape moral responsibility. Yom Kippur won't let us! It bars all the doors, strips us of our defense mechanisms, buck-passing and rationalizations and bids us repeat *Al Chet* [prayer of atonement] fifty-two times for every conceivable sin."

Not for Rabbi Gold the realm of pure ethic. To him, in his

overheated temple in his overheated town, the rules of life come clear and consistent from the past. "The Torah teaches us," he says, " 'thou shalt not hate thy brother in thy heart.' Yet some of us permit ourselves to fall into the trap of hating another person, and it is a trap. Step number one, we feel guilty. It's difficult to face the people we wrong because every time we see them we are reminded of the wrong. To defend our self-esteem, we begin to hate them. We feel compelled to look for faults to justify our hate; we find some, for no man exists without fault. What a vicious circle hatred travels. A Yiddish saying describes this perfectly, *Zeh nor vi er est zich op lebedigerhayt. See how he is eating himself up alive.* So tonight, we pray for the sins we have committed before thee O Lord—needless hatred."

The prayer books and programs beat furiously back and forth. The crowd in Temple Beth Sholom, at least four hundred people, is sweltering without the air conditioning. Rabbi Gold pauses to apologize for the heat. The silken prayer shawls weigh on the men like fur.

A rabbi here would have no luck in abstract ethics. This is a pragmatist's town. Rabbi Gold does not intend to spend the sermon in analogy and theory. He has something specific to say about hate. "We must clamp down hard on those inciting to riot and racial strife," he tells the hustlers, the solid middle-class men, who go to prayer in the synagogue at Las Vegas. "Whether they represent George Wallace, the Klan, the Birch Society. . . ."

Hank Greenspun grins tightly. His front-page column in the *Sun* this morning charged Birch influence among the local police.

"The Birch Society; or whether it is Adam Clayton Powell, Stokely Carmichael, SNCC, or Black Muslims." The single Negro in the choir wears a face that is blank, but not bland. The colored chorister is playing it cool in the temple. Rabbi Gold talks of the "bigots of black power" demonstrating to keep a white principal out of a Harlem public school. Well, the rabbi tells the listeners, Jews have to strengthen the hands of Martin Luther King and Roy Wilkins, leaders of the nonviolent struggle "for humans."

People have asked, the rabbi says, why all this rioting, looting, burning and bloodshed? "We Jews have suffered similar hardships. But *our* fathers worked hard, saved every penny to send children to college. We too had ghettos, and we suffered for many generations without looting and burning."

It is a hard question the rabbi has posed in the hot night. "Yes," he says, summoning up common remembrance. "We knew what it meant to be hated, to be kept out of guilds where we could learn a trade, and off the land, so that we couldn't be farmers, and out of universities where Jews could learn art, science, medicine. We too were slaves in the land of Egypt. Pharaoh stereotyped us as lazy, shiftless Hebrews. Later, anti-Semites characterized us as dirty Jews, and the Communists called us capitalists and cosmopolitans. But unlike the unfortunate, jobless or frustrated residents of Negro ghettos in Watts, Chicago, New York, Philadelphia, we happened to have the benefit of history; a long tradition, a strong culture, an incomparable religion, a sense of pride in our own worth, our Torah, in our closely-knit family units. Acts of violence were against our tradition, done by the *Pogromchik* [Jew-killer], a *shikerer goy* [drunken Christian]. *A Yid tit duss nisht*. This a Jew does not do."

Rabbi Gold pauses. The heat is getting worse. Some people have quietly gotten up and walked out.

"Black power," the rabbi says, "is a manifestation of bitter frustration. The Negro of America has not had the history, the closely-knit families, the consolation of culture, Torah. We were blessed and lucky and, last but not least, our skins were always white. We could pass.

"Consider the turtle. He makes progress only when he sticks his neck out. Thousands of white and Negro Americans are sticking their necks out for freedom and justice—and though some heads are bloodied in the process, they will continue to do so."

Rabbi Gold has no answer, really. He has gone as far as he can. There is no special significance to the Negro activism except that it is the way things are and it needs understanding before an abrupt refusal ever to give one more cent to the N.A.A.C.P.

The heat has become unbearable. Men are standing in the foyer, their prayer shawls still on, and the *yarmulkes,* talking quietly. "Well, a good new year, let's hope," they say to one another. "Isn't it a shame about the air conditioning?"

Inside, the rabbi turns from black power to hunger, complacency, envy, gossip. "Yes, my friends, we have sinned," he says, "and we must accept individual responsibility and collective responsibility for our sins of commission, omission, and permission. Because God gave us freedom of choice, we are not only responsible for the past, but we are capable of changing our future."

Outside, the men are talking about fasting. Not many intend to. "Pretty good sermon, wasn't it," Hank Greenspun says. "He said some things that needed to be said."

Probably to a young Negro activist, the sermon would be offensive, just as to a high theologian it would be simplistic and to an Orthodox Jew it would be heretical. But Rabbi Gold is speaking not to Negro activists nor to theologians nor to the ancient Orthodox; he has been preaching to the Jewish congregants of Las Vegas, Nevada, lost in the desert or found. And in those terms, his Yom Kippur services are a success. They bring people together. They may make some think. The evening has been honestly wrought. From the cello played with too much vibrato to the rabbi wrestling with the undefeatable issue of Negro activism, everyone had done the best he could.

And life goes on. When the services end, the musician, who had had to argue at the door, cannot be found. He has left early. "It was the heat," he explains a day later, without embarrassment. "In all that heat I couldn't stick it out."

## THE MOTTLED FACE OF GOD

The rabbi, whose name is Chaim Karo Vrotchnik, is eighty-seven or eighty-eight or eighty-nine years old. He is not certain any more. He does not remember when he was born, if he ever knew, which is itself not so certain, he has to admit. When you think about it, the important thing is being born at all. It is important that God has taken the time and the trouble to create you and it is a miracle that He is merciful enough not to strike you dead at birth. He himself was first-born, the rabbi remembers. He knows that.

"Darling," Rebba is calling. "You have an appointment to see someone—not a *goy*—at three o'clock."

"All right," the old man says. Phlegm chokes him. He does not attract many visitors any more. "All right," he says. "All right."

"I have to go shopping now." She is sitting at his side; still she calls. "You will be all right, Chaim, if I go." Rebba draws herself up straight—she is proud of her carriage—and walks into a large round foyer that opens off the sitting room. The rabbi sits in the window seat, curved like the window itself. Beyond are his lawn and his elm tree, dappled with sunlight.

When she has gone, slamming both vestibule doors, the rabbi picks up his cane and makes his way toward the high old bookcases that Rebba designed "to be made of cedar for a rabbi's books." He reaches for the shelf where he keeps the twenty-one volumes of his Talmud, bound once in 1914 and rebound, as a special gift from the congregation forty-three years later. But, even as he begins to read, he wanders.

He cannot remember it all, in the *shtetl* or why they had had to leave, or even who the Czar was any more, but still he can picture Mother, her head covered, swaddling the one who died. The baby lay on a pillow and Mother was singing and wrapping the swaddling loosely so that the baby would be warm and comfortable. And someone else, an old aunt, was saying, "Poor Baby, he lies there so nice and warm, but he looks like an Egyptian Mummy. He can't move." It was a boy, of course. Avram.

Soon, in another winter, the snow of Russia fell soft and white and killing. Avram, older now and full of laughter, was soaked with snow coming back from *cheder*, the Hebrew school. Chaim had not been with him. Because he had not known a lesson, Chaim was being beaten by the *cheder* rabbi, who had a pointed nose. While Chaim squirmed but did not cry in the hard grip of the *cheder* rabbi, Avram went home by himself, a short distance, but lingered in the snow. The next morning there was the fever. It was so swift. Something was boiling in Avram's chest. By night-time he could not cry, but only whisper; then not that; then nothing. *Ech,* it was too hard. It made his own phlegm come; that was why he had proceeded to this city in the high desert, this remote place called Long Ridge. There was no snow.

What the Lord does is for the best, Rabbi Chaim thinks. He knows that as he knows his name, from the old *cheder* and the Talmud. They wanted him to be a scholar, he remembers. So he would be a scholar. The *cheder* rabbi said, fine mind but lazy. Chaim knew that he was not lazy. He worked hard. It was the mind that was not so fine.

"The literary club," Rebba is saying. So, the rabbi thinks, she is back so soon. "They are considering taking a Negro member."

"An excellent idea," says the rabbi, "if he is a literary Negro."

"I think no," says Rebba. "I don't see why all of a sudden we should *have* to have a Negro."

"Why should we not have to have a Negro?" the rabbi says.

"You are going to tell me," Rebba says, "that once it was important that there be a Jewish couple in the Literary Circle. Yes?"

He has not intended to tell her that. "Yes," the rabbi says, keeping the peace.

"It is altogether different," Rebba says. "When I came here, it was from London, where my family had been for many years. And who was more learned than you? They knew how brilliant you were. And we had culture. Look who we had behind us. Maimonides and that one you like in your Talmud, Rabbi Akiba, and the Torah. Is it the same, having such people as us, as having a *schvartze?*" Rebba's face is long and strong; she sets her dentures hard against each other, making her chin protrude.

The rabbi makes no answer. In truth, he does not understand the *schvartzes.* Why don't they build their own schools instead of integrate? Why ask the white people for help? What do they expect? What do they want from Jews? The rabbi has known very few *schvartzes.* The man who swept the temple—he remembers Rucker—and once, on a summer in Maine, an artist, a painter, but that painter did not fool the rabbi. He was a painter so that he could paint the naked bodies of women. Naked black women and naked white women were not important, but a *schvartze* staring at a naked Jewish woman is not good.

Rebba is making a cup of tea. Her body is thicker now. Sometimes life is better without the eyeglasses. She brings the teacups on a tray and fills them and puts them down in front of him on a little black mahogany table. "What should I tell them, Chaim, about the *schvartzes?* Sip, my darling," Rebba says.

"What is it you have to tell them?"

"Well, nothing at all, but simply this," Rebba says. "Sooner or later, one of the young ones is going to propose a Negro family. They are talking about it already."

"So they talk," the rabbi says. He bites into a piece of sponge cake. "To talk is not to act."

"But it is a beginning, Chaim, and then they will act and then there will be *schvartzes* in our group."

"Would that be such a terrible crime?" the rabbi says.

"You know what the people will say," Rebba calls across the china teacups. "They will say if the Reb himself does not want a Negro, there must be something to it, because the Reb is a fine and considerate man."

The rabbi wants to suspend the discussion.

"They will say that the Reb is a man completely free from prejudice," Rebba says.

"Thank you," the rabbi says, "but I have my prejudice for The Law."

"Exactly," Rebba says. "We do not need to join with black brigands." She reaches across the teacups and the sponge cake, and pats his hand.

"There is nothing so important, so complicated as The Law," the rabbi says. "It is the tent under which we have always lived."

"So many of your young men," Rebba says, "have become such wonderful lawyers and judges." Tap goes her hand on his. Tap tap.

What is it Law says about the *schvartzes*? Here, in this country, it says equality. But the black violence he reads about, not only in the lay press but in Jewish publications, clearly is not legal. What does Law have to say about that?

The violence of a state is to be expected, and from the old times there have been proper ways of fighting back. When Hadrian of evil memory decreed that the Palestine Jews were subject to so-called imperial law and proscribed the practice of Judaism on pain of death, the rabbis knew how to respond.

"Nothing must stand in the way of self-preservation," the ancient rabbis decreed, "except for these three. *Idolatry.* Thou shalt have no other gods before me. *Immorality.* Thou shalt not commit adultery. *Bloodshed.* Thou shalt not kill." And Rabbi Ishmael added: "Only the public profession of idolatry is to be resisted. Private matters are suitable for compromise."

Are the men who today make the laws of Mississippi as

evil as Hadrian? Rabbi Chaim thinks not. If only he had a
pulpit, again, the rabbi thinks, because now he has something
to say about the *schvartzes*. Where they are oppressed, they
can take lessons from the Jews: Resist without giving up the
right to self-preservation. Try to avoid the futility of violence,
the sin of violence, and accommodate to a governing law,
however hateful. Hadrian is passed, forgotten, except for pillars of stone. The Jews remain. It has been willed by God.

The Reb came to live in this city, here called Long Ridge,
late in the year of 1905, after hard suffering; sometimes in
dreams the suffering recurs. His family left the little village in
Russia when one day his father came back from the butcher
shop, blood on the right side of his face. Chaim wondered for
a minute if it was the blood of an animal; he had seen animal
blood on his father often, but beneath the blood-matted beard
his father's face was odd. Mother knew at once. She ran to
him. "Zalmen, Zalmen!" In dreams Chaim could still hear his
father's voice saying one word before that night of lamentations. *"Goyim!"* he heard his father say.

Afterward, they moved to Vilna where they lived with another family and his father had bad times, but still Chaim
was to be the scholar. The father wrote his brother in New
York and at fourteen Chaim had gone, leaving the family
and Europe in the final decade of the nineteenth century.
Chaim traveled by foot and by cart until he came upon two
fences of barbed wire and a river frozen white. That was the
border. It was terrible crawling under the barbed wire and
feeling the brittle snow, cold and jagged against the face. He
must have made noise, but it was a dark night and anyway the
guards, *goyim*, probably were drinking. The Reb laughed at
that years afterwards. *Goyim* and drinking. Who knew why?
Even the fine ones, the professors, had the weakness.

The Rabbi wears a short, neatly-trimmed beard and a
broad well-trimmed mustache. It pleases him to be part of tradition and to be modern as well—to wear a beard, but not a
long one. He is fond of the old ways in his privacy with God,
but he does not believe that a man has to display Judaism in
his garments to show Judaism in his heart. That is for the
Hassidim, the mystics. Chaim is a rabbinic Jew. He remembers Vilna, city of the learned Gaons.

What Chaim wants most is to understand the nature of

God. Indeed, God has spared him, as He spared Isaac, so that he might spread understanding. Chaim believes that he is an instrument of the Lord. Does he himself then understand God?

Sometimes, in younger days, he felt that he did, with vision so wide the horizon became a grain of sand.

Sometimes he understood with a consciousness of fire that flamed endlessly, never flickering.

Sometimes he understood hearing a voice whose whisper was louder than ten blasts of thunder.

In younger days.

Now he is old. He has not been granted the old age of Abraham.

Certainty is gone; and vision. He knows no promise. For the old rabbi now, only questions remain.

At *cheder* in Russia, the teacher said: " 'And God created Heaven and earth,' The Torah tells us, so we can be certain that it is so." Chaim was satisfied. He liked the sense of sureness. Besides, those who asked questions were beaten.

The teacher in America beat no one. That was the most important difference Chaim found after his great journey. In the *cheder* in Brooklyn, the teacher whined, as though he was afraid, and boys talked continuously.

"Please, I must have silence," the American teacher said.

The boys continued to talk. One, stronger than anyone else, wandered about.

"I must have attention," the teacher said.

Chaim was amazed.

Uncle Menachem sent him to public school for a time, where Chaim completed his mastery of English, and excelled. The year was 1899. After that, continuing an arrangement with Chaim's father, the uncle enrolled him in a Yeshiva, to begin serious studies toward the rabbinate. Uncle Menachem had three daughters and Chaim had passed the age of seventeen. His cousins stirred uneasiness; Chaim was busying himself entirely with a search for the nature of God.

The teachers of theology at the Yeshiva told a moving story. As they explained it, first came Abraham, the father of all the Jews for all time. Abraham lived in a world not so very different from our own, and he had a vision.

"Imagine," one impassioned teacher said, "a brilliant castle.

A castle not lit from without, but from within. Can you imagine such a thing?"

Chaim nodded.

"Seeing that castle you would know, without having to enter it, that here is a seat of the mighty."

"I suppose so," Chaim said.

"It is not *suppose*," the teacher said. "It is *certain*."

"Yes," Chaim said. "You are right."

"Abraham with his vision saw the universe as you might see this castle," the teacher said. "The universe is more towering and more brilliant than any castle. Considering all the universe, Abraham realized that here was the seat of the Lord our God. Abraham considered the universe and asked himself if all this could exist without a directing mind. Is that clear to you?"

"I will say when you are finished," Chaim said.

"Very well. Abraham *inferred* the existence of God. This was the most important moment in the history of the Jews." The teacher's eyes grew bright and hard. "Before that moment, there were no Jews, because it was only after Abraham inferred that God existed, that God chose to reveal Himself. You will repeat with me . . ."

Together Chaim and the teacher said, "The Lord looked down upon him and said, *I am the master of the universe.*"

The teacher smiled. His eyes were soft again. "You understand, Chaim? God did not reveal Himself until Abraham *inferred* His existence. God revealed himself as a reward. And all the Jewish people for all time are inheritors of God's reward to Abraham."

"That is very fine," Chaim said.

"You are satisfied?"

"There is still something."

"*Nu?*"

"About the creation."

"Ask."

"I do not understand who created God."

"Nor do I," the teacher said.

"*You* don't!" Chaim cried.

"I will get some things for you to read," the teacher said.

Certain things, Chaim learned from the Talmud, were forbidden. Many of the ways of God were beyond man's understanding. They had to be accepted on faith. The Talmud suggested that trying to solve questions beyond the scope of man distracted one from the important tasks. Besides, it could be dangerous. Chaim read of three wise teachers who sought too deeply: "Ben Azzai gazed and died; Ben Zoma gazed and became demented. Acher cut the plants"—became an apostate. And he read the cold warning of Ben Sira:

"Seek not out the things that are too hard for thee, and into things that are hidden inquire thou not. In what is permitted to thee instruct thyself; *thou has not business with secret things.*"

There was no one he could turn to in the home. Chaim enjoyed his Uncle Menachem, but a thinker the uncle was not. He owned a shop that sold bolts of cloth and he had succeeded well enough to buy a small home in the Borough Park section of Brooklyn, but he had no thoughts about God's mysteries. He was one of that company of immigrant Jews who combined personal ignorance with a respect for learning. Chaim liked the uncle without feeling kinship.

Chaim occupied a bedroom by himself. Uncle Menachem was very insistent on Chaim's privacy. Evenings, before he went to sleep, the uncle, his face gray with weariness, paused at the door to look in at Chaim studying tracts. He smiled, and ever grayer, went to bed.

One evening, he came like death itself. "Chaim, I have solemn news to tell you," he said.

Chaim felt annoyance. He was eighteen years old and, insistently, did not like to be disturbed. Then he saw the uncle's face and thought, which one is dead?

"Your father," Uncle Menachem said. "His lungs were never strong." Uncle Menachem started to cry. Chaim got up and closed the door, and led the uncle to bed. He felt that he should cry, too, but it had been so long ago, four years, and distant. He said, "I wrote my father two letters every month."

"I know, I know," Menachem said. "Always remember your father's sacrifice."

Chaim could not remember his father's face. Perhaps, he thought, as he watched the uncle weep, this was because he had been trying so hard to see the face of God.

Rebba is calling again. He opens his eyes. He is lying on the brass bed by the bedroom window. It is not cold. The window is open slightly and he hears warblers chattering as they play in and out of the row of plane trees that separate his house from the place of the delicatessen man.

Rebba stands at the door. "I will help you down."

"I am capable," the rabbi says.

"Eh," Rebba says. "Your rest was good? Did you consider the Literary Circle further?"

The rabbi sits up and clears his throat. "The Negro couple must be judged entirely as individuals. Of that I am certain.

"I would suggest that we then admit the Negroes to the Circle, but not as full members. They would have a subsidiary role—auditors. It would be made clear that others are there to exchange ideas and that Negroes are there to learn. They have generations to catch up with."

"Your visitor," Rebba says, "is coming soon." She grasps the rabbi firmly under one warm and pulls him to his feet. "You must come downstairs now," she says. "Don't worry when you talk to him, Chaim. I shall stay right at your side."

"Without you," the rabbi says, starting forward with two short, shaky steps, "I would be a wanderer in the desert without manna."

Four girls lived in the uncle's house in Brooklyn. Hannah. Fagele. Dora. He cannot remember the name of his fourth cousin. The house, wood frame, wood-planked, sat in a row of similar houses on Corey Street, thrown up in haste, side by side, and painted green. Corey Street began at a trolley-carline and ended in farms. He walked to the far end one day and saw a herd of goats.

The men of his block in 1901 were like the uncle; they had made a small success, a little money. Chaim rode the trolley, which was new, to the Yeshiva, feeling adventurous and heroic. It was odd; he had not felt at all adventurous on the long, redolent boat ride from Europe.

He was, as the uncle put it, "the only one of the young generation to have a room to himself." The four girls shared. He was, also, as the uncle put it, "the finest Yeshiva scholar, without a doubt, on the entire block and maybe two blocks." He had been given the room for study.

"So. How goes the school, scholar?" Hannah said to him. Two years older, she was the impudent cousin, pretending to question, really mocking.

"It is hard to explain to a girl," Chaim said.

Hannah smiled at him. The corners of her thin lips played.

"Women do not study what I study," Chaim said, "for complicated theological reasons."

Hannah's hair was light brown. Her eyebrows were thin, and arched high over pale green eyes. The other cousins were dark. A hint of *shicksa* shone in Hannah's face.

"In the complicated theology," Chaim said, "it is considered not possible for a woman to comprehend certain important things. And not only that, it is not even considered proper for them to try."

"I know you are studying Talmud," Hannah said. "Jacob Schatz studied Talmud before you were even in this country. He told me what it is."

"That is not proper," Chaim said.

Hannah cocked her head slightly, raised the brow over one eye and smirked.

"So because Jacob Schatz does an improper thing," Chaim said, "do not think everybody will."

"I find things out," Hannah said. Her skin was fair.

"You cannot understand," Chaim said.

Hannah gazed steadily. She did not move or speak. Chaim suddenly wanted to see her breasts.

He blushed and turned and clumped away. He felt that she stared after him. He was glad, upstairs, for the privacy of his own room.

Afterward shame assaulted him in waves. It was not the first time, but Hannah was a cousin. Chaim shook his head. He went to his books and found the story that he wanted in the Midrash. The story would protect him and comfort him, he muttered, but his head continued to shake from side to side as he bent over the book—his eyes were already worsening—and began to read.

"God deliberated" (Chaim read) "from what part of man to create woman. He said, 'I must not create her from the head that she should not carry herself haughtily.

" 'Nor from the eye that she should not be too inquisitive.

" 'Nor from the ear that she should not be an eavesdropper.

" 'Nor from the mouth that she should not be too talkative.

" 'Nor from the heart that she should not be too jealous.

" 'Nor from the hand that she should not be too acquisitive.

" 'Nor from the foot that she should not be a gadabout.

" 'But from a hidden part of the body that she should be modest.' "

"Chaim, you are napping sitting up?" Rebba is standing over the window seat, calling at him.

"No, darling," the rabbi says. "I was not sleeping." He takes the old woman's hand and strokes the inside of her wrist.

"You are trembling, Chaim," she says. She runs a small, square hand over his brow and down his neck. "You have no fever."

"No, no. It is nothing."

"The visitor will be coming soon. You are well enough?"

"It is nothing." He places the old woman's hand in his own.

"I am going upstairs," Rebba says. "I shall put on a nice dress, for the young men, that you can be proud of me."

"I am all right now," the rabbi says. "It is only my years." He hears her singing harshly on the stairs.

Chaim brought the Vilna cough with him to Brooklyn. It grew neither better nor worse on Corey Street. When he was tired, bending low over the books, the cough seized and shook his chest. That was why his chest was thin. "Like a chicken's," Hannah said to the other girls, loud enough for Chaim to hear.

Uncle Menachem scolded her. Later the uncle came to Chaim's room and said, "I want you should go to a doctor."

"It is nothing, Uncle," Chaim said. "I have always had it."

"Friday afternoon," the uncle said. "I have made the appointment with an excellent man. You will arrange for time away from your studies."

"No," Chaim said. "I have always coughed this way."

Uncle Menachem's gray face angered. "So did your father," he said.

The physician, whose name was Geldthaler, thumped and thumped and scowled and thumped again. "Has anyone in your family had lung complications?" he asked.

"My father, I believe."

"Phthistic?"

"Please?"

"Has he grown thin?"

"He is dead."

Geldthaler resumed his scowl. "I will talk to you with your uncle," he said. "Put on your shirt and call him in."

In the end, the two of them, the uncle and the doctor, were facing Chaim.

"If you are to be a rabbi," Doctor Geldthaler said, "it will have to be in the West where the air is dry. My fee—the diagnosis has not been an easy one—is fifteen dollars."

The uncle bit his lip and slowly counted out three bills.

Actually, it was not difficult to find a place. Several groups of Jewish merchants, within the larger communities of the West, claimed the need for a rabbi, as soon as they felt established. Denver, Phoenix, Salt Lake all had temples. The merchants sent word to seminaries and Chaim had a choice of at least five medium-sized congregations in cities Geldthaler said were medically acceptable. He could not, of course, pursue strict Orthodoxy. But he could be a Conservative rabbi, which was also acceptable.

"Select the city that is closest," Uncle Menachem said. "That way we will not be lost to each other."

But Chaim remembered the snows of Vilna, and chose Long Ridge because it was farthest south. Afterwards, he had never seen his uncle's face so mournful.

"You will miss us, at least, Chaimele? A little bit you will miss me and the girls?"

"Yes, Uncle, of course," Chaim said. It struck him that the cough from Vilna was in one way a mitzvah. At least in Long Ridge he would be far away from the haughty, inquisitive, mocking temptress who wanted to lure him from his God. He would be beyond the reach of cousin Hannah.

Eyes closed, as he perches on the blue window seat, the rabbi sees Hannah as she was sixty-five years ago, head cocked, one eyebrow raised, smile mocking.

He shakes his head.

Who would have thought that he would gaze on Hannah thus, as an old man?

As Chaim found it in 1907, the Long Ridge Conservative Congregation, called Beth Israel, Place of Israel, was housed in a plain stone building, and administered by a rabbi who had lost the power of speech after a stroke. Chaim communicated with his predecessor by note, but even so, it did not take him long to realize that the rabbi was stupid. Chaim had more tolerance for *goyim* than for a stupid rabbi.

His own first sermon, declaimed to more than 100 congregants, was an angry challenge. They were all going to have to
confront God some day, Chaim said. As he was their rabbi,
he wanted the confrontation to take place as properly as possible. They might not like what they saw. They might see
nothing.

Did they know the story of Hadrian and Rabbi Joshua
ben Hananiah?

Hadrian had demanded of Rabbi Joshua in ancient days to
behold the God of the Jews.

Impossible, Rabbi Joshua said. But the Emperor was not
satisfied with a direct answer.

Then you must come outside at noontime, Rabbi Joshua
said, and stare with fixed gaze at the sun. The Emperor
agreed, but when the hour arrived, he stared and turned
away. He found the sun too strong.

Chaim's voice rose and his story built to a crescendo. He
told it in the city of Long Ridge as if he were Rabbi Joshua.

"So, you admit you cannot look at the sun, which is only
one of the ministering servants of the Lord. How much more
beyond your power of vision is God Himself?"

What this meant, Chaim told his congregants, was that no
man can *expect* to have a vision of God. But it is the *duty* of
every Jew to seek that vision, even if, like Samson, he loses
his sight.

The congregation reacted with pleasure and distress. Long
Ridge was a cattle and mining center. It catered to the needs
of prospectors and cowboys. While Jews did not run the bars
or the whorehouses—most sold dry goods and groceries—
they were affected by the atmosphere, the dusty air, the angry
summers, the squatness of a city under mountains. Here was
a problem for the men of Beth Israel to discuss. How did
moralizing suit their lives? Was this new rabbi going to fit?
Would he adapt himself where necessary? If not, the men of
Beth Israel agreed, send him back fast. The men of the
congregation, eighty Jews in a city of 27,000 selected a delegation to call on the young rabbi with a series of questions.
The delegation numbered three. When they found him,
Chaim was studying the Torah. "Yes, yes," he said. "Come
in." He was wearing his white prayer shawl and *yarmulke*,
and perspiring in the late spring heat.

"I am Marcus Hindman, Rabbi," the leader of the three began.

"Yes, Mr. Hindman," Chaim said. "Please be seated."

"We would like to ask," Hindman said. The men took time selecting seats in the sparsely furnished room, in the cottage they had given the rabbi behind the stone synagogue.

"Ask," Chaim said.

Hindman pulled a slip of paper from a vest pocket and read: "Must the religion of our fathers be practiced as it always was? Or can it grow and change?"

"Aha," Chaim said. "It cannot be the same always, but it does not grow by change. It grows by interpretation.

"The Torah, which I was reading when you called, is unalterable. But man's interpretation of the Torah grows with each generation. In that way our religion does grow. But as the Torah is constant, it does not change."

"I see," Hindman said. "My next question: Is the foundation of our religion ethics or the belief in God?"

"What is your occupation, Mr. Hindman?"

"Marcus Hindman Clothing. I sell to men."

"You ask very complex questions for a clothier."

"Thank you."

"You are referring, of course, to Isaac Mayer Wise, and the Germans and Reform," Chaim said. "As you know, I am not a Reform rabbi. But I did not hold with all the old ways for this new country. As many as we can keep, we should keep. Not all," Chaim said. "To answer, the belief in God and Torah is basic. Ethics, however, flow out from those beliefs."

Hindman looked at his paper again. "Can a man, whose ethics you dispute, be in your view, a good Jew?"

"Why not? A Jew is a Jew. Goodness and evil we shall all be discussing for many years, and we shall never agree. Nor in a single lifetime is there need."

For the first time Hindman smiled. He crumpled the paper as if to throw it away, thought better and stuffed it into a pocket. "In a small town such as this," he said, "it is important that we have the respect of the Christian community."

"I know nothing of such considerations," Chaim said.

"No matter," Hindman said. "The portion of the Christian community that is important to us will respect you and your thinking. If that is not important to you, it is to us."

Chaim shrugged. "Am I being hired by the Christian community?" he said. "What is this concern with *goyim?*"

"You will see, Rabbi," Hindman said. "Things are different out here."

Chaim was annoyed. "If I am to put my head inside a noose," he said, "I would rather do that in my first pulpit than in my last."

Hindman and the others chuckled. Abruptly, it struck Chaim that he had been on trial, and that the chuckling was the signal that he had triumphed.

"You have studied, Rabbi," Hindman said, "while we have been out here working fifteen hours a day and longer for survival, without enough time to think. In your studies, have you come across anything that explains the purpose in life?"

"Rabbi Akiba," Chaim said, "taught that the Golden Rule was the fundamental teaching. Ben Azzai believed that the fifth chapter of Genesis . . ."

The old man sitting on the window seat makes a braying noise. He is laughing. Who knew less about the purpose of life than an absolutely self-occupied young man?

When he was twenty-six, Chaim married the first time, quickly and well. Naomi Gewanter had black hair, a strong broad nose and a high trilling laugh. Her father had profited from a variety of land purchases. Chaim liked her laugh and relished her gentility. For no other reasons than these, he stood with Naomi in the autumn of 1911 under the wedding canopy and crushed the glass with his shoe.

Naomi pleased him. She had read many English novels, she played simple Mozart on the piano her father gave them, and she was wiser than he about the body. She made him brush his teeth every day and bathe as often as three times a week.

Her laugh (to his ears) rang like a bell. Her figure was pleasant, but the broad nose and a strong wide chin dominated her face. When he began to love her, her face became more soft. He noticed her flickering smile now, not her chin.

Lust bothered Chaim. Lust was danger for any man, but particularly for a rabbi. Was not his life a dedication to inquiring after the nature of God? Lust distracted him. Besides, was not lust part of the nature of animals? And if he allowed himself to be seized by something animal, was he not moving away from the search for God?

Chaim fought battles within himself as he lay with his new

wife. Naomi was patient, although sometimes afterward she cried. When she became pregnant, Chaim told her that they must lie apart until the boy—he was certain it was to be a son—was born. They would name the boy Avram, Chaim said.

To celebrate, they moved into a large new house, with a gabled roof, rare in Long Ridge. Naomi busied herself making curtains and waiting for Avram. Chaim preached and studied. The congregation was growing: eighty families; one hundred; one hundred and eleven. Beth Israel grew through Chaim's intensity. "God is not subject to change. God is absolute and eternal. He surpasses description. His power has neither end nor limit. Hear O Israel, the Lord is our God, the Lord is One."

Avram was stillborn. The Rabbi would have endured, although not easily, his brother dead again, had not three days afterward mother followed son. Naomi died with a grunting noise, unlike a bell.

*Sh'ma Israel*, the rabbi prayed. *Hear O Israel, the Lord* . . .

Now he lived in a too-large house with broken prayers.

On the blue window seat, the old rabbi is mumbling to himself in Hebrew. He is quoting the second chapter of the Book of Habakkuk. "The Lord said, 'Write the vision and make it plain upon the tables. The just man shall live by his faith.' "

Congregation Beth Israel was dwindling. It was reduced again to eighty families. With Naomi dead, the rabbi lived entirely within his mind.

How could God have let such a death occur?

There was no answer in Talmud or Midrash or Torah, at least so far. The rabbi studied Talmud, Midrash and Torah again.

Rebba came to see him, during an afternoon of winter rain, on what she said was a personal matter. The rain had pasted black strands of hair against her forehead. "I have a problem concerning faith," she said.

"So I understand," the rabbi said.

"I have been living in widowhood."

The rabbi nodded.

"The great sisterhood, although I am a young woman,

twenty-nine." Of all rabbinic duties, Chaim liked personal counseling least. He knew that she was widowed; so were several other young women of Beth Israel. God's will. *Nu?*

"What I want to see you about has to do with sin," Rebba said.

"What is sin?" the rabbi said.

Rebba flushed. "You are the rabbi, are you not?" she said. "Why should *you* ask?"

"So you should answer."

"I know what sin is," Rebba said, and smiled.

"What is it you wished, please?" the rabbi said. He would give this woman five minutes from his books.

"First, perhaps, a towel, so I can dry my hair. The rain is terrible."

"Yes, of course."

He found a white towel and watched as she patted the dark hair. She stood in front of him, body straight, legs slightly apart. As her arms moved, he saw the lines of her breasts. It had been very long. "Sit here by me," Chaim said, suddenly. "Sit here. Right here."

She crowed afterward, "We both know what sin is, do we not?"

He was silent, unable to believe.

"You owe me nothing," Rebba said. "That you must understand. You took me because you had need. I answered with giving, as a woman should. It pleased me, Rabbi."

"I am sorry for what I have done to you," Chaim said.

"You have done nothing to me," Rebba said, "and if I should become pregnant, I will go to Toronto, Canada, and give birth there."

"Toronto?"

"The closest place away from here where I have family," she said.

"You will go nowhere," Chaim said. "We will be married in the synagogue. We have not sinned." He meant, but never found a way, to ask what sin she had intended to inquire about in the beginning.

Rebba had an intense, almost violent, sense of order. She found the house with the curved window, moved them into it and set about reorganizing their lives. Breakfast at 8:30 sharp. Dinner at 6:15. Empty the pants pockets. Stack the coins on the bureau. Lay out tomorrow's clothes. "You can do many more things than you have, Chaim. There is a whole world beyond our congregation, which, by the way, should be growing faster than it is. Do you know that fifty-seven thousand people live in Long Ridge."

"For a rabbi there are only two worlds," Chaim said.

"Three hundred families at least should be in Beth Israel," Rebba said.

"The world of studies and the world of synagogue," Chaim said. He fought off change. He had his Talmud. If she disapproved of all his hours at study, she did not say. She would wait.

One day she told him breathlessly that she had been to a doctor who said something was not right inside and could not be fixed.

"There are other doctors," Chaim said.

"Not for this, Chaim. I cannot have children."

So, Chaim thought, I am to die without issue. He wanted to remember his own father. The chain was broken.

He was not a devious man. When he thought of Rebba, it was with sympathy. That evening he sat gloomily in a chair she had purchased; the arms roared up in lions' heads and the legs became lions' paws. She fell at his feet on the blood red Sarouk rug and cried, *"Kindele, kindele, kindele!* Where are my children?"

He patted the black hair gently. "What God does is for the best. That is a foundation of belief."

Her shoulders were shaking. Her hand squeezed his knee. "Besides," he said, "we do not have such a bad life."

"It is not everything I want," she said, still weeping.

"So, we shall make it what you want," the rabbi said.

"Then we must go out into the world more. It is very important not to be cooped up. We must go forth, and Chaim, your knowledge shall be our children. It is what we have to leave to the world."

"Such leavings even a worse-yet world would not deserve."

"It pleases me to make you cheerful," Rebba told him.

The Literary Circle came first. The Circle began as a reading group for faculty of the State University at Long Ridge. After a time, a lawyer who had studied at Cambridge asked to join. A physician with a wife who published poetry followed; and a newspaper editor with an astonishing memory for Browning. The professors and their wives enjoyed receiving applications; they enjoyed even more the process of screening applicants. Presently an outer group coalesced around the original Circle. Membership was limited to thirty and the Literary Circle assumed significance independent of literary things. After a time in 1929, Rebba was able—the Rabbi never found out how—to have the Circle invite him to speak on the meaning of the Talmud. She beamed, as she showed him the invitation.

His lecture lasted for one hour and twenty minutes. In a small amphitheater at Long Ridge State, he spoke of the forerunners of the Talmud, the Sopheric Movement begun by the Babylonian Jew Ezra; he led the Literary Circle through Persian times and introduced them to the Perushim, the Pharisees, who were so wise they withdrew from ordinary men; he mentioned Hillel. "You know, of course," the Rabbi said, "how Hillel met the challenge when asked to tell all Jewish law while standing on one leg?"

The Literary Circle did not know.

"As Hillel put it, 'The Golden Rule of Leviticus; all the rest is commentary.'"

He explained the need to supplement the Bible. "The Holy Text often requires clarification. The Bible allows for ending marriage by divorce, but it does not specify grounds. It prohibits work on the seventh day, but leaves work undefined. Is writing a letter work? Are my duties in the synagogue work? Must an army stop defending its country on the seventh day? So there was need for the Talmud and to fill this need rabbis prepared the Talmud over the centuries."

Afterwards, the rabbi was led to the Faculty Club for an informal reception. He clutched Rebba's arm tightly in the strange, crowded, *goyische* room.

"Would you consider—I know you are busy—joining the Circle? Coming regularly and taking part in our discussions?" The leaders of the Literary Circle had been conferring at the faculty bar. Their speaker was a tall and handsome woman, whose dark hair was salted with gray.

The rabbi touched his beard. He was not certain what to do.

"We will be delighted," Rebba said.

For her, it was a triumph. For the rabbi it was an unalterable changing point. For the first time in his life—he was almost fifty—he was committed to something secular.

To his surprise, he enjoyed the Circle. He listened attentively to a discussion of T. S. Eliot's indictment of Hamlet. Without fuss, he began to read the play. Shakespeare's language was strange and that made progress arduous, but Chaim was a student. He read *Hamlet* twice and then announced to Rebba, "There is no doubt in my mind, this Eliot with his objective correlative is like the rabbi who was so happy to find a good donkey that he rode the animal ten leagues in the wrong direction before he stopped to think where he was going. Eliot is making a mistake."

Within the next few years, with the Depression raging, the rabbi agreed to join three other organizations: the Long Ridge League Against the Ku Klux Klan; the Long Ridge Youth Council; and the Ministers' Interfaith Committee. All met irregularly.

The rabbi understood the Ku Klux Klan in a parochial way. He knew that it was anti-Semitic. One of his congregants, a lawyer named David Steinberg, told him that in the villages around Long Ridge, no jury would decide for a man who had a Jew for a lawyer. In Jackson Center, twenty-seven miles southeast, the Mayor himself was a Klan leader. He burned crosses in front of the county courthouse.

The Long Ridge League Against the Klan was busy, with memos, leaflets and petitions, preparing a program to counter Klan influence. There were debates and discussions, none of which seemed forceful to the rabbi, and then, for reasons beyond the memos and debates of the Long Ridge League, abruptly the Klan waned. *Mine enemy supporteth me*—the Long Ridge League waned, too.

The Youth Council tried to help the children of the Mexican and Indian families that were crowded into Southwestern Long Ridge and who had a consumption rate triple that of the rest of the city's children. The Council members included a Presbyterian minister, small, dark and brusque; a large, brooding Spanish Catholic priest; and a variety of laymen who seemed (to the rabbi) all to be in the field of sociology.

Some time after the rabbi joined, John Boardmer, the Presbyterian, invited him to tour the Mexican area, "to see what we are up against."

"This is astonishing," the rabbi said, "but I myself have

never been in that part of the city." It was 1935, twenty-eight years after he had arrived.

"Tuesday afternoon, then," Boardmer said, with what the rabbi thought was a tone of excessive command.

Boardmer called for the rabbi by car, a black La Salle, and they drove for twenty minutes toward the South Mountains far beyond Long Ridge. It was a clear afternoon in March. The minister was silent, and the rabbi occupied himself gazing at the mountains which rose, without foothills, bare and brown.

Because he was looking into the distance, the rabbi did not notice the neighborhood change slowly, block after block. He was surprised when Boardmer stopped the car in front of a row of houses brown as the mountains.

"Mud huts, rabbi," John Boardmer said. "Ever seen anything like it?"

"Yes," the rabbi said. "Just as bad."

Walking within was walking into stench. Smells of urine, feces, sweat, came out of darkness. The rabbi could not see very well. Children were lying on straw.

"Hello, Mamita," Boardmer called, "did they bring your food Sunday?"

The woman answered in Spanish. The rabbi did not understand what she said. A child was coughing. "Good boy, good boy," the rabbi said, into the direction of the cough. The hut seemed dusty as well as dark and redolent. He was having a difficult time adjusting his eyes. The child coughed again and the rabbi began to cough himself. He turned and bent by the force of his own coughing, spun out of the stench into the street, hearing, as he fought for his own breath, the Mexican child call after him, *hicahicahicahicahah*.

Broadmer did not ask the rabbi into other houses. Instead, they went directly to the La Salle. As they drove back, with the South Mountains behind them, the minister said, "You mentioned that you've seen places like this before?"

The rabbi's throat rasped. He nodded.

"Where, may I ask?" Boardmer said.

"In the town in Russia where I was a child."

"Oh?" Boardmer said. They proceeded silently up Fronton Street; downtown lay ahead. "Well," Boardmer said, "will you help?"

"What can I do?" the rabbi said.

"Funds," Boardmer said. "For food, mustard plasters, everything."

"Beth Israel Congregation is not as wealthy as you may think," the rabbi said. "I will try, however, to do as you request."

"Thank you," Boardmer said, and turned down Claridge Drive toward the far east side of Long Ridge, where most of the Jewish families lived.

"You will understand," the rabbi said, "that although what we saw is pitiable, our Jewish families are not without problems and it is a point of my belief that the Jewish charities come first."

Boardmer started to say something. His face went white. He pressed his lips tightly and drove on. At the rabbi's door they muttered curt goodbyes.

The rabbi saw Boardmer from time to time when the foremost religious body in Long Ridge, the Ministers' Interfaith Committee gathered. They seldom spoke.

"Chaim," Rebba is calling. "We have a visitor." The rabbi blinks and blinks. It is a fine, pleasant afternoon. He is sitting on the old green chair with the lions' heads at the end of the armrests and claws at the base of the legs. "Yes," he says. He rises very slightly when the visitor enters. He stares hard through his glasses. Dark hair, large dark eyes, large cranium and a curving, broadening nose. The visitor is Jewish. "Yes," the rabbi says, enthusiastically. "Come in. Sit down."

Rebba roosts on the couch, also green. She nods her head. Bosom and rump tightly corseted, she looks like twin cocoons.

"You want to know about being a rabbi?" the rabbi says.

"Yes."

"For yourself? You want to become a rabbi?"

"In a way."

"He doesn't want to become a rabbi," Rebba says. "He just has some questions, Chaim."

"We do not have enough real rabbis," the rabbi says. "Fakes, we have plenty. And slickers. And *goyim* pretending to be Jews. But if you are a bright young Jewish boy, truly Jewish, it is a wonderful opportunity."

"The rabbi has lectured at several colleges here," Rebba says, "including the Methodist College. Do you know," Rebba says, "that when anyone in the city, Jew or *goy*, has a difficult question, the man they turn to for an answer is the rabbi?"

"A citizen of Israel," the rabbi says, unasked, "is an Israelite, but not necessarily a Jew since that is a matter for civil laws."

"Even professors come to him," Rebba says. She rises from the green couch, twin cocoons on sticks, and moves to the blue window seat. The rabbi's chair is in front of her. She barely pauses. She leaves the window seat and perches on an arm of the rabbi's chair. Beyond, outside the window, daylight beckons.

The rabbi smiles vacantly.

"Let me show you our house," Rebba says.

"Show him the house," the rabbi says, hoarsely. Now, for no reason, he feels exhausted. At eighty-seven or eighty-eight or eighty-nine, weariness assaults him with such suddenness that he thinks he understands something of dying. It will be like a great weariness, mightier and more sudden. But is it that way for a child? Had death been weariness to Avram or to the baby? And since death is one thing can death also be many things?

He would not mind. It does not frighten him any longer to die.

Rebba walks the visitor into the small dining room. The man remains a pace behind the old lady, who does not know that in her corset, she reminds him of cocoons. "I want to show you pictures of the rabbi," she says, whispering. "You should see them."

In the small dining room there are four pictures of the rabbi, but the room is dominated by a large oil painting of Rebba as a young woman. She was dark-haired then, and creamy-skinned. The tops of firm breasts pushed up over a lavender gown. Her face was set in a defiant pout. It would be something to turn that pout into a whimper of passion.

"Well?" the old lady says.

"Lovely."

She nods. She is not going to let go. "I was a pretty young woman when that was painted. My people were from London and before that, Austria. Western Europe. Not like the rabbi from the East. You like my painting?"

There is an odd little smile on her face. It is impossible to reconcile the soft, dark woman of the oils with the two co-coons rustling in corsets.

"I was some girl," Rebba says to the visitor. She looks at him with her old woman's face and forgets.

She winks.

Rebba has set out coffee cake and summoned the rabbi, who walks very slowly, very heavily. But when the visitor offers an arm to help, Rebba clucks, "*Neh, neh, neh.* The rabbi is still strong. He can walk by himself."

The rabbi's hip pains him. Baths have not helped. He clutches the chair in the dining room and sits slowly, closing his eyes and wincing. He groans. He does not remember the visitor until he opens his eyes again.

Tea, served hot and strong, makes the rabbi feel better. He sucks it through a lump of sugar held between his teeth. He smiles at the visitor. "You will like Long Ridge," the rabbi says. "It is a nice city. We do not have so many problems, like other bigger cities."

Rebba is ignoring her own coffee cake. "In this enlightened city," she says, "the rabbi is a leader."

The old man removes the lump of sugar, sets it on the white tablecloth and begins to speak in a strong voice. "It is for us," he says, "to show by example. That is our sacred obligation. In the covenants with God, in the covenants of Abraham and Jacob, we were chosen to show the ways of godliness and virtue and to bear witness. We do not proselytize. We do not ask for converts. It is for us to show the others by our lives, but if the others choose not to learn from us, what can we do?"

"We can only do what we can do," Rebba says.

"It is hard enough," the rabbi says, "just being chosen. That He, Blessed be His Name, should give such a tremendous responsibility to our people, is that not enough?"

"The rabbi has spent his life studying the ways of God," Rebba says. "He has studied everything from the Creation forward."

The rabbi speaks loudly: "As the letter *beth* is closed in on all sides and only open in front, you are to regard as closed to inquiry what was before the creation. What is open begins with the time of creation."

"His understanding has impressed everyone," Rebba says. "One day an anti-Semite tried to attack him with words." Her small mouth moves steadily, even when she is not speaking. "Isn't it always there?" she says. "Scratch a Turk and find a Tartar. They're all the same. But if anyone tried to touch the rabbi in Long Ridge ten thousand Christians would rise up in his defense."

"Really?"

"At the least," Rebba says. "Maybe twenty thousand."

The old man has closed his eyes.

"It makes you wonder," the visitor says, "about Auschwitz."

The rabbi's scream, there, in his own dining room, is a terrible, long, wild, wailing cry. "Arrriiiyeeeee."

Rebba stands up, shuffles to the rabbi and throws both arms around his head. He yields. His head is tight against her bosom. His mouth remains open. The scream does not die. It eases as he draws breath, living in its echo in the little room. Then he screams again and cry and echo blend. "Eeearriiyeee." The rabbi's third scream is not so loud, and he begins to weep. His shoulders and chest shake. Gigantic tears appear under the thick eyeglasses and roll down his cheeks toward his beard. Rebba's hand is on his neck and he begins to sway back and forth, left to right, right to left, with great expulsions of breath. The rabbi is trying to stop crying because he has something to say.

He draws a breath and says, "We are not worthy that God should help us. But I hope He will help us even though we are not.

"A boy," he says, "like you, sat here, asked questions. A German boy. A rabbi. They burned him up."

"I remember," Rebba says.

"The secret things," the rabbi says, "belong to God. They are revealed to us only as He pleases. Everything is in the hands of God, except the fear of God." The old man slumps. "Excuse," he says.

Rebba walks the visitor to the door. There is a vestibule in the old home with a rack for umbrellas. There is little room to stand. Rebba faces the visitor, touching him.

"Take an umbrella," she says. "It is supposed to rain."

"Thank you."

"Our storms this time of year can be quite violent," Rebba says. "I want you to take a taxi. You have money?"

"Yes."

"It is beginning to rain already," Rebba says. "I have a credit card with the taxi company. Will you stay long? If you will be here long, I will help you out. There are a great many things that I know." Her hand is on his. She slips her fingers up the wrist, under the shirt, and squeezes the visitor's skin.

A mountain storm has burst upon Long Ridge. The rabbi is in the chair with the lions' heads. It is another day, or another hour, or another minute. He is not certain and he is not concerned. The rabbi remembers and his memory is like a silent prayer. *From the tops of the rocks I see Him, and from the hills I behold Him. Lo, the people shall dwell alone and shall not be reckoned among the nations. I alone am Chosen to bear witness. Adonai.*

*Who can count the dust of Jacob? Let me die the death of the righteous and let my last end be like his. Elohenu.*

But even as he thinks these words, the old rabbi knows that they are wrong and that his heart is wrong and that God has found him out.

Of his days, which exceed the allotted, how many have been spent inquiring after the nature of the Almighty? Some few meager winters of short light; some days of boyhood. But he knows as he sits in the lion-armed chair and prays to God, Blessed be He, to be granted the soft death of the righteous, that he has fallen from the paths of righteousness. He has sought after transient things and he has walked among *goyim* and he sat with the so-called Jews of so-called Reform. Each was a sin. He does not know which was the worst. His God would tell him; his God who stretched forth the heavens and laid the foundations of the earth, whose voice rends mountains, shatters rocks, whose bow is fire and whose arrows are flames.

The rabbi weeps now for his sins.

It is not Rebba who has been evil. He has been evil. He has sought temporal things and hunted the praise of men and lusted for women when he had been charged by Him, from birth, only to inquire after His nature. His shield was the clouds and His sword was lightning and His spear was a torch and His vengeance was more terrible than the sound of lamentations.

*Whom do you speak for, Chaim? the thunder says.*

*I cannot lie, the old man cries. I speak for the Jews.*

*Are all the Jews in you, old man? the thunder asks.*

*I cannot lie, the rabbi says. I cannot.*

Rabbi Chaim speaks for the Jews and he fails for the Jews and his sins are grave and unpardonable. He was cast as a young lion, his fingers clutch the ends of the chair, but he has sought the praise of men, the ruts of women and spilled his seed.

How evil he has been. How weak in spirit. How obtuse in the pulpit. How dense amid the books. How slothful at Talmud. How proud.

*I have found you out, says the thunder.*

His is an evil that the Lord God, Blessed be He, has not seen in all the centuries. His is the greatest evil, a life without fruit, and a pride without bending.

The Lord God, merciful and Blessed be He, has mounted a punishment for the evil in Rabbi Chaim. It is a punishment wisely made by He whose voice rends mountains and whose bow is fire.

*You are in all Jews, saith the thunder, and all Jews are in you.*

It is a punishment meted to all the Jews as a warning against the sinful life of Rabbi Chaim. It is a terrible punishment, he knows, but it is just.

It is Auschwitz.

Rebba hurries into the room calling, "Chaim, Chaim, are the windows closed? We are having a terrible storm."

She is startled by the way he is slumped so uncomfortably in the chair and for an instant she is not certain whether her husband is alive or dead.

# Part Four

*Things Profane:*

*A Mercantile Heritage*

DESPITE THE MOVING IMPACT OF THE FAITHFUL remnant, Jews, like most Americans, are secular people. Surveys suggest that they are somewhat less religiously involved than northern Protestants and substantially less involved than Roman Catholics. Apparently Jews do not attend religious services as frequently as either group. Fewer affiliate with congregations. More express disbelief in a God. The Jewish survival drive concentrates on this world, not another.

Although intellectuals are often the most evident and articulate of Jewish Americans, the great majority of Jews cannot be called learned. More than half of all the heads of American Jewish households spend their lives "in business." Sociological categories are neither complete nor mutually exclusive and it is possible to find Jewish intellectuals who work as office managers. But characteristically, the American Jewish businessman is neither an intellectual nor a scholar. He respects intellectuals. He believes in scholarship. He offers admiration and grants. But the respect is external. The dedication of the American Jewish businessman, like that of most of his Christian colleagues, is overwhelmingly commercial.

In the late Edward Lewis Wallant's novel, *The Pawnbroker,* Sol Nazerman, who survived a Nazi death camp and now grants usurious loans in Harlem, is asked why Jews "come to business" so naturally. Nazerman's answer bristles with intensity. "You begin," he says, "with several thousand years during which you have nothing except a great bearded legend. You have no land to grow food on, no land on which to hunt, not enough time in one place to have a geography or an army or a land-myth. Only you have a little brain in your head and this bearded legend to sustain you and convince you that there *is* something special about you, even in your poverty. But this little brain, this is the real key. With it, you obtain a small piece of cloth—wool, silk, cotton—it doesn't matter. You take this cloth and you cut it in two and sell the two pieces for a penny or two more than you paid for the one. With this money, then, you buy a slightly larger piece of cloth, which perhaps may be cut into three pieces and sold

184

for three pennies profit. You must never succumb to buying an extra piece of bread at this point, a luxury like a toy for your child. Immediately you must go out and buy a still larger cloth, or two larger cloths and repeat the process. And so you continue until there is no longer any temptation to dig in the earth and grow food, no longer any desire to look at the limitless land which is in your name. You repeat the process over and over and over for approximately twenty centuries. And then, *voilà*, you have a mercantile heritage."

American Jews sell washing machines and manufacture electric coffee percolators. They design peasant blouses, import chateau-bottled wines and distribute buoyant golf balls guaranteed not to sink when topped into a water hazard. They subdivide estates and arrange mortgages and build hotels on the Boardwalk. They produce etched glass lighting fixtures and spectacularly lit musical comedies. They organize mutual funds and sell insurance and lend money and own almost every sort of store and shop on earth. In a nation where business reigns, where the ultimate hero is neither poet nor warrior but that bland, happy gentleman who started with nothing and through unspecified means has made a million dollars, the Jewish business achievement is considerable. There may well be more American Jewish millionaires than paupers.

But Jewish business success is ringed by irony. Sol Nazerman would be amused. The irony has been forged to his temper.

Jews do not generally share the American worship of a successful business career. They take comparatively little delight in their acquired skills of buying and selling. "Look, I'm not knocking money," says the proprietor of several discount stores in New York City. "I got it and I'm glad. But I hope for better things for my kids." Some of the most prosperous Jewish businessmen see business as nothing more than a platform from which their children can advance into the professions and into the arts.

Jews have proven their business capabilities for millennia under oppressive conditions and it is not surprising that they have achieved business success in the large freedom of America. But anti-Semites have turned the Jews' inventive and pragmatic ways against them, robbing Jews of pride and self-esteem. Although one hears of the thrifty Scot and the shrewd Yankee, similar attributes are distorted by the anti-

Semite. He speaks of "the scheming and conniving Jew." Unfortunately, Jews, as well as Christians, are shaped by anti-Semitism. "I hope," the wealthy New York Jewish businessman says cheerlessly, "that my kids will end up doing something better than making money."

A second irony is that Jewish business success in the United States has taken place against the resistance of American industry. "There are just no Jews in giant industry," says a securities analyst from Chicago. "I have studied the big companies and I know. They won't let us in." The situation is not as sweeping nor as consistent as the Chicagoan maintains, but he is not completely wrong. As far as can be learned, there *are* no Jews on the highest executive levels of Bell Telephone, Standard Oil of New Jersey, U.S. Steel, the Metropolitan Life Insurance Company, or E. I. DuPont. There is none near the top of most of the other hundred largest American corporations, either. There has never been a Jewish chief executive or vice-president at any major automobile manufacturers. In view of the Jewish mercantile tradition, such a consistent absence of Jews is remarkable. A variety of factors contributes to the continued absence now, but there is no doubt what created the condition originally. It was anti-Semitism.

The American Jewish Committee, that staid, secular organization of Jewish moderates, publicly proposes a name for what many corporations privately practice. Committee spokesmen refer to "executive-suite" anti-Semitism. "The way things work," a committee researcher suggests, "is pretty standard. In old-line entrenched industry—say the utilities—where there were no Jews at all thirty years ago, a few token Jews get in today. They have a hell of a hard time. They are restricted to the lower levels. They never make policy. You can call that an improvement, but we are not very pleased with it.

"Then there's the other kind of industry, innovative industry, where new ideas, new products are important. Things are somewhat more equitable there. Jews have a much better chance here, and why? Because their brains are needed. Is that anything new? Sometimes, you can find a kind of schizoid scene at a single company. Plenty of Jews in research and development. The deep think departments. No Jews in sales or in management."

From the corporate side, one hears a variety of explanations and excuses, but not denials. In the days after World War I, an official of the New York Telephone Company explained that there were no Jewish telephone operators because "the work requires reaching all over a switchboard and Jewish girls have short arms." Today a major telephone executive says, "We insist our top people learn the business from the bottom up, and face it, Jewish boys don't want to be phone linemen." The words are different; the mental process is unchanged.

Across decades of systematic exclusion, Christian executives have adopted life patterns which admit no Jews. Many of the executives live in all-Christian communities, play golf at all-Christian clubs and, except for random contacts on planes or in restaurants, exist in perfectly sheltered homogeneity. They then say vaguely that "Jews wouldn't be happy in a setup like ours," or, more frankly, "Hell, Jews would spoil things." Sometimes the sentiment is even stronger. "I'll tell you just how we feel," a vice-president for sales of an oil company has remarked, after a drink on the terrace of his golf club. "Two things we don't want in our outfit are felons and Jews."

With years, the problem has become more complicated. The Ford Motor Company earned the distrust of the American Jewish community in the 1920's when the first Henry Ford underwrote the massive American circularization of *Protocols of the Elders of Zion,* a Czarist Russian forgery which purports to reveal a Jewish plot to dominate the world. Since the old man's death, his company has taken care to mend its ways. Not only is the director of Ford's scientific laboratories a Jew, but the company has defied an Arab boycott by erecting an assembling plant in Israel. Recently, as part of its continuing talent search, Ford sent scouts to both Yeshiva University and Brandeis, seeking young men to try out as potential executives.

The forays failed. The scouts got no one. Not a single student at either Jewish-sponsored university wanted to go to work for Ford, a full generation after the company had reversed its policy. "They're still damn clannish," a Ford executive exclaimed.

The disabling effects of bigotry are not easily healed, and the ambivalent position of the Jew in American business—enormous success in a limited area—would persist for some time even if the leaders of American industry were willing to abandon their historic anti-Semitism. There is no evidence that appreciable numbers of them are.

In the sophisticated complex of response to anti-Semitism, a reaction most common to American Jewish businessmen is the donation. It is only slightly hyperbolic to suggest that when a Jewish businessman feels threatened, he reaches not for a gun or a club, but for a checkbook. Threats to Jews have been endemic in our time; American Jewish philanthropy is now an establishment with an annual "gross national product" of $725 million.

The intensity with which most Jewish Americans reacted to the 1967 Middle Eastern War surprised many people, including many Jews. But as Israel engaged the forces of Egypt, Syria and Jordan, an old terror returned. Remembering Auschwitz, American Jews believed another massacre of innocents might be at hand. They poured $175 million into a hastily organized Israel Emergency Fund, within six weeks.

At the roots of this reaction lie traditions and patterns of Jewish life which extend backwards in time and beyond the borders of the United States. Charity—*tzedakah* in Hebrew—is an historic duty of a religious Jew. The medieval Sephardic teacher Maimonides, a major influence on Jewish thought, set down eight distinct degrees of charity. According to Maimonides, the highest order is the gift that helps the receiver to become self-supporting. The scale descends—giving anonymously out of high motives, giving publicly to community charities—down to the lowest step: giving grudgingly, which still is better than giving nothing at all.

How much necessity influenced Jewish theology and ethos is uncertain, but for centuries the Jews of Europe needed to have their own charities. No government, no class, no line of princes in Christian Europe could be relied on to defend Jews. If aged, indigent Jews, if Jewish orphans and widows were to enjoy any protection at all, Jews themselves would have to provide it. If the Jewish sick were to be treated, Jewish physicians and later Jewish hospitals would be essential. *Tzedakah* plus necessity. Long before the first tides of Jewish immigration reached America, European Jews had developed extensive communal services for themselves.

In America, more than sixty-four Jewish-supported hospitals offer a total of twenty thousand beds on a non-sectarian basis. (Typically, private-room rates are exorbitant and clinic ces are low.) In every major city one finds Jewish community centers, Jewish social services and Jewish homes for the aged. Although American, these institutions have their roots not in the modern welfare-conscious United States but in the Europe of the anti-Semite and the pogrom. They are transplants that have grown. And not morality, nor tradition, nor the American scene raised Jewish charity to its present state of affluence. The dominant growth factor was Hitler.

During the 1930's, when every Jew on earth was threatened, American Jews poured hundreds and hundreds of millions of dollars into defense organizations established to save Jewish lives. In many cases the money was invested in the hope of rescuing a relative from Austria, Czechoslovakia, Poland or the Balkans before the Nazis came. Only a handful were saved.

The enduring side effect of the effort was that the American Jewish philanthropic establishment, fed enormously, grew gigantic. Three years after Hitler's corpse was burned, or at about the time when the Jewish charitable system might have faced hard going, the state of Israel came into being. In 1948, the year of Israel's birth, American Jews contributed $200,721,000 to their various community philanthropic campaigns. Most was an offering to Zion. During the five years before the Middle Eastern War of 1967, community campaigns still drew about $125 million annually.

Although that figure works out to a contribution of about twenty dollars for each Jewish-American, including infants, the evidence is strong that fewer than half of the adult Jews of America actually give anything at all. Much of the money comes in large chunks. In some areas of the American Jewish business community contributions of one hundred dollars and up are all but mandatory.

The organization of Jewish fund drives in the United States follows clearer lines than the organization of almost anything else within the nationwide Jewish community. Throughout most of the country, the charities collect through federations. The individual contributes once to a central fund, which allocates. Parts of each dollar go to resettlement of Moroccan Jews in Israel, to a local hospital ward, to Jewish cultural organization and Orthodox Jewish schools. Almost invariably, most of the money, about sixty per cent, goes overseas.

In New York City, by far the greatest source of funds, the

United Jewish Appeal, primarily overseas, and the Federation of Jewish Philanthropies, primarily domestic, collect separately. Elsewhere the drives are usually combined. These so-called Federation fund appeals, under professional guidance, are held annually in more than eight hundred American cities and towns. The local groups are joined in a national Council of Jewish Federation and Welfare Funds but they retain autonomy in making local allocations within national guidelines.

Success varies with both the energy of the fund-raisers and the nature of the Jewish community. Cleveland, a city of endless Negro slums, is "a good area," for Jewish fund raisers. The Cleveland Jewish community, almost exclusively suburban, donates an average of seventy-five dollars per person. Detroit is another "good area." Los Angeles is not.

Why does the Los Angeles area, with a population of almost half a million Jews, contribute no more than Greater Cleveland, home for at most one hundred thousand? Professionals point to the diffuse quality of Los Angeles and to its pervasive sense of impermanence. (A typical native Californian hails from Indiana.) But conceding these things, the professionals still wring their hands. Fund-raising has not yet yielded all of its mysteries.

"Generally," one explains, "we can be reasonably concrete about what a successful program requires. We know, for example, that the community must have people with means. We can't run major fund drives among paupers. Then we do best in established communities, like Cleveland, where families have settled in and giving has become a tradition. In places like that you find people with a strong Jewish consciousness and a strong communal consciousness as well. Finally, as you can guess, you had better have a well-run apparatus."

In a typical large city, Chicago, the organizers send committees fanning like patrols through every avenue of Jewish life. Fund-raising groups are appointed for each of Chicago's Jewish city and country clubs, the Standard, the Covenant, Briarwood, Bryn Mawr and the rest. Others hunt in the business community. Distinct fund-raising committees, established by Chicago's Combined Jewish Appeal, work in Accounting, Alcoholic Beverages, Amusements, Automatic Merchandising and Auto & Auto Leasing—in all, fully sixty-eight committees wring the business community dry of cash and, possibly, charitable impulses.

"The universal objective," in the description of one New York fund raiser, "is to make it impossible for a man not to give. You appeal to whatever you think is best: fear, vanity, sympathy. You want results. Vanity is usually the best of all."

One technique, popular in most large cities, is the publication of a so-called *Book of Life,* which is widely distributed throughout the Jewish community. After a few pages of words and pictures on the purpose and good works of charity, the *Book of Life* becomes a roster of names. Everyone who has contributed at least a minimal sum, perhaps five dollars, has his name listed in agate type. Conversely, anyone who refuses to give is identified by exclusion. "A *Book of Life,*" says a fund raiser, "is one of the most effective ways to nail the stiffs. Not only that, it makes everybody give a little more. Look, you're in business. You're doing good, or you want everybody to think so. What are you gonna give, five dollars? Like hell. Giving is a form of boasting, too."

Few people justify all the strong-arm and guileful techniques of Jewish fund raising. Instead, advocates of the charitable establishment point to the ends. They talk of Mount Sinai Hospital in New York, Michael Reese in Chicago. They talk of orphans who have found homes, disturbed children undergoing treatment, crippled widows busy and seemingly content learning how to work looms. They talk of Israel.

The point is not that the American Jewish philanthropic establishment would rate high on the scale of Maimonides. It would not. The point is that Jews, specifically Jewish businessmen, are unique among recent immigrant groups. Whatever the reasons, they pursue philanthropy and take care of their own communal needs, with a positive excess of zeal.

## NOT QUITE BABBITT

As far as an outsider can tell, Morton I. Applebaum, businessman—a leading and public-spirited businessman according to the *Franklin City Sun*—is more or less like Hank Cavanaugh or E. J. Baggott, who are also described as business leaders in the *Sun.* Mr. Applebaum's box adjoins the Baggott family seats at the home games of the Franklin City Thunderbolts of the All-American Football League. He serves with Mr. Cavanaugh on the Franklin City Community Chest. But forty-seven years of life, most of it spent in the affluent and

moderately tolerant Midwestern metropolis here calle
Franklin City, have convinced Mr. Applebaum that he is n
like Baggott or Cavanaugh at all. He is a leading Jewish bus
nessman, another thing.

The awareness works within Mr. Applebaum in compli
cated ways, although he is not a very complicated man. If h
were capable of tragedy, he would say that his own was t
have wrought a wholly American success story only to fin
that in the end he felt less native than when he began. M
Applebaum does not articulate such things. He is disincline
toward introspection, contained on serious matters, althoug
generally ebullient. He is ambitious.

Mr. Applebaum founded and retains the controlling inter
est in The Original Music Shoppes, a chain of six retail store
selling high-fidelity equipment, phonograph records and
limited line of expensive television sets. The Music Shoppe
are successful largely because of Mr. Applebaum's busines
abilities. He was able, through hunch or luck or both, to an
ticipate the American vogue in high fidelity. That was the cir
cumstance which began his movement from the lower middl
class to affluence. Another might have served as well. It wa
just a question of finding a field for his skills. Mr. Apple
baum is comfortable with money and unafraid. Almost all o
his stock market transactions have gone well. He bough
Xerox as it was rising and Georgia-Pacific, which soon after
ward split twice. He invested heavily in Franklin Fields,
cooperative garden apartment development catering to retire
people. Franklin Fields, with huge and sometimes misplace
glass walls and pervasive wrought iron railings, is garish, bu
Mr. Applebaum considers it handsome. He is gifted with in
nate commercial taste. *Liebestod, The 1812 Overture, Hava
naise* and Liszt's *First Piano Concerto* are his announce
preferences in serious music. Privately, he prefers to hear th
Zero Mostel recording of *Fiddler on the Roof,* which he ha
played 131 times, by actual count, wearing out two pressings
He is particular about accounts and numbers.

He suspects that within a year, or certainly two, his per
sonal holdings will exceed one million dollars. That day h
plans to celebrate in an unusual way. He is going to present th
secretary-treasurer of The Original Music Shoppes, a square
backed and serious Presbyterian named John Knox Collins
with a two-week vacation trip to Israel, all expenses paid

"compliments of the boss." Mr. Applebaum is the possessor of a belligerent generosity.

Morton Isaiah Applebaum is his full name, and he will not change it. His son is Barry after a grandfather named Baruch, and his daughter is Sherrill, after his own Grandmother Shlotka, who helped raise him long ago. He is more consciously Jewish now than he was when the children were born. He is sorry he did not call the boy Baruch, or Moshe.

This morning, crisp autumn, purrs at Morton Applebaum in his sprawling house in the suburb called Laurel Hill. An automatic timing device activates a hidden stereo receiver and light music suffuses the master bedroom. Mort extends a large, square hand, throws a small lever, and brightly printed drapes part with a vexing motor noise. He would like to have that noise eliminated. He will speak to Knox Collins later in the day. Morning, beyond the half-glass bedroom wall, is bright.

"Got-tammit," his wife says. "Got-tammit. Morning." Her eyes are closed, but her mouth is beginning to smile and Morton touches Vera on the shoulder. He is proud of Vera. He considers the way his hand sits lightly on her flesh. Vera is Viennese and creamy. "Doll," he says. "Got-tammit," Vera says, still embraced by sleep.

A doll is the image Morton retains of her. He knows that she is brighter than he in certain ways but she can be a child about money, and if he did not look after things, they would all starve.

"Don't go got-tammit," Morton says, mimicking, "until we see the market pages in the *Sun*. Then we'll see whether we have something to got-tammit about."

"Ach," she says, awake now and bored at the thought of stocks. She rolls away from Morton, toward her right side, then moves in a writhe onto her back. She reaches her arms up behind her head, clasping her hands high above. Vera is getting somewhat fleshy in her upper arms, but the underarms show no stubble. She is a meticulous woman. Her face, oval and pale, lies in a frame of long dark hair.

The excerpt from *Les Sylphides* ends and an announcer's voice invades their bedroom. "This recording, like many others, is available at discount at The Music Shoppes."

"Say it like you mean it," Morton says.

"What is that?" Vera says, squirming under a pale blue sheet. She is remarkable, Morton thinks, and why don't announcers sell harder. She is forty-four years old. He clutches her shoulder. "No," Vera says. "No."

He slips the hand under the blue sheet and under the frilly ivory gown and Morton strokes his wife's bosom until she breaks into a giggle. He holds her then, firmly, easily, and with his other hand seeks out and finds the metal lever in the headboard. The drapes, whirring too loudly, close again.

"Morton, Morton, no," Vera says tolerantly. The day, although ultimately crowded, begins pleasantly for Morton Isaiah Applebaum.

He has had to struggle for this. That is something he wants his children to understand. He does not want them to be fighters like him, and only partly schooled. What he wants for his children, he says, is that they should have some learning and be wonderful persons, not fighters. It was for the children, he says, that he put $87,768 into this enormous flagstone and glass house, for them that he hired the Frank-Lloyd-Wright-nik to design and for them that he selected Laurel Hill. Here is a place where there were plenty of *goys,* but you could still be Jewish and not be ashamed. It is the second-best location in Franklin City. Crestwood, the best, is still restricted.

Morton prays, doubting God, at Temple Sherith Israel, Remnant of Israel, and Barry is going to go to dental college and Sherry is majoring in English poetry, which Morton underwrites although it is not a practical thing. Morton donates $500 a year to the temple and considerably more to the Consolidated Jewish Appeal of Franklin City. It is a long time after Hitler, but now there is Nasser, and what the hell did America do? Morton asks. It is easy to give, he says. Give or die, that's what it is, when you're a Jew. He wants Barry and Sherry to understand about charity. Listen, he says, charity is the one thing he hopes that Jews never lose in America, no matter how well off they are. What is the word the liberals use? Integrated? No, that's color. Assimilated.

Vera is in the bathroom, with its side-by-side sinks and separate anteroom for the john. They rarely use the side-by-side sinks, with side-by-side mirrors as the architect intended. Sinkside intimacy embarrasses them both.

A mirror faces the bed. Morton Applebaum is in excellent shape for forty-nine. Golf helps a little, but what is it Sam said at his last checkup? Sam said he could play golf nine times a week and not be in shape like Mort. Sam was fatter than he wanted to be. Mort liked fat doctors. It kept things a little more even, and Sam Tedesco was a fat doctor who smoked.

Mort Applebaum shoots in the high seventies, and he enjoys tournaments and betting. He is a good gambler, with a gambler's realistic grasp of his own limitations. He bets accordingly. Once he played with E. J. Baggott, during a hospital fund drive, built vaguely around the Franklin City Open. Two days before the professionals took over the Greenwood Club, a charity tournament mixed pros and amateurs in competition. The amateurs had to pay fifty-dollar entry fees. All the proceeds, a little over $1,700, were given to Shawandanga County Hospital.

Mort Applebaum outplayed E. J. Baggott by a wide margin, driving thirty to forty yards farther, although E. J. was as big as he. "Look, Applebaum," E. J. Baggott said, after Mort had driven 230 yards from the eighteenth tee. "It's my club, and the way you're playing I simply must reserve the right to buy drinks for you."

Mort had Scotch, the pro who joined them ordered beer and E. J. Baggott drank martinis. Baggott was a lean, sinewy man with thin fair hair and high cheekbones. "People say I look like a Texan," he said to the pro, a dark, heavy Southerner. "I tell 'em, when they say that, they better smile. That's not at all my style, if you understand me."

The pro nodded and finished the beer. When he left, Baggott began to talk to Mort Applebaum about Jews. "I have seldom—I can't say never, even to please a first-class golfer like you, Applebaum—met a Jew I didn't like. I find them an astonishing people."

"Those that are left," Mort said.

"Exactly, and have you ever considered that that's why they are astonishing? A hyped-up process, so to speak, of survival. You're a versatile guy. Now where the hell are the Jews who aren't like you? Smart and tough and able. I'll tell you. They probably are dead. Killed in some massacre they weren't smart enough or tough enough to live through. Obviously, your forebears like you were a different breed of Jew."

"You know," Mort said, "I bet I could take six strokes off

your game if you played with me for a week." He did not want to listen to talk about Jews any longer.

E. J. Baggott did not understand. "I know what you're getting at," he said. He drained his glass and held it out for his second martini. "The first thing you *should* be getting at is why there aren't more Jews in National Electronics and I can tell you, you're a businessman, hiring Jews is more trouble than it's worth. But what you *are* getting at, is why you haven't been asked to join Greenwood."

"I haven't asked you to join Burnt Oaks," Mort Applebaum said.

E. J. Baggott held his glass up and waved it slowly back and forth. "Now don't be a smart ass, Applebaum," he said. "There's that kind of Jew, too."

Morton stared darkly straight at Baggott. "What I'm getting at," Baggott said, "is that the small town I really began in, Ramseyville up in New England, had this club that excluded Jews. And I thought that was wrong. It was the only club in town.

"I was going to a Jewish doctor then, Jack Eckman, and there was a Jewish accountant, first-class fellow, and I spoke to them about it and they didn't think about what I said for even a minute. They both said that asking Jews into the Ramseyville Club would be a mistake.

"*Look,*" they said to me, "*Mr. Baggott, we want you to know that we respect you. That's the first thing. And second we respect your ideas. But in this one case, Mr. Baggott, you are wrong. As a Jew, we're telling you, you are wrong. You have a doctor in here, right? That's fine. And an accountant, okay. But does it stop there? You are going to have other Jews wanting to come into the club, too. Only they won't be like us. They'll be kikes. Now Mr. Baggott, if there is one thing that we cannot and will not stand, it is to be a member of a club that lets in kikes. So if you let the kikes in we would have to resign, and what you'd end up having in your club was no Jews, only kikes. You wouldn't want that and neither would we. So do us a favor, Mr. Baggott, and do yourself one, too. Don't invite us to join your club. We don't mind driving a little to play our golf.*"

Baggott sipped at his martini. "There's a certain kind of Jew," he said, "is the most sensible kind of guy on God's green earth. I'm telling you, Mort, I mean it. I got a lot of respect for the Jews."

"You got a big mouth for a horseshit golfer," Mort Applebaum said and got up and slammed E. J. Baggott in the back with a closed fist and walked away.

Over the two speakers in Morton Applebaum's bedroom, KLAB, Franklin City's fine music station, has been playing The Heart of the Symphony, Selections from the Great Works of Beethoven, Brahms and others. A rushed and raspy interpretation of the third movement of Brahms Third is playing when Vera comes out of the bathroom, wearing a purple wrap he does not like but cannot criticize when he should have told her twenty years ago, not now, that he did not like purple.

She emerges and walks to her night table, far across the room from the bed. "You are pretty good for an old man," Vera says, sitting. She tosses her head and dark hair falls down over her shoulders. The purple wrap is open in the front. She begins to comb her hair. "Morton," she says.

"Yeah. What is it? I got one helluva lot to do today."

"About the dinner." Tonight they are going to attend the annual fund-raising dinner of the Consolidated Jewish Appeal.

"I'll be home early."

"How much are we going to give?"

"Depends."

"I think you should give a thousand dollars more than last year. Twenty-five hundred. Because of the war."

"Depends," Mort says. "I got to move."

"I have a busy day myself," Vera says. "Hair dresser at two-thirty and Dr. Kramer at four."

"Something wrong?"

"Shots only. My monkey glands, Dr. Kramer calls them."

"Fifty-dollar Kramer is what I call him," Morton says, and although their marriage is good, their moods are now in conflict and they exchange hard looks, neither retreating.

His black Continental waits in the carport, alongside of Vera's white T-bird. He likes the Continental's lines better than a Caddy's. The slab sides have—he doesn't care for the word but what the hell else is there—class. Besides, he heard at a national Jewish fund dinner once that a Jew might just as well not buy a General Motors car. It was nothing definite, or even very extreme. It was just that given a choice, why not buy a product of Ford or Chrysler. They were more willing to employ Jews. Mort took the advice, but a few months later he also took the suggestion of his broker, Dave Klein, and bought two hundred shares of G.M. at seventy-one. Mr. Applebaum is an incomplete idealist.

He could employ a driver for the black Continental. There is plenty of money for that. But he enjoys sitting at the wheel of the big substantial car, with its air conditioner, its stereo tape player, its automatic seat, its power brakes and windows, its robot speed control. He does not like traffic but he has achieved a position where he can live by likes and dislikes. He never leaves for the office until 9:45, by which time Kennedy Memorial Freeway, which he follows downtown, is pleasantly clear.

When Applebaum arrives at his office in the main Original Music Shoppe, Knox Collins, his assistant, is waiting beside the free tube testing machine, near the front door. He is slim, thin-lipped, with a thin, curving, but not Jewish nose, on which sit spectacles. "Well, come in," Mort Applebaum says. "Don't just stand by the door."

Collins grins quickly.

"Problems?" Mort Applebaum says.

"Nothing you can't handle."

Applebaum grunts. Collins has wanted to tell him something. That was why he was waiting at the tube testing machine near the door. The two men walk briskly back through The Original Music Shoppe, past the record sections, and the Hi-Fi Stereo Department until, at the start of Quality TV and Consoles, they climb a flight toward a second level.

Applebaum's office, behind the musical instruments department, is small and panelled in a glossy wood. He does not spend much time inside the office and he does not know what kind of wood it is. Awards hang on the walls. Morton Applebaum has been second vice-chairman of the Consolidated Jewish Fund Appeal; he has headed the "Campaign Cabinet" and been chairman of the Special Gifts Division. A scroll goes with each job.

He flicks a buzzer on a long, modern walnut desk and says, "Coffee, dear. You?"

Knox Collins shakes his head.

"One coffee, sweetheart, thank you very much. Now, Knox."

"I got some word on that speaker company, Global Electronics," Collins says. He pulls a small pad from a pocket and checks notes as he talks. "You may be right. They may be having some troubles. The advertising manager of *Stereo Magazine* can't get any kind of commitment from Global."

"Nothing at all?"

"That's right."

"You see, Knox. The first thing they cut back on is the advertising. It never fails. A small outfit like this Global, or giant like G.M. When they're in trouble, they pull back and hope. I don't know how good that is, but that's the way they all react."

"Global does business out in Long Island City, which is right near Manhattan, and they bank at Long Island City National." Collins was reading from notes. "They're a New York State Corporation, chartered eight years ago, and I'm trying to get a line on their stockholders."

"Forget it. Just find out who makes their cabinets."

"Ahead of the list of stockholders?"

"Knox," Mort Applebaum says. "A speaker system is only as good as the cabinet you put it in. People making stuff as fine as Global have got to have a first-class cabinet maker. Well maybe, just maybe, they're behind in their payments to him. Then they're really broke. See if you can find that out."

The door opens, and the secretary, a pretty red-haired divorcée, brings coffee. "Here you are," she says. Mort Applebaum fails to acknowledge. He is not trying to be rude. He is concentrating. Global loudspeakers are very possibly the best in the world. His hunch that the decline in their advertising means that they may be in trouble, looks good. Mort Applebaum, who likes to go to fat doctors who smoke, relishes doing business with people who are in economic trouble. He may never have cut a jugular but he likes the sight of one bared before him.

Morton did not, as he enjoys pretending, grow up in a jungle. The neighborhood was hard but not so hard as he is inclined romantically to remember it. The Irish and the Poles, who liked to wait for Jews and beat them up, were not two blocks away as Mort claims, but seven. One had to go out and hike to trouble in the old neighborhood. Still, trouble was not very far away.

Papa had a little bakery shop. He and Mama worked hard until Mama died when Mort was six and Papa was forced to work harder. He was not a joking man. With better luck, he might have been a clothier or even a lawyer maybe, so he said. As it was, he worked so hard, Mort did not see him often. Mort was a big boy, who could care for himself and he was not afraid of many things. When he was very little, two or three, he wrestled with Saul, his brother who was five years older, and although he did not win, he sometimes made Saul cry. He did not cry readily himself.

The Applebaums lived in a small gray house on Ninety-Fourth Street, near the corner of West Boulevard. Franklin City had been designed around an enormous central hub, the City Circle. Four boulevards, spokes in the wheel, ran from the Circle, taking their names from the directions. Most of the Jews, East European immigrants, lived near West Boulevard between Eighty-eighth and One Hundred-and-First. They were an enclave ringed by non-Jews. The Russian colony was a bad and drunken bunch, according to the Jews. The Poles were not much better. The Irish, who lived on West above One Hundred-and-First Street, could be the best and the worst of all the *goyim*, the most vicious anti-Semites and the most steadfast of *goy* friends.

Mort Applebaum was a proficient basketball player. He enjoyed the game and although he was not fast, he could start quickly. He was strong and when he dribbled the ball, moves were always suggesting themselves to him. They all ended with an animal drive toward the basket. He was a fair shot and a relentless driver. "Moose," the other boys called him, "Morty the Moose."

He played indoors and out, at playgrounds in the neighborhood and at a cellar gymnasium, and he made the Borem High School varsity when he was a sophomore.

"Such a waste," his father said. "You should want to become something, a lawyer. What are you becoming? A basketball player." His father looked at him narrowly. He did not really know his second son. "What is that with your hand?"

Mort had a habit of making the motion of bouncing a basketball with his right hand, even when he did not have a ball. "Setting up a give and go," Mort said.

"What's that?"

"Nothing, Papa."

Mort Applebaum has been musing in the office, also a waste. He presses the buzzer. "Red," he says to his secretary.

"Get me Global Electronics in Long Island City, New York. Find out who the president is and put him on."

She is back quickly. "The president is Emory Taylor, and he's on the line."

"Mr. Taylor?" Mort says into the phone.

"Yes."

"I heard your speakers at the last Hi-Fi Show. First class. Maybe we can make a deal. How's business?"

"A little slow right now," Emory Taylor says. His voice is deep and even.

"Well, maybe I can help you out. We have six stores here. We do a fair volume, handling quality stuff."

"Are you asking for an exclusive distributorship?"

"I'm asking for a price."

"We wholesale at forty per cent of list."

"No," Mort Applebaum says. "We don't get list out here."

"I thought . . ."

"We don't get list. I'm thinking in terms of a hundred speakers, maybe two hundred in the long haul. But if the price is no good, we can't make any deal."

"I'll talk to my partner."

"Call me," Mort Applebaum says. "Between four and five today, please. My girl will give you the number." He talks to the secretary, then buzzes Knox Collins on the intercom. "I've got Global calling back at four. You got to check with the cabinet maker by 3:30, otherwise I'll duck it." He hangs up. It is after eleven. He begins to light a cigar. The buzzer sounds. "Sidney Fetterman, for you on three."

"Sidney, boy. Why aren't you working?"

"Hello, Mort," Fetterman says, breathlessly. "Listen, we want to hold a meeting tonight, just a few of us, after the Fund-raising dinner."

"After? Who meets after? What about?"

"Christmas intruding into the schools," Sidney Fetterman says. He is the principal of Rhodes Junior High. "I've been in and around some of them and the situation is getting worse and worse, with the crèches and the hymns, and no matter what the Supreme Court has decreed some of us feel we have to take some action on a local level, to protect our kids."

"Good," Mort says. "You can count me out."

"Out?"

"*O* for out, *u* for out and *t* for out," Mort says.

"This is an important issue," Fetterman says.

"This is a Christian country."

"We have several Unitarians with us on this thing, and a Quaker."

"But people won't notice that," Mort Applebaum says. "What they will notice are the Fettermans and Applebaums."

"It is a question of the right thing, of protecting kids from being Christianized in a secular place."

"No," Mort Applebaum says. "You may be wrong and you may be right, but the question here is something else. How would it be for the Jews? That's the real question. And the answer, and you must know it as well as I, is that, right or wrong it would come out that Jews are attacking Christmas, and that would be terrible."

"Mort." Fetterman is pleading.

"No, Sidney. Goodbye."


Mort Applebaum was a good enough high school basketball player for the State College at Robertson to award him a twenty-five dollars-a-week living allowance above room, board, books and fees. Athletics at Robertson were organized to the point of segregation. Varsity athletes had a small dormitory to themselves and were fed at a year-round training table.

Mort roomed with an even-tempered, small-town Slavic American named Eddie Falkowicz, who wanted to change his name to Eddie Falk. Eddie, a football lineman, had no neck. But his face, atop the thick square body, was a pugnosed, blue-eyed mask of innocence. Mort wondered how rival linemen felt after getting one of Falkowicz's fists in the gut and looking up and seeing the pugnose and the mild blue eyes.

Eddie was going to coach. That was why he was working toward a degree. Mort talked vaguely about law.

"Why do you want to do that?" Eddie asked.

"Family," Mort said.

"What do they care what you do?"

"They care."

"You got to make money, is that it?" Eddie said.

"No. They want me to be a lawyer."

"Well, I mean," Eddie said, "neither one of us is exactly a wonder with the books. How you gonna make law?"

"I don't know, Eddie. It bothers me."

Ed missed his girl. He told Mort he had been sleeping with

her all through his senior year in high school. He showed a snapshot of a pretty, round-faced blonde. "I never slept with anything looked that good even once," Mort said. Eddie laughed and rumpled Morty's hair.

A few nights later, at the training table, Harry Durnan, a half-back, began talking about the war in Europe. It was early in 1940. "All we ought to do is stay out of it," Harry Durnan said.

"Damn right," said Larry Tannehill, an end.

"Oh, I don't know," Mort said.

"We got our oceans," Tannehill said. "Why do we have to go crossing them looking for trouble?"

"I don't know," Mort said. He was trying to think. "I don't know. But maybe we're just going to have to."

"I kind of thought *you'd* say something like that," Harry Durnan said.

"What do you mean?" Mort said.

"What do I mean?" Harry Durnan said.

"What does he mean?" Larry Tannehill said.

Harry Durnan touched his nose.

"Now wait a minute," Mort said. "What the hell?"

"You know what I mean by *that,* don't you, Applebaum?" Harry Durnan said. He had begun to tap his nose.

"Goddam right," Mort said.

"Take it easy, Morty," Eddie Falkowicz said.

"How can I take it easy with that kind of talk?" Mort said.

"Yeah, Morty."

"It's a lot of shit, Eddie."

"Yeah, Morty. Sure." The blue eyes looked blandly at Mort.

"Well, why don't *you* tell 'em," Mort said. "You tell 'em it's a lot of shit."

"I can't, Morty."

"Why not?"

"They're talking the truth," Eddie Falkowicz said.

"It's a Jew war," Harry Durnan said.

"He's right, Mort," Eddie Falkowicz said. "You may be my roomie and my buddy but that doesn't change the fact. What's happening in Europe is a Jew war."

It annoyed Mort a year and a half later when the Army of the United States elected to send him, not to Europe, but to the Pacific Theater.

Restless, Mr. Morton I. Applebaum walks out of the office toward his store. His gait is rolling, awkward and powerful. His hair, still black and thick, forms a widow's peak above a long nose on the long moose face. He passes the desk where his secretary sits typing. The V of her printed blouse opens too deeply, showing a ribbon of white. "Now, dear," Mort says. He leans over and carefully closes her blouse. She gasps when his hand touches her skin. He fixes her eyes with his own, and the secretary blushes.

Clerks bob and nod as Mr. Applebaum strolls through his store. "What's number one?" he asks the store manager, a pudgy, perspiring man named Lefkowitz. "The Monkees is what the charts list," Lefkowitz says.

"And what do we have in the window?"

"Yeah," Lefkowitz says.

"What we got in the window is The Supremes."

"I'll redo the window tomorrow," Lefkowitz says.

"Try tonight."

"Okay. Yeah. Sure."

Applebaum turns and walks back to Knox Collins' office, which is larger than his own. Collins is working over statements. "Hey, I'm going to lunch," Applebaum says, "and maybe get in a quick eighteen. See ya by around three. You'll get that cabinet man, before then, probably."

At Burnt Oaks, he has a date with Harry Altman, a thin, left-handed redhead, who struggles profitlessly in real estate. Altman is a fine natural golfer, but under pressure his game collapses into wildness. Mort Applebaum has taken Altman's measure. He is thinking of Altman's golf and humming to a stereo-tape cartridge of *The Sound of Music,* as he parks his black Continental in the Burnt Oaks lot, between Dr. Kramer's big green Mercedes, MD-101, and the red TR 4-a that Sam Shaver, from the Consolidated Fund Appeal, gave his blonde wife last spring.

Attendants park members' cars at Greenwood, the Christian country club where E. J. Baggott once offended Applebaum. Burnt Oaks, Franklin City's principal Jewish golf club, is less formal than Greenwood and less immediately attractive. Burnt Oaks is newer. Its greens are not as lush. Its landscaping is scrubbier. Its trees are younger. The view from the Burnt Oaks clubhouse, a converted mansion in the Spanish-Moorish style, is merely pleasant. Greenwood offers a spectacular sweep toward a horizon of long brown hills.

Harry Altman is sipping a scotch and soda when Mort Applebaum spots him in the locker room.

"So early?" Mort says.

"I got some business on my mind."

"And I suppose I don't?" Mort Applebaum says. "I suppose I'm not in business?" He grins. *"Schicker,"* he says to Harry.

They are going to play ten dollars Nassau, a mild form of gambling, which can cost the loser thirty dollars. Any gambling challenges Mort Applebaum. He does not enjoy golf nearly as much when he cannot bet on himself.

"My honor," he says, standing at the first tee. "You remember, Harry. From the last time." The first at Burnt Oaks presents a long slow dip that extends to the base of a steep rise 210 yards out. Mort swings his driver back and forth, loosening his big shoulders.

He walks up to the ball. "Gonna go for the bird," he says. His drive sails out not high, grabs the air, climbs, slams into the crest of the rise, and bounces forward, out of sight down toward the green. Mort looks innocently at Harry Altman and says, "Tweet, tweet."

Harry Altman's swing is an uncoiling. He lashes out, but something imperceptible has gone wrong. The drive sails out straight, but suddenly dips and slips to the left. "Damnit," Harry says.

"This is the ancient and honorable game of Oh, shit," Mort says. "You'll settle down."

Altman does not and Mort, playing calmly, wins four of the first five holes. Except for Mort's light needling there is little communication between the men. In the beginning, they are working as much as playing, seeking an advantage. But after Mort Applebaum draws far ahead, he paused to light a cigar. "Whatsa matter with you today?" he says at the sixth tee. "The money worrying you? You need thirty bucks that bad, I'll lend it to you." He is annoyed. He prefers close victory to a rout.

"I need more than thirty," Harry Altman says. "I want to talk to you."

"Yeah," Mort says. "Wait'll I drive." Abruptly, Mort's guard is up. A man can be skinned on a golf course as painfully as anywhere else. He pushes the drive and it fades to the right, landing in rough, near the bank of a narrow stream.

"Too bad," Harry says.

"The name of the game is Oh, shit."

"I'll tell you what I wanted . . ."

"Drive," Mort Applebaum orders. "We'll talk walking."

Harry slams the ball long and straight. He falls in step with Mort and after a pause, begins to explain. "I got a great chance for something good, Morty, and I want to give you a crack at it."

"I'm listening."

"You know the houses up on Parker Boulevard? I can get hold of thirty of them in pretty good shape. Decent plumbing. Not many violations. And it won't take too damn much cash."

They are striding along the bank of the stream toward Mort's ball. "Who wants 'em, Harry?" Mort says.

"What do you mean?"

"You know what I mean. The neighborhood is going colored, Harry. You know it as well as I."

"You know what is S. R. O.?" Harry says.

"Standing room only," Mort says.

"Single room occupancy," Harry says.

"Meaning?"

"Those buildings up on Parker are going to get converted to single room occupancy. The city is going to move all these colored welfare guys into them, one welfare guy to a room."

"It's a beautiful day, Harry. I am taking money from you. The grass is green. What are you talking to me about welfare for? I don't come out here for a headache."

"You know what welfare allows as rental in S. R. O.'s Mort? Eleven dollars a room a week, that's what. One of those old houses on Parker, I can break up into ten rooms easy. That's a hundred and ten dollars a week, from the city. Guaranteed. No collection problems. Four hundred and forty dollars a month. Thirty buildings. You know what that comes out to, Morty?"

Mort knows. The thirty houses on Parker Boulevard will gross $13,200 a month from the Franklin City Welfare Department. The developing proposition bothers him. He does not want to think about it. "I'm gonna use a two-wood and hope to hell I reach the green."

"The figure is thirteen-two."

Mort chews on his cigar and glares at Harry Altman. "Not when I'm getting ready to hit."

The wood is short. Harry Altman makes a clucking sound of disappointment, and hits his own second shot well. "I figure," Altman says, "that we can get those houses, if we move quick and quiet, which I can do, for between three and four hundred thousand, with about a hundred thousand cash. You can figure out that's a pretty good return."

Mort has been figuring. The cash outlay comes back within eight months. The total investment is covered in two and a half years. After that, if Altman is right, the slum houses on Parker Boulevard will be an annuity.

"I mean, it's one hell of a deal," Harry Altman says.

"So why are you talking to me?" Mort says.

"I'm talking to you about scratch, Mr. Applebaum. I don't have a lot. I gotta hustle. I don't have a chain of stores." The thin, redheaded man grins briskly. "And then there's friendship, too. I want to let you in on a good thing."

"Forget the friendship. Business is business." Mort hits a wedge short to the green, and walks after it. He is away. His first putt is very weak. His second, for par, slides four feet past the hole. He is thinking about the income from the houses on Parker Boulevard. He would be able to turn the profits from the stores over to the kids so they would never have to worry, they could do what they wanted, and he and Vera could live pretty well on the money from the houses. Welfare money. That's what it would be.

"Hole out," Harry says.

"Yeah." Mort bites the cigar, and rolls it with his tongue, and tramps after the ball, big feet pounding the green. He studies the short putt and misses it. The ball stops at the lip of the hole. He twirls his putter, then taps the ball home with the handle. He has taken a seven for the par five hole.

"No," he says.

"What no?" Harry Altman says.

"I don't want to be a slumlord."

"Oh, shit," Harry says.

"The name of the game," Mort says. "Putt, *schlemiel*."

Driving back to his office above The Original Music Shoppe, Morton Applebaum does not hum or play a stereo tape. He has won the match, but he considers the day's golf spoiled. Mr. Applebaum does not like to walk away from money and he would not have rejected Harry Altman's proposition without investigating it, except for one of his primal business rules. Mr. Applebaum believes that a man cannot long mix clean money with dirty. "Before long," he says, "everything you got, even the money you give the temple, gets dirty, too." Mr. Applebaum sees himself as hard but fair; he looks at his business record as tough but supremely clean. For practical reasons, he means to keep it that way.

After his discharge in 1945 as Corporal M. Applebaum, worth three hundred dollars, he had no pragmatic values, and he had lost his ideals. He had suffered through a bloody, brutalizing war as a foot soldier in the South Pacific Islands and his earlier life now appeared irrelevant. When he came back to his father's house, it looked smaller and grayer than he remembered; his father, too, was smaller and grayer. Mort had not been home for two hours before Mr. Applebaum started talking about law school. His brother Sandy had graduated, Papa said. Sandy was already in practice. Mort Applebaum, sitting in the small living room, unpraised in paratroop boots, shook his long head and trudged out to escape the callous baker who was his father, and to begin several weeks of drinking.

When his money ran out, he took a job at sixty-five dollars a week, for a small agency called Ace Brokerage, which sold Negroes insurance policies on the installment plan. Ace Brokerage covered life, cars, and personal belongings, for premiums that included interest and fell due once a week. Mort thought that he was being hired as a salesman, but the position turned out to be collection agent. He stayed because he thought sixty-five dollars a week was a lot of money.

Mort was sipping coffee in a little colored diner one afternoon when he saw Vera Schlesinger's picture in the *Franklin City Sun*. She had been elected campus queen of Franklin Junior College. Looking at her picture, Mort said afterward, was his best moment in a long time. He went to a Junior College dance to meet her, arriving in his Army clothes and trooper's boots and campaign ribbons, and approached her easily and asked what he was supposed to call a queen.

Vera smiled. Her skin was clear and very white against the darkness of her hair. Her face was long but soft; her nose was thin, with thin nostrils flaring sensuously. Her mouth was wide; Mort still had a soldier's sure belief in what a wide mouth meant.

"Would a queen dance with a corporal in soldier shoes?"

"I have an escort." She nodded toward the slim, round-faced boy at her side.

"Pardon me," Mort said, and he and Vera were dancing. She led the conversation, asking about the ribbons. "Nothing to talk about here," Mort Applebaum said. He remained silent and just before the dance ended, he said, "Vera, where do I call you?"

"My father, Karl Schlesinger. The only one in the book."

She made him take her to a movie on the first date, a sentimental woman's story called *To Each His Own*, which bored him and would have driven him from the theater, except that he enjoyed gazing at Vera and he liked the way she clutched his hand when he gently placed it on her thigh.

Afterward, the elegance of the living room at the Schlesinger home impressed him more than he wanted her to know. The house itself was brick, behind a fine spacious porch furnished with cane rockers. The living room, filled with rich, overstuffed furniture, was divided by a Knabe baby grand. He sat on a couch covered in dark red velvet and felt oddly glum.

"Why do you still wear those boots?" Vera said.

"I still feel like a soldier."

"It has been a terrible war," Vera said. She turned her head and smiled at him warmly. She looked very young, although her bust was full.

"Don't tell me, lady, I was there."

"Do you like music?"

"Sort of."

She went to the piano and played a dozen bars of a Chopin mazurka.

"Good," he said. "Very good. You took lessons."

"I took lessons, yes," she said. "My father was a music teacher in Vienna."

"Ain't that something?" Mort Applebaum said.

"You had a bad war?" Vera said.

"Bad enough."

"Don't tell me," Vera said. "Don't think about it too much. Wait. I will see if Papa has some good Scotch."

She sprang up and he watched her leave, not much butt, and he heard her feet on the stairs. There was a lot of blue china on little end tables, and in the bookcases. He had never seen china like that before, pale blue with a kind of raised ivory design.

"Ja, ja," the tall old man was saying, as he came down the stairs in a patterned silk robe. He had gray hair and a large mustache. "So ver iss diss soldier?" he said. He strode across the room and took Mort's hand. "Maccabee," he said. "For a Maccabee, good Scotch." Karl Schlesinger bent toward a sculptured fruitwood cabinet, which he opened with a key. "From before the war," he said. "And very well aged. Almost as old as Vera, almost twenty-one."

They drank the Scotch straight. "For too long there haff been too few Jewish fighters," Karl Schlesinger said. "Too few. We must haff another drink, *aber nicht du, mein kind.*"

"I'm old enough," Vera said.

"Are you still a professor, sir?" Mort said.

The tall old European looked pained and drank his second Scotch. "You young people," he said, ignoring the question. "You do not need an old man. You can amuse yourselfs, *nicht wahr,* Vera? However, I warn you. She is a sensible girl." He looked sternly at Mort then suddenly smiled. "Good night," Karl Schlesinger said and tramped off.

"Damn," Mort said, after Mr. Schlesinger was gone. "It must be something fine to have a father like that."

"He was much more than he is now before Hitler made him run," Vera said.

"My father is throwing me out of the house. He wants me to be a lawyer, and I don't. I just want to make some money. I want a decent life. I want the war out of my life. I want a business of my own."

"It should be a right business," Vera said.

"I haven't much thought about what business."

"You can't make a happy life out of indecent business."

"What makes you so sure?"

"Papa," Vera said. "He would not tell you what he does. He was afraid you would find out that he is not a teacher in this country. He was afraid you would find out what he does."

Mort's jaw fell when Vera told him that her father was making his comfortable living as a director of Fidelity Insurance, the principal rival to Ace Brokerage which sold policies at usurious rates to underprivileged people.

By the time he reaches downtown, Mort Applebaum has tuned the radio in the Continental to KSTA, a rock and roll station, to find out if Herb Alpert is closing in on *More of the Monkees.* Mr. Applebaum expects a hard argument from the speaker manufacturer. He particularly wants to win and he is getting himself ready, clearing his mind of everything but business.

"I got some information for you," Knox Collins tells Mr. Applebaum in the little shiny-wood panelled office where Mort works. "It wasn't that rough finding out, after all."

Applebaum waits.

"The people at Global subcontract their cabinet making. An outfit called Artcraft makes Global's cabinets. Artcraft hasn't been paid in four months. They're talking about going to court."

Mort Applebaum lights a cigar, nods Collins' dismissal and buzzes his secretary. "Get me the report of our loudspeaker sales for the last six months." She appears with files and a cup of coffee.

Mort has gone over the reports twice and planned his strategy carefully before the president of Global Electronics telephones at 3:55. What he can offer, Emory Taylor says, is one hundred speakers that list at $425 for $200 each, provided a one-third deposit is sent immediately.

"Deposit?" Mort Applebaum says. "Who knows from deposits? As a matter of fact, I want some on consignment."

"We don't really know The Music Shoppes. We've never done business with you before."

"Look us up," Mort says. "National Credit has our rating. And U.S. Small Business. Anyway, lemme see, lemme think. Wait'll I light a cigar, will you? Talking business always gets me nervous." Mort puts down the telephone for precisely twenty seconds. Then he says, "Look, Mr. uh, Taylor, your company is a little rich for my blood."

"Well, maybe we could waive the deposit, assuming everything is all right."

"Good," Mort says. "Now what do you think is a fair price for a hundred Global Imperial speaker systems."

"If you pay promptly, $20,000."

"I'm talking about the ones you advertise at $425 list."

"I know what you're talking about," Mr. Taylor says. "If you can't pay within thirty days, we will have to charge you $23,000."

"Please don't dun me until you make the sale," Mort says. "Wait a minute. The cigar is out again." He waits thirty seconds this time. Then he announces, "The Music Shoppes of

Franklin City are prepared to offer you $10,000 cash within ten days for a shipment of one hundred speakers."

"I couldn't think of it," Mr. Taylor says quickly.

"Maybe your cabinet maker could."

"What?"

"I'm offering you a deal, Taylor, that can save your business. Don't get cute with me, or I swear, I'll call up your cabinet maker, whom you haven't paid in ten months and tell him you're walking away from an awful lot of dough."

In the end Emory Taylor takes $11,500 for one hundred speakers, each of which, he agrees, will bear the special label, in gold on black, *Music Shoppe Soundmaster.*

"A hard bargain," Knox Collins observes pleasantly, afterwards.

"I don't usually like to make 'em that tough," Mort Applebaum says, "but that guy tried to fake me. Acting as though he hadn't checked on our credit the minute we hung up this morning." He stretches lazily. "Besides," Mort says, "I've got a special reason for this one, a kind of need to make big money today."

When Mort Applebaum arrives home, at Laurel Hill, Vera is curled on the bed, a spray of yellow flowers planted in her hair. "Good day?" he says, reaching down and clamping a hand on her bottom.

She curls away. "I had an injection there. I'm sore."

Mort takes off his jacket and loosens his tie.

"I'll get the martini," Vera says.

"No. No martini. I have serious work yet."

"Oh? How much are we going to give tonight?"

"I promised a couple thousand. Maybe I'll make it just a little more."

Vera says nothing. She has asked to have the living room redone, in massive stainless steel pieces, which will cost four thousand dollars and Mort has said they had better wait. But it is not right to approach him now.

"I gotta take a shower," Mort says.

When he returns, in a blue terry cloth robe, she is sitting before her night table, with its hinged mirrors, brushing her hair. She is wearing lacy, black bikini underpants. She stops brushing when she sees him and holds a strapless white brassiere before her breasts. "Hook me, Morton," she says.

"Yeah," he says. "Hey, they don't match. Your top and your bottom are different colors."

"Well," Vera says, "we can have that as our secret. 'Underneath the elegant gown, her underwear doesn't match'." He laughs and that seems to be what she wanted. She smiles warmly. "How much are we going to give tonight?" she says.

They were married five months after they met. He left the Ace Brokerage immediately. For a time he sold second-hand cars. Then, at her urging, he took two education courses. Finally he combined the money her father had given them with a loan from a branch of the Veteran's Administration, and began The Original Musical Shoppe selling records, instruments and sheet music in what had once been a stationery and candy store. Business was slow. Even with Vera working, they did not make progress for more than a year. Then Mort decided to cut his record prices by twenty-five per cent.

Vera thought he was wrong. She thought that at best they would have less money and at worst they would go out of business. But Mort's decision and the sudden popularity of long-playing records coincided. The result was boom for The Original Music Shoppes. Vera retired to have babies and Mort's financial supremacy in his family was assured.

He is wearing a tuxedo and he has hooked her into a soft blue gown, carefully designed so that the small fatty pads on her pectorals are concealed while a long line of cleavage is displayed. Their first extravagance this evening was hiring a tall Negro chauffeur named Oliver. Mr. Applebaum will be able to drink freely if he pleases because Oliver, who has wavy hair and wears a tan uniform, is to drive the Continental. Oliver has worked for the Applebaums before. He opens the door smartly, but inside the car he says, "Could I ask what this boat set you back, Mr. Applebaum?"

"Would you believe fifty-eight hundred dollars?" Mort says.

"Hooo-weee," Oliver says.

"Same car costs most people sixty-two hundred."

Oliver maneuvers the Continental down the Applebaum's driveway. "We have to pick up my father," Vera says. "Mr. Schlesinger. He lives at 610 Eighty-Fourth Street."

Oliver is silent.

"Off Farnsworth," Vera says. "Do you know where that is?"

"Sure he does," Mort says.

"I live on Eighty-Second off Farnsworth," Oliver says.

"Class stays with class," Mort says, quickly.

They drive down Farnsworth, a street of pawnshops, credit furniture stores, cramped bars and ancient trolley tracks intermittently covered with asphalt, and turn into Eighty-Fourth, a street of homes. Patches of lawn before many brick houses are gone to weed. Trees line the sidewalk, but two or three are dead; the city has not yet bothered to take them down. The Schlesinger house, near the middle of the block, is still well-kept; its porch has been freshly painted. A family of Negro women sits on the porch of the adjacent building. One, very fat, sips beer out of a can. Oliver jumps out and opens the door for Mr. Applebaum. "Yessuh, yessuh," cries the fat woman on the porch. "We love to see that good trans-poh-tation in our neighborhood."

Katherine, Mr. Schlesinger's housekeeper, answers the door. "Yes, yes." She smiles at Mort. "Come in." She is Czech, Mort remembers, or Hungarian.

Mort walks into the living room, which seems dark. The huge ebony Knabe is too large for the surroundings. A baby grand would fit more suitably. Wedgwood is everywhere but Mort Applebaum no longer likes Wedgwood. Vera has told him that its blue is too assertive. The room is a collection of old pieces of furniture, some too fragile, some with squat fussy legs, all with too many layers of polish. It is impossible for Mort to conceive of being impressed by a room like this.

He sits in an overstuffed ancient couch and when he tries to get up, the pillow surrounds him and he falls back. "Damnit," he says, as Katherine reappears, helping Mr. Schlesinger down the last two stairs.

Mort leads the old man out the door and down the white stone steps. "Hey, Karl," calls the fat colored lady on the next porch. "Karl, you doan do nothin' naughty now, you heah?"

For a number of reasons, a private party exclusively for so-called Appeal Leaders always precedes the annual dinner of the Consolidated Jewish Appeal of Franklin City. The party is an occasion for successful members of the Jewish community—*the bourgeois elite,* as old Karl Schlesinger describes them—to gather and celebrate communally their position. It is also a time when Samson Raphael Shaver, the twenty-one thousand dollar a year executive director of the

Franklin City Jewish Federation, makes last-minute checks to make sure everything at the formal dinner will go as planned.

The Appeal Leaders gather, self-consciously at first, in the Crystal Lounge of the Franklin Plaza, moving toward the bars which have been set up at each end of the sprawling oval room. Former Judge Julius Pollack, of the Judicial Committee of the Lawyers Division, comes forward to greet Morton Applebaum's party with both arms extended. "What a pleasure!" he exclaims. He embraces Vera and old Karl Schlesinger, and shakes Mort Applebaum's hand.

"Will we be fortunate? Are you speaking again this year?" Vera says.

"Ah, Vera," Judge Pollack says. His hand is on her shoulder. "I hope for a special eloquence. This is such an important year." Pollack is a short, round man with eyeglasses and a white mustache. He looks carefully at Vera, then looks beyond, says "Pardon me," and is off.

"That guy will be running for something on his deathbed," Mort Applebaum says.

Karl Schlesinger brightens. "For his life, perhaps, Morty?" the old man says.

Soon Vera is talking to her cousin, Dr. Bruno Dornberger, of the Physicians and Health Sciences Division of the Consolidated Appeal. Mort excuses himself to speak to Arnold Levinson of the Insurance Men's Group. "I'm getting in some new speakers, Arnie," Mort says, "and I'll give you a price."

"I'm happy with what I got, but maybe, if the price is real good, maybe I'll come down and look around," Arnold Levinson says. "I been meaning to have a talk with you anyway."

"What about?"

"Stereo."

"And what else?" Mort says.

"All right. I'll confess. You twist my arm I'll talk about insurance."

"You know," Mort says, "my father-in-law has gotten all my insurance business for years. He's the guy who set me up in the beginning."

"Well, I'll be perfectly candid with you," Levinson says. "I don't know how good an idea that is. We're all fond of Karl, but he is an old man, and out of touch."

"Morty." The voice behind him is intimate and urgent. Applebaum wheels. Samson Raphael Shaver is standing there with a small pad in his hand. "Excuse me, Arnie. This is business."

"Oh," Arnold Levinson says. "Sure."

"I have you down for two thousand dollars," Samson Raphael Shaver says. "Is that all right? I don't want to embarrass anybody."

"Sure," Mort says, quickly. "Fine. No sweat."

"Thanks," Shaver says, moving away, pad open, making a note.

Mort Applebaum turns from Arnold Levinson and looks over the room. Two crystal chandeliers hang overhead. Crystal fixtures protrude from the walls as well. The large central portion of the oval, down three small steps, is guarded by a silver metal railing. Leaning on the rail, talking intensely to Judge Julius Pollack, is Harry Altman, the redheaded golfer. He and the Judge shake hands, just before Sam Shaver approaches with open pad and the rotund former judge turns away.

Mort moves back to Vera, passing Dr. Bruno Dornberger. "Bruno," he says. "I have some new speakers coming in that I know you'll think are great."

"What kind are they?" asks Dornberger.

"Made up special for us," Mort says. "Really outstanding."

Sam Shaver has come up close behind Bruno Dornberger, open pad in hand, whispering. "Excuse me," Dornberger says to Mort. "Pardon me."

Vera is animatedly talking to two other women when Mort finds her. "You aren't drinking, Mort?" she cries.

"Not yet. Maybe later."

"Ladies and gentlemen, ladies and gentlemen." Samson Raphael Shaver, his voice no longer soft, is standing on top of the staircase. He is slim and shiny-browed and his face triangulates to a pointed chin. "First, on behalf of the Consolidated Jewish Appeal, I want to welcome most cordially all you Leaders, and second, I promise you that I will not make a speech."

There is a light scattering of applause. Almost a hundred people are standing in the room. Most are in their middle years. The men are generally more attractive than the women.

"Instead of a speech," Sam Shaver says, "I am going to propose a toast. You all have drinks?"

Some of the Division Leaders continue talking, but others

move toward Shaver, gathering in a vague semi-circle several steps beneath him.

"You may have noticed," Sam Shaver says, "that the price of drinks here is a little high. Two-and-a-half bucks is a lot of champagne, let alone Scotch.

"Well, I'm happy to let you know that Gilbert Wacker, who manages the hotel—you all know Gil, from Congregation Beth David—well, Gil is taking his fee for the Crystal Lounge, which I don't mind telling you is $250, and turning it back to us, as a contribution."

There is a light burst of handclapping.

"What about the booze?" someone calls.

"The liquor," Shaver says, "has been donated by Eugene Shapiro and Leo Wax of our Alcoholic Beverage Division, and almost all the cash you *shickers* have been plunking down to get stoned, also comes back to the fund as contributions. Keep your receipts. You'll need 'em at tax time.

"But now for the toast. Here is what I propose. A toast to the brave men and women warriors of Israel"—someone starts to applaud and is shushed—"and a toast to the generous men and women of the Leadership of the Consolidated Jewish Fund of Franklin City. In other words, ladies and gentlemen, a toast to our heroes and a toast to ourselves."

A few minutes later the Appeal Leaders begin their march into the Grand Ballroom of the Franklin Plaza, Samson Raphael Shaver is employing his intimate voice again. Walking with Vera, Mort distinctly hears him say to Arnold Levinson, "Less than fifteen hundred would be a disgrace."

The Grand Ballroom of the Franklin Plaza, 190 feet long and 145 feet wide, is crowded with more than eight hundred members of the Franklin City Jewish Federation, most chattering in their assigned places before a seat on the dais is filled. A formal march of group Leaders to the dais has become a dinner tradition. Jerry Tanzerman of the Public Relations Division takes the microphone and requests the guests, who have paid fifteen dollars a ticket, to withhold applause until he has introduced everybody.

The introductions take three minutes. "Here is your Leadership," Jerry Tanzerman begins. "The Honorable and Mrs. Julius Pollack, Judiciary; Mr. and Mrs. Mordecai Tannenbaum, Automotive Industries; our fine Executive Director, Sam Shaver; Dr. and Mrs. Phillip Sands, Plastics and Chemicals Division; . . ." Mort is a Leader of the Recordings and Instruments Division. Karl Schlesinger, like several other "respected veterans," is introduced by name. "He needs no affiliation." Tanzerman's pace is brisk. The introductions do not lag. The respected veterans have not yet reached their seats when Rabbi Samuel Kalmanoff, Conservative, offers his benediction.

"Dear God," says Rabbi Kalmanoff, one of the few men in the Grand Ballroom wearing a *yarmulke,* "another year of trial for this your people, trial by fire in Thine ancient desert whence come our laws, trial by libel in the United Nations whence come our hopes, and yes, even trial for us here, who amid plenty, know and remember our heritage of heartsick and woe. Bless us this evening as we meet for Thy high purpose, *Tzedakah.* Amen."

Although the banquet offered by the Franklin Plaza is not kosher, neither is it belligerently anti-kosher. Even the most secular members of the Federation would agree that the meal should not include ham, pork, or marine animals without scales, such as shrimp. The four-page menu, its cover adorned by a blue Star of David, lists Herring Supreme, *Potage au Poulet;* Prime Ribs *au jus;* Fresh Garden Peas, Whipped Potatoes, Choice of Greens or Aspic Salad, *meringue glacée,* Demi-Tasse, Tea or Milk. At the bottom of the page, in gray type, the menu mumbles, "Kosher food available on request."

Mort and Vera Applebaum sit in the second row of the three-tiered dais. Older men occupy the front. To Mort's right is Crystal Freitag, Harry Freitag's wife, a chubby woman who has not been getting on well at home. Vera sits next to Ralph Lifschitz, a large-browed accountant with whom she grows quite animated. Mort concentrates on the food, which is ordinary.

While *meringue glacée* is still unfinished on most dais plates and unserved through much of the Grand Ballroom, former Justice Julius Pollack rises to speak. He taps a knife handle against a glass for order. He taps four times.

"Ladies and gentlemen," Judge Pollack announces into the microphone. "We have a full, and we hope rewarding, evening ahead, which is why I feel it is important that we start early. I wouldn't want any of you to miss *The Late Show*, or *Johnny Carson*.

"Seriously," Pollack, corpulent but resolute, announces into a clamor of murmurs and clattering silverware, "it is hardly necessary for me to remind you that this is a particularly important year for us as Americans, as Jews, and indeed an important year for Jews everywhere. Your presence here testifies to your own awareness of the importance of the night." He smiles pleasantly. "You and I all know that nobody is going to get out of here for free."

The murmur is laughter now. Judge Pollack is weaning the audience away from the ordinary banquet dinner served at the Franklin Plaza.

"On behalf of your division Leaders, who are seated here on the dais, personally for myself, for Sam Shaver, our fine Executive Director, and—this above all—for all the thousands of people you have helped, let me begin the formal part of the evening by saying *Thank you*." The 876 guests, gathered in the ball room, applaud.

"Do I have to tell you about Jewish traditions of charity?" Judge Pollack says. "I think not. You all know the Christian Trinity. Well, there exists a Jewish Trinity, too. The children of Israel are beholden first to study Torah, second to pray, and third—and every bit as important—they are bound to act with charity and kindness toward the less fortunate. That is as important as the other two. That is why we are here."

The judge has lowered his voice. The audience is serious. "I remember," he says intensely, "walking the streets, which I like to do, in an Orthodox neighborhood in our community, a not very fashionable neighborhood. There was a little boy, no more than ten or twelve, who had just been given some coins by someone I judged to be his grandfather. As I watched, the boy passed a man soliciting funds for a Yeshiva in Israel, with a *pushky*. Now, the coins meant a good deal to that little boy. Obviously he was not wealthy and he looked at his grandfather questioningly and said, *"Do I have to?"* Judge Pollack pauses and sips a glass of water.

*"Do I have to?"* the judge repeats, "and the grandfather looked at the child and said, *"A Yidloch kind musste geben*, A Jewish child must give." The judge sips water again. "You are all Jewish children before me tonight," he whispers, "and I ask only that you remember the old man's simple, moving words. *A Yidloch kind musste geben*."

"Thank you," the judge says, *"and may God Bless you."*

"Good," Mort says to Vera. "Very good. That guy gets better at that speech every year."

It is time for reports. Administrators of hospitals, schools and special institutions march to the microphone and explain how they have used grants from the Consolidated Jewish Fund. "I know you all have important things to say," Judge Pollack says, "but my gavel comes down in two minutes. At three minutes, it comes down on your head." The audience laughs. The reports are delivered almost as quickly as ordered.

"And now," Judge Pollack says, after Rubin Berman, D.Sc., supervising director of the Franklin City Home and Hospital for the Hebrew Aged, concludes his report ungaveled in two minutes and twenty-two seconds, "we have a real treat." Against the wall of plate-glass doors, the main entrance to the Grand Ballroom, two men are hurriedly erecting a large screen. "I hope," says the judge, "you will bear with us briefly. We are trying to arrange this filming so that as many people as possible get a good view."

The lights dim slowly. "Turn around," the judge says. "Turn around." The screen is in the back of the room. There is a harsh sound of furniture shifting, and creaking and, with the lights not finally dimmed, the screen jumps to life with the title *No More Must Die!* Within seconds, the loudspeakers carry the stirring muted strains of *Hatikvah,* an anthem for Israelis whose title word means "hope."

A child, white-faced, enormous-eyed, is standing with his hands held high. He is a European child, wearing a long and too-large coat. Three Nazi troopers, enormous beside the white-faced boy, train rifles at him. One Nazi calls commands. The child listens earnestly, with a terrible wisdom. He seems to understand that his hope, *Hatikvah,* is to listen precisely to this brutish German and do exactly what the brutish German says. The child neither trembles nor weeps. He only listens with ancient concentration. And then, as one of the Germans springs forward, the boy follows a command and reaches into the baggy pockets of the too-large coat. He has been told to empty them. Of what? Guns? Inflammatory pamphlets? Hand grenades? Staring at the commanding German, the boy pulls from his pocket a collection of rolls. Bread. He has been trying to smuggle rolls through the *sturmdrangen* lines into the ghetto of Warsaw, where some-

one else, other people, are hungry. And he has been caught
and he is guilty. Two *sturmdrangen* roughly lead the child
away.

"This boy," a narrator says in somber, understated tones,
"is dead. He was gassed and his corpse was burned in a death
camp in Eastern Europe. If he had any gold teeth, they were
saved.

"We do not know this boy's name.

"We do not know his dreams.

"We do not know even to whom he was carrying the rolls.

"We know only that he was a brave boy, who would have
made a fine man, just about now, right about now.

"But he is dead."

Vera Applebaum looks away. Mort clenches a big fist and,
not realizing he is doing it, begins to pound the table. Tears
are starting down the nose of chubby Crystal Freitag beside
him.

"This," the narrator says over the loudspeakers, "must
never be allowed to happen again. And,"—a martial bugle
shrills—"it need not." Suddenly the screen is filled with tanks,
crossing a desert. Jet fighters bridge the sky. Their engines
wail. From inside a tank the desert passes at frightening
speed. A statesman is talking. Someone is making a speech at
the United Nations. And then back in the desert, tanks, bearing the Star of David, hurtle onward.

"A Sinai campaign," the narrator says. "Heroic, brilliant,
lifesaving. No. Not the most recent one. Much of the recent
film remains classified. But here is an earlier campaign, when
Israel was threatened and struck first and showed the world,
who wondered about docility in Europe, that Jews can fight."
The narrator pauses. Israeli marksmen shatter an Egyptian
tank. A Mirage jet hammers bullets into an Egyptian gun em-
placement. Another Egyptian tank explodes in smoke.
"Jews," the narrator says, "can fight like hell."

There are more pictures of the Sinai campaign of 1956.
Then photographs of gloomy Egyptian prisoners, captured
Russian-made equipment, Israeli forces cheering General
Dayan and then, at this moment of victory a sudden, ghastly
picture of inmates of a Nazi death camp.

"All this," the narrator says, "in a single generation. Death
and birth. Despair and joy. Holocaust and triumph. Which
shall we choose?"

The film slides into sequences of Jewish children studying, Jewish aged at hospitals, Jewish immigrants arriving in Israel. "The choice is not always so dramatic," the narrator says. "Sometimes it is not life and death, but ignorance or education, idleness or usefulness." And then, just as the audience's attention is beginning to wander, Israeli tanks again charge across the screen. The noise of their cannon rises to a crescendo that suddenly yields to silence. Once more the white-faced boy fills the screen, but now he is still and frozen under the guns of the Nazis.

"If you do not want this ever to happen again," the narrator says, "and you cannot drive a tank, you will do the next best thing." The camera moves closer and closer to the white-faced boy, closer and closer to his eyes. "Please," the narrator says, "give."

The audience is silent, then erupts into applause and Judge Julius Pollack, dabbing at his eyes says, "I'm turning this over now to our wonderful Executive Director, Sam Shaver."

"I begin," Samson Raphael Shaver says, briskly, striking while the mood is still intense, "after that fine and moving film, by asking for something big. The movie said it all. All right. The tanks don't run on water, and even water is expensive over there. The anti-Semites didn't all die with Hitler. I want to begin with a gift of fifteen thousand dollars. The Soviet Union probably gives more than that to Nasser every minute. I know it's a lot. But I won't settle for less." The trim aggressive man looks hungrily about the room, but he is only pretending to search. He knows that there will be not one gift of fifteen thousand dollars but six. His canvassing is careful and precise.

"Ah," he says. "Jerry Lassinger right here on our dais. His hand is up. Most of you know him. Lastwell Suitcases. You probably own some. Mr. Lassinger makes them, and he's going to sign a pledge card promising fifteen thousand dollars for the Consolidated Jewish Appeal. What's that, Jerry? Wait a minute. I see. Ladies and gentlemen, the contribution is made not by Mr. Lassinger, personally, but by the Lassinger Foundation. We understand. Thank you very much, sir." Sam Shaver applauds. The others join.

"Wait," Sam says. "Dr. Kanterman. Ladies and gentlemen, Dr. Morris Kanterman, a skilled and dedicated surgeon at our own Sinai Hospital—Chief of Surgery, I might add—is also signing a fifteen-thousand-dollar-pledge card, on behalf of the hospital medical staff. Thank you, Morris. Thank you very much, good Doctor Kanterman."

Sam Shaver controls the pace. He gets fifteen thousand dollar pledges from another foundation, and from a lawyer, and from three brothers who own a meat-packing business, and from a man who inherited a loan company. He moves down to ten thousand dollars. Four pledges, arranged in advance, come in promptly. The tanks and the Nazis and even the dead boy of *No More Must Die!* are receding in memory now. The fund raising, under Shaver's conducting, assumes expanding vitality of its own. A wild mood sweeps the room. People are talking of fifteen and ten thousand dollars casually. The same phenomenon occurs in well-run gambling houses and at stock brokerage firms.

Mort Applebaum calmly lifts a hand. Vera starts, but remembers she is on the dais. Sam Shaver spots Mort, and questions with a look. Mr. Applebaum nods. "Another ten thousand dollars from Mort Applebaum of The Music Shoppes. They sell records. This *is* a record. Thank you, Mort."

"Yeah," Mort says.

Vera is speechless.

"Now," Mort says, "I want to do a little drinking."

"Can we afford it?" Vera says.

Most of the gifts down to two thousand dollars have been prearranged. There are a few surprises for Samson Raphael Shaver, all pleasant. At the two thousand dollar point, he can afford to speculate, and he turns to a list of cards arranged in front of him. There is one card for each dinner guest who in past years has contributed five hundred dollars or more. Each card lists a man's name, occupation, gifts for each of the past three years, the division to which he belongs and his table number.

"Harvey Kleiner," Sam Shaver says into the microphone. "I haven't heard from you, over there at table twenty-six. What are you, pro-Arab? Come on, Harvey. You used to give five hundred dollars. Are you game to triple it now?"

Harvey Kleiner begins talking excitedly to Martha Kleiner. "You had to come," he says. "You had to come to this dinner to show off that goddamn dress." He stands up and bellows. "Yeah, yeah, you got my fifteen hundred!" He sits down. "One night at home," he says, "this woman can't stand."

"Harvey, as many of you know, is in our Accountants Division. Come on, you money-changers. Come into the temple. Eddie Rosen, table one-oh-one, five hundred dollars last year and the year before—what do I hear from you?"

"A thousand!" Eddie Rosen shouts.

"Good," Sam Shaver says, "good. We've not twisting arms. Don't give more than you can afford. If you had a slow year, you shouldn't be ashamed.

"Milt Polansky, table seventeen, another five-hundred-nik. What do we hear, Milt?"

"Seventeen hundred and fifty dollars," Milton Polansky says, "and I would like to say something about that wonderful film. . . ."

"You've said it with your donation. Art Schoen, Art Schoen, table sixteen. Art Schoen."

"He's sick," someone calls.

"Well, let's all remember that," Sam Shaver says. "Art Schoen is sick. Ike Robbins, from our Dental Division. Dr. Robbins, table fourteen, can you brace us, the way you brace teeth, with something more than five hundred dollars."

"Seven-fifty," Dr. Robbins says.

"All right, all right," Sam Shaver says. "Only what you can. We can't all give as much as the Israeli warriors. What we can."

"A thousand," Dr. Robbins calls.

"Better," Sam Shaver says. "Asher Josephson, Alcoholic Beverages, table nine. The surveys tell us everyone's drinking more. Up to two thousand dollars, Ash?"

"How's fifteen hundred?" Josephson calls.

"Five hundred light, but we'll take it," Samson Shaver says. "We're going to be taking everything we can get tonight, because we all know we've got a worthy cause. The cause is life.

"All right, Sam Benadgin, table twenty-two, Real Estate. What do I hear from you Sam? . . .

"Milt Karasik, table thirty-one, Law . . .

"Sheppard Goldman, table twenty-four, Drug Division . . .

"Herschel Mayer, table twelve, Men's Clothing . . .

"I don't want sentiment," Sam Shaver says. "That's for tomorrow. There's only one thing I want to hear tonight, gentlemen. We all know what that is."

"One thousand dollars!" Sam Benadgin cries.

"Twelve hundred!" hollers Milt Karasik.

"I hear you, gentlemen," says Samson Raphael Shaver, "and I am gratified."

Safely chauffeured home after three double Scotches, Morton Isaiah Applebaum sits on the bed in his undershorts and wonders how to tranquilize his wife.

"You didn't even ask me," Vera says. "Not once did you ask what I thought we should give away." She has undressed in the bathroom and emerged in a high-necked flannel robe that reaches her ankles. "There are certain things we must have for the house," she says.

"It's no sweat," Mort says. "This afternoon I made a deal for loudspeakers with some outfit in New York. I faked the guy from here to Cairo."

Vera stares at him. "Ten thousand dollars was too much."

"It goes out monthly," Mort says. "For the next year it's gonna be $833.33 a month, that's all."

"We still have to pay."

"Over this next year, my deal today will make us thirteen and a half thousand."

"So?" Vera says. "There is thirty-five hundred dollars left over?"

"Damn right," Mort says. He stands and paces, swaggering in his shorts.

"I want to make some changes in the living room," Vera says.

"Sure thing," Mort says, still swaggering.

In a moment he lies down beside his warm and handsome wife, who has become terribly expensive, and thinks, placing a hand on the back of her neck, what high pleasure it is to have the money to do the things you want, and to be able to give the things you want with a grand gesture, and to possess the things you want, with clean money, without a single dirty dime. He lies musing, watching a smile play on Vera's face and it amazes him in his struggle toward sleep, when he is seized by a sense of uselessness approaching melancholy.

The limitations American mores impose on Jewish businessmen vary from community to community, affected as much by change as by history. The bigotry of the executive suite and the country club are random cruelties, constant only in their power to disrupt. Given Babbitt's hat, but barred from Babbitt's cloakroom, the American Jewish businessman is robbed of final nativity in his own land.

New York City is a semi-separate country, part of the United States and yet distinct. More vital, neurotic, sophisticated, intense and cultured than any other city in America, New York is also more Jewish. Almost two million Jews make their homes within its five boroughs. According to demographers, the Greater New York area houses 2,381,000 Jews, roughly half of all the Jews in America.

The Jews of Greater New York are not a minute minority. They make up a quarter of the regional populace at large and forty per cent of its middle- and upper-income groups. Because Jews are so numerous and so evident around New York, it is common to conclude that New York Jews have absolute mobility. They do not. As most aware New York Jews concede, full mobility is a metropolitan illusion.

Through numbers and concentration, Jews have been able to dominate certain areas of New York business: clothing, printing, food, general retailing. But New York is crowded with bastions from which Jews are barred. It has more such bastions than any city in the country.

Beyond exclusion from corporate directorships, clubs and simple high-level jobs at hundreds, or thousands of companies, Jews in New York are also systematically prevented from purchasing cooperative apartments in certain buildings. They are denied access to certain favored vacation spas. They are as sharply restricted in New York as anywhere else, despite all the evidence of Jewish achievement in New York City.

The illusion relates to size. New York is so big that a Jew, barred from three companies, may very well find a position at a fourth. Turned down at one building, he can purchase a cooperative duplex in another. He can now even buy a vacation home in East Hampton, in clear sight of the Maidstone Club, a links from which Jews have been barred and which has been called, in retaliation, the Maidstein Club.

New York City does offer absolute mobility to a Jew, provided he limits his movements to areas where other Jews have gone before. In a city as large as New York that makes for an enormous arena. It also makes for the metropolitan illusion of mobility, which for many Jews is as satisfactory as the real thing.

But it is the belief of Louis (Duke) Hurwitz, a lawyer and businessman in Sioux Falls, South Dakota, that he has found a deeper freedom than he could have won in New York City. "In my thirty one years here," Hurwitz says, "I've never heard or sensed anything that you could call anti-Semitism. Of course, I'm not the sort who goes around looking for it."

Sioux Falls, a clean and quiet community of almost seventy thousand, supports two country clubs: the Minnehaha, for its most established citizens, and the Westward Ho. Duke Hurwitz is a member of Minnehaha. Both Sioux Falls clubs accept Jews.

Hurwitz is a trim, bespectacled man who speaks with a flat Midwestern accent, and who grew up in Iowa. "When I first came to Sioux Falls, I was accepted and able to make a living right away," he says. "To be frank, I got a certain amount of legal business from Jewish families established here and I got a certain amount, too, from Christians, who thought I was smart *because* I was Jewish. The concept isn't true, but when I set up my practice in the 1930's, needless to say I did nothing to discourage it."

Within a few years, Hurwitz joined the law firm of Davenport, Evans and Smith. There he quietly prospered, expanded his business interests and in time sent children off to college and lost them when they said, "What are we going to do with our graduate degrees back in Sioux Falls?"

"That," Hurwitz says, "is not a Jewish problem. It's a general problem in a community such as ours, where there really isn't much work for the Ph.D." Hurwitz is a moderate Republican possessed of a streak of independence. His determined and successful fight to prevent the Gideon Society from distributing free New Testaments in the public schools cost him no friends, he says. Recently when Sioux Falls right-wingers formed a chapter of the John Birch Society, they invited Duke Hurwitz to join.

Hurwitz declined. There are excesses to everything, even acceptance.

As variously as American communities attempt to dictate the path its Jews shall walk, so Jews themselves variously accept such dictates or challenge them. In many, but far from all, communities of under one hundred thousand, the easy freedom Duke Hurwitz describes, applies. Further up the scale, among medium-sized and large cities, patterns are less free. Everywhere they can be significantly altered by the impact of a single man.

Rochester, New York, the home of Justice Harry Goldman, was dominated by Eastman Kodak, Inc., a chemical and camera complex. Kodak's record is free from charges of liberalism. Although at least one Jew, Garson Meyer, has been prominent in its chemical division, Kodak historically has not sought to hire Jews. The club structure of Rochester reflected the executive structure of its largest business. The freedom of Rochester Jews was limited.

About ten years ago, Kodak's primacy was challenged by Xerox, a younger company and manufacturer of equipment that copies documents by an ingenious process. Like the technique it utilizes, Xerox is innovative. The company employs not only Rochester Jews, but Rochester Negroes. Where Kodak sponsors *The Ed Sullivan Show*, Xerox underwrites the televising of *Death of a Salesman* and *The Rise and Fall of the Third Reich*. Xerox is a huge corporation, reflecting many disciplines and many talents, but some of its success and some of its progressive viewpoint trace to the gifts and outlook of Sol M. Linowitz, a warm and cultured lawyer and the former Board Chairman of its International Division.

Linowitz, now the United States Ambassador to the Organization of American States, reportedly was able "to weave a web of patents around the Xerox process that will be two hundred years in the untangling." Whatever, Sol M. Linowitz, who looks Jewish, whose name sounds Jewish and who is a religious Jew, became the number two man in an enormous American corporation.

Both Linowitz's parents were born near the Polish border of Austria; his father enjoyed modest success in America as a fruit importer. "The Jewish respect for learning is all bound up with Jewish humor," Linowitz says, discussing his childhood. "You know, you had to play violin at your Bar Mitzvah. And what did you play? *My Yiddische Mama.*" A smile lightens his long dark face. "This is humor," Linowitz says, "but it reflects a respect for the things which make a learned person, or at least make a man who tips his hat to the arts."

Linowitz was himself a child violinist. "If I had practiced hard all my life," he said, "I might have been able to play in the second strings of a major orchestra or just possibly in"—his voice drops in mock awe—"the first violins.

"I gave concerts," he says. "You know how Menasha Skulnick goes. I didn't give concerts." Linowitz holds one hand high. "I gave concerts." The critical hand drops down toward the floor.

Humor covers earnestness. "The moral force of Judaism," Linowitz says, "is vastly complex, and when issues come up such as Vietnam, one does not say, now what does the Jewish religion teach about this? But if you remember Micah and if you are not too presumptuous and you don't take yourself too seriously, you may find your Jewish heritage reminding you that there are no simple answers to complex issues and that out of both the respect for learning and the religious sense, you had better think through serious questions before you venture the *Chutzpah* to offer a solution."

During the years when he worked in the predominantly gentile business community of Rochester, Sol Linowitz was persuasive evidence that Jews, even Jews who take Judaism seriously, can be creatures of worth and dignity. Several years ago, the University Club of Rochester invited him to become their first Jewish member.

"No, thank you," Linowitz answered, in effect. "If you want to accept Jews as members, fine. Invite several, but I am not going to be your Jew."

Accepting Linowitz's challenge, the University Club and at least one other superChristian stronghold in Rochester relaxed barriers. There were no casualties. The climate between Jews and Christians in Rochester, still imperfect, is better than anyone can remember it.

"Why, Kodak," someone points out, "is sending recruiting teams to Brandeis University these days. We figure they may be trying to find a Linowitz for themselves."

During the 1930's, the community of Detroit was as tolerant of anti-Semitism as any major city in the United States. Even though the first Henry Ford recanted the anti-Jewish libels printed in *The Dearborn Independent*, the weekly newspaper he purchased in 1919, recantation is a limited remedy. The old libels lingered and, in addition, new ones issued weekly from the Shrine of the Little Flower in suburban Royal Oak, where Father Charles Coughlin, the Roman

Catholic "radio priest" preached brazenly anti-Semitic sermons.

Currently, Detroit is a city of other disturbances, but the relationship between Jews and Christians in its business community has improved. To some degree, the improvement corresponds to the rise of an unusual Jewish industrialist named Max M. Fisher, whose immigrant father drove a peddler's cart near Salem, Ohio. Big, pragmatic Max Fisher earned his fortune through petroleum. He is the largest single stockholder in the Marathon Oil Company. "With a fellow like me," Fisher says, "there's never been any question whether I was Jewish or not. I've got the map of Jerusalem written all over my face."

Comfortable in his living room that overlooks a golf course, Max Fisher continues. "Now I won't try to tell anyone that there wasn't anti-Semitism around here once, and that there isn't some today, but it is not nearly as bad as some people have made it out. Any responsible journalist who wants to know about hiring policies at Ford and Chrysler can walk in, ask 'em, and get straight answers." (One who did, was told by a Ford executive, "Our policy is that we are opposed to anti-Semitism. There are unquestionably individual anti-Semites in our organization, which is enormous. But the company policy is to fight anti-Semitism where we find it.")

When Max Fisher settled in Detroit, it was generally believed that a Jew trying to do business with the big auto companies would be turned away. But Fisher developed a system for making gasoline available in the Detroit area more reasonably than anyone else, and demonstrated that, perhaps at the urging of cost accountants, the big companies were willing to deal with a Jew who could save them money.

His business success has been paralleled by his increasing community service, and prosperous Max Fisher now requires a full page to list his affiliations and community activities. These include directorships at the Detroit Museum of Arts Founders Society, the Detroit Symphony, and the Detroit Board of Commerce. He is a former president of Detroit's biggest secular charity, the United Foundation, and for all his hearty football-oriented Americanism, he has been chairman of the national United Jewish Appeal. On the way to his fortune, Max Fisher became a devout Zionist.

"And to tell you the truth, I respect him for it," says a conservative automobile executive. "I respect almost everything about Max. He's a straightforward guy. Nothing devious about him. You never have to wonder how he stands. You know," the executive says, "he's done a lot to open eyes around here to what kind of people the nicer type of Jew can be."

The benevolent presence of Max M. Fisher does not sway the extreme anti-Semite. Indeed, the extremist invents libels to explain Fisher's success. But the presence of Fisher may influence the "doubtfuls," lined up on the borders of anti-Semitism. They are more numerous and can be as dangerous as fanatics.

Even though Max Fisher's clubs include Bloomfield Open Hunt and Detroit Yacht, Jews have not been welcome to join the Detroit Athletic Club, the "D.A.C." of ten thousand business conferences, nor to gather with the golfing group at Bloomfield Hills. The influence of one individual on community attitudes is finite. "But a point about *our* town, the thing about Denver," suggests a Colorado stockbroker, "is that we've never once had a major national Jewish leadership figure like Max Fisher here. Maybe that's why things are the way they are."

Denver is a city where Christians and Jews might be well-integrated with one another. Jews have lived in Denver almost since its beginning. The city has had an interesting and attractive roster of Jewish residents, ranging from a white-bearded patriarch cattleman named Robert Lazard Miller, who rode horseback through the Denver stockyards, to a goateed, surviving patriarch, Rabbi C. E. H. Kauvar. Under editor Palmer Hoyt, *The Denver Post* is forward-looking. One of the most famous American charities, the National Jewish Hospital, located in Denver, provides treatment for thousands of consumptives, of all faiths, without charge. Yet on the testimony of its Jewish residents, the community of Denver is completely and rigidly separatist. "I don't mean," said a businessman in 1967, "just that the Denver Club won't take Jewish members, or that the country clubs are either all-Jewish or all-Christian. I mean, there doesn't seem to be much mixing anywhere, beyond necessary business contacts. We must be fifty years behind the times."

No one is certain why Denver, sprawling under the Rockies in the open West, pursues parochialism. Some blame the

Ku Klux Klan, which once possessed such power that it was able to block appropriations to the University of Colorado. Almost non-existent now, the Colorado Klan left a heritage. Some mention Denver's isolation from large population centers; it is a five-hundred mile drive to any other large city. A number of Denverites say that they feel "cut off." But talk usually comes back to the question of Jewish leadership. "If we had someone who made it really big" is a fair summary of comments. "If we had Fisher here, or Linowitz or anybody who'd get damn big, and have the guts to shake things up a little, Denver would be a better place for everybody."

Although its private clubs have grown more biased in the last fifty years, San Francisco, supposedly cosmopolitan, is reasonably well-assimilated. But so is Dallas, a city which is supposedly narrow and provincial. Joe Golman, a Jew, has been Deputy Mayor of Dallas. The curious local "super government," The Citizens Council, includes Jewish businessmen and employs a Jewish publicist, Sam Bloom. Anti-Semitism is not a simple matter of right and left, nor even of worldliness and provincialism.

As a movement, anti-Semitism has been quietly adopted by the American business community. At the moment, the movement appears to be declining. Unfortunately history, even American history, argues against forming cheery postulates from the tendencies of a few decades.

The second generation of American Jews fled menial and manual jobs so universally that there is no longer a substantial Jewish working class. Through a period of tremendous economic growth, Jews were able to leap upward, from clothes-cutter to lawyer, from tailor to electronic engineer, from peddler to store-owner or financier. It is consistent with American ethos to assume that upward mobility is continuous and that the third generation of Jews will go still farther ahead, almost automatically. Actually, there is nothing automatic about advancement and in a sense, the third generation of Jews, the grandsons of immigrants, confront more difficult problems than did their fathers.

Second-generation Jews, moving up, had the advantage of position. They started low. In addition, their rigid and sometimes simplistic values—hard work plus education equals success—suited American demands. These values and the circumstance of growing up poor fused into an enduring drive.

But third-generation Jews, the beneficiaries of so many driven successful parents, confront a more complex amalgam. Success itself is not an ideal to many of them. It is a reality, as tangible, as pleasing, and as demanding as a completely air-conditioned home.

On a number of occasions, groups of Jewish college students, gathered around tables in residence halls at midwestern universities first spoke of their parents and backgrounds with an air of superior tolerance. But as the evening proceeded and the talk became more frank, it was remarkable how their backgrounds held them chained.

"There are certain things I heard at home that I thought were wrong," said the willowy daughter of a New England physician. "There was always talk about my marrying someone Jewish. For a long time I thought, I certainly will not. But now that I'm nineteen, I've changed my mind. Marriage is complicated enough even if both people come from the same background and besides, why *not* marry somebody Jewish? I'm proud of my heritage. I try only to go with Jewish boys."

"I'd thought that I was going to teach law," said the son of an attorney from Illinois. The boy had a face without lines under straw-blond hair. "But, look, man," he said, "why fight it? The money is all in practicing. I drive a damn nice little Triumph. Maybe I'm spoiled, but I don't feel like giving up the good life that I'm used to."

An earnest, bespectacled boy from Ohio said that his father was in the scrap business in Columbus. "I tell him," the boy said, "that I'm not going to college to learn to be a junkman. But I'm sort of kidding. My father's done a lot for me and I've got to be ready to do as much for my own kids. If I end up being the only Jewish junkman in Ohio with a Masters in Business Administration, it'll be a laugh, but I have responsibilities I have to live up to."

These young people are products of households which, whatever their differences, shared a preoccupation with children. All were raised in webs of protectionism. Either or both parents wanted and demanded that the children succeed, be attractive, be secure, become educated, remain Jewish and, perhaps above all, preserve the family's hard-won respectability. The children were not encouraged to become actors, professional athletes, poets, libertines or disc jockeys. Responding, they developed into imitations of their parents. But where the parents had to struggle to crash the middle class, the children were born there. They have only to hold a place already won. That is all they propose to do. As a result they are predictable and, at length, dull. "Some of them," one Jewish economics professor remarks of his Jewish students, "are dull enough to be fifth-generation Protestants."

Young Jewish rebels do not often follow an expected course; a number make a partial revolution. With name-changing and plastic surgery, any American with means can choose not to be Chosen. Would-be rebels opt out of Judaism readily, rejecting the lofty Judaic elements preached, if not always practiced, in their homes. But many accept the other element, American materialism. Some become hustlers.

One quality of the Jewish hustler, who believes he has broken with the past, is insensitivity to the needs of other Jews. He identifies less with other Jews than he does with other hustlers. He may well be a hustler not because he is Jewish but in spite of it. He enjoys hustling. The ancient compassion is buried. *Tzedakah* is unknown.

He says to hell with the fatcat suburb where his fatcat parents raised him. He says to hell with the fatcat parents. He says he is a different kind of cat. But for all the arrogant, rebellious words, he—like Dad and Mom and Dr. Lieberman next door (and Mr. Wilkes across the street)—covets the buck.

## MARGINALIA

The walls are papered in peppermint stripes which match the stripes on Myron Berman's tapered shirt. "I've got seven shirts exactly like this," Myron announces to the newspaper reporter who has come to interview him, "and when the shirts wear out, I'm gonna change the wallpaper." Myron laughs. "What do you drink?" he says, and pushes a button on a free-form desk.

"Scotch," the newspaper reporter says.

"Don't let me bribe you, baby," Myron Berman says.

"With water," the reporter says. "I don't sell out for just one drink."

Myron laughs again. "That's a good one," he says. A pug-nosed blonde waitress, wearing a hip-high skirt and black lace tockings eases into the room. "Scotch and *aqua* for him, and he usual for me," Myron says, "and on the way out, show the ress your waggle."

The girl turns and walks away, pumping her hips enthusiastically, the way ice skaters do, cranking toward full speed.

"She used to dance for me," Myron says. "Good can, bad eet."

Myron Berman's office, in the night club called La Vie en Rose, is overwhelmingly obscene. The peppermint striped wallpaper is crowded with photographs of hard-looking girls, most of whom are naked. Some grin brassily. Others pout. A few of the girls in the pictures press their hands against their breasts and gaze open-mouthed. "I suppose," Myron says, "you want to know about the obscenity charge and my arrest."

"That's what my editor sent me here for," the reporter says. "Charley Feldman. He says, get a Sunday feature on what's a nice Jewish boy doing facing an obscenity rap."

"Jewish got nothing to do with it," Myron Berman says. "But sure, I'll tell you anything I can, provided you don't try to make me look bad or dirty." Myron leans on the free-form desk. He is a short man of thirty, small-featured and immaculate. His fingernails glisten and he wears a vest. "What we are trying to do here," he says, "is come to grips with something important. All of us. Me, the dancers, everybody. As I see it, the issue is not that I, Myron Berman, and she, Marilyn Esther Wolf, jointly conspired to commit an obscene act. The issue is deeper than that." Myron sits forward. "Is there any such thing as obscenity? That's got nothing to do with being Jewish or what. It's something bigger. It's basic."

"I didn't mean to offend you," the reporter says. "Our Sunday editor, Charley Feldman, is Jewish himself."

"I'm not through explaining," Myron says.

The office door opens and the waitress walks in and puts the Scotch and a pony of brandy on the desk. "Thanks, Charlene," Myron says. "You're doing just fine, baby." She turns to go and Myron says, "You certainly got a nice ass." Charlene looks back, smiling harshly.

"Over here," Myron says to the reporter. "I want to show you Charlene's picture on my wall."

The girl retreats.

"Let's get back to that obscenity point," the reporter says.

"Take your time," Myron says. "We got no hurry. Take your time, feast your eyes and drink your drink."

In the North Beach section of San Francisco night-clubs are an economic staple. Daylight exposes the age and shabbiness of buildings in the district; by day North Beach is quiet and full garbage pails stand beside doors. But at night, cabs prowl, lights beckon, doormen urge and tourists surrender to extravagant claims of wickedness.

Across years, the North Beach clubs have changed names and styles and decor to suit tourists, and enrich or bankrupt a variety of owners. With time, it has become increasingly difficult to determine the ownership of the clubs. Rumors in San Francisco suggest that they belong to a mixed band of politicians, or that they are Mafia property, or that they are a secret profitable possession of some of California's oldest families. No one is certain. The owners have no offices in the clubs. Only the managers are visible, and the dancers.

The girls appear in the bottoms of bikini bathing suits and dance the frug or twist or swim. They work on stages and on bartops and between tables, twirling arms and breasts above the tourists' heads. Recorded music plays. The bands are gone. The beat goes rum-rum-bippety, rum-rum-bippety, rum-rum-bippety, rum-rum.

Myron Berman is the youngest of the men who manage nightclubs in San Francisco. He is also the brightest and the most ambitious. He worked as a show business columnist for a throw-away newspaper at sixty-five dollars a week, selling mentions in the column for two to five dollars, before becoming manager of La Vie en Rose, for a flat fifteen thousand dollars a year. He needs every cent he earns. He makes alimony payments of $613.75 a month.

When he was hired, Myron recruited girls who were particularly attractive, particularly busty and for whom he devised unusual costumes. One bikini bottom was spotted leopard. Another was zebra-striped. A Negro dancer wore a bottom of white silk. The girls were lively and word spread that the entertainment at La Vie was worth the four-dollar minimum. Receipts climbed, which pleased Mr. Crocco, the short gruff man who had hired Myron. He was the agent for "a group," Mr. Crocco said. "You must be a pretty bright guy to do so much business," Mr. Crocco told Myron, who beamed. But presently as the novelty of toplessness waned, receipts at La Vie fell.

"Maybe I was wrong. Maybe you're not so bright," Mr.

Crocco said then. "Maybe you, with the fancy office, aren't so smart."

"Don't worry," Myron said. "Just don't worry."

"I am worrying," Mr. Crocco said, "and you better worry, too."

An idea came to Myron, the following night. He drank three ponies of brandy, cleared two visitors from his office and sent for Marilyn Esther Wolf, the bustiest of his dancers. He told Marilyn to get undressed.

"Can't you wait, Mike?" she said. "I got another show to do."

"Just undress," Myron said. "Just undress and turn around a couple times."

She took off a pink chemise and a bikini top and a pink bikini bottom. She had huge breasts and swelling thighs and buttocks.

"Would you do something like that out there?" Myron Berman said. He pointed toward the club, beyond his door.

"I don't know," Marilyn said. "In the altogether?"

"You've been a model," Myron said. "Look, fifteen dollars more a week. That'll make it ninety-five dollars even."

"Well," Marilyn said. "All right. But no publicity. You have to promise me that."

A motion picture called *The Girl on the Red Velvet Swing* lent Myron inspiration. Marilyn was to sit naked, rocking for five minutes, to a slow beat version of the song "Night Train," perched on a *black* velvet swing.

The idea did not excite Mr. Crocco. "You can do just so much," he said. "The cops, even the cops *here,* only let you get away with just so much."

"Can't you fix the cops?" Myron said.

"I fix nothing," Mr. Crocco said. "You want to get yourself arrested, you got some girl willing, go ahead."

On the second night of the performance, called Nude Descending, two San Francisco plainclothesmen served summonses on Myron and Marilyn. The girl wept. She said she was crying because her name was going to get in the papers and her family would see. But the club's attorney, Eddie Cohn, explained in one sibilant sentence, that all she faced was a civil charge, and that the worst the judge could do was sock her $250, which the club should pay anyway, and, besides, there was a silly kind of glamor to this sort of publicity that was significant. With Mike, the lawyer said, matters were different. Technically, he faced a criminal charge. He could get thirty days in the workhouse.

"I consider myself a rebel with a cause," Mike Berman announces to the reporter from the *San Francisco Sun*. "My cause is that obscenity exists only in obscene minds. When my case comes up in a couple of months, I'm going to tell exactly that to the judge."

"You from around here?" the reporter says.

"South," Myron says, "near San Diego."

"Are your parents still there?"

"Leave them out of this."

"Okay," the reporter says.

"I consider myself a rebel against them, too. Mainly against them, maybe. You ready for another drink?"

"Sure."

"My parents are what you call typical upper-middle class," Myron says. "My father's got a law degree, but he's in the liquor business. My mother's in all the clubs. Hadassah. You know what Hadassah is?"

"I think I've heard of it."

"Hadassah," Myron says. "The plural of *yenta* is *Hadassah*. Jewish joke. It's an organization of Jewish ladies. Upper middle cass. The Jewish D.A.R. Well, my parents put on this front of being the most moral, apple-pie, sweet square things, but they're not. They can be killers, do you know what I mean?"

Charlene reappears with drinks and Myron ignores her. "They almost killed me. I'm no dope, right? No idiot. You can see that, can't you? Now don't use any of this about my parents. I'm just telling you for background, so you can understand. But mother, Miss Hadassah Virgin of the ages, tried to cut my balls off. You want to know how?"

The reporter sits erect. "How?" he says.

"She wouldn't let me be a man. In school, I get a B, it should be A-minus. I get an A-minus, it should be an A-plus. I want to study English, she says I got to be a doctor. My father sits there like he don't care. Maybe he's got a dame downtown. Good God, I hope so.

"I'm twenty years old and a junior at U.S.C. and I knock up a girl. I'm in love with her, as it happens, but anyway, I knock her up. I go to my Mom and tell her. She said she always wanted me to be honest with her. She said she didn't care what I did, as long as she heard it from my own lips. I tell her about the pregnant girl, my wife-to-be, and Mom looks hurt, terribly hurt, as if I knifed her. As if I stuck it into her. But she'll help me. I'm her son. She owes me that. *What's the girl's name,* she wants to know. I tell her, *Carol McKenna.* All of a sudden, Mother don't look hurt any more. She's furious. *A shicksa, you slept with? Not a Jewish girl? A lousy tramp of a shicksa?* And all of a sudden, because I went to bed with a girl I loved, I'm a dirty, lousy, no-good bum."

Myron finishes his brandy. "You don't know me very well, mister."

"Flagg," the reporter says.

"Mr. Flagg, the one thing you'll find out about me is that I despise hypocrisy. When I found it in my own parents, I took off. I mean I'm not in touch with them any more at all. And that costs, you know. I had to have a little analysis a while ago.

"I go to my Dad, after this happens. I tell him I got a problem with this girl. My old man don't care whether she's Jewish or Coptic. He just sees dollar signs. He tells me *You got into it, kid. You get yourself out.* I say, all the time you made me go to Hebrew school they taught me charity and looking out for the other person. My father says *Charity has a place. That's what the Federation is for. But you're talking about something else, and son, a dollar is a dollar. I can't run our home like a charity bazaar.*"

"I wish I could use some of this," the reporter says.

"I don't know," Myron says.

"Well there won't be room for all that personal stuff, anyway," the reporter says.

"Yeah. Don't use it," Myron says. "Any other questions?"

"The bottomless girl is still working?"

"That's right. We reached what you'd call an accommodation."

"She still comes down on the swing and everything?"

"Look, kid," Myron says. "The cops aren't looking to make trouble. They don't want to close us up. We got the word, and this is strictly between you and me, that they don't care what she wears as long as she wears something, down there."

"So what's she wearing?"

"A band-aid," Myron says.

"What?" the reporter says.

"I swear to God," Myron says.

La Vie en Rose occupies the site of a speakeasy that, after prohibition, became a nightclub called The Barbary. The Barbary was a barn of a club, three tiers high, with two huge, polished mahogany bars and a surfeit of mirrors. Presently the Barbary became The Gay Nineties; down came the mirrors and up went paintings of plump, pink nudes. Fifteen years ago, La Vie en Rose supplanted The Gay Nineties and began offering commercial jazz and comedy, with limited success. Big money came with the topless dancers.

Now, as the reporter walks in at the main level with Mike Berman, the history shows its marks. The bartenders are gone, but the heavy wooden bars remain. A bare-breasted girl is dancing on each. Both have small breasts and appear to be bored. At the rear of the main level is the bandstand, built for The Gay Nineties, bandless now, on which a topless Negro girl writhes gracefully.

"We got the upper tier closed tonight," Myron says to Mr. Flagg, the reporter. "Tuesday is always slow."

The center of the main level floor has been cut away, and a wrought-iron railing guards the edge. Below, two other topless dancers work on smaller bars. In the center of the lower level is a pit, into which Marilyn Esther Wolf, the bottomless girl, descends.

"I'd like to talk to the bottomless one," the reporter says.

"I dunno, kid," Myron says. "An arrest for obscenity is not something a girl wants advertised. Come on. We'll sit by the railing. That way you can see the broads downstairs, too."

La Vie is lighted by dim lamps and small spotlights playing on the dancing girls. The music rattles over loudspeakers, fed by an endlessly repeated tape. Mr. Flagg, the newspaper reporter, gapes at the Negro girl. "Nothing," Myron says. "Wait till you catch Marilyn."

One by one, the small spotlights in La Vie en Rose go out. Bare-breasted girls bounce down from bars and walk briskly toward dressing cubicles. Finally the Negro girl is dancing alone in her white bottom on the abandoned bandstand. When she is through, the audience applauds lightly.

"No more than forty-five here," Myron says. "My arrest probably keeps some of the middle-class squares away."

"Night Train" beats slowly, and a spotlight finds Marilyn Esther Wolf, in pink chemise, on the black velvet swing. Her meaty legs are crossed above the knee. She holds a swing rope with her right hand. Her left arm is drawn across her bodice. The swing descends slowly and Marilyn stares into the light, the corners of her wide mouth smiling slightly.

The audience watches in total silence. The swing descends. Marilyn holds the swing ropes with both hands. Long black hair trails down her back. Her bodice falls open. Her breasts are white and enormous.

"Mah-ma," a man says.

Marilyn swings to and fro. Her face is long, thick-lipped and sensual. She shudders and the chemise falls from her body. She is swinging, a dark Jewish girl, with enormous breasts and shaven pubis, rocking naked on a swing behind crossed legs.

"Couple of tank cars," says the man.

"Don't forget the band-aid," Myron says to the reporter.

Marilyn's long face, still smiling into the spotlight, is vacant now. Her dark eyes hollow away.


What Marilyn does while she is swinging is remember things. It is easy once you learn the trick. You stare at the spotlight and then you can't see very well, and you stare a little to a side of the light and you can see nothing, but the music is pleasant and the rocking is gentle and it is a good time to remember home.

She comes from Brooklyn. It bothers her that people think it's a joke when they find out. She doesn't know what Brooklyn is like now, but when she grew up there on Union Street, in a big private house, it was very respectable. The house was four stories high. Grandpa, who started the business that supported them, was sick and had to stay in bed all the time. He lived on the ground floor with Grandma. All the rest of the house was for Mama and Papa and Marilyn. It was good to be an only child with four adults.

Grandma always wanted her to eat. Grandma was always feeding her, blintzes and flanken, and chicken soup and borscht. Whatever happened, Grandma said, eat and everything will be all right.

No, Mama said. Mama was arguing with Grandma. "It isn't as if she were a boy," Mama said. "She'll have a figure to worry about. Childhood eating habits are important and I'll thank you not to make my daughter a chronic overeater."

"Have a little more chicken," Grandma said, ignoring Mama.

"No," Mama said. "The child has already stuffed herself and chewed with her mouth open. How will you ever be a lady, Marilyn?"

Mama liked to dress her. The way Grandma always made her eat, Mama always made her try on clothes. Pink was Mama's favorite color. Since Daddy was in the business, Mama could get all the children's clothing she wanted, but Mama said that Dad, and Grandpa before him, worked very hard so she could have these clothes.

"Yes, Mama."

"I dress you up so you look pretty, Marilyn."

"The boys will come soon enough," Grandma said.

"Not for any boy am I dressing Marilyn," Mama said. "Would boys appreciate this little flowered print? Such delicacy. See the ruffle lines around the neck. No boy could appreciate that. I dress you for me, Marilyn, so you will be a daughter I can be proud of. You understand that, Marilyn, my darling? I dress you to make a little doll for my very own."

The spotlight cuts suddenly and a recorded wolf howl carries over the loudspeakers at La Vie en Rose. Marilyn's act is over. Act One. She will go out on the swing four more times tonight. The show at La Vie en Rose is continuous.

"I got to talk to her," Mr. Flagg, the reporter tells Myron Berman.

"Okay, okay, you can talk to the help. But I don't see how it will do much for your story. The story's right here. The story's me."

Myron introduces the reporter to Marilyn Esther Wolf at a side table, far from the rail. It would be awkward and possibly illegal for Marilyn to go walking across the main level floor after her performance. She wears the pink chemise she wore on the swing, but the light where they sit is poor and Mr. Flagg cannot tell whether she has put on underwear. Her face, from this close, is older than it seemed when she was swinging. The nose is broader. Coarseness is invading Marilyn Esther Wolf, who is about to become twenty-eight years old.

"Jesus Christ, I need a Scotch," Marilyn says to Myron. She smiles at Mr. Flagg. "What's your first name?"

"Benson."

"Well, Ben, you can have a Scotch with me, if Mike says it's okay, but you can't touch me. That's the law. If they catch an entertainer touching the customer, or vicey-versey, they can close the place down. I'm learning a lot about the law lately."

"If you promise not to touch me," Ben Flagg says, "I'll promise to try not to touch you."

"He's cute," Marilyn says to Myron Berman. "Look, if you write anything that I say, could you do me a favor? Could you promise not to use my name?"

"I'll use it, but in a way you'll like."

"No. It's not that. It's not something you'd understand."

"With her it's a family thing," Myron says.

"A Jewish family thing," Marilyn corrects. "You don't come from a Jewish family, do you, Ben?"

"Not exactly."

"Well, you can't imagine this, but I've got an uncle in Brooklyn and I can just hear him after he reads a story about me, saying, *that is work for a Jewish girl?*"

Ben Flagg stares silent, noncommittal. "Fuck the rules," Marilyn says. "If I have another drink, I may let you touch me."

"If I don't tell your uncle?" Ben Flagg says.

"No," Marilyn said. "Touching is something else. Touching is Mama."

"Do you drink a lot?" Ben Flagg wants to know.

"I write," Marilyn says. "Did Mike tell you I'm a writer?"

"I mean, do you have to get tanked to get on the swing?" the reporter says.

"I might fall off if I was smashed. But right now I want another drink, Mike." Marilyn finishes the first drink and says to the reporter, "I write short stories."

"I write them myself once in a while," Ben Flagg says. "You want to let me see what you got? We publish fiction in the Sunday section."

"Oh?" Marilyn says. "That's right. Look, I got some."

"Lemme come around and maybe we have lunch tomorrow and you show me what you got and we'll see."

"Some of my writing is really good."

"Where's the can, Mike?" Ben Flagg says.

After the reporter gets up, Myron puts a hand on Marilyn's shoulder and says, "I warn you. You know he's only coming around to lay you."

"So?" Marilyn says. "Is that so awful? Does that mean we can't have some good writing talk? He is a reporter. He makes a living writing."

"He's also married," Mike says. "Didn't you see the ring?"

Marilyn waves an arm wildly. "Thirty-five hundred miles I come from Brooklyn," she says looking up at the ceiling, "to work for a swinger. Such a swinger. I haven't seen such a swinger since Mama died."

On the black velvet swing, Marilyn looks at the light and then a little to the side and remembers that Mama was a very moral person and hardworking and efficient and not once could Marilyn remember seeing Mama be affectionate to Dad. Sometimes he tried to kiss her, and she let him but Mama always went stiff and set her teeth and sometimes afterward, after those sometimes, she came to Marilyn for a little talk. She told Marilyn about dressing; even though Marilyn was fourteen now, that was still not too old for pink. Mama gave Marilyn a big brass bracelet and a matching necklace and helped Marilyn do her hair swept up, in a way that made her look older, and when Mama stepped back to see her girl, she said she wanted to cry. "So grown up," Mama said, "and so luscious." And Mama gave Marilyn a kiss on the forehead.

Marilyn smiled at Mama. "I guess I'm going to have to worry about the boys," she said.

Mama set her teeth and said, "I want to explain something, Marilyn. You're a very attractive young lady, nicely groomed, and you can wear good jewelry. It goes well on you, like pink.

"Sure you are going to have to worry about the boys," Mama said, "but they are something every girl has to worry about. That's why every girl has to be good."

"I'm good," Marilyn said.

"What a boy sees in a pretty girl is not what your mother sees, Marilyn. He may see something a little different. A little —you know—dirty. And he could be a very nice boy. It's just that he can't help it. It's just that he is a boy, and thinking those kind of thoughts is a part of being one of them."

Marilyn felt herself turning red. "I don't understand," she said.

"You know about babies," Mama said. "You know about having them."

"Yes."

"The pain is terrible," Mama said. "You have no idea. Think of your monthly cramps, only a hundred times worse. A thousand. Boys don't understand about that. Men, either. When they see a woman, they think about what they want and how they can get it, not how much it will hurt the woman."

"Even Jewish boys like Marvin Weinberg?"

"Even Jewish boys," Mama said.

Marilyn gasped before she asked the next question.

"Even Daddy?" she said.

"Especially Daddy," Mama said.

Ben Flagg is more interested in Marilyn's second act than he was in her first. Myron Berman has moved him back to the table near the rail and the newspaperman sits forward, hand on chin, staring at the great pale breasts. "Jesus," Flagg says to Myron. "Geez-zus. She's not your girl, or anything like that?"

"Take it easy," Myron says. He is put off by this reporter, but he may have him hooked and if he has Ben Flagg maybe he has Flagg's editor, and maybe he has the story, and to hell with the trial, Myron thinks. If he gets the right newspaper story, he'll be all right, nationwide.

"Look, Ben," Myron says, "when we get done watching here, there's something I can show you. And you can write it up some time, but not real soon."

Flagg is lost, staring.

"It'll be terrific, but you can't write it up now."

"Sure," Ben Flagg says, all teeth and eyeglasses. "Any way you want to play it, Mike."

"Okay. Let's get back to that side table. She's about through."

Marilyn glides in, sober, poised, carrying a folder. "I got one short story here to show you, Ben."

"I can't buy," Ben Flagg says. "I don't do the buying for the paper."

"But you can help." Marilyn puts the short story, which is

four pages long, on the table near the center light. "You can read it now," she says. "It's called *The Funeral.*"

*The Funeral* is not a good short story. Along the margins and at the end of *The Funeral*, a teacher has written comments. The comments are like the story. They are not good, either. They are preoccupied with detail, and miss the whole.

"I don't know," Ben Flagg says. "I've had a couple drinks. It might be hard for me to concentrate."

"Just try," Marilyn says. "I'm only asking you to try. I mean, it isn't a very long short story."

*The Funeral* describes the death of the mother in a Brooklyn Jewish family, as her only child, a daughter, sees it. The mother is a dominant woman, but her cancer is painful and she lies at home dying slowly, weeping. A doctor comes every day and gives the woman injections. But she dies. The daughter cries and cries. She knows that her mother's death is something she will not get over, ever, and she wants to dress up for the funeral. She knows how important it was to her dead mother that she dress very beautifully, and she decides that for the funeral she will wear a pink dress, her mother's favorite. But the father, who is shadowy, insists that pink is not suitable, and that she will have to wear black. The daughter does as she is ordered, but cries out wildly, at the end, at her shadowy father. "I hate you. You wouldn't let me wear the pink, and dress up pretty for *her!*"

"The thing is," Marilyn says, "the family is *Jewish*, and Jewish families are very close."

"Yeah. I got it. I get that," Ben Flagg says.

"The stuff I have to show you," Mike Berman says, "is psychedelic."

"Well, I better go get dressed," Marilyn says.

"Undressed, you mean," Mike says.

Marilyn feels let down. Showing a short story is an intimate thing and the reporter's failure to react strips and embarrasses her. Even Professor Goodstein, at the University Extension, liked *The Funeral*. It was her best short story, he said. Marilyn Esther Wolf walks dully into the dressing room and places her best short story, *The Funeral*, in a drawer in her night table. She would not allow the *San Francisco Sun* to publish it, she decides.

She certainly went through a crazy time when her real Mama died. Daddy shriveled. She had always thought so much of Daddy; she thought that Mama hurt him, but now, when he was left alone, and free, there was nothing there. He was routed out with work. When he came home, he sat before a newspaper, saying nothing. Even when Marilyn told him that she wanted to quit Long Island University, Daddy did not put down his *New York Post*. "For a woman," he said, reading, "college is not as important as for a man. Your mother never went to college at all."

Marilyn went to live in Greenwich Village with another girl. They were going to be dancers. Papa said he would help her out for a year, but before the year ended, the girl friend was married and Marilyn had stopped taking money from home. She liked the feeling of living alone, and she found that she could support herself as a photographer's model.

She had an affair. One of the photographers started her. He was older; she liked men who were older. He took her to a party and afterward, in her one-room apartment, he said, "Can I put you to bed?"

"What do you mean?"

"Undress you and put you to bed."

"Well, I guess so," Marilyn said. "You're all right."

"Just like you were a little girl."

"Oh yes," Marilyn said, enthusiastically.

She developed a relaxed, anesthetic attitude toward sex. It was something nice to do for people who were nice. She had no deep sense of sexuality. When she lay with a man, she felt neither commitment nor pleasure. She would whisper to herself, over and over, I'm doing something nice for someone nice.

Five years after the first affair, a married photographer named Ira Cohen announced to Marilyn that if he ever fell in love with anyone beside his wife, it would be with her.

"Why do you say that?" Marilyn asked. They were sitting on the floor of a loft, where Marilyn had posed, nude, except for a white apron, sitting on a three-legged stool. The photograph was entitled "Milkmaid," and the joke was that Marilyn leaned forward, so that her large breasts swung.

"I was looking at you while you were posing and I can tell, looking at you, that you're a real woman," Ira said, "which is what a real man needs."

He expected a wildness in Marilyn, and when she failed him, he said he was going to find out what the reason was, if it killed him.

"There isn't any reason," Marilyn said. "This is the way I am."

"No," Ira cried. "There's more to you, more to all of us, than we realize. What are you, Marilyn? You a Jewish girl?"

"Sure I'm Jewish."

"I've outgrown it," Ira said.

"How can you outgrow Judaism?" Marilyn said. She sat up in bed, and Ira fell toward her breasts. She pushed him away and said, "I want to talk." She put on a robe and went to a pile of square orange cushions that stood in one corner of his studio apartment, where, he said, his wife never came. He followed, reaching for his pants, and sat in a canvas chair, under two bullfight posters.

"I believe in Zen," Ira said.

"Judaism is the Golden Rule," Marilyn said. "I learned that at Sunday school in Brooklyn. How can you outgrow the Golden Rule?"

"Zen is large," Ira said. "More huge. What is the Golden Rule exactly, anyway?"

*"That which is hateful to thyself, do not to thy neighbor,* is what they taught us in Sunday school."

"You see that," Ira said. "Zen is bigger. It doesn't concern itself just with people. It deals with nature and the universe. The idea is to be natural, understand, and passion is natural. The idea is to be a natural part of the universe." Ira Cohen recited:

> The Being still as stone.
> The Mind as dead leaves silent on a tomb.
> Here is understanding
> Beyond striving toward content.

Marilyn was not sure she understood the poem, but she liked the part about dead leaves on a tomb. Her own mind felt like that to her sometimes. Ira lent her a book on Zen, which she found heavy and confusing, but to please Ira she agreed to follow Zen philosophy, too.

Ira would not permit her to use her diaphragm. "It pollutes a natural thing," he said. Marilyn had always been very careful, but the naturalness seemed to be important to Ira and it seemed to be right. Ira said she was getting wilder now, although she felt no more than before.

After she missed the second period, Marilyn knew that she

was pregnant. She didn't mind. She was afraid, but she didn't mind. With Mama gone, it was almost her duty to have a baby. "I hope it's a girl," she said to Ira Cohen.

He was big and black-haired with a blue chin that hurt her cheek. "Jesus Christ, what the hell are you talking about?" Ira said.

"I hope we have a little girl," Marilyn said. "I suppose you want a boy. Most men do, I suppose."

"Where the hell did you get that idea?" he said. Very suddenly he was stamping up and down the bare little apartment.

"I just supposed," Marilyn said, "that most men would like to make something like themselves. That's natural."

"You know I'm married," Ira said. "She won't divorce me. The lawyer says I've got to wait her out."

"We can still have the baby," Marilyn said.

"How?" Ira said. "The lawyer says it could be years. How can you have the baby?"

"I'll just have it, that's how," Marilyn said. "You're always talking about being so integrated with nature and here we are with a real chance, Ira."

"Look, Mar'," Ira said. "I know you're right in theory. I agree with you. But for God's sake, we got to be practical. I mean we're not set up to raise a kid. I mean it wouldn't be right, not so much for us, but it wouldn't be fair to the kid."

"I want my baby," Marilyn said. She began to cry.

"Now, look," Ira said, "you can cut that crap out right now. There isn't any baby. You know that as well as I. You know what there is. A frog maybe, or a fish."

"I want my baby," Marilyn said.

"I'll tell you what, Marilyn," Ira said, evenly. "You can have your baby, but I got this one condition I got to stick you with. You and your frogfishbaby in your gut, get the hell out of my pad. I don't know you. I don't want you. I don't want to see you again."

She got up and stopped crying and went back to where she had been living before. The next afternoon, a man with a beard rang her bell and handed her an envelope. In it was $250 and a note from Ira. "My lawyer says you've got this coming."

It was the Zen, Marilyn thought. She could never let herself stop being Jewish. She had to leave. A photographer gave her the names of some people in an art school in San Francisco who would take her in. She spent most of the money

Ira gave her by buying a first-class ticket. Through the long
flight, she thought how phony Zen philosophy was. You
couldn't be sure about someone who followed Zen. At least
with a Jewish person, you know where he really stands.

The art school was a series of lofts. There were three or
four other girls and four or five artists. They all slept on the
floor of the lofts and there was an easy sharing of money and
women. Marilyn's man was Pete and sometimes Greg. They
talked about Zen, too, but they didn't care that she was Jewish or try to convert her. When the other girls found out she
was pregnant, everyone except Noreen told her to have an
abortion. "I'm Catholic," Noreen explained.

"Well, look," Marilyn said. "I'm Jewish."

"*Nu?*" Pete said.

"Well, I want to keep the baby. You know, like Noreen's
Catholic, I'm Jewish."

"Man," Greg said, "we don't care watcha are, long as ya
swing."

"You don't understand," Marilyn said.

"*Nu?*" Pete said.

"I want my baby to be Jewish," Marilyn said.

"Ain' he got enough trouble jus' bein' colored?" Greg said.

"What's *nu?*" Pete said.

"Give her some more wine, f'chrisake," Greg said, kindly.

They collected one hundred dollars and told her Noreen
would go to Mexico with her. Marilyn took a little wine in
the morning and felt crazy drunk, just from three small
glasses. Noreen had to help her on the bus.

He was some kind of spic Mexican with a thin black mustache and high cheekbones but he wore a white jacket like a
real doctor and he asked her questions in the same cold way.

"Date of last period?"

"I don't know exactly."

"Previous births?"

"None. I didn't have any others, Doctor. I'm not the kind
of girl that gets into trouble."

He nodded, rising and handed her a short white gown.
"Get undressed," he said, "and put on this, please. You must
pay me now."

She counted out the ten tens. She was glad that the Mexican doctor took the American money. She could tell now that
he was a really nice man. She stood up and took off her
blouse.

"There is a screen."

"Oh," Marilyn said. "You see I'm a model and I pose for artists all the time so it doesn't mean as much to me as it probably does to your other patients."

She lay on the table on her back, her legs strapped into supports. He was a nice man. "There will be no pain," he said.

"Oh, I know that," Marilyn said. "You know, at first I didn't think I wanted this, but now that I've met you and all, I'm really glad. It wouldn't be right for the little baby, not having a real father, would it?"

Another woman was in the room. Marilyn was startled to see that the woman was wearing street clothes, a black flowered dress, not whites. "She will help with the gas," the man said. "Do as she says, and there will be no pain."

"I trust you, Doctor," Marilyn said. "I really do, and this is the right thing I'm doing, isn't it?"

Some sort of cone came over her mouth and something began to stab inside her toward her baby. It would stab her baby. It would kill it. Marilyn tried to close her legs but they were strapped. She writhed.

"Breathe," ordered the woman's voice.

"No. I will not let you do this to me. Get away from me. Get out of me. Get away from my baby." Marilyn shrieked a long desperate cry and the Mexican abortionist heard a rasping moan.

"Out?" he asked.

"Yes, now."

He had Marilyn's womb scraped clean in four minutes. She hardly bled at all.

She has come down from the ceiling again and the rubes press around the rail in a crush. It is later now and the rubes are loud. They come from Ottumwa, and Albert Lea and San Jose and they are churchmen who try not to beat their wives, and back home, add *Pardon me, ma'am* whenever they mouth a hell or damn. But they are not home, the rubes are at La Vie en Rose, drinking in the half-light, and they press against the rail, looking down at the big, beautiful boobs the Lord God of Israel has given Marilyn Esther Wolf, who is childless. The rubes say:

"Anything over a mouthful is a waste."

"Hey, girlie. Uncross your legs."

And the rubes giggle.

The girl on the swing does not hear. She is rocking back and forth pretending that she still wears the pink chemise and that out there, beyond the light, seeing the chemise, is Mama. The girl on the swing knows that she has been bad. She has let men touch her and that is why they have taken her baby away. But Mama is talking nicely to her. "Good girl, good girl," Mama is saying.

"Yes, Mama," Marilyn says. "No one can touch me while I am on the swing."

Myron Berman has taken the rube reporter into his office. "This idea of mine is psychedelic," Myron says. He puts a screen in front of a patch of peppermint wallpaper and turns on a machine that projects light through two wildly colored, concentric discs. The discs rotate at different speeds and the screen crawls with slowly changing blobs of purples, greens and yellows.

"That's my next idea," Myron says. "I get a lot of girls, and put them up on the bandstand, bottomless, and then I run these crazy patterns on their cans. Like LSD without the headaches. How do you like that?"

"You gonna use this instead of Marilyn?" asks Ben Flagg.

"After a while," Myron says. "You can't ride one horse forever. Besides, when my obscenity case comes up, the judge may really make us drop her act."

"I wonder what will happen to Marilyn then," the reporter says.

"Mister," Mike Berman says, "I'll tell you one thing I believe. Business is business. A dollar is a dollar. I'm not running any charity bazaar."

Troops of right-wing demagogues claim to know the Jew as businessman. Reshaped, his heritage distorted, he makes a splendid frame on which to mount a diatribe.

*How can the Jew in business be moral, when he knows no Christ?* the Rightist demagogue inquires. *Observe the aggressions of the Jew. Good Christians do not push that way. The Jew, who knows no Christ, lacks standards or morality. Venality,* says the demagogue, *thy name is Israel.* But this is not merely talk from the right or from the gutter. "Let us," proposed one famous theoretician, "look at the real Jew of our time.

"What is the Jew's foundation in our world?

"Material necessity.

"What is the object of the Jew's worship in this world?

"Usury.

"What is his worldly God?

"Money."

The composer of this catechistic exercise was not Hitler, raised on the catechisms of Austrian Catholicism, but Heinrich Karl Marx, founder of Communism, born a Jew in the Rhineland town of Treves. In his tract, *The Jewish Question*, Karl Marx had more to say. "The Jew has emancipated himself," he observed, "not only by taking to himself financial power, but by virtue of the fact that money has become a world power and the practical Jewish spirit has become the practical spirit of Christian nations."

Although these passages can be regarded as illuminating Marx's mental processes, their present significance is to be found elsewhere. They have shaped an absurd alliance of Marx and the extreme Right.

Even in the United States, hardly fertile country for Leftism, Jews have published radical newspapers, delivered radical speeches, formed radical unions and run for office as radicals under the anti-materialist banner of Marx.

Such activities disturb the right-wing demagogue and, when he is done attacking the venal Jewish businessman, he turns to the Jewish radical.

*A grave danger of all we hold dear*, says the demagogue, *lies in the international atheist Marxist Jew*.

*The danger*, cries the demagogue, *is the real Jew of our time*.

The right-wing demagogue does not know that he is quoting Karl Marx.

No Jewish Left survives in America. To be sure, there are individual Jewish Leftists, but Jewish Leftism as a body is no more. At least two factors smothered it, and a third—Negro anti-Semitism—works against its revival.

Generally, Leftism in America has been describing an extended decline. Running as a Socialist, as well as a Progressive, Robert LaFollette drew 4,822,856 votes for President in 1924; eight years later in 1932, the combined vote of the Socialist, Socialist-Labor and Communist parties exceeded one million. In 1948, drawing on a substantially increased electorate, Henry Wallace was unable to swell that figure significantly. The decline of the American Left, considered by itself, is highly complex. The Jewish Left has slipped along with the larger general descent.

A specific factor moving Jews toward Right and Center has been their remarkable second-generation success. "My father was a Socialist," the Jewish owner of a fruit canning factory reports, "but for only one reason. He never saw a thousand dollars in his life. Give any Socialist a thousand—make it ten thousand these days—and right away he becomes a capitalist." The businessman himself is a moderate Republican, as far from the Left as he can go without coming uncomfortably close to right-wing demagogues.

Historically, leaders of revolutionary movements, such as Marx, have often come from the successful middle class, but the middle class is no breeding ground for a radical rank and file. Rank-and-filers come from underneath, marching for bread or recognition or freedom. Most Jews have won all three in the United States. They feel that their marching days are done.

The most popular of recent liberal causes, the Negro effort toward full citizenship, once was vastly popular with Jews. No longer. Extreme and vocal elements of the Negro community have adopted anti-Semitism as an article of their manifesto and young Jews, joining Negro movements, may presently be shocked, disenchanted or abused.

One Negro, who operates a successful business in Harlem, preaches the characteristic *Black Case Against the Jew*. "The Jew is guilty," he says, "of living a lie in America. He is trying to become a part of the white Protestant majority.

"The Jew knows Christianity doesn't work, but he won't say so out loud. He tells the colored man to pray. The Jew knows that won't do any good. You think he prays himself? He works like hell.

"The Jew comes into a colored neighborhood and sells a clothes washer for $299. Same washer goes for $169 in a Jew neighborhood. The Jew comes and tells the colored man, *Ten dollars down and just tell me your job and you got the washer*.

"Now, the colored man signs a paper and the Jew who owns the store, he sells that paper to a credit company, which is Jewish, and when the poor Afro-American can't make some payment, a Jew lawyer draws up a summons, and a Jew marshall comes around with it. The Jews take the washer away so they can sell it again, and the poor Afro-American, he got maybe two bucks in his pocket, and he's failed his family and he wants to run, and he feels so bad. He just goes down to a liquor store and puts the two bucks into booze. The guy who sells him the pint, he's another Jew.

"You maybe got some fancy words for shit like that. I got but one. Slavery. The Jew is slavemaster for the whole United States."

Although there are elements of truth in this speech, they are distorted and wrenched from context. It is true, for example, that home appliances generally carry higher price tags in Negro neighborhoods where it is also true that higher crime rates, inferior fire protection, and the possibility of riot inflate the cost of staying in business. It is true that Negro men have been shamefully served by the American—not the Jewish— business community. It is true that some Jews exploit some Negroes. But it is as foul to picture Jews as "slavemasters" as it is to describe Negroes as "baboons."

More than a million-and-a-half Jews from Eastern Europe reached the United States between 1881 and 1910. They fled a Russia increasingly obsessed with anti-Semitism. One Russian plan would have settled "the Jewish problem" in three steps. One third of the Jews were to emigrate. One third were to be converted to Eastern Orthodoxy. One third were to be murdered.

Their situation in Czarist Russia sent hundreds of thousands of Jews toward the Left. According to Rabbi Bernard Bloom, "Socialism was to the Jew of the Russian Empire, what Reform Judaism was to the Jew of the Western World." Both ideologies enabled Jews to escape medievalism.

But after reaching America, the Yiddish Left flashed with more color and more vigor than Reform. At the turn of the century and after, a vital Yiddish Left flowered in New York City; a few of its advocates survive today. Some gather in the lobby of the Atran Center for Jewish Culture, which was once the home of Stanford White and now houses the steadfast unionists of the Jewish Labor Committee. There, beside pillars of marble, anti-capitalists beat the air with fragile hands. Still they proclaim the old slogans. *Mir kempfen gegen krankheit, fri-zeitigen toit, un capitalismus.* We fight against sickness, premature death and capitalism.

The old Jewish Left remains, only as an influence and a memory. It did not presage the so-called New Left. Its issues are dormant or dead and the grinding questions of this time were not considered or imagined a generation ago. There has been a blurring of political lines, and no one believes any more that the theories of Marx or Lenin or Trotsky, promulgated by Jewish labor *bunds,* will heal man's faults.

The Jewish anti-mercantile heritage in this era is most evident in intellectualism, to which political belief is only incidentally appended. But if there arose in America, tomorrow, a strong crusading Left with causes clear, and a body purged of anti-Semitism, it would find immediate Jewish response and support.

The evils of sickness and premature death, and the inequities of capitalism, have not yet been put to route.

## JACOB AND MANYA, OLD WARRIORS OF THE LEFT

Their aristocracy is expended in a yellowing apartment building, set against a littered hummock in the Bronx. No word but yellow fits: dirty yellow bricks, streaked yellow hallways and near the elevator shaft, the smell of urine. There will not be Jews in this neighborhood for very long. Negroes have come and Puerto Ricans, and the young Jews have moved away, beyond the trolley tracks that are partly buried in asphalt.

Last winter, somebody in the neighborhood was said to have been raped. Nobody knows who it was, but everybody is sure that it was somebody. Jacob and Manya heard the stories but did not know whether to believe them. It would be terrible if the stories were accurate, but, truth to say, not important to them personally.

"We do not get out so much any more," Manya explains. "We do not feel any danger in our apartment."

"What?" Jacobs says. "What is she trying to tell you? I have to clarify things sometimes on her behalf."

"He is a little deaf," Manya says.

"It is not so cold, she is right," Jacob says.

The aristocracy of tea-time is theirs, with sugared cookies, crumbly soft for ancient gums, but no one to pay court.

"It is pretty hard for me," Jacob says, "now that I have to follow the activities of the labor movement without being able to participate in it. It cannot be helped, but that does not make it easier to accept."

"We will have some tea, yes?" Manya says. "Mr. Linderman likes his tea very much. Yes, Jacob?"

"Yes," Jacob says. "Do you ever hear of De Leon?" he asks. "He is not in fashion for many, many years, so I thought maybe you had not heard."

"I will bring the tea later," Manya says, "or perhaps you would prefer to sit in the dining room for it. Jacob—Mr. Linderman—has certain things he would like to talk to you, he has prepared. So after he is through, then the tea. Is the sofa comfortable? It cannot be. I will get you a straight chair. You will hurt your back."

The books in the small, rectangular living room date from the time when people purchased books in sets. In a heavy, black wood case, the complete works of Dickens stand darkly bound. A sense of darkness, without morbidity, pervades the room. Oddments of dark metal lamps lob light. The windows are heavily draped with a dark cloth. A sagging couch on ancient legs, crooked and bowed, is upholstered in black.

"There is a fine straight chair," Manya says. "And I will get it for you." The mahogany is heavy but Manya will accept no help. She is a small woman, but apparently she manages easily, even down the two steps that lead from the foyer. "This," she says, "will be just the thing for your back."

One wall, opposite the bookcase, bears a plaque and scrolls in frames, three scrolls in all. They were given to Jacob by unions, or as he likes to say, by workingmen. Jacob is ninety-three years old now. The old workers, even the unions themselves, are dead.

"How is your chair?" Manya says. "Good, I am certain. I have not sat in it for so many years myself without knowing."

A dull gold plaque hangs above the bookcase, marked: "To Jacob Linderman, from The Workers Hospital." They were all Socialists then, the patients and the nurses and the doctors, all Socialists sixty-five years ago.

"Do you know where I was born?" Jacob says. "I was born in Russia in 1874. You would never believe I was born in Russia with my speech."

Jacob's head is like a bird's, an alert, blue-eyed, friendly, bright-browed bird. The eyes, behind his glasses, are clear. His forehead slants back. The dome of his head is large but delicate. Jacob is a bird without evil.

"He was very young when he came here," Manya says. "Very young!" she shouts.

"I was Bar Mitzvahed already," Jacob says. "I was more than thirteen years old. Where I came from in Russia, a small town, everybody was religious. There wasn't anything but Orthodox there *Chasid* and *mismagdim*. All Orthodox." Jacob draws in his breath. He has been gathering his thoughts for several days because it is important that somebody understand now. He has been careful to recollect everything exactly right. "I began to work in 1889 the year after I got here. I went to school for one year. One year only. Then my father had to put me in the sweatshop because he needed every little bit of help I could give him. The two-and-a-half dollars a week that I was earning at that time was a great help.

"Whenever I came to the sweatshop in the morning, I found people already working. I came earlier and earlier. Seven o'clock. Six-thirty. But there was always someone ahead of me. There was no union, no regulation of hours and the earnings were not certain. Do you understand what that means?"

In the Bronx of the 1960's, the young Jews are gone and the sad-faced man at the Bronx Association for Judaism has had to hire a New York City policeman to stand in the doorways on nights when there are lectures on 'American Judaism Today.' "Otherwise," the man from the Association says, "no one will come. They are afraid. The *schvartzes* and the spics."

With the policeman, six or seven souls appear. "We have fine lectures," the man says. " 'Intermarriage: Curse or Blessing?' 'Church, State and Education.' " Years ago the people of the South Bronx poured from their homes to hear, for fifty cents or even more, lectures on the topics of the day, delivered by men of authority. Now the lectures attract only old-timers. The young have fled.

It is gone, the old neighborhood, and perhaps it was never very much anyway. It is gone in 1967. Turbulence and change, and cities die. But in the living room, amid the old lamps, Jacob, the gentle blue-eyed bird, has gone back to the Lower East Side and the factories of eighty winters ago.

To Jacob, the bosses were an unconscionable lot. Jews? Hah. Lice.

It was wrong. That much you could tell in your bones. You did not have to have an education to know the wrongness of it; all that you needed was a little *foregefil in di bayner* (feeling in the bones).

Each morning when he was fourteen years old, Jacob arose for work by six o'clock. Mama set the breakfast, bread and cheese and milk, on the wood-topped kitchen table. There was little talk at breakfast. The Lindermans were subdued by common weariness.

Jacob left with his father. That was the nicest part of the day. Walking down the four flights and starting down the street with Papa, two men (Jacob thought) going forth into the world. Four blocks from the house, Jacob had to turn. Two gruff goodbyes, man-to-man. After that, the day was never again so pleasant.

The boss who employed Jacob, for $2.50 a week, was Mr. Nachman. The loft on Leonard Street where Jacob worked, learning to sew broad patterns, was called a sweatshop, and in summer it possessed a human reek. But in the long winter there was no sweat. The loft was cold; almost as bitter as outside, and some mornings in the loft you could see your breath.

Everyone spoke Yiddish, the boys, like Jacob, and the men and the women, horny-handed and unfeminine, whom Mr. Nachman employed for special fancy stitching. Mr. Nachman was on the margin of the marginal business of making cheap clothing for women. He did not own the loft in which his employees worked, not the material on which they worked, nor the tools he had them use. Everything was "contracted for." Mr. Nachman lived on loans and rentals, borrowings and maneuverings and secret petty thefts.

A Turk worked in the factory with Jacob, an oily, black-mustached Jew who told Jacob that he had come from Smyrna. Jacob found the man repellent but exotic. The Turk was not a good worker and soon was fired, but before he went, Jacob tried to help him. It was difficult because of the language problem, but Jacob tried.

"*Mein Freund.*"

"*Nicht versteh.* No understand."

Ah, Ah! Jacob clapped his hand to his head.

*"Verstehen sie a bissel?"*

*"Nein, nein."* The Turk stood up. He was a very short man, Jacob realized suddenly, wide but very short. He seldom spoke. He had seemed stolid as earth, with his earth-colored skin. Then, in a week or ten days at the most, the Turk was gone, and no one knew where, or cared.

"Why did you bother with him?" one of the other boys asked later.

Jacob did not know. "Because he couldn't speak Yiddish," he said, "more than a few words."

"So?"

"A man has to speak Yiddish," Jacob said. "It is very important." Jacob was becoming certain of his ground.

"Why is it so important?"

"Don't be an idiot," Jacob said. "Don't you understand? How is it possible for a Jew to be a real American if he cannot speak Yiddish?"

Near the brown tenement on the cramped block the Lindermans shared with eleven hundred Jewish immigrants, Jacob and his father prayed at a small, white Orthodox synagogue. The synagogue stood apart from the sameness. It rose only one-and-a-half stories high, but there, among tenements, its low-domed roof assumed a dignity that it did not deserve, and would not have won among grander structures—nor even, perhaps, under the bare hills of Judea.

The interior of the synagogue was a corridor, lit by candles. There were no pews. Toward the rear, a raised platform had been erected from which the rabbi, a Lithuanian with thick features and modest attainments, led prayers. Sometimes, in the synagogue, the men and boys talked among themselves. They did not agree on many things or very often, and their discussions were sometimes so heated that the Lithuanian rabbi sternly ordered quiet, or, alternatively, raised his prayer chant to a higher wail. The disagreements were all on specifics; all the men conceded that they shared a sour destiny.

One morning in the year 1888, before the great snow, dozens of small circulars appeared on the floor of the synagogue. No one had any idea how they got there. The rabbi himself was mystified. But someone had placed circulars announcing the appearance of "a new and important newspaper." Its title was *Der Americanishen Arbeiter,* The American Worker, and it would be printed once a week in Yiddish. It was dedicated to the American-Jewish laboring man, and to his children, and to *their* children in a better world. The circular aroused the men. They said it was about time somebody started a paper. But the Lithuanian rabbi went from person to person saying over and over that he was upset. "How did those crazy circulars get into my synagogue?" was what he wanted to know.

Weeklies and monthlies were sprouting; on the Lower East Side of Manhattan it was an almost revolutionary time. The year 1889, centennial of the French Revolution, was one that the Socialists in America invested with current significance. They held a convention to celebrate and, there, openly demanded for the first time that the American workers' day be limited to eight hours. *Der Americanishen Arbeiter* reported the Socialist convention in Yiddish. Workers, *Der Arbeiter* reported, *should* share in profits. Workers *should* have a say in management. Workers *should* struggle to make the manufacturers accept their rights. These ideas stirred Jacob, but not so much as the thought of an eight-hour day. Only eight hours for work! Six hours for sleep. Why then, the time he would have for reading and even writing. He wanted an eight-hour day so badly that he embraced all of the principles advocated along with it. At fifteen, Jacob Linderman became a Socialist without realizing it or even knowing precisely what a Socialist was.

The first May Day Parade in the United States was held in 1890. The thousands of men and women who were to march milled about Union Square, bearing placards with hand-lettered slogans of the day.

*Solidarity Now and Forever*
*Freedom for the Workers of the World*
*Workers Arise and Triumph*
*We Demand an Eight-Hour Day*

Each of the unions in New York City was represented by a group bearing a banner. Against the gray city buildings, the flags made a fine show of color, blue and white and—everywhere—red.

Jewish union men, the workers from the New York garment industry, comprised the largest ethnic contingent. The garment men, too, had the finest of flags; among Jewish cutters and tailors there was no want of sure hands. Jacob's union, which had only just been begun, had a white flag, with a blue wreath around the red letters that proclaimed "A.C.U."—Associated Clothing Union. The white silk billowed and caught the sunlight. As the group swung into rank and started marching, in and out of step, some of the older men sang.

There had never been anything like it for the Jews. That was what Jacob's father told him as they strode, side-by-side. Five years before, in the *shtetl*, they had lived with tyranny and poverty too terrible to recall. Now, here was freedom. You could hear it in the songs and see it in the flags and feel it on the air that bore the music. There were tears in his father's eyes. Jacob saw, and so there were soon tears in his own eyes, too, as the Jewish workers sang to the tune of "Tannenbaum:"

> The people's flag is deepest red.
> It's shrouded oft their martyred dead,
> And when their blood grew thick and cold,
> They dyed its stain in every fold.
>> Then raise the scarlet
>> Standard high
>> Beneath its folds, we'll
>> Live and die.
> Though cowards cringe and traitors fear
> We'll keep the red flag flying here.

The brave and naked Socialism of May 1, 1890, terrified and angered the contractors and the manufacturers in Jacob's garment industry. The businessmen conspired to protect themselves and one day Mr. Nachman, the boss, came to Jacob, who was by this time sixteen, and said, *"Mensch."* Mr. Nachman smiled and Jacob felt uneasy.

*"Mensch,"* Mr. Nachman repeated. He clapped Jacob on the shoulder and held, skinny shoulder in claw hand, and smiled.

"Yes, sir," Jacob said, ducking downward. He was trying to get free of Mr. Nachman's grip.

"I want the people who work here should be happy," Mr. Nachman said.

Jacob wrenched as hard as he dared but the claw would not release his shoulder. Jacob stood straight and tall. He was five inches shorter than Mr. Nachman.

"So I have decided," Mr. Nachman said, "that we shall here have a workmen's society, which will provide special benefits for all."

"Such as?" Jacob said.

"Funeral benefits," Mr. Nachman said. Mr. Nachman was bald and the planes of his face curved downward, nose, lips and seemingly, even the brows. "Mr. Nachman," Jacob said, "I hope to live a long time."

"Of course," Nachman said. "I was only using that as an example. I want there should be a society of only my people. The Nachman Workman's Society, we shall call it. Then you will not have to join other workers' societies where the blood-suckers come and suck the money from good honest workers, and you know about the anarchists, Jacob. They throw bombs."

"You are speaking to me, Mr. Nachman, of this society you propose for some special reason, is that correct?"

"No special reason," Nachman said. He had meant to ask Jacob to lead the Nachman Workman's Society. What better leader of a little union than this pale, blue-eyed boy who fluttered and who jumped, actually jumped, whenever you shouted "Hoo." But Mr. Nachman was not so sure any longer.

"I feel that I must tell you, sir," Jacob announced, "that I could never join any society organized by you, not for any personal reason but because we are of different classes."

"Hooo!" Mr. Nachman cried.

"I am a worker," Jacob said, his voice quavering, "and you are a member of the bourgeoisie. I can join no society started by you." Mr. Nachman's round face darkened. Jacob had seen it like this before and cringed. Mr. Nachman raised a hand. He glared at Jacob. "Goddam dirty Red!" he said "You're fired!"

Although the loss of $2.50 a week was a serious matter to the Linderman family, Jacob's dismissal became insignificant within two weeks. The manufacturers and the contractors who had found out that the workers were meeting and organ-

izing, responded by shutting down the entire garment industry, in a lockout. It was August, ordinarily a busy time. Most
of the bosses had something put away. And on a Tuesday,
hot even at dawn, without any warning to the men and
women and boys of the ghetto, all the lofts were closed.

Jacob was stirred. On the second night of the strike, Jacob,
sat at the wooden table in the kitchen of the tenement flat and
wrote a long and furious article in Yiddish. He called the
story, *Di Opzogen Fun An Erlichen Bocher*—The Firing of
an Honest Boy. He wrote simply and angrily, unconsciously
using the Marxist phrases which he had been hearing so frequently. The boy, as Jacob told it, was a diligent artisan. The
boss was an exploiter. The boy was permitted to hold the
tools of production but not to share in the fruits of his
labors. Jacob started writing at ten o'clock at night and by
two in the morning he was finished. He sat up for hours,
rereading and making little changes in what he had written,
breathing the stale air of the kitchen, unemployed, weary and
too happy with his new craft even to notice the half-undressed
women rustling in the apartments across the courtyard when
dawn came.

After no more than the first bites of his breakfast cheese,
Jacob bolted down the tenement stairs and rushed to the office of *Der Americanishen Arbeiter,* seven blocks away. The
newspaper was housed in the store front of a low brick building. This early, its office door, on which the word Arbeiter
had been lettered in gilt paint, was locked. Jacob stood on the
sidewalk, nine yellow manuscript pages under his arm, waiting. Finally, near ten o'clock, a man with a sinewy neck and
thick hairy forearms, walked past Jacob and put a key into
the door.

"Sir," Jacob said, in a soprano tone that startled him. His
nervousness was vast. "Sir," he said in a high tenor, "I have
with me an article by an excellent journalist that it would be
very much to your advantage to publish."

The man was having trouble with the lock. "And who is
this excellent journalist?" he asked. His voice was deep and
full, but not frightening.

"By name, Jacob Linderman," Jacob said, "and he is an
excellent journalist."

"I know a great many excellent journalists," the man said,
"but I have never even heard of Jacob Linderman."

"I am Jacob Linderman," Jacob said.

The door sprang open. "And I am Herman Markowitz, editor of *Der Americanishen Arbeiter*. Leave the article and I will let you know this afternoon. It is our policy to read the work of excellent journalists promptly." Herman Markowitz cuffed Jacob gently on the shoulder. The man must have been six feet tall.

Herman Markowitz accepted Jacob's article at once and even raised seventy-five cents to pay him. He invited Jacob to take tea with him and afterwards, for all the long months of lockout, the *Arbeiter* office was home for Jacob. Now, when someone asked him what he did, he answered with furious pride, "I am a journalist."

In implementing their lockout, the manufacturers made one serious mistake. They turned not only against so-called "tailors"—the button-sewers who were mostly recent immigrants—but they also turned on the cutters. Garment cutters were men of considerable acquired skill; many had been in the United States for ten years or even longer, learning to shape "raw goods into garments." Marcus Adler, the president of the Manufacturers' Alliance, proposed a simple plan to destroy the young Associated Clothing Union. He would lock out everyone for a month, then each manufacturer would recruit a fresh labor force. Each of the new workers would be required to swear that he would not join any union except one organized by his employer. Marcus Adler, who wore a *pince nez* and a trim goatee, thought that making the men swear on an Old Testament would be a dramatic and anti-Socialist touch.

Before the factories could be reopened, Marcus Adler had to send emissaries to the cutters and the tailors, to find recruits for his new labor force. The emissaries talked too much and Jacob, in the offices of the *Arbeiter,* learned a new, unpleasant sounding word. Scab.

He was not really a good reporter because he was afraid to talk to strangers, but he followed specific directions very well and was able to formulate an intelligent line of questioning once the dialogue was begun. As he went out, Jacob discovered something that struck him as peculiar. The tailors, the greenhorn button-sewers, were having second thoughts about the union. Life here was not so bad, some of them said.

But the cutters were different. They had been in America for half a generation longer than the tailors. Compared to the

Irish or the Germans they were still timorous, but some of the ghetto fear had been peeled away. The cutters told Jacob they would not go back to work with any *cockamamie* promises about unions. There were no scabs within the cutters, and if any wanted to scab, he knew that he would not be safe from the anger of the others. So there were none. And without cutters the bosses could not reopen the woman's clothing business in New York.

The union organized various committees to help the workers. Jacob served on the committee that was charged with obtaining contributions of food. On the day when he began to forage, Jacob's first stop was at Katz's Green Grocery, four-and-a-half blocks from the offices of *Der Arbeiter*. Herman Markowitz had told Jacob what to do. He knew Jacob's reticence and had provided a speech, which Jacob memorized.

"Mr. Katz," Jacob said to a plump, round-headed, bespectacled man at the grocery. "I bring you greetings from the honest artisans of the Associated Clothing Union. Greetings."

The roundfaced man was bent, arranging boxes of vegetables on the floor. He looked up. "Katz ain't here," he said.

"No?" Jacob said.

"Yeah," the roundfaced man said. "Katz has gone away for a long time."

"Who are you?" Jacob said.

"Klopman," said the man. "I am Klopman."

Jacob walked the four-and-a-half blocks back to *Der Arbeiter* and explained. "A short, roundfaced man?" Herman said.

"Yes."

"That's Katz. He knows about the strike and he's afraid that the union wants something for nothing. Try him again, Jacob, and finish your talk and don't let him interrupt. Whatever he tries, do not let him interrupt. Is that clear?"

Back at the grocery, the roundfaced man was still arranging boxes of greens. "I told you Katz ain't here," he said.

"Mr. Katz," Jacob said, in a high quaver, "which I happen to know on excellent authority that you are, I bring you greetings from the honest artisans of the Associated Clothing Union, even though you attempted to lie to me. Greetings."

"I am a poor man," Mr. Katz said. He stood up and wiped his hands on his apron.

Jacob remembered that he had been told not to let Katz interrupt, so when Katz spoke, Jacob started to hum.

"On behalf of the workers of Associated Clothing, locked out against their wishes by the bosses," Jacob continued, "I have come to enlist your support."

"All right, all right, already," Katz said. "Don't try to convert me."

"Tum, umm, umm," Jacob hummed. "We do not ask that anyone make great sacrifices," Jacob said. "Only from each according to his abilities and to each according to his needs. This is our motto and belief, of the workers—your customers, Mr. Katz, before the cruel lockout, and your customers again after the lockout, provided you retain their good will."

"How much do you want?" Katz said.

Jacob flinched and hummed. "Tum-um, tai-tiddy-tiddy-tai-um."

"Come on, come on!" Katz shouted, raising a fat round fist.

"Tum, tum, don't strike me," Jacob said. "A fair portion of food is all that is required. A fair portion of food for the starving workers."

"All right," Katz said. "Why didn't you say so? I am a working man myself."

"That is something to be proud of," Jacob said.

"Yeh, yeh," Katz said. "I will give you food. But nothing fancy, you understand. All you want, but *bebelech*. Beans. Workers do not have to eat like czars."

"On behalf of Associated—" Jacob began.

"I got work to do," Katz said. "Get out of here already."

"Yes, sir," Jacob said.

"And what is it with you and that crazy singing, tell me?" Katz said. But Jacob was gone, happy and sleek, to the next grocery store, a block-and-a-half away.

The men held firm. It amazed Marcus Adler. There was no industry; it was closed down at one of the busiest times of the year. It was madness to keep the *drek* locked out any longer. There were other ways to punish them, Marcus Adler said. He would find ways. He would learn more, and the more he knew, the better he would be able to fight them. With these militant words, the manufacturers surrendered and fully three months after it began, the bosses' lockout against the Associated Clothing Union collapsed.

Herman Markowitz offered Jacob a real job. "You say you want to be a journalist," Herman said. "What does your father say?"

"He would be proud for there to be a writing man in the family."

"There is not very much money in labor journalism," Herman said.

"I was earning only $2.50 a week at Nachman's."

"Not exactly the point," Herman said. "I will be able immediately to pay you four dollars a week. But Nachman or his successors will be making clothes for a long time. A labor paper is not even so stable as the labor movement itself, and as you see, the labor movement is hardly stable."

"I understand what you say," Jacob said, "but can you understand that stability is not now very important to me? I live at home."

"You have a girl?" Herman asked. "It's time, you know."

Jacob blushed. "I don't have any interest in trivial things," he said.

"What I am trying to say," Herman said, "and I'm afraid I'm not saying it very well, is that I'm asking you to join me in an unstable industry, with no past, with a shaky present, and a future tied to the future of a labor movement that may be outlawed by the capitalist Congress tomorrow."

"Such an honor," Jacob said. "How can I thank you?"

Marcus Adler realized soon after the lockout that the mistake had been attacking the greenhorn tailors and the American cutters together. The cutters were a problem for some other time. For now, Marcus Adler proposed giving them everything they wanted. At the same time, give nothing to the tailors. The first step in breaking the Associated Clothing Union, according to Adler, was to cement a wedge.

Herman Markowitz had a bitter comprehension of Adler. "He is the worst kind of exploiter," Herman told Jacob, "because he has intelligence. Some exploit as pigs wallow, but this man knows better. He is not an emotionalist, Jacob, but a rationalist, a man of filthy, calculated greed."

"Should I write an article?" Jacob said. "I know plenty of people who have worked for him and will talk to me."

"No article yet," Herman Markowitz said. "First, we strike Adler's firm."

Adler Garments, occupying three floors in a five-story building on lower Jamison Street, was one of New York's leading manufacturers of cotton underwear for women. The first of the Adlers had emigrated from Bavaria during the

1850's, started the business, profited handsomely and died childless and young. Marcus Adler, his nephew, was pleased to be a second-generation American. He was intolerant of immigrants generally, and of Jewish immigrants particularly, which was a convenience in the family business. Almost all of the employees of Adler Garments were immigrant Jews from Eastern Europe. "Dirty," Marcus Adler said, "and *drek*, with their filthy Yiddish papers and their smelly beards and their women who never bathe."

Intolerance relieved Marcus Adler of the necessity of seeing the workers as human beings. Privately, he was warm, if domineering; generous, and at times, even sensitive. He had played the cello for six years as a boy and although now card games were his hobby, he sometimes wished that he had time to go to concerts. Wines were important to him also. He loved to pour a small glass of fine white Alsatian wine for his wife. These splinters of Marcus Adler's behavior would have surprised the immigrant Jews who worked for him. To them, he was invariably arrogant and rude.

Adler knew that a strike against his company was coming. He also knew (it was good business to know things) a great deal about *Der Americanisher Arbeiter* and Herman Markowitz. He had even heard the name of Jacob Linderman. Adler knew because he had hired spies and instructed them to listen everywhere, even in the toilets. His foremost agent was a Roumanian cloth cutter with ambitions to become a manufacturer. Adler promised the Roumanian help in the future; for the present, he provided $1.50 for every report of value. Because the Roumanian had a fine ear for gossip, Markowitz's strike was not going to surprise Adler Garments. Indeed, Herman Markowitz would have been startled to know that Adler Garments actually welcomed it. Marcus Adler had been preparing for some time. Everything for the cutters. Nothing for the tailors. It was a quiet new slogan among the bosses.

On a brisk November evening in 1895, four hundred clothing workers met with Herman Markowitz at a three-story red brick building called Freiheit Hall. Two white stone doric columns and a white stone pediment framed the entrance. The building had been designed to look important.

"This man Adler," Herman Markowitz told the few hundred workers gathered in Freiheit Hall, "is trying to destroy us. Would you like to know how?"

"Yeh," said an old cutter near the platform. "Yeh. Tell us how, Mr. Writer." Jacob was sitting on the platform. He was supposed to write down Herman's speech, word for word. He wished Herman had written it out himself so that he could enjoy the meeting. The union flag stood on one side of the platform and the American flag drooped on the other. The workers were tense. Herman was excited. Jacob felt the vitality in the hall. "Hsst," he said to Herman. "Hsst, hsst. It is important."

Herman turned his head slightly, but held on to the lectern with both hands. He was not relinquishing the attention of the audience. "Should I write down what *they* say to you?" Jacob whispered. Herman shook his head, slightly, decisively. "Very good," Jacob said aloud to himself. "Only what you say to them."

"I will tell you what Adler and the rest are trying to do," Herman said, "and it makes no difference if I am a writer or not. It even makes no difference to me that I am a Jew."

The word startled them.

"What does make a difference," Herman said, "is that I am a worker and you are a worker and all workers are brothers everywhere in the world."

"So," said the old cutter, "a Chinaman is my brother?"

"The Chinaman as much as anyone else is your brother, just as long as he is a workman," Herman said. "This man here wants to know about the Chinaman. What are you, mister? Tell me what."

"Roumanian," said the old cutter.

"All men who work are brothers," Herman cried. "That is the most important thing there is. Now, along comes this Marcus Adler, a smart man. He owns a business. He owns a house for himself in Brooklyn. He has a little garden in the back, where he plants flowers." Herman lowered his voice.

"This Marcus Adler is a smart man, you say, because if he was not smart how could he be a manufacturer and have so many things?

"I will tell you how he has so many things.

"He has stolen them from the workers!" Herman was suddenly roaring. "From the sweat of your brows and the cunning of your hands, he has stolen his fortune, this Marcus Adler. From you, and from your women, and even from your children. This boy here, Jacob Linderman, by my side, could not even be educated properly because of the greed of men like Marcus Adler.

"I will tell you about Marcus Adler. He is not your brother. Is the wolf brother to the sheep? Is the lion brother to the lamb?" Herman was bellowing and the bellow came back, "No!"

"This wolf, this lion, this jungle creature, this boss Adler," Herman said quietly, and the audience went silent so it might hear. "He is trying to drive brothers apart. He is trying to drive apart the cutters and the tailors by pleasing the cutters and spitting on the tailors." Herman himself spat vigorously. "What are we," he called, "idiots that we cannot see?"

"He is the idiot!" someone shouted.

"You are right!" Herman shouted back.

"He is the *schlemiel!*"

"Yes," Herman said, "but not so fast, my friends. Not so fast. What we must do to defeat this man, you know as well as I."

From around Freiheit Hall came cries of "Strike!" A short, red-faced Polish Jew; a tall and sallow Hungarian; a portly Russian. Together they were all calling, "Strike!"

"Strike!" Herman echoed. "Not a strike by cutters or a strike by tailors, but a strike by cutters *and* by tailors. A strike by workers, the free men of the world!"

When Herman put the question to a vote, the strike carried by acclamation. "Unanimously," Herman pronounced.

Afterwards, Herman invited Jacob to join him over tea. Glowing Jacob, sipping, asked what the issue behind the strike was, and Herman beamed with pride. There were two other men beside him. He turned to them. "With this one, there is no nonsense," Herman said. "Straight to the issue, never mind the speech and song and dance."

Herman put down his tea glass and bit off the end of a cigar. One of the other men quickly struck a match. "There are, of course, as many issues as I care to create," Herman said, "but only one issue is real. That is the survival of our union.

"For our union to be born without some violence would not be possible," Herman said. "You cannot have childbirth without labor. If there is pain now, it is for good later, for a greater good. Our means are justified by our ends. Without the strike, without the painful violence, our little union might not be born. So that is the real reason for the strike. The cause is birth."

"Which, of course, we cannot now tell to the workers," Jacob said.

"Not yet," Herman said.

"You didn't tell them tonight," Jacob said.

"Very good, Jacob," Herman clapped Jacob on the head and laughed. "Listen to the word, not the voice."

"What will be the reason we announce, Herman?" one of the men said sternly. "We are going out on strike tomorrow morning."

"I don't know the reason for the strike," Herman said. "I haven't decided yet." Herman Markowitz's ego was at work.

The cause he finally chose was vague. "Losses to workers as a result of the recent inexcusable lockout" led the list. Under Herman's directions, Jacob wrote an article accusing "the manufacturer Adler" of impairing the rights of workers. In all, Jacob reported, 180 men, women and boys were employed at the Adler Garment Company. "At the very least," Jacob wrote, "the boss Adler should be made to pay out $1,000 to the union to distribute among the 180 people who were so cruelly damaged during the unfair lockout. That way, bosses everywhere will understand: no more lockouts."

A day later, Herman erupted into talk. "I have got word," he said, "from Adler. And you thought, and I thought, myself, that we would hear nothing, but here he wants to see me tomorrow at his home and in absolute private. He says he has to save face. It is to be a secret meeting. He says that he will offer a settlement to please us all. One thousand dollars."

"But you said we could not have a union without violent birth."

"We can have a union without further pain," Herman said, "if I win the marvelous settlement I have proposed." Once more, Jacob was exposed to the ego of a man who demanded that in all accounts of debates, the winning remark be credited to him.

Jacob felt uncomfortable and oddly calm. It was the first time in their relationship that one of Herman's enthusiasms had left him untouched. The claim, Jacob thought, was artificial. How could an artificial claim produce one thousand dollars? It did not make sense.

But on the following afternoon, Herman returned from Brooklyn, excited but controlled, carrying a check. "Look at this," he said to Jacob, who read, "Pay to the order of Herman Markowitz, one thousand dollars and no cents."

Jacob blinked. "The strike, then, is over," he said.

"Soon," Herman said. "First I will cash the check to make sure that it is good. Then, I will distribute the money—more than five dollars to each of us, it comes out—and *then* the strike will be over." He looked hard at Jacob. "I suspect a trick," Herman said. "I suspect the check is not good. I will cash it at once and, if it is good, we shall celebrate with schnapps."

Herman did not come back that day. Jacob did not see him until 3:15 the following afternoon, when he walked casually into the office.

"The check," Jacob cried, "was it good?"

"Good?" Herman said. "Why yes, of course it was good. Every penny."

"You have the money?"

"All of it. Every cent," Herman said. "Get the strong box."

"Where have you been?"

"Walking," Herman said. "Wondering about Adler. I will feel better when the money is in the strong box. I promised you schnapps."

Jacob had never seen a thousand (or even a hundred) dollars before. His blue eyes glazed as Herman slowly counted the money, fitting it into all the sections of the strong box.

Then Herman slumped dully at his desk. "Schnapps," Jacob said.

"If you wish," Herman said.

Jacob poured two small glasses, cried "To the union!" and drank, feeling the liquor burn against his throat. Tears came to his eyes. He shook his head and blinked. For a few moments he was unable to see. When Jacob opened his eyes, he was startled to find three men marching into the office. He did not know any of them. Two were policemen.

"Herman Markowitz?" said the man in plainclothes.

"Yes."

"Is that your signature on this check?" The man waved the thousand-dollar check from Adler.

"Let me see," Herman said. He examined it. "Yes," he said, "that's my signature all right."

The policemen stood, hands at their sides, primed and ready. Herman, for all his muscle, was no bigger than either of them.

"Herman Markowitz," said the man in plainclothes, "I place you under arrest."

Herman lurched to his feet. "What charge?" he said. "What charge?"

"Extortion," said the man.

Herman roared, deep, wordless, terrifying, and Jacob jumped back. He had never before heard such a frightful noise. Herman lunged toward the policemen with his roar. What did the policemen know about the labor movement and entrapment and betrayal and a life lived as means to an end? Herman's roar did not say any of these things to the policemen, who chopped short blows to the neck of the man who had lunged at them head down. The blows were rhythmic and carried astonishing force. One-two, one-two. "Uh," Herman said, not so loudly any more. "Uuuh." One-two, one-two, the billies battered against his neck. "Oooh," Herman sobbed, spinning crazily.

The policemen, in a precise movement, grabbed him under both arms and, trailed by the man in plainclothing, marched out of the offices of *Der Americanisher Arbeiter,* dragging the fallen editor behind them. Jacob overheard the man in plain clothes tell the others, "Not as tough as he figured, that big kike."

Jacob was an improving journalist. He possessed sensitivity, writing competence and a willingness to innovate. The earliest Yiddish labor journalism in America was a collection of the minutes of meetings. As Jacob saw them, the articles all read: "Decided so and so; decided so and so; decided so and so. Unanimous." Jacob's reporting included not only the decisions but descriptions of the discussions that had gone before. His writing was plain but clear, and anyone reading his articles carefully in *Der Arbeiter* knew not only what happened but also how certain things had happened, and sometimes even why.

Jacob's account of the capitalist beating of Herman Markowitz, published in *Der Arbeiter,* made some men actually weep and yet, with their eyes tear-bright, the leaders of the Associated Clothing Union were happy to see the editorship pass on from Herman Markowitz to Jacob Linderman. Herman's ego had bothered them all. "He was primarily a self-glorifier," one of them said.

"I must state clearly, gentlemen," said Jacob, who was twenty-one years old, "that I cannot take over *Der Arbeiter* for very long because I am not a professional editor."

The men had quick answers. "So, who said anything about permanent?" And, "Surely, Herman will be coming back."

"No," Jacob said. "I do not think he will be coming back again." The memory of the beating was alive. First, watching the truncheons, Jacob had been choking in his own fear. Then, as Herman called out in pain, Jacob heard *him* as the young one, the child overwhelmed by anguish and, he understood now, he had been certain that Herman groaning was Herman dying, writhing through childhood toward the common womb. Who would have thought birth and death were so close?

"What do you propose," Jacob said to the union men, "in the event that Herman does not choose to return?"

"Then, we shall hire another professional editor."

"Good," Jacob said, "or rather, excellent. I accept the assignment under the provision that I shall be permitted to resign without hard feeling as soon as you are able to hire a professional to replace me."

"Agreed."

"Superb," Jacob said. "You understand that there are aspects of journalism of which I am deeply ignorant?"

One of the men patted Jacob's shoulder and said that they understood. He was a white-haired, bespectacled tailor, genial and plump, who could not read or write a word of English.

The first campaign of *Der Arbeiter,* under the editorship of Jacob Linderman, was to exonerate Herman Markowitz. As Jacob envisioned it, the campaign would have additional consequences. It would restore the Associated Clothing Union and it would expose Marcus Adler as a fraud.

Jacob began with a polemic. He wrote:

The history of all hitherto existing society is the history of class struggles.

The proletariat alone is a really revolutionary class. The other classes decay and finally disappear.

When commercial capital occupies a position of unquestioned ascendancy, it everywhere constitutes a system of plunder.

Beyond slogans, Jacob's essay called for unity, strength and courage without violence. Through the rest of the newspaper, he placed fund appeals and testimonials to Herman Markowitz from workers who knew him. He printed 1,750 copies of the paper, charged two cents each and to his amazement, the issue sold out. It was a triumph.

Unfortunately, in succeeding weeks, the impact of Jacob's articles lessened. The triumph, like the beating, became a memory. Herman Markowitz remained in jail.

In February 1896, Jacob was speaking to the committee of workmen who had urged him to edit *Der Arbeiter*. Now they wanted stronger articles attacking Adler.

"Why must you be so gentle, Yakov?" the plump white-haired tailor asked.

"He must have proof, Velka, don't you understand?" said another workman, with a steely and luxuriant head of hair.

"Proof?" said Velka the tailor. "For what? For what, we already know. That Adler is a louse. What is this proof?"

"Proof," said Jacob pleasantly, "is what we must have."

"You are precisely correct, young man," said the workman with the white mane. "I am Feigenbaum. Perhaps I can help you to get it."

"How so?" Jacob asked.

"Watch the man Adler constantly and secretly."

"For what?" Jacob said.

Feigenbaum outlined a number of possibilities that secret observation of Marcus Adler might reveal. The most likely, he said, was that Adler was keeping a whore somewhere in the Bensonhurst district of Brooklyn. It was well known that Adler was a bottom pincher; even the ugly seamstresses had felt his hand. Bottom-pinching, Feigenbaum said in his positive prolix way, was the inevitable giveaway of the whoremaster.

Jacob could barely bring himself to think seriously of prostitution and he would not discuss it. He blushed.

"Is it agreed?" Feigenbaum said. "I am to observe Adler secretly and to write my observations in the form of an article which *Der Arbeiter* will publish."

Jacob wanted to shout, no, that is not our way in the labor movement, we are not vile. The blush still burned strong. Their eyes were on him. He nodded curtly.

"I'm glad I have your approval," Feigenbaum said.

Almost from birth, the Jewish labor movement was fractioned. There were the Marxist activists who wanted revolution now, and the syndicalists who wanted a general strike now, and the anarchists who wanted an end to government now, and the Social Democrats who were gradualists, and the religious laborers and the atheist workers, and there were those who were combinations of one or several or who went from group to group, cross-pollinating. But there was a hard center in each group, believing that in their way and only in their way could the Jewish worker find salvation. Jacob had drifted into a group of evolving Centrism. (It was accident that he had drifted in, but will kept him where he was.) The Centrists believed in a workers' state realized by elections. They believed in strikes but not in violence. They were not actively religious, but neither did they oppose religion. They believed in the amalgamation of the Jewish labor movement with the non-Jewish labor movement. They were middle-of-the-roaders while the road was still being built.

Feigenbaum had drifted toward the Centrists from an anti-religionist bund. He shared the atheism, but it seemed to him that some of the men were so concerned about the rabbis that they lost sight of the greater enemy, the bosses. Feigenbaum had a sure, self-satisfied contempt for religion. It was sufficient for him to say, "What are we afraid of a few stinking rabbis for, anyway?" He had no need to consider the power of religion further.

Steely-haired Isaac Feigenbaum claimed to have followed Marcus Adler for six consecutive weeks. But the article he handed Jacob presented nothing new. It stressed the abominable conditions in Adler's shop, the opulence of Adler's home and, in the one section of passion, commented on Adler's dutiful trips to a synagogue. "This abuser of workmen," Isaac Feigenbaum wrote, "sweatshopper, strike-breaker, exploiter, arrogant man, has the temerity to cloak himself in supposed righteousness and wear the skull cap and pray, as if that way lay virtue, this abuser of workmen, this *layzige yarmulke* [lousy skullcap]."

Jacob concentrated so hard on making Feigenbaum's writing readable that he did not concentrate on anything else. As soon as *Der Arbeiter* appeared, Marcus Adler, through his son Harold, a practicing attorney, brought suit for libel. The complaint did not mention *Der Arbeiter's* attacks on the sweatshop. It was based only on the defamatory phrase: "*lay-*

*zige yarmulke*," a pure and simple example, Harold Adler said, of derogation.

As Jacob walked into the court, he saw Harold Adler, young and elegant. Marcus Adler managed to look bent and humble beside his son. Briefly, Jacob wondered why Feigenbaum had not bothered at any time to mention that the old man had a son.

In the Bronx, seventy years afterward, Jacob, who has grown aged and become Mr. Linderman, is sitting in his straight-backed chair trying to explain.

"I will get the tea," Mrs. Linderman says.

"It was bad enough to use such language among Jews," Mr. Linderman says, "but it was much worse when Adler's son used it against us, my paper and myself, to the jury that was trying our case."

"Why was it much worse?"

"I do not hear." The question is repeated, louder.

"Ah. Why? Always a fair question. So. It was worse because they were all Americans on the jury. Not Jewish at all. The Jew understands that you use such terrible language among Jews without meaning it. The non-Jew takes it literally, as a religious fake, a hypocrite, a liar. He does not understand that we can shout among ourselves and call each other names but in the end we are together as one against the *goyim*."

Manya is coming back. "I have put the water to boil," she says. "Yes, Jacob. Tea, Jacob."

"We were convicted," Mr. Linderman says. "I and the others, we were convicted as we were bound to be. They told the Americans on the jury our language was terrible, anti-God, and that the worst was that a Jew should use such terms against another Jew, as if *layzige yarmulke* could be used against a *goy*. What did the Americans know, that such language was common, that they could stand outside Siegal's on Fourteenth Street any night and hear it, as the men marched off to Union Square to have their debates."

"But the worst," Jacob says, "is that Christians should have been allowed to sit in judgment.

"And what do you think the *goyim* did?" Mr. Linderman, the old bird, is sitting so straight his bottom does not seem to be touching the chair. "They found for the religionists to the sum of, I shall never forget as long as I am on earth, six thousand dollars. And there it was, a great victory for the terrible Adlers. Herman in jail, being beaten God knows how often by the Irishers, and the Adlers had their victory. Do you know how much six thousand dollars was then?

"We could not raise it. They made an assignment. The Adlers had our paper and the presses. After 1896, there was no more *Der Americanisher Arbeiter.*"

"Will you have cookies?" Manya asks.

"No, thank you."

"I order them special from a bakery far uptown."

"Manya," Jacob says. "The man is trying to work."

"Is it so bad he should work with a full stomach?"

"I am trying to explain important things."

"Would you mind waiting, only a few minutes, for the delicious cookies?" Manya says. She has transparent eyes—pale, gentle, without luminescence, incapable of anger. She flutters away in an unhurt retreat.

The dining room table in the yellowing apartment in the Bronx stands in the rectangular foyer raised two small discreet steps above the long dark living room. Wrought-iron railings, curious on thin wooden balustrades, guard the steps, and Jacob, untired by his reminiscences, lays his hand only lightly on the railing as he ascends.

The foyer is as bright as the living room was dim. Two standing lamps project cones of light up and down, and a fixture glows in the ceiling. Yet it is a small foyer. A hallway opens from one side. Next to the opening there is an incongruous little alcove. The dining table, long and thin, matching the room, is covered by a blue and white checked cloth. Manya has placed a bowl of artificial flowers at the center, near two plates filled with sugared cookies, and an old samovar, polished silver, on a polished silver tray. Above, the walls of the foyer bear more scrolls from Jacob's life. Within the alcove hangs a black and white photograph of Abraham Lincoln.

"I don't suppose, I mean, it is not possible," Jacob says, "you have ever heard of Daniel De Leon?"

"Jacob," Manya says. "Your tea."

The old man's hands tremble slightly when he lifts a cookie to his mouth, but he eats tidily, with no spilling of crumbs.

"De Leon had a brilliant mind," Jacob says, "although he

was not of the labor movement. He was an associate, or an assistant, professor of economics at Columbia University. He was born in Venezuela but he studied in various European universities; he knew European languages and he was able to make a brilliant career as a professor. But he heard something about the labor movement—not much, but something. He told me he remembered when the workers first paraded for the eight-hour day how his friends spoke of working men with contempt. He told me that he became interested and began to look around, and, as he himself put it, for three years he stopped writing new lectures for his class and devoted himself to a study of the labor movement. He not only studied it, he joined it.

"He believed—we all believed then—in certain principles, you understand, which are not so popular now, although some actually are law. I suppose you could call these principles, Socialism. The question then was how to achieve a Socialist state? Many Socialists believed it would be achieved through gradual passing of laws to modify the American society. De Leon, however, had a different point of view. He wanted the unions not merely to be workers' organizations, but to prepare to govern as soon as the Socialists won the election. In other words, as soon as the Socialists won, the power would be given quickly, by a batch of laws, to the unions, which would represent all the people. So the unions, as De Leon saw them, were not merely organizations of workers. They were the government of the future."

"More cookies?" Manya says.

They are excellent cookies that she has brought from far uptown into her declining neighborhood of restless Negroes and caterwauling Puerto Rican women who have never heard of Daniel De Leon.

"Yes, thank you very much." The sugar grates the tongue, but pleasantly. Is it odd that Lincoln hangs in the alcove? One would have guessed Theodore Herzl.

"Before he died, it was 1914, De Leon and I did not agree on everything," Jacob says. "One day, when I held office in some small union, he asked me if I thought my lining up with them was justified. I told him, yes, and he said that was all he wanted to know. I could see then that he was coming to understand that you cannot get people to accept views by force. He realized, unfortunately, too late. One time, I asked him to come and speak to my group of workers. He wrote back, 'The will is there, but the power is not.'

"I organized a memorial meeting. It was very large and well-attended. So, that was his end. And the Socialist Labor Party, De Leon's party and mine, came to a standstill with his death. It could make no headway. The reason was that they kept on using the language of De Leon, quoting him and printing his articles, brilliant in their time, but after a while, failing to express the current situation.

"I complained to the Socialist Labor leaders. I was an admirer of De Leon, but I was trying to show that time brings its own demands that cannot be disregarded. At one point, there was a meeting about the war, the First World War, and, citing De Leon here and there, they said that the position of the party was to be in favor of labor everywhere, so they could not support either side in the war, and I said:

" 'Perhaps it is too much for us to except Socialist policies, as we knew them once, always to be fitting in all other times.'

"To them that was heresy, and I had to leave the Socialist Labor Party. Of course, the rest of the labor movement still viewed me as a radical. They would have none of me either. I was a young man, a union man, in exile."

During the exile he met Manya Margolies. He took a job at Shumkin's Department Store on Fourteenth Street, which he had passed often on the way to the rallies and the parades that began in Union Square. He was short and dapper, with a hint of elegance now. A sister had married a relative of Shumkin, and the relative introduced Jacob to Shumkin himself, an iron-haired asthmatic man, who said that he certainly understood what Jacob had gone through because he had been a Radical Socialist himself once, but had outgrown it. He wheezed into Jacob's face, making Jacob muse that the man should have outgrown not the Socialism but the asthma.

At Shumkin's, for the first time in his life, Jacob held a position at which he stood rather than sat. If this were a promotion, he joked, his feet did not rejoice. He was assigned to the first floor, and there he walked for ten hours a day, six days a week, the fresh boutonniere, which was issued each morning, curling as the day progressed. Walking on the first floor was tolerable because, if nothing else, the air was good. Large, expensive fans had been positioned about the first floor to show customers that Shumkin's was a store that cared about their comfort. There were no fans on the other floors, but by the time the customers found that out, it was difficult to escape.

Jacob supervised twenty-one salespeople, mostly women. With a pleasure he concealed from everyone, Jacob began to realize that some women found him charming. He was gentle, and in the context of Shumkin's Department Store, erudite. Still, admiration was a small reward for such boring work.

One day, the head floorwalker, a cousin of Shumkin's, but without the asthma, approached. "Linderman," he said, "I have to take you down to the basement."

Jacob's face drooped. He remembered the air.

"Nothing against you. We are pleased with your work, but the floorwalker in the basement cannot get along with the help. They have been threatening to quit and Christmas is coming and we want that you should reestablish order."

The feature of Shumkin's Christmas display in the basement was a cage filled with live South American monkeys. Jacob noticed them at once. The smell pervaded the entire basement; Jacob quickly suspected that it was a fundamental cause of employee unrest.

Each night, at Shumkin's, the floorwalkers filed written reports. Jacob's commentaries from the basement, literate statements on odor and human sensibilities, were stamped "received" and, like all the other reports, filed away unread.

One stifling afternoon Manya Margolies fainted. Manya, petite and brown-haired, had been selling cheap men's neckwear adjacent to the monkey cage. She revived as Jacob was ministering to her, shaking drops of cool water into her face. When she opened her eyes, she looked at Jacob with adoration.

Moved, Jacob marched up to see Shumkin, who was not in. Instead, he had to speak to the head floorwalker.

"Since you are ignoring my daily reports," Jacob said.

"Good man, we are ignoring nothing."

"You know about the monkeys and the smell."

"Indeed we do, but we advertise the monkeys. Customers come to Shumkin's to see them. Salespeople we can always get. New monkeys, who knows?"

"At least a fan," Jacob said.

"You are right there."

The fan, a huge machine, was fixed permanently into the

floor facing the monkey cage. Shumkin had finally looked over Jacob's reports, and they had frightened him into authorizing the big expensive fan. Somewhere Shumkin had read that circulating air was essential to the life and health of South American monkeys.

Jacob worked at Shumkin's for a long time. That part of the labor movement in which he was interested regarded him as a deserter of De Leon and would not have him. The Gompers' labor movement, as Jacob called the more conservative groups, he would not have.

Once, some neckwear people he had met through Manya came to see him in the store and asked him to take over the management of a new union. "After five o'clock," Jacob said. "I cannot talk about it here."

They met in a little park, and Jacob opened the meeting by making a speech. "You see what my job is," he said. He took the boutonniere from his lapel, threw it to the pavement, and stepped on it. "I am quite unhappy in this line of work. They pay me eight, ten dollars a week. I am sure you would pay me more."

"Our last manager," one of the neckwear workers said, "was paid some thirty odd dollars."

"*Nu?*" Jacob said.

"Not enough, apparently."

"What do you mean?"

"We caught him stealing."

"So?"

"Believe me, Mr. Linderman, we are not going to pay you less than we paid the thief."

Jacob smiled warmly. Warmly smiling sparrow. He was sorry for what he must say. "I have had some disputes in the labor movement, which you cannot understand. I appreciate your offer very much, but because of the disputes, I cannot accept. If I take office in your union, the people who are fighting with me will fight you, because of me, and I have no right to expose you to that."

Soon afterward, Jacob married Manya. It surprised him when a new uncle came forward with one thousand five hundred dollars, enough money to start a Yiddish labor weekly newspaper. "I don't know if we shall make as much as thirty dollars a week," Jacob told the bride, who still looked at him with awakening adoration. "But we surely shall make enough to live."

At the table, over tea, Manya says, "Isn't his memory remarkable?"

"It certainly is."

"He never makes a mistake, not even on the smallest detail."

"The memory is better than the legs," Jacob says, "but I have neglected to explain certain aspects of anti-Semitism which are significant. The Jewish workers, you see, were always restricted to certain industries. Specifically, garments. I can remember in 1914, the year De Leon died, there was a national convention of clothing workers in Nashville, Tennessee. How did the convention come to Nashville, which was not a clothing center at the time? The people in charge of the national union wanted to keep the convention far away from what they called 'the troublemakers.' And who were they? The troublemakers were the active Jewish people in the big clothing centers, New York and Chicago."

"Even then," Manya says, looking up from her tea and speaking with abrupt, immense ferocity, "they called us names."

Jacob was riding the train out of Louisville to Nashville. The excitement—it was the second longest trip of his life— had subsided and, as he stared out of the window, disappointment nagged at him. He had hoped, or somewhere he had been told, that he would see real mountains in Kentucky but now that they had crossed that absurd little river, the Ohio, there were only hills such as one might see in New York State. And the railroad car was chilly. They had told him that the South would be warm. He had brought only light clothing.

"Jacob, Jacob." One of the young union boys from New York had run up to him. "There is a woman in another car. You must speak to her." The face Jacob saw was dominated by brown eyes and filled with pain.

The cold whipped through Jacob's jacket as he walked between the cars. It was something to feel the way the train was swaying out here. Really something. Another car, warmer. Again the cold. Terrible, and the noise of the wheels. Who would have thought steel wheels on steel rails should make so much noise?

She was in the next car, talking in strong level tones to a little group. He recognized her at once. It was not anything that he would forget afterward. She had no face. All of the blank anonymities of the crowds had come together; the pallid women in the unreal posters, the heedless women marching past when De Leon spoke in open air, the odd creatures in the advertisement drawings that were the very height of capitalist distortion. It was all their faces that this woman wore. So, it was none. "Good day," he said. "I am Jacob Linderman of New York City."

"I have heard about you, I am afraid."

Jacob was shaking with anger. He shook so violently he thought surely everyone must notice. He was ashamed. He did not know that his will had grown so strong that the shaking was confined within himself. It was as if the brain vibrated in violent lateral motions but the skull itself did not move. There was nothing for anyone to notice, no way to detect the brain in motion, except perhaps through the eyes.

"Madam, I understand you have some concerns," Jacob said, "about the roles of myself and my friends at this convention, to which we, at some expense, have come?"

"Leave it to a Jew to mention expense."

"State your concern," Jacob said.

"Concern? It's something we know. You Jews are going to the convention to throw out the Christians."

Jacob wheeled. The vibrating in his head stopped. He started to walk from the car. "Mr. Linderman," the boy called, "why don't you answer her?"

He wanted to answer with hands at her throat, clawing, but it was wrong. Violence settled nothing. All his life this woman had been waiting for him—the anti-Semite was always waiting somewhere—and now that it had come, this meeting, he could not fight back without becoming as bloody as they, for all his principles, for all his books.

There were tears in Jacob's eyes. He did not want the boy to see. "I know of propaganda along such lines," Jacob said quickly. "It is not economic theory at all. It is nonsense."

Not as the first order of business, but soon afterward the convention expelled the delegations of Jewish clothing workers from New York and Chicago. There was, a beefy speaker said, no place in the great brotherhood for troublemakers.

That was the expression he used. It was the same term Jacob heard later from an assistant to Samuel Gompers, the Jew, when Jacob tried to prepare an application for the Associated Clothing Workers to join the Gompers' American Federation of Labor. The application was rejected.

In the end, they had to exist as an independent union, the syndicalists, the faltering followers of De Leon, the conservative Socialists, the anarchists, the Communists and the great Centrist majority who cut and tailored cheap clothing for women in sweatshops that grew more redolent every year. The big unions pretended that the Associated did not exist. The fantasy seemed to please the big unionists. It made them feel more American, more like capitalists themselves, like the big bosses in the big industries who were all Christians, down to the last Mellon or Frick.

In 1919, the big unions found out about reality. That was the year of the great Carnegie Steel strike. Suddenly pitted against great industry and the Federal courts, the big unions needed as much money as they could find, and the desperate steel workers sent a delegation to ask money of the little Jew tailors' union in New York.

Stirred by the steelworkers' troubles, and intent on proving their merit to the men who had rejected them, the tailors and cutters raised one quarter of the total collected throughout the entire American labor movement. Jacob himself presented the check for one hundred thousand dollars to a representative of the A.F. of L. ending his brief talk with words from a placard of the first May Day. "Solidarity now and forever," Jacob said.

The man from the A.F. of L. walked out of the room quickly. "He did not say thank you," Jacob said afterwards, over and over again. "We gave him a hundred thousand dollars and he did not say thank you. Where were his manners?"

"Why did you come here and speak to us, although it has been delightful," Jacob says in the foyer that is ablaze with light, "when you should be speaking to the young?"

Manya, pouring more tea, shakes her head and clucks at deaf Jacob for his rudeness.

"I cannot really find a young Jewish labor movement as such."

"Ah," Jacob says. "That is correct. An excellent answer."

Manya stops shaking her head. Jacob was asking the question to teach.

"What you also cannot find," Jacob says, "are great national labor leaders who are Jewish. Jews are not permitted to reach the top of industry or labor, either one. Lawyers, yes. We have always had plenty of important Jewish labor lawyers. You have heard of Lee Pressman and Arthur Goldberg. But lawyers are not leaders and even today, a Jew cannot be the head of the C.I.O."

Jacob sips tea to moisten this throat.

"Dear, it is late for the gentleman," Manya says.

Again, Jacob holds his ancient spine straight. "The function of a union is not simply to bargain collectively," he says. "It is to provide for all the needs of its workers. For good housing and for medical care and for education. And so I ask, with so much rape and murder, never mind the ethnic theories, are the unions doing enough educating among the Negroes and the Puerto Ricans?

"But I can only ask," Jacob says. "I cannot answer. The time has come when the labor movement proceeds without my help."

"A sad day for him," Manya says loudly.

"No," Jacob says. "That is foolish sentimentalism. It is not sad at all; only inevitable."

Outside, in the cold night, two Irish policemen have picked up a Puerto Rican boy for loitering and have walked him into a deserted subway staircase. One holds his arms, the other beats a nightstick on his shins. The Puerto Rican howls from pain.

Two Negro teenagers come at a run. They are armed with aerials torn from parked automobiles. They size up the situation. They stop and stand their ground. One calls again and again, "Git fuckin' Whitey!"

"You're next," bawls a cop, slapping a hand toward a holster, and the Negro teenagers run in terror.

Soon, in the burning of a handful of candles, in this old neighborhood where Jacob has spent sixty years, it will be as though no Jewish students walked with their books and as though Jacob himself had not lived so that the class struggle might end. All will be undone in violence, in the burning of a handful of candles, here, under the yellowing building, where Jacob and Manya live in twilight.

# Part Five

Survivors

ALTHOUGH IT RUNS AGAINST THE STATED POL-
icies and philosophies of the United States government, anti-
Semitism cannot properly be called un-American. American
history may be told as the rise of an enlightenment, within
which bigotry holds an ineradicable place.

Anti-Semitism was one of the first of Europe's exports,
reaching the New World well in advance of the most adventurous Jews. Some historians maintain that a number of sail-
ors serving Columbus and later explorers were "Marranos,"
Spanish Jews converted to Roman Catholicism under the
pressures of the Inquisition. Such records are sketchy, and
with reason. During the Inquisition, "Marranos" did not generally proclaim their ancestry.

It is certain that no *practicing* Jews settled in what was to
be United States territory until the middle of the seventeenth
century. Then, on one of the last days of summer, 1654, a
French bark named *St. Charles* docked in the Dutch colony
of New Amsterdam at the foot of Manhattan Island. Aboard
were twenty-three Jews, refugees from the Portuguese who
had descended on the growing community of Recife.

Dutch Jews migrated to Recife, in what is now Brazil,
about twenty years before. They prospered in the local sugar
business and built a white stone synagogue under tall palms.
But early in 1654, the Portuguese laid siege to Recife. When
it fell, the Portuguese, proud of their own Inquisitional ways,
ordered all the Jews to leave within three months, on pain of
death.

Some Jews returned to Holland. Others settled in the West
Indies. The twenty-three who finally reached New Amsterdam endured a harrowing escape. They were the last to leave
Recife. Now, in the haven of another Dutch possession, they
hoped for security. It did not come without a desperate struggle.

Peter Stuyvesant, Governor of New Amsterdam, was in-
fested with medieval prejudices. On September 22, 1654,
Stuyvesant wrote his employers, the directors of the Dutch
West India Company:

"The Jews who arrived would nearly all like to remain here, but learning that they (with their customary usury and deceitful trading with the Christians) were very repugnant . . . we have, for the benefit of this weak and newly developing place and the land in general, deemed it useful to require them in a friendly way to depart; praying also most seriously in this connection, for ourselves as also for the general community of your worships, that the deceitful race—such hateful enemies and blasphemers of the name of Christ—be not allowed further to trouble this new colony."

In time, Stuyvesant's request was rejected. Pressed by the Jewish community of old Amsterdam, and aware that New Amsterdam needed colonizers, the directors of the West India Company decided that the Jewish refugees could be admitted. As a concession to Stuyvesant, however, the Jews were not permitted to build a synagogue; they had to confine worship to their homes.

Bickersome correspondence between Stuyvesant and his employers ensued, but records indicate that by 1656, two years after their arrival, Jews had won a measure of acceptance in the new community. In that year, Asser Leeven, one of the twenty-three, appeared before the magistrates of New Amsterdam with a petition for citizenship.

"As he keeps watch and ward," the magistrates ruled, "the Jew is a Burgher."

Stuyvesant's defeat was undramatic, and citizenship in North America, with all its rights and all its future, fell to Asser Leeven in the ineloquent legalisms of the era.

American anti-Semitism never holds ascendancy for long. Greater traditions assert themselves and dominate. But the struggle between liberation and inquisition, between egalitarianism and caste, has been tempestuous. Democracy is not created by fiat, even by fiats as stirring as the Declaration of Independence or the Bill of Rights. Where Jefferson, Madison and Washington speak for freedom, the other side of America has spokesmen, too. Their names are Henry Ford, Ulysses S. Grant and Cotton Mather.

Mather, the preeminent figure in Puritanism at the beginning of the eighteenth century, was a man of episodic brilliance. He entered Harvard at the age of twelve; by manhood, he spoke seven languages. In a sixty-five-year life, he wrote four hundred fifty books, including a biography of his father, Increase Mather, an account of smallpox inoculations in New England and a study called *The Negro Christianized*. Whatever his gifts and modernity, Cotton Mather burned with the timeless fires of fanaticism. He was a leader of the Salem witchcraft trials, and once he wrote that Jews were "the convicts of Jerusalem, the outcasts of the land."

Mather believed that Jews, unlike witches, did not have to be burnt. They should be saved. In the summer of 1696, he recorded in his diary:

"This day, from the dust where I lay prostrate before the Lord, I lifted up my cries: For the conversion and for my own having the happiness at one time to baptize a Jew."

Subsequent pages brim with similar entries, but when it came to these specific cries, Mather's Lord proved to be satanically deaf.

Jews came to Newport, Rhode Island, in 1658, from Communities in the Caribbean and in Holland. The first charter of Rhode Island provided that no person should be "molested, punished, disquieted, or called in question for any difference of opinion." In Roger Williams' words, it was "God's will that freedom of worship be granted to all, whether pagans, Jews or Turks."

But the years that followed were difficult for New England. In 1675, the region was disturbed by war with Indians. Soon afterwards, reports spread that the Catholic French were planning an invasion from Quebec. In 1690, investigations began into a Popish Plot to seize Massachusetts. And in 1692 came the witchcraft trials. As the eighteenth century began, New England was variously insecure, xenophobic and neurotic. It was all but inevitable that Roger Williams' temperate laws of Rhode Island should be rewritten. In 1719, the right to vote was summarily withdrawn from Rhode Island atheists, Catholics and Jews.

For most of the rest of the century, the developing colonies, slowly coming into conflict with England, were wrenched by conflicts among themselves. Even as Mather raged in New England, the Quakers of Pennsylvania accepted Jews almost as equals, the mixed Protestants of South Carolina accepted, or adjusted to, the Jewish community at Charleston, and in Virginia the seeds of enlightenment were being sown. Despite New England's Puritanism, Maryland's narrow Catholicism and general Anglican arrogance, the eighteenth century saw the concept of religious liberty establish itself in America. In light of recent European history, no development in modern times has been more critical to Jewish survival.

Jews themselves, however, were not critical to the development. The generative American movement was neither concerned with, nor motivated by, any single minority or religion. Its vision was greater, for all mankind, with all sects, religions, creeds and groups—except Negroes and red Indians —pursuing happiness as equals before the law.

Excluding slaves and Indians, approximately four million people lived in the colonies at the time of the American Revolution. Their number included approximately two thousand Jews. Stated differently, Jews were not the 2.9 per cent of America they reportedly constitute today. They were one twentieth of one per cent. Out of every ten thousand Colonists, five were Jews. Proportionately more Jews are alive in Germany.

Almost all the Jews lived in coastal cities. Charleston, New York, Philadelphia, Newport and Savannah are the sites of the first five synagogues in the United States. A smattering of Jews fought in the Continental Army, or in militias, and a lesser number were Tories. But few citizens in Revolutionary America had ever met a Jew. Only one Jew is recorded to have done significant work with the Founding Fathers.

Haym Salomon, who probably reached America in 1772 as the first Jewish immigrant from Poland, served the Revolutionary Government as "Broker to the Office of Finance." Based in Philadelphia, after having fled the British in New York, Salomon sold securities for the new government in unstable and inflationary times. He appears to have been a remarkable salesman and, beyond that, a man of generosity.

"I have been a pensioner for some time on the favor of Haym Salomon," James Madison wrote Edmund Randolph of Virginia, in 1782. "The kindness of our friend near the coffee house is a fund that will preserve me from extremities, but I never resort to it without great mortification as he obstinately rejects all recompense. To necessitous delegates, he always spares them supplies."

But Salomon's American experience was not entirely happy. He left a Poland that was regressing toward the middle ages under the dominance of increasingly bigoted Jesuitism. As Polish anti-Semitism increased, Salomon's relatives asked him for funds and to provide room in his house for a young cousin. He had to refuse. Despite his skills at selling Colonial securities, he was unable to amass capital for himself. In 1783, in pain and embarrassment, he advised relatives in Poland to remain there because "your *yikhes* [family dignity] is worth very little here." Two years later, Salomon died, leaving a wife and four children, and a variety of securities in the Continental Government. They were virtually worthless.

Bills offered in Congress to provide for Salomon's family were repeatedly rejected. Historians cannot agree why. Some suggest that one of Salomon's sons was pushing an unjustified claim. Others say that the reason was anti-Semitism.

Neither the Declaration of Independence nor the Revolution it produced was sufficient to drive Matherism from the various state governments of America. On August 14, 1776, a month and ten days after the Declaration was issued, the State of Maryland adopted a constitution which provided that "all persons professing the Christian religion are equally entitled to protection in their religious liberty." Protestants had long since established themselves in this Catholic colony, and in a practical sense, Maryland Christians were offering religious liberty to other Christians.

The North Carolina Constitution, adopted December 16, stipulated that "no person who shall deny the truth of the Protestant religion or the divine authority neither of the Old or New Testament" was to hold public office. Here, Protestants offered equal opportunity to other Protestants. The Georgia Constitution of February 5, 1777, required that all legislators be Protestant and the Massachusetts Constitution, adopted on June 16, 1780, shows well the scars of Matherism. It protests that "every man in all times may find security" in Massachusetts laws, but goes on to make it "the right as well as the duty of all men in Society publicly and at stated seasons to worship the Supreme Being, the great Creator and Preserver of the the Universe." Masked as a document of liberty, this constitution actually established a state religion in Massachusetts, and later made clear what that religion was. "Every denomination of Christian," it provided, "shall be equally under the protection of the law."

But elsewhere, in New York and in Virginia and, most important, on a national level, a larger spirit was abroad. The Federal Constitution of 1787 bears witness.

Article VI, section 3 of the Constitution placed the great wall between church and state that still stands strong. The article provides that "no religious test shall ever be required as a qualification to any office or public trust in the United States." The language is firm, direct, unequivocal. Four years later, when the Bill of Rights was adopted, the First Amendment guaranteed universal religious liberty in language that has become famous: "Congress shall make no law respecting an establishment of religion or prohibiting the free exercise thereof."

Now the end of discriminatory state laws was ordained, which is not to say that it was imminent. Following Federal lead, state and local lawmakers rewrote and erased at varying rates of speed. New Hampshire was the last of the Matheristic holdouts to delete a discriminatory provision from its constitution. It was not until 1877, one-hundred-and-one-years after the Declaration of Independence promised liberty and equality to all Americans, that the Jews of New Hampshire were allowed to run for state office.

A variety of documents survives in which the Founding Fathers correspond with Jews. At the time of George Washington's inauguration the settlement in Richmond had increased the number of Jewish congregations in the United States to six. Every one dispatched a congratulatory letter to the first President.

Washington answered all courteously, even warmly. His response to the Newport Congregation concludes by weaving the words of Micah into an eloquent and compassionate statement, from a man not always associated with either quality.

"It would be inconsistent with the frankness of my character," Washington wrote, "not to avow that I am pleased with your favorable opinion of my administration, and fervent wishes for my felicity. May the children of the stock of Abraham, who dwell in this land, continue to merit and enjoy the good will of the other inhabitants, while everyone shall sit in safety under his own vine and fig tree and there shall be none to make him afraid. May the father of all mercies scatter light and not darkness in our paths and make all in our several vocations useful here, and in his own due time and way everlastingly happy."

In 1818, the new Mill Street Synagogue was consecrated in New York City, an occasion which one of its leading congregants, Mordecai M. Noah, used to write a number of Americans. Noah described the consecration, expanded into general Jewish history and spoke out for religious liberty. Thomas Jefferson, then seventy-five years old, personally replied from his mansion, Monticello.

"Your sect," Jefferson wrote Noah, "by its sufferings has furnished a remarkable proof of the universal spirit of religious intolerance inherent in every sect, disclaimed by all while feeble, and practiced by all when in power. Our laws have applied the only antidote to this vice protecting our religions as they do our civil rights, but putting all on an equal footing. But more remains to be done, for although we are free by the law, we are not so in practice. . . . It is to be hoped that individual dispositions will at length mold themselves to the model of the law."

Despite the encyclopedic range of his knowledge, Jefferson was no scholar of Jewish history. He had numerous Jewish acquaintances, one of whom, Commodore Uriah Levy, preserved Monticello as a memorial after Jefferson's death in 1826. But among the Founding Fathers, John Adams of Massachusetts, the second President, and Jefferson's rival and friend, appears to have been the most ardent Judeophile. Adams once described Jews as the "essential instrument for civilizing nations." Characteristically, John Adams' response to Mordecai Noah was particularly cordial.

From Quincy, he wrote, "I have had occasion to be acquainted with several gentlemen of your nation, and to transact business with some of them, whom I found to be men of as liberal minds, as much honor, probity, generosity and good breeding, as any I have known in any sect or religion or philosophy.

"I wish your nation may be admitted to all privileges of citizens in every country in the world."

It had been a heartening century. Almost precisely one hundred one years before the Adams letter, another Massachusetts man, Cotton Mather, still lusting for converts, was writing hotly in his diary:

"I heard of a Jew in this place. I would seek conversation with him."

There were probably no more than fifteen thousand Jews in the United States during the 1830's, when the national population was approaching seventeen million. Most were Sephardic, Jews of Spanish and Portuguese descent. But with the 1840's, and a massive exodus of Jews from the German states, the first large wave of Jewish immigration reached America.

Liberalism was a grave problem for Europe in the 1840's, when the "perfect peace" of Metternich was destroyed. Revolts and revolutions erupted about the continent, in France, where Louis Philippe was overthrown, in Austria and in the disunified provinces of Germany. The German uprisings, in Hannover, Saxony and elsewhere, were efforts to secure greater freedom and constitutional government. After early successes, the liberals were defeated and old regimes, returned to power, often more autocratic than before.

Jews were among the liberals of Central Europe and a number fled to America, as revolutionaries embracing a revolutionary country. But a larger factor in the exodus was that familiar concomitant to unsettled times, rising anti-Semitism. Jews were reportedly beaten in the streets of Bavarian villages. In other areas, they became again objects of scorn. The tide seemed to be running against the Jews of Germany. Before the Civil War, between one hundred and fifty and two hundred thousand had become American immigrants.

Generally, the German Jews possessed a dedication to *Kultur,* and there were certainly intellectuals among them, but the great majority were business people. They settled in cities from New York to San Francisco and went to work as merchants. Some ultimately were able to establish fortunes. The Schiffs, Loebs, Warburgs, Lehmans are affluent Jewish families with German roots.

Approximately seventy-five hundred Jews fought in the Civil War, six thousand of them for the North; but the war itself disrupted the integration of Jewish immigrants into American life. Like all wars, it exacerbated tensions, promoted mistrust and fortified extreme positions. On July 22, 1861, Congress passed a law requiring each Army chaplain to be "a regularly ordained minister of some Christian denomination."

Jewish protests began immediately. One group, the Board of Delegates of American Israelites, dispatched a Dutch emigré named Arnold Fischel to lobby in Washington. That December, Fischel was able to win Abraham Lincoln's promise to "try to have a new law broad enough to cover what is desired by you in behalf of the Israelites." In July, 1862, the discriminatory clause was eliminated. The most brazen act of official anti-Semitism to be found in American history followed this small victory by a few months.

As Major General in charge of large areas of Kentucky, Tennessee and Mississippi, Ulysses S. Grant had been having a frustrating time. He lost badly at Shiloh in April of 1862, and in November, his march on Vicksburg stalled. Smuggling and profiteering were rife along the borders, with Army officers particularly guilty. That a few of the civilian profiteers happened to be Jews can hardly be used to justify Grant's actions.

On April 10, 1862, from his headquarters at La Grange, Tennessee, the general issued an order "to all the conductors on the road that no Jews are to be permitted to travel on the railroad southward." Grant called Jews "an intolerable nuisance." Unchecked, he and his staff grew more bold. On December 8, an aide, Colonel John V. DuBoise, ordered "all cotton speculators, Jews, and other vagrants having no honest means of support," to leave the district. The campaign reached a climax on December 18, with the issuance of General Order No. 11:

"The Jews, as a class violating every regulation of trade established by the Treasury Department and also department orders, are hereby expelled . . .

"Post commanders will see that all of this class of people be furnished passes and required to leave, and any one returning after such notification will be arrested . . .

"No passes will be given these people to visit headquarters for the purpose of making personal applications for trade permits.

"By order of Maj.-Gen. U. S. Grant."

The classic behavior pattern of an anti-Semite is to attack all Jews—in Grant's phrase—"Jews as a class." The anti-Semite is blind to Jews as individuals of varying beliefs and varying worths.

One worthy Jewish business man, Cesar Kaskel of Paducah, Kentucky, found himself expelled from his own home under the terms of Grant's order. Kaskel led a delegation that sent a furious petition to Abraham Lincoln on December 29. Carrying out Grant's order, the petitioners wrote, "would place us as outlaws before the world. We respectfully ask your immediate attention to this enormous outrage on all law and humanity."

No record survives of a direct reply from the President. However, five days later, the War Department dispatched an order to Grant. It read:

"A paper purporting to be General Orders, No. 11, issued by you December 17 has been presented here. By its terms, it expels all Jews from your department.

"If such an order has been issued, it will be immediately revoked."

Six years later, as a candidate for President, Grant's alleged anti-Semitism became a campaign issue. "I have no prejudice against any sect or race," he insisted then. "Order No. 11 does not sustain this statement, I admit, but then I do not sustain that order. It never would have been issued if it had not been telegraphed the moment it was penned, and without reflection."

Anti-Semitism, as most American Jews encounter it today, did not exist at the time of the Civil War. The closing of clubs to Jews, and the related closing of other areas of social life, commerce and education, were refinements still reserved for the American future. During the 1860's, Joseph Gratz, a devout Reform Jew, was elected president of the patrician Philadelphia Club. In New York City, the Seligman brothers, Joseph and Jesse, who were wealthy bankers, helped found the Union League. The Seligmans were German-Jewish immigrants. Despite the presence of individual anti-Semites, American society at large was mobile and open. Jews were not barred from favored places because they were Jews.

The founder, or at least the patron saint, of contemporary American anti-Semitism, is Henry Hilton, a businessman reportedly connected with the Tweed Ring, who was afterwards appointed general manager of the Grand Union Hotel in Saratoga Springs, New York. Possessed of stately elms, natural baths and a racetrack, Saratoga had become a fashionable resort. The Grand Union was its most luxurious hotel.

In 1877 Joseph Seligman of the Union League arrived at the Grand Union on vacation. The room clerks turned him away. Hilton had issued instructions that "no Israelites shall be permitted in the future to stop at this hotel."

One of Joseph Seligman's close friends, the Reverend Henry Ward Beecher, quickly denounced anti-Semitism from the pulpit of his Plymouth Church in Brooklyn Heights. "What have the Jews of which they need be ashamed," Beecher asked, "in a Christian Republic where all men are declared to be free and equal? . . . Is it that they are excessively industrious? Let the Yankee cast the first stone. Is it that they are inordinately keen on bargaining? Have they ever stolen ten millions of dollars at a pinch from a city? Are our courts bailing out Jews? . . . You cannot find one criminal Jew in the whole catalogue."

The futility of reasoned defense is recurrent.

*Hath not a Jew eyes?* asks the defender.

*Indeed,* says the anti-Semite, *the better to leer at my daughter.*

Even if Beecher's arguments had been more powerful and less defensive, they would have failed. They were running against a rising wave of American xenophobia, of which anti-Semitism was both a symptom and a part. The immigration boom was underway.

In both 1871 and 1872, Congressmen considered taking action "to control the immigrants." Several states adopted anti-immigration laws, which the Supreme Court had to invalidate in 1876. Newspaper editorial writers began making distinctions between old immigrants and new. Without the xenophobia that accompanied mass immigration, the Hilton-Seligman case might now be nothing more than an example of overt rudeness. With it, the incident became the starting point for a campaign of anti-Semitic restrictions in America that was not halted for almost seventy years, until after the Second World War and the exposure of Hitler's final solution to "the Jewish problem."

No one knows how many Jews emigrated to America during the late nineteenth and early twentieth centuries. Estimates range from two to three million. The best guess seems to be that which puts the immigrant total at about two-and-a-quarter million, or more than seven times the number of Jews who lived in America before the huge wave from Eastern Europe broke.

Not all these two-and-a-quarter million Jews were East Europeans. Not all the earliest Jews had been Sephardic, nor had all the immigrants of 1848 come from Central Europe. But the great majority of the so-called third wave came from Russia, Polish provinces, Hungary and Roumania, areas of

Europe which were in common depressed, unenlightened and increasingly anti-Semitic. The third-wave immigrants knew no drawing rooms, no teas nor even Reform Judaism.

Most left Europe for pragmatic reasons. "Pogrom" is one of the very few words to have entered the English language directly from the Russian. In Russian, it originally meant devastation, and escape from the devastation of pogroms both real and threatened drove hundreds of thousands of Jews to the United States.

Avoiding conscription was another motivating force. The prospect of service in the anti-Semitic army of an anti-Semitic czar led thousands of Jewish youths to plot escapes. But probably the overwhelming consideration leading Jews to America were the twin conditions of poverty and hopelessness. East Europe offered Jews an existence with no dream of betterment; beyond that, the existence itself was miserable. Hunger, skimpy clothing, dying infants, men worked out by thirty-five were realities in many of the *shtetls*.

So the Jews left. By the latter half of the nineteenth century, word of American freedom had extended even into impoverished, unemancipated Eastern Europe, and Eastern Jews came to America bearded, unwashed, pediculous and fervent. In America they found a variety of poverty which differed from the poverty of Europe. It allowed hope.

Most of the Jews settled in their port of entry, New York City, where they made clothing, wheeled pushcarts and, as Jacob Linderman recounted, became Socialists. Their lives were mean but free and the sudden release from European bondage produced some of the most remarkable ghettos in history. Nelson Glueck, the archeologist, has likened these refugees to people who have been too long in a desert. "When they escape," Glueck says, "and finally approach food and drink, they spring forward ferociously. Their table manners may be less than perfect, but how could it be any other way?"

On the lower east side of New York, and in a region of Brooklyn called Brownsville, the emigrés scratched out livings, worked, connived and passed enormous ambitions to their offspring. Some of the children became professors and lawyers and musicians, delighting the parents. Others, out of the mean neighborhoods, became prize fighters. Still others were gamblers and a few grew up to become killers. One hyperbolic, but significant, story has Professor Morris Raphael

Cohen, the late philosopher, and Louis (Lepke) Buchalter, the late murderer, growing up in a ghetto tenement side by side.

Vitality was the special quality of Jewish life. One gets a sense of it in the realistic novels of Abraham Cahan, long the editor of *The Jewish Daily Forward,* and in Michael Gold's impassioned *Jews Without Money.* "Excitement," Gold wrote, "dirt, fighting, chaos! The sound of my street lifted like the blast of a great carnival or catastrophe. The noise was always in my ears. Even in sleep I could hear it; I hear it now."

Noisy, resolute and vital, the Eastern European Jews troubled other Jews, who had been living in America for years. They were poor relations, turned up at the wrong time, embarrassing—the way an unsuccessful uncle from Brooklyn embarrasses his nephews in Roslyn Heights, Long Island, when he arrives unannounced at a formal dinner party and begins spouting jokes in Yiddish at Christian neighbors.

The *Ostjuden,* Eastern Jews, appeared to threaten the German-Jewish hope of complete assimilation. They might, by their very difference, revive American anti-Semitism. To many German Jews, they seemed an unpleasant amalgam of anarchy, dirty socialism, hair and Orthodoxy. In 1886, the Conference of Managers of the Associated Hebrew Charities, dominated by German Jews, passed a resolution of commentary on *Ostjuden* in New York. It read: "We condemn the transportation of paupers into this country . . . all such as are unable to maintain themselves should forthwith be returned whence they came."

Today, the vast majority of American Jews traces to East European forebears. Most of what is classed as simply Jewish —*Fiddler on the Roof,* gefilte fish, the rising inflection of speech—is *East European Jewish.* It is alien to other Jews. No Jew who came from Seville had tasted borscht.

But ninety years ago, the climate of the United States was inhospitable to such distinctions. As immigrant roles grew, the times became right for hardening distinctions of occupation, class, religion. In 1879, two years after the Grand Union Hotel barred Joseph Seligman, Austin Corbin, president of the Long Island Railroad, announced plans to transform Coney Island into a stylish resort "forever free from Jews." By the 1880's, according to William Dean Howells, property values on better Boston streets dropped as soon as a

Jew was allowed to purchase a house. In 1893, Seligman, that sturdy founder of the Union League Club, decided to resign. His son had just been blackballed for being Jewish.

The college quota system, limiting the number of Jewish students, first began appearing shortly before World War I. Anti-Semitism in hiring followed soon afterward. In 1916, Jacob Schiff, the New York financier, withdrew as a director of a large employment agency which was "discouraging" Jewish applicants. By the time Congress terminated unlimited immigration in 1924, anti-Semitism had assumed a respectability. It was, in fact, an important part of the new snobbery in the presumably respectable American life. Into this climate charged a great industrialist, issuing spleen.

Henry Ford purchased *The Dearborn Independent* on January 11, 1919. Within a year, this previously obscure paper had embarked on the most ambitious, fanatic and best-financed campaign of anti-Semitism in the history of the United States.

In May 1920, *The Dearborn Independent* published the first in a series of ninety-one articles entitled: "The International Jew: The World's Problem." Pivotal material was that odd, durable forgery from Czarist Russia called *The Protocols of the Elders of Zion*, which claimed to be based on the minutes of a secret meeting "of the leaders of the world Jewry."

A premise of the *Protocols* was that "the Jews" were planning to dominate the world. Proceeding further, the editors of *The Dearborn Independent* were able to impute dark implications with polemical skill and paranoid zeal. They depicted Jews as a monolithic group with monolithic values and the one great purpose of domination. Jews sought to control industry; they already dominated the world of finance. Jews were "loose"; they were the creators of pornography and the misleaders of youth, the more swiftly to undermine the United States. "Who are the masters of musical jazz in the world?" *The Dearborn Independent* asked. "Who direct all the cheap jewelry houses, the bridge-head show parks, the centers of nervous thrills and looseness? It is possible to take the showy young man and woman of trivial outlook and loose sense of responsibility, and tag them outwardly and inwardly, from their clothing and ornaments to their hectic ideas and hopes, with the same tag. *Made, introduced and exploited by a Jew."*

During the ninety-one consecutive weeks in which *The Dearborn Independent* published these anti-Semitic attacks, its circulation rose to seven hundred thousand copies. Some sold by subscription. Most were given away free by Ford dealers. Ultimately, in 1927, Ford disavowed the articles in a public statement. "I am deeply mortified," he wrote, "that this journal has been made the medium . . . for contending that the Jews have been engaged in a conspiracy to control the capital and the industries of the world . . . I deem it my duty as a honorable man to make amends to the wrongs done to the Jews as fellow men and brothers." That same year the Ford Motor Company placed one hundred fifty-six thousand dollars worth of advertising in Yiddish and Jewish newspapers. Also in that same year, the articles from *The Dearborn Independent* were translated and reprinted in German. Five years earlier, a correspondent for *The New York Times,* interviewing Adolf Hitler in Munich, had noticed a picture of Ford hanging on one of the office walls.

Modern American anti-Semitism, growing wild for half a century, inherited a ninety-one chapter demonology in the 1920's. No longer were Jews scorned merely as foreign, hirsute, overshrewd or as the committers of an ancient, abstract deicide. *The Dearborn Independent* had argued in issue after issue: *The Jews are out to take over the world. The Jews are a menace here and now*.

To growing thousands of Americans, the charges seemed to possess substance. Their appearance in print, their repetition, seemed to lend them validity. To others, only part of the accusations were accurate. With ponderous liberality, they pleaded that not *all* Jews were bad. Then the Depression struck, and the tone of American life grew strident.

During the 1930's, when ten million men were out of work in a Depression that seemed chronic, it was a relatively easy matter for professional demagogues to whip American anti-Semitism toward its climax. Fritz Kuhn, Fuehrer of the Nazi German-American Bund, organized Bund chapters in every major city in the United States. Gerald Winrod, a Fundamentalist preacher from Kansas, found one hundred thousand readers for his anti-Jewish newspaper, *The Defender*. Father Charles Coughlin's *Social Justice* did far better. Its circulation reached one million and Coughlin's sermons, attacking "Bolshevik and international Jews" were broadcast over a national network that, at its height, numbered 475 stations.

Anti-Semitism hammered at the American consciousness. City street corners were loud with anti-Jewish speeches. *Kike* was the cry from the platforms, while hustlers milling in the crowds handed out throwaways advertising rubber truncheons as "kike-killers." Jews were baited, insulted and beaten on the sidewalks of New York.

It was a curious time. A Jewish child at school was reverently taught of Washington, Jefferson and Madison, but all the while he found himself in a society that appeared hellbent on embracing the reviving fanaticism of Mather, in which Jews were fit only for salvation, or the nascent fanaticism of Hitler in which Jews were suitable for nothing except cremation.

## HERRENVOLK

Saul Lederman does not consider himself very Jewish, in spite of his name and his long curving nose, and the intensity that seizes him when he finds himself confronting a German in an argument. Saul Lederman prefers to say that he is neither Jewish nor non-Jewish. He is, he says, a practicing intellectual. It amuses Saul, who is forty-two, bald and given to complicated self-deprecation, to quote one sentence from *Mein Kampf. I had ceased to be a weak-kneed cosmopolitan and become an anti-Semite.* "My knees," Saul says, after a deliberate puff on a cigarette, "were good enough for me to run relays for Columbia, so I'm ahead of Hitler there. But I'm certainly behind him in the rest of it. I'm still aspiring toward cosmopolitanism."

Saul lives in New York City and intends to live there always. He belongs to no Jewish organizations and subscribes to no Jewish magazines. He has been in synagogues only on three occasions and he does not intend to go again, either in life or after death. Saul Lederman does not believe in any god, by any definition. With a faith he can neither articulate nor justify, he believes in humanity in spite of itself. It is a thin faith, and Saul has lived an intense, demanding life. He wonders now if the vague throbbing ache that sometimes starts between his left elbow and shoulder could be, so soon, he is not ready, the first murmurings of the coronary ahead.

By craft, Saul Lederman is an editor. By avocation, he is a student of poetry. Of the two hundred books he has edited, he is proudest of two volumes of sprung rhythm, *Cold Sunlight* and *Autumnal Hymns*. The author, dead now, was an epileptic woman whom Saul Lederman had never met. Saul does not write himself. He tried deeply when he was younger, but the results were not satisfactory. He remembers the plots of three attempted novels that did not begin very well. There were drafts and struggles and cruel surges of hope and then he studied the drafts, and placed them in manila envelopes which he concealed in a bedroom bureau drawer. "It seems," Saul said to Clara, his wife, a chubby straw-haired girl from Mason City, Iowa, "that my critical taste exceeds my creative ability."

"It seems," Clara said. That was how she was always, echoing and always echoing the wrong things. What he should like to have been told was that his critical taste was rare, or to have been asked how it felt to see the world with Keats' sensibilities, and to be flawed by wanting Keats' pen.

Still, he misses Clara in the remembering morning, when the apartment is vastly empty, and the FM music is trivia and he is not up to playing his own recordings of Beethoven or Schumann. It is difficult for a man who has known family for most of forty-two years to live suddenly and by his own choice alone, so that he must walk out of his own home to address another human being face to face.

Saul's defense has been to routinize mornings, although he dislikes routines. He awakens at 8:30 in a light blue bedroom, sits up facing books, and trudges toward the narrow alcove of a kitchen. There, he sets a pot of water to boil. Then he showers and shaves, lathering luxuriously with mug and brush. After dressing, he proceeds to add hot water slowly to a filter coffee maker. The trick, say the instructions, is to maintain water temperature at 190 degrees. In between turning the burner on and off and pouring, Saul occupies himself with *The New York Times*, avoiding book reviews because it is not yet time for work, and eating the same dry cereal he has liked for thirty-six years. As a concession to his arteries, the milk he adds is skimmed.

The mornings are mindless and not unpleasant, unless he has drunk heavily the night before. Saul holds liquor well but pays afterward with wracking hangovers that leave him quivering. No religion, he suggests, has ever been strong enough to sustain hope in a man alone during the first hour of a hangover. "If there were," he says, "I'd enlist."

By 9:20 this morning, he is out of the apartment building, twenty stories of identical windows and identical air-conditioning vents squatting on top of one another on East 63rd Street in Manhattan. He tests his voice with a "yessir" at the doorman, and begins loping across town toward the offices of the New Caxton Press. He has a ten o'clock appointment with Peter Warrens, the president of New Caxton. Warrens has come across a book he wants Saul to edit, and Saul has come across an author he wants New Caxton to publish. The two men endure each other edgily.

New Caxton is housed in a commercial equivalent of the building where Saul lives, forty-seven floors of glass, bound by garish plastic panels, rising above Third Avenue. Caxton's offices begin on the thirty-fourth floor.

"Morning. Coffee?" Peter Warrens says to Saul. Warrens is big and bland-faced behind eyeglasses. Except for a huge oak desk, his office is equally bland.

"Thanks, no," Saul says. "Just had a few cups. I've got some poems here, from a young Negro. I think we ought to have a look. They're called *The Rose is Gross*."

"What the hell is that supposed to mean?" Peter Warrens says.

"It's from a sentence by Pound. *If they don't understand poetry and they don't feel music, what can they understand of love, compared to which the rose is gross*."

"Pound is a goddamn anti-Semite," Warrens says. His father's name was Warhaftig.

"The poems aren't."

"Read me one," Peter Warrens says.

"What?"

"I don't want any slick, aesthetic presentation. Here. Give me the script." Warrens reaches over the oak desk which once belonged to Hoover or Coolidge—Saul can never recall which—and seizes the loose-leaf notebook in which the poems are bound. He opens it and points. "Read," he orders. "This one," he says. "The one he calls *A Pair of Coppers*."

I have wept for a lady who died to meet my tears.
I have wept at the grave of a friend, melting ice years.
But my father.
      Oh, brave, unslaving dark sonsaving man aloof.
My father is ashes, interred beyond grief's watering.
The urn, dull copper
        Like his skin,
Is rustproof.

"Cute," Peter Warrens says. "A bonbon. Very good. But
we don't stay in business publishing bonbons."

"Lyrics are his real forte," Saul says. "His name is Marshall Booker, and he writes these fine, gentle, flawed lyrics,
and when you get all done and you realize that these poems
are about love and young manhood in a black jungle, with
rats and roaches and incest all around, the impact becomes
enormous."

"Maybe," Peter Warrens says. "Maybe. With the right introduction. Maybe we could get Baldwin to write it."

"No," Saul says. "He doesn't want that. This is Marshall
Booker's work, and he doesn't want anybody else writing in
it."

"In that case, you can tell Marshall for me, I said *oi vey*."
Warren laughs. "I got something for you," he says. "Have I
got something. A German woman's diary, day-by-day, of the
decline and fall of Hitler's Reich, seen from the inside, mind
you, and by a woman. I want you to read it right away."

"I'm not sympathetic," Saul says.

"Well, now this does *not* happen to be anti-Semitic," Warrens says. "Not at all. It's a story of decay. And more than
that. Before you're done, the woman becomes a kind of German Anne Frank."

Saul smiles thinly. "From whom is this German hiding?"
he says. "From Jews?"

There is no topping Peter Warrens in his own office.

"I've got a busy morning," he says. "Was there anything
else you wanted?"

Saul shakes his head.

"This German thing could sell," Warrens says, "and big.
Look it over. See if you can work out a way to bring it to
New Caxton standards. I've seen a little and it's kind of
rough. But if you can make it go, maybe I can come up with

some way to publish your colored friend's poems, without it costing us too goddamn much."

Peter Warrens buzzes for his secretary. He looks up at Saul and says, "I'm sending the Kraut in to see you. It'll help you to meet her before you read her book."

At 2:15 P.M. she appears in Saul's office, tall, but not so tall as she seems, and commanding in a black flaring coat and a black witch's hat, above long, straight blonde hair. "Hello," she says. "How do you do? I have heard about you from Peter. I'm so glad he has arranged this meeting. I'm Herta Cohen."

Slowly Saul looks up from his gray steel desk. "Oh," he says. "Excuse me. I was reading." He closes Marshall Booker's *The Rose is Gross* and glares at his secretary. "Jeannie. Take Mrs. Cohen's coat." Jean Rawson stares helpless, shrugging. She has been told repeatedly that all visitors must be announced, even those sent by Mr. Warrens (especially those sent by Mr. Warrens).

"So," Herta Cohen says. "I have barged in. I am afraid I am not one for all the graces."

Under the coat she is wearing a white dress on which a white design is vaguely patterned. She walks to Saul's bookshelf. "So," she says. "You do not mind? I think you can tell so much from a man's library."

Saul drops into his black leather chair and says, "Two coffees, Jeannie."

"Poetry. So much poetry," Herta Cohen says. Jean Rawson, trim and shy, retreats. "You can't tell very much from an editor's office library, Mrs. Cohen," Saul says. "Much of it is simply what people send—other editors and publishing houses—and what he's been forced to edit himself. Won't you sit down?"

Herta Cohen moves in long mannish strides, but gracefully. She holds a satchel. As she sits, she places the satchel on Saul's desk, opens it with strong, deft hands and gathers the manuscript which spills.

Saul notices two typing errors on a page. "It's generally a good idea," he says, "to put the thing in a box. Most authors do."

"You flatter me," Herta Cohen says. "I'm no author, to be sure. I mentioned this to Peter Warrens at a party, and he

read a page or so and he said this was something Saul Lederman must see. He thinks a great deal of you."

"We all have dark thoughts."

Herta Cohen does not smile. Jean Rawson brings in coffee.
When the girl has gone, Herta Cohen says, "It isn't any good,
to be sure. I have fantastic guilt that I should waste your
time."

"Peter, who is the president of New Caxton Press, has instructed me to read your work. Peter pays my salary. There
is no time-waste at all."

"Well, he is not here and I am here," Herta Cohen says.
She clutches Saul's arm. "I am embarrassed to be making a
demand. I do not like to make demands of men. I only ask
you to tell me the truth, even if it is brutal, horrible about
my diary."

Grabbing women discomfit Saul. There is the clear temptation to grab back, but that is not what many of them want;
some want to wriggle away. They court the pleasure of rejec-
tion. And yet, for a man not to respond is vital weakness.

The hand rests on Saul's arm. He leans back slightly. "Perhaps," he says, "you can make things easier all around by
telling me how this book came to be written."

"Ah," Herta Cohen says. "Ah, of course," as though Saul
has said something profound. Cool green eyes fix his, and
Herta squeezes his arm. "I was living in Germany of a good
old Cologne family, when the war came, and we had hard
times, particularly in the end. It is no more pleasant to be
bombed as a German than it is to be bombed as an English-
man or even, to be sure, as an Israeli."

Saul stiffens. "Were you a Nazi?"

"I was a child."

"When the war ended, how old a child were you?"

"Eighteen."

"As I get the picture," Saul says, "there were never more
than five or six Nazis in Germany. But they worked hard."

"I was in Hitler Jugend," Herta Cohen says. "Bund
Deutscher Maedel. Bund of German girls." She throws her
head back and the blonde hair swings. She is not bowing.
"What else was there to do?"

"If only Streicher were alive," Saul Lederman says.

"Why do you say such a terrible thing?"

"So I could tell him I have found a Nazi who is named
Cohen."

"Our family name was Lieber," Herta says. "I have been married to a painter. Perhaps you know his work—Frans Cohen."

"No, I don't know him at all," Saul says. He drums long fingers on the desk. "What I thought was that after the war you might have changed your family name to Cohen as an act of contrition."

She gazes at him for a long time. "How odd," Herta says, "for you to be so ungentle."

It was odd, and how astonishing for Herta to have noticed right away. What he remembers first of life is a red brick home in Jamaica, Queens, inhabited by intellectuals, who talked of revolutions and were quite incapable of violence. His father, Jesse, had inherited money, and become a professor of constitutional law. Rosie, his mother, taught piano, and sculpted and painted and was hostess at parties which attracted gentle people. It was a savage Depression time, but not to Saul.

When he was old enough, Saul would curl on the window seat, a dark ornament with wide, dark eyes, devouring party conversation. By his ninth birthday, he knew the names of Shakespeare, Whitman, Housman, Toscanini, Shelley, Picasso, Koussevitzky, Gibbon, and had heard the Theory of Surplus Values.

Except for parties, and sometimes at dusk, his mother was busy. Saul was raised at the full bust of Bertha, a Bavarian woman, who crooned to him and baked him lemon cookies and bathed him and sometimes, but not often, took him to St. Jude's Roman Catholic Church, where, with great intimacy in the pillared dark, the two lit candles for Bertha's mother who had died long before in Germany.

There was no religion at the Lederman home. Saul was aware of being *ein kind*, long before he found out that he was Jewish.

But he caught cold easily and the public school was crowded, and Rosie Lederman had high ambitions for her boy. After a few years of shuttling, she enrolled him in Jamaica Preparatory Academy, an elementary school for boys which, according to its principal, Miss Ernestine Cokes, was "Episcopal by orientation, but welcomed worthies of any faith." Miss Cokes extended an ancient hand to pat Saul's neck.

What bothered Saul first at Jamaica Preparatory Academy were the daily chapels, when he had to join the others singing songs. They seemed to know them but he, for all his assiduous piano-playing at home, had never heard any of the melodies before. He had to apply himself for more than a week, until he could join in a chorus:

*Cast thy burden upon the Lord,*
*And he will sustain* (two, three, four) *thee.*

He was not comfortable with the music nor with the psalms that Miss Cokes cried from her chapel pulpit in a high baritone voice:

*My God, my God, why hast Thou forsaken me? Why art Thou so far from helping me and from the words of my roaring?*

It was all Saul could do to keep from giggling. He did not know that these words had been written by a Jew. He did not even know that he was the only Jewish boy in his class.

He got along easily with his classmates, establishing himself before the first Christmas when he made a lunging catch of a forward pass thrown by a seventh grader named Fats Linscott. "Jeez," Fats said, in the next huddle. "What's the matter, kid? Can't you catch a pass without falling down?"

Sanford Anson, a dark-browed boy who was president of the student body said, "Shut up, Fats. The kid made a good catch." Anson patted Saul's bottom, and winked.

That was all it took, or would have taken, for acceptance, had not the times been against a Jewish boy outnumbered in a Christian private school. Two years later, in the fifth grade, an Irish Catholic joined Saul's class. Francis Doheny, strawhaired, bespectacled and fleshy-faced, was the first devout anti-Semite Saul Lederman had met.

Frannie Doheny, disciplant of Father Coughlin, grasped the concept and the details of the Jew scheme to dominate the world which he had learned from his own father and from Father Charles Coughlin's radio sermons and from reading the newspaper, *Social Justice*. Soon after Frannie Doheny started carrying *Social Justice* into Jamaica Academy, everyone in class became aware that Saul Lederman was a Jew.

Doug Kincaid, the class leader, had shared with Saul a distrust of older children and a specific dislike of Fats Linscott. Doug's baseball swing ended, when he missed, with the bat motionless above and behind his left ear. "Hey, look at Pose-o!" Fats Linscott would shout. "Hey, Pose-o, hold that pose!"

One afternoon long after school and a hard catch, Saul and Doug were experimenting with swings that stood in the graveled playground behind Jamaica Academy. They were twirling. Suddenly Doug said to Saul, "Hey, Izzy."

Saul blinked.

"Hey, Izzy. You look like an Izzy." Doug Kincaid said. He smiled wide and Saul saw the braces in Doug's teeth, with rubber bands behind them.

"What are you calling me Izzy for? Why don't you call me Saul or Lederman?"

" 'Cause you look like an Izzy," Doug Kincaid said.

Saul said, "I've got a name. You've got a name. Call me by my name."

"No," Kincaid said.

"Why not?"

"You look like an Izzy, you look like an Izzy," Kincaid said.

Saul's face sagged, and by the following afternoon he was "Izzy" or "Iz" to everyone in the class.

Saul remained friends with Kincaid, but it was not what it had been.

The willingness was gone. Now Saul accepted Kincaid as class leader, arbitrator, matchmaker only because he had no choice. Kincaid was suddenly crueler; he matched Saul against pudgy, dull, bullish Harvey Boyd one snowy afternoon with jubilant meanness. "C'mon, Izzy!" Kincaid shouted over the muffling snow. "Look at Izzy. He sticks his tongue out when he swings."

The fight damaged neither Saul Lederman nor Harvey Boyd, but it made them play the role of enemies. Two months later, in a pushing contest on a line in the gravelly yard, Boyd called Saul Lederman a dirty Jew.

Saul looked beyond Boyd to the backsteps of the school. Doug Kincaid was trotting down. He waved. "Hiya, Iz."

"I want to talk," Saul said. "Let's get over there by that tree." Under an ash, Saul told Doug Kincaid what had happened. Doug grinned. Saul saw the braces and rubber bands again. "Well, maybe you are a dirty Jew," Doug said.

"Well," Saul shouted, "you're a dirty whatever your religion is."

"Well, you are, well, you are," Doug Kincaid said. His grin was wider still.

"Well, you're a dirty Presbyterian."

Saul was rolling over and over in the gravel. He had guessed right, and even though he did not win the fight, it pleased him to discover that Douglas Kincaid did not like being called a dirty Presbyterian, any more than Saul liked being called a dirty Jew.

In 1937, when Saul was a sixth grader, a second Jewish boy joined the class. Saul was elated. His sudden hope was that the nickname "Izzy" might shift to the newcomer. What he failed to understand was that "Izzy" had become a term of familiarity. Andy Gottlieb, the Jewish newcomer, had not earned the right to have a nickname.

Gottlieb turned out to be little help. Small incidents, which Saul had come to accept, shattered Andy.

Toward noon one winter day, the class was reading the science textbook aloud in sequence, when Francis Doheny was blessed with an important paragraph. "In 1883," Doheny announced in triumph, "Louis Pasteur discovered the cure for rabbis."

Suppressed giggles spurted. "Oh, Francis," said Miss Derlaine, the teacher. "You know that's not how to pronounce the word."

"All right," Doheny said. "Rabies."

"Good," Miss Derlaine said. "That's correct."

Andy Gottlieb raised his hand and left the classroom, looking toward Saul Lederman as he left. Saul waited for a minute, and then followed.

In the boys' room, Andy was shaking with emotion. "Did you hear that?" he said, his back against a urinal. "Did you hear what that rat Doheny said?"

"Sure. I heard it."

"You know, he did it deliberately."

"Sure."

"Well, what are we going to do about it?" Andy Gottlieb said.

"I don't know," Saul said. "What can we do about it?"

"I'm going to tell my father," Gottlieb said.

"Now, how can you do that?" Saul asked. "That would be snitching."

Miss Cokes was gone and the new principal, Mr. Dowell from Massachusetts, was making a number of changes. He was able to eliminate the chapels but the trustees of the Academy insisted that Mr. Dowell institute an equivalent devotional. Mr. Dowell decided on a program of daily classroom prayer. It was a simple idea. Each day classes would start with a student reciting a prayer of his own faith. The boys would rotate; everyone in turn would have a chance to say the prayer that meant the most to him.

Privately, Saul Lederman panicked. As yet, he had no scruple against praying. His problem was simple and practical. He knew no prayer to say.

Pleas to great God rotated throughout the class without incident. Kincaid prayed and Boyd and Doheny, and suddenly it was the turn of Saul Lederman. That morning Saul woke early, chilled with tension. What he needed was an excuse to stay home. But that was risky. His father could be stern and so could Mother, if he turned out not to have a fever. All at once, the alternative was simple. He could write; he would write a prayer himself. He knew the form. *Thy, Thee, Amen* and *Thou.*

Sitting in bed, Saul composed an extended tribute to God, which ran for five minutes, well beyond the necessary time, and which, in the fullness of its emotion and piety, moved him. But at breakfast, he had forgotten the first prayer and had gone to work composing another. Over eggs, the eloquence of dawn eluded him.

Usually, he arrived at the Academy early enough for a game of catch, or at least gossip, in the gravelly yard. But this morning, Saul marched to the classroom, sat down and began to think. He had not moved very much or thought at all by the time Miss Derlaine arrived and nodded formally for him to begin.

He rose and stood before the class. The blackboard was to his back. He bowed his head and clasped his hands before his abdomen. It was a familiar posture. He half expected to hear an adult voice pronounce a benediction.

He was alone. He looked up without raising his head. They were all there, Kincaid, Boyd, Gottlieb, Doheny and the rest, heads bowed. He saw Miss Derlaine, her head bowed, too, her hands tightly clasped on her desk.

"Uh, Almighty Father, may Thy, uh, almighty glory lasteth in Heaven forever. Amen."

He stood still. The teacher looked up. Amen must end the Jews' prayers, too.

He walked back to his desk. Heads bobbed up. Doheny was smirking; he would have smirked at a lordly *Kol Nidre*. Books were opening. Miss Derlaine started to speak about compound sentences. Saul had mounted a dull morning as though it were an adventure, but the next time it was his turn to pray, he stayed at home and then, for no reason beyond the transcience of things, the prayer program was dropped. It was only decades afterwards that Saul felt hot fury against himself for not having stood there and told them, like Ingersoll or Sinclair Lewis, that prayer was not his way; and, indeed, if his name had been Ingersoll or Lewis, rather than Lederman, he might have had the courage to do so.

Graduation from Jamaica Academy was held at St. George's Episcopal Church in Queens, in June of 1940, as France fell. It was a fine, dark-bricked old church and at the graduation, the principal speaker, a minister, said that a commencement was not an end but a beginning. A hard beginning, too, he said, for these young people. Look at the world into which they were going. The minister spoke of the evils loose in Europe and said that he hoped that when these young people had children of their own the world would be a better place to send young people forth. As for himself, the minister said he wanted to apologize: adults everywhere had been falling down.

Jesse and Rosie Lederman liked the talk, but Mrs. Carleton Kincaid IV said over and over again, "I don't think it's really fair to the young people to have to hear such things."

Douglas Kincaid had been valedictorian. Saul Lederman's contribution was to recite *An Old Athenian* oath, which he did with legs set wide, hands clasped behind his back, speaking in an affected drawl.

*We will never bring disgrace to this our city by any act of dishonesty or cowardice, nor ever desert our suffering comrades in the ranks.*

In the Blitzkrieg spring of 1940, Saul Lederman was not fooling himself any more than he was fooling Francis Doheny. Drawling Athenian though he might pretend to be, at Jamaica Preparatory Academy, he had learned that he was a Jew.

Herta Cohen's diary has engrossed him. In it she has managed to mask the fact that the Liebers are Germans living under Hitler, or at least to remind the reader so infrequently that his sympathies are not disrupted. The Liebers of Cologne were intellectual, musical, agnostic; politics appears to have been irrelevant to their lives. Dr. Lieber was a lawyer. Marta, the mother, was a dominant woman whose heroines were de Staël and Clara Schumann. Sometimes she condemned Clara for not marrying Brahms.

From her ninth birthday forward, Herta Lieber intended to become a painter. She would be Germany's first great woman artist. The family encouraged her and Herta was studying with a young Swiss, a secret idolator of Klee, when war broke out. Herta wept, because she would not be able to continue studying in Paris.

In the diary, Herta disarmingly concedes her time in Hitler Jugend. She and a friend, Traudl Auerbach, served together and occasionally tried to be daring. While standing in formation and giving the Nazi salute, they sometimes were brave enough to rest the heels of their hands on the shoulders of the girls who stood in front of them.

After random remembrances of girlhood, Herta's diary skipped years. The time would have to be bridged, Saul decides as he reads, or filled. Then the diary resumed in a bomb shelter where Herta, crouched on her haunches, was so terrified of the fire raid outside that she lost control of her bladder. Her parents were dead. They had been incinerated in an earlier bombardment. Herta had very little money. For a time she had worked in a factory, preparing glazes, but the factory was destroyed and then there was no more work.

The startling thing, to Saul, was the way Herta was a completely different person in the two sections of the diary. At the beginning one could see her, shining-faced, long golden-haired, striding with her sketching pad and making drawings of Rhine scenes, or the cathedral, or the statue of Friedrich Wilhelm, or a tree. But the Herta of the second section no longer sketched. She was hard. The sentences in the diary became short and understated. She described each odor in the bomb shelter, where she was trapped for three days, and the hysteria of Traudl, and afterwards how, she, Herta, had to offer herself to men, although the sex act frightened her.

In the third section, describing events after the war, Herta was yet another creature, cunning and contained. She had to exist on her wit and her body and she had accepted the facts of existence. No trace of the artist endured. Slowly, and with horror, Saul gleans from the entries that Herta Lieber had become a whore.

She was neither good-hearted nor likeable. She made her escape from rent Deutschland by seducing an intensely religious G.I. into a marriage that was to get her to the United States. The soldier, Ward Tallimer, promised Herta "a good life in the good city of Chattanooga." The final entry in the diary, penned when Herta was a new bride, read:

*I do my homework at the Post library. I am relieved. There are ten grounds for divorce in Tennessee.*

In 1943, Saul was resigned to entering service. He had even begun to look forward to being drafted. The Columbia campus teemed with naval cadets, and Saul's friends had left, one by one. Alan Lindbaum. Larry Fried. Gene Camwell. Bobby Conlin. They had been his classmates and now the only ones from the old group were himself, Mel Linsky, who'd had asthma as a child, and Xerxes Perderbatore, of Madras Province.

On February 11, 1944, in Grand Central Palace, Saul stood in undershorts waiting for the physical examination, and as he looked around at the inductees, feeling proud of his tall, well-conditioned body.

After a while, an ophthalmologist told Saul to take off his glasses and to read a chart. The man studied Saul's eyes through an ophthalmoscope. "Wow," he said.

"What do you mean 'wow?' " Saul said.

"You've got some combination," the doctor said. "Myopia and astigmatism."

"I shoot well enough to play jayvee basketball," Saul said.

The ophthalmologist looked past Saul at an Army corporal. "We won't need this one," he said, "until we're fighting the Nazis for Herald Square."

"What do you mean?" Saul said.

"Next," the corporal hollered.

The return to Columbia was humiliating. He told no one that he had been classified 4-F, except Mel Linsky, his best friend. Mel punched him joyously. "Only *schlemiels* get shot at," Linsky said.

"Call Herta Cohen," Saul tells Jean Rawson, his secretary.

"That witch?"

"Just get her, please."

"Yes, sir," Jean says, working sarcasm.

The telephone voice of Herta Lieber Cohen is deep and breathy. "So. You have read it. So quickly."

"Not read all the diary," Saul says, "but skimmed, and I'm calling to let you know I like what I've skimmed."

"How fantastic. You like it."

"It fascinates me. Of course, I'll be interested in some other professional opinions. It may need a lot more work. Are you willing?"

"What?"

"To work."

"Of course. How fantastic."

"Well," Saul looks at the calendar on his desk, "the next thing is for you to make an appointment to stop by again some time next week."

"I could never stand that. I could never stand such a wait to hear more. I must see you sooner."

"When?"

"Soon. At once. I want to talk. Tonight."

"I may have a late appointment," Saul says. "Tonight is out."

"Then you can have an early appointment," Herta says. "You will come here at six. You are divorced. I will have dinner, special."

"All right Herta. That's very nice. I'd like to meet your husband."


As a collegian, young, intellectual and 4-F, Saul was Jewish and he was not. He was a Jew only among Christians. He spoke no Yiddish; its sounds were coarse to him and whinnying. His mythology was drawn from Athenians, not from Hebrews. He rejected religion; he would no more have worshipped Yahveh than Holy Mary, Mother of God. Zionism disturbed him. It ran against his idea of American. He had heard Mel Linsky describe him as a *"goyische* Jew."

Linsky was a gifted student, but oddly crippled. He said that he wanted to become a mathematician and once he spent weeks fashioning pipestems into bizarre shapes and dipping them into soapsuds. He was studying minimum surface areas, and Saul had never seen him so roused. But Mel said he could not make a living as a mathematician. Instead, he was going to have to become a doctor. "It's the only thing for a Jew in a country like this," he said.

Saul and Mel Linsky played football on the same intramural team and softball together on South Field, and ran track and dated together and went to baseball games. Mel was a good gambler, and a good creator of bets. On a cloudy day at Yankee Stadium, Mel would bet against rain before the fifth inning. Or he would bet total doubles, taking DiMaggio, Henrich and Gordon against all the Red Sox. He bet with confidence and often won.

One day, when they were juniors at Columbia, they stood in their gray sweatsuits, sweating but strong, walking around the outdoor board track set on the snow. "I want you to come to a dance with me tonight," Mel Linsky said.

"What kind of dance?"

"There'll be a lot of stuff there," Mel said. "It's for *Habonim*, my Labor Zionist group."

Saul walked ten or fifteen steps. "You know I don't believe in that business, Mel," he said.

"It's not religious," Mel said. "Nothing like that. Socialist like your mother."

"I don't want to go to the dance," Saul said, "any more than I want to go live in Palestine."

"Goddamn," Mel said. "If you don't own the ball, you just don't want to play."

Saul stopped walking and put his hands on his hips and shook his head. "All right, Mel," he said. "I'll go to the dance with you. I'll go to see the Zionist stuff."

It cost a dollar to attend. A wiry young man, in a short-sleeved shirt, sat at a bridge table, guarding the entrance to a windowless basement playroom intensely lit by fluorescent tubes. "Get up the buck, get up the buck," the young man said with heavy frivolity as Saul trailed Mel, and Mel's girl, Naomi Korngelt, into the over-bright room. "The money will buy tractors for *kibbutzim*," the man said.

Mel and Naomi drifted away. Saul saw them standing against a wall, talking excitedly to another couple. Mel was using his hands as he spoke. Naomi, square-shouldered and flat-bottomed, stood gazing at him, her straight legs wide apart. She wore brown pants and a man's plaid shirt, open at the throat. Although she was not fat, Naomi must have weighed 150 pounds.

Saul knew no one in the room. There were twice as many boys as girls, and the girls wore dungarees and baggy slacks. They were not groomed. They were young Zionist functionals who wanted to emphasize that they had no time for permanent waves or lacy underwear. One girl, dark hair falling long over her shoulders, was an exception. Saul stared. The girl looked back, blinked, and walked to the man at the bridge table and began whispering. He nodded once and clenched a fist. Saul saw veins bulge in the forearm. Then the girl joined a group; soon she was talking to Mel Linsky and Naomi Korngelt.

"Hora," cried the man behind the bridge table. "Hora." He jumped up and walked to the center of the playroom and clapped. The group, the curly men and utilitarian women, formed a circle around him and a big, black-haired man who wore a *yarmulke* played records. Everyone skipped and danced in a tight circle in the overbright room. There was a surging. The song resounded.

*Tzena, tzena, tzena habanot ur'ena hayalim bamoshava.*
*Tzena, tzena habanot ur'ena hayalim bamoshava.*

Saul did not understand the lyrics. *Come out, come out, come out girls and see. Come out, come out. Do not hide from Army men anymore.*

He did not know the words, but the rhythm was foot-stamping and sexual. A girl in brown-checked pants had taken Saul's right hand without looking at him, and he was dancing in the circle. Saul's left hand was in the grasp of a chubby, black-haired boy, who grunted as the circle spun.

*Tzena,* Saul heard, *tzena, tzena, tzena.*

The other dancers shouted and sang along and, then, as if by signal, they sat on the floor. The wiry man who had collected dollars rose to speak.

"*Shalom,*" he said, "*shalom.* I have to catch my breath."

The man leaned against the pine-paneled wall, panting. "We should only put as much energies into Youth *Aliyah* as we do into our hora.

"We have some new people here tonight," the man said. "We therefore must be guarded, a little bit." He stared at Saul. "Can we talk? Or are you going to report us to the State Department?"

"He's okay," Mel Linsky said.

"Let him tell us," the group leader said.

The pretty, dark-haired girl whispered to the functional girl who had taken Saul's hand. They giggled.

"Well," said the leader. "Are you with us?"

"I'm here, aren't I?" Saul said.

"Just say you're with us."

"I don't know yet."

"Join with us and within five years you'll have a wonderful new life in Palestine. *Shalom*."

The leader talked about a camp in New Jersey where young people were being trained to fight and farm. The talk was intense, but Saul found his mind drifting. He gazed at the black-haired girl. She was enraptured.

"If you drive a tractor, you can drive a tank," the leader said. "And when we have won our land," he said, "we will make the desert blossom."

Mel Linsky's face was shining. Later he gobbled coffee cake and clapped Saul on the back. "Well," he said. "How do you like our world? We'll get you to Palestine yet."

"I don't think so, Mel."

Mel Linsky glowered. "It's going to come down to us or them."

"Who's them?" Saul said.

"The anti-Semites. All the *goyim*. They'll have every Jew kicked out of America by 1970."

In his late teens, during World War II, Saul was impersonally close to his parents. He respected their intellectualism, but he was intimate with neither of them. The Bavarian woman had raised him for his busy mother. His father regularly offered him one weekend day, but Jesse Lederman, Professor of the Constitutional Law, was a formal man, not given to intimacy.

Saul's sense of being Jewish was waning. His experiences at Jamaica Academy seemed distant now. In inner monologues, he looked to find roots. What moved him most, he asked. Shelley and Keats. Kelly and Sheats. He laughed. Who wrote *When I have fears that I may cease to be?* Saul saw himself as sprung from lyric Housman *for she and I were well acquainted and I knew all her ways,* and Brahms' strings throbbing after horns, and Hamlet, choired by Gielgud. *But to meeee, what is this quintessence of dust.* And Thomas Wolfe, whose lines were reachable, whose lines were just what Saul himself could write.

> Who is there in this world of hollow men
> On nights when nature's murmurings are stilled
> Who has not raised his fist and cried to gods,

Too full of years and death to understand,
*Why must it be? Why have you made it so?*

*Poem of Youth,* the most ambitious writing of Saul's life, was unsuccessful. When Saul was finished with fifteen stanzas all in blank verse, he wanted to read them to someone. He tried Naomi Korngelt and she said, "It must be very beautiful, Saul. I only wish I was smart enough to understand it."

"It's not so hard," Saul said.

A week later, in the living room in Jamaica, he proceeded to read *Poem of Youth* to his parents.

They heard him out. Then his mother said, "Saul. Dear Saul. My Saul."

"Yeah, Ma."

"It is your misfortune to come from such an educated home."

He waited. His father gazed blankly at a wall.

"If you had an ordinary mother, who didn't know Homer and Milton and Whitman, and you went to her with your little epic, she would be terribly impressed. Poor Saul. It's your misfortune to grow up here with me."

Jesse Lederman got up and walked into his den.

Saul married Clara Swift, of Mason City, Iowa, without loving her, because she accepted him wholly and was comfortable. She was blonde and snub-nosed and studying for a graduate degree at Teacher's College. He could not remember proposing to her, or when their relationship first turned toward marriage. He said one evening that he did not want to marry for a long time and she said, "Yes. We shouldn't rush into it." As far as Saul could trace it, afterwards, the unchallenged "we" was his acceptance.

Saul's mother disapproved of Clara; his father said nothing but, in the end, prevailed upon Judge Hirsch to perform the service. Bland, comfortable Clara stood by, while Saul worked as a junior editor and failed successively, to become a poet, a novelist and a short-story writer. The failures took ten years. She bore a daughter.

Then, abruptly, in the middle of a desultory affair with an older copy editor, his fourth affair in two years, Saul told Clara that he wanted a divorce. She cried, and said she didn't understand, and what would become of Vicki, and he said

that if they all continued to live together nothing would become of any of them.

"I'm drying up," he said, "you're drying up. There's got to
be more to it than this."

"There's got to be more," said Clara, always echoing.

He won a raise from Peter Warrens, twice-divorced himself.

"Well," Warrens said. "You've joined us. The Alimony
Slaves Society. That makes you an ASS. It's a good thing
you're working for me. Maybe I can help you out a little."

Warrens gave Saul an increase to twenty thousand and
Saul moved into the modern yellow brick building, where the
windows squatted on top of one another.

Herta Lieber Cohen is waiting at six o'clock in a mirrored
corner of the enormous old apartment where she lives with
her second husband, the painter, Frans Cohen. She rises for
Saul, and standing in a floor-length, bright red skirt, leans
forward to be kissed.

Saul gently pecks.

"I have worked hard for dinner," Herta says. "Don't I get
more than that?"

Saul considers a smoked panel of one mirror.

"Would you help with the martinis, please," she says.
"Frans is delayed." Herta leads Saul from the mirrored alcove
to a bar, in the large foyer, under an awning striped green and
white and red.

She opens a panel and Saul steps behind the door. "I
should get for you a little crimson jacket," Herta says.

"I'm afraid you don't understand the way things are," Saul
says. "The Germans are the bartenders. The Jews are the employers."

She looks at Saul and says, "You are serious?"

"No, but a German governess brought me up."

"It is a terrible thing, and very American, that you do,"
Herta says.

"What is that? Not use enough Vermouth?"

"No, it is what you have done again."

Saul stirs.

"You substitute wit for conversation," Herta Lieber Cohen
says. "It is clever and amusing but there is no interchange of
ideas.

"I have known Brecht. I admired him and introduced myself to him; in the late years he was witty but ideas gave him chest pains. He was becoming Americanized."

"Be grateful, then," Saul said, "you've found an editor of minor wit."

Herta drinks elegantly, holding a crystal goblet with her right pinky extended. "There was something between us on the telephone and there is something between us now, but if you want anything to develop, you cannot be afraid and hide with wit."

He has flipped up the panel and moved close to the barstool on which she sits. Herta leans forward, and Saul strides away, into the living room where, under a high ceiling and artfully lighted, six of Frans Cohen's paintings hang. "I know nothing at all about art," Saul Lederman says.

She enters slowly, pausing as the doorway frames her. Herta, too, becomes artfully lighted. The golden hair falls down her back. "Frans is a fabulous painter," Herta says, "and when you meet him you must ask him to tell you what he sees when he looks at a model." She strides to a set of sketches of a dark-haired nude leaning backwards. "You look at the abdomen," Herta says. "Frans has put hair there. Gauguin and Michelangelo did not. If you respect their integrity and Frans'—and I tell you, Frans is an honest painter—then it is obvious that the three men did not see the same things when they looked at a cunt."

Saul cannot quite believe what he has heard.

"So," Herta Cohen says, "this is not what you expect to find here and from me?"

"Come here," Saul says. He clutches her and kisses. Slowly, Herta opens her mouth.

"I forget," she says, presently. "You make me forget everything. But I must not. I have to look after the sauerbraten."

"Your mouth," Saul says, "is very soft."

She rises, smiling, and he makes another drink for each of them, and they sit at a small table in the mirrored alcove. She has flavored the sauerbraten with dry wine, onion, peppercorns, bay leaves, sugar, sour cream and gingersnaps. "This is how we served it in Cologne when I was a child."

Saul eats ravenously. "I loved this when I was a kid myself," he says. A spot of gravy spills onto a lapel and Herta is up at once. She dips her napkin into cold water and begins rubbing. "Ach, ach, how you need someone to look after you." She kisses him lightly on the cheek, and rising, places both arms around his head. She presses his face gently against her abdomen, and strokes the back of his head. "I must get for you coffee," Herta says.

The coffee is black and strong. Herta moves her chair close to Saul and stares at him, as though she were trying to see behind his eyes. Saul drinks the coffee. "Where is the artist?" he says.

"What?"

"Your husband."

"Out on Long Island for a few days. He will not be here."

"A man with faith."

"Why should Frans have anything to worry about? He has the most magnificent set of genitals."

"A lot of good they do you here and now," Saul says.

"I can think about them, and maybe that does good."

*"If you can think, and not make thoughts your master."*

"Please," Herta Cohen says. "I am serious. Come sit beside me on the couch, and kiss me the way you did before, and, please, be as serious as I."

Saul finds it difficult to accept what is going on. He expects at any minute Frans Cohen, the artist, to burst into the house and he wants to take Herta to bed and she is waiting, but is she, and wouldn't it be something if Frans Cohen, the artist, found them in bed? "If we shacked up and your husband came home," Saul says, "he could paint our picture."

Herta grabs Saul at the ribs, almost pinching and pulls him toward her, and kisses him hard. "I think I need another drink," she says. "Or two."

When he returns with the drink, she asks him about his marriage. "It was once and it is not," Saul says. "Gone. *Faded flowers of friendship faded.*"

"But surely there are residues of affection," Herta says. "You didn't, as I, have to be married to escape an insane country."

"A miniscule residue," Saul says. "The affection between us is insignificant."

"Do you still go to bed with her?"

Saul does not want this woman invading Clara's privacy.

"Could you go to bed with her if you wanted still?" Herta asks.

"Can't most men go to bed with most women if they want to badly enough?"

"After the war, you know, to live, I went to bed often," Herta said. "You know—you have read about it. Counting Germans, I have gone to bed with about three hundred, and I can tell you that there are only two kinds of men. There are the bangers, who have to leave the bed with a semi-erection, and then there are the ones who tremble when they come."

"How do you categorize your husband?" Saul asks.

"He has some other difficulties," Herta says. "My principal rival for his genitals is another artist, Karl Muhlbeck."

"Shocking," Saul says.

"Not so. Not at all."

"I mean you're a handsome woman."

"Tell me more," Herta says, "about your wife."

He begins to talk vaguely, about personality differences. "No," Herta says. "No. You are not being honest. Remember what I have told you about wit. All relations, yours and mine, yours and Frans', when you meet him, should be an exchange. Perhaps in your marriage there was no exchange."

"There was in the beginning," Saul says, "but I was interested in my work, and I found after four or five years that we didn't have anything to talk about. It happened suddenly."

"You have children?"

"One. A girl."

"You had her after you and the woman had nothing to talk about?"

"Yes."

"You have had a hard time," Herta Cohen says.

"You're damn right I've had a hard time, but it's been my own choice, and if I miss the kid, what the hell. I chose to do it like this, to make my way by myself. What is the worst, the most dishonest thing, is for a marriage to go on when it is no marriage at all. To pretend love is an obscenity."

"It is interesting," Herta says, "that we should be so much alike. You have wanted certain things. Your integrity. You have been willing to have hard times and loneliness. We are alike and from such different worlds."

"What was it like growing up in Cologne?"

"Narrow winding streets and too many idiots."

"I grew up with a pack of idiots in Queens," Saul says. "They were a terrible bunch, but they had the power to hurt. That is the damnedest thing. The damnedest fools can hurt as much as any worthwhile person."

"You know of Schiller?"

"Of course."

"Schiller wrote to his muse, I have always remembered it, *What would I be without you? I do not know—but I shudder to see what hundreds and thousands are without you.*"

"You remember that," Saul says. "Marvelous. Damn few women can remember lines. I walk around with a filing cabinet for a brain.

"That's stirring, what Schiller wrote. I read something today by Pound. *If they don't understand poetry, if they don't feel music, what can they understand of this passion*— he means love—*compared to which the rose is gross and the perfume of violets a clap of thunder.*"

"We are, I say, so similar," Herta says. He leans toward her and the kiss stirs him; her worldliness stirs him. She opens her mouth to kiss, like all the rutting schoolgirls and like little Jeannie Rawson, but she is not like them at all. She has lived and he knows her wildness.

He draws back his head. *Her lips suck forth my soul. See how it flies.*

"Do not always quote someone else so much," she says. She pulls him to her, and kisses him again.

"Wait a minute," Saul says. "Now look," he says. "Maybe it is important that we do spout quotes. We have a certain intellect. We ought to live by it. I'm fed up with a world where the other side is making all the claims. *It is important,* the other side says, *to be religious. When an agnostic dies, have a rabbi pray. That way nobody will be offended.* But it is just as important to be irreligious. More even. And with intellect, the other side is always telling us to blend into the terrain. Don't be too bloody bright. Don't be defiant. I say the hell with it. I can quote five thousand lines, and I'm damn well going to quote, no matter what the other side says."

"Ach," Herta says. "Ach." She draws an arm around him.

"If you decide to walk a solitary, difficult way," Saul says, "that's overwhelmingly important. To believe in man, not God. To believe in the intellect. To believe in the superiority of a special group, intellectuals."

Herta smiles and shakes her head, stirring the golden hair. "The Chosen People," she says.

"*Herrenvolk,*" Saul says.

"Ah," Herta says. "The similarity between Germans and Jews could only end the way it did."

Fragments of a poem arrest him.

> . . . in the moonlight,
> it is as if we had never been young.
> . . . . It is from this
> That a bright red woman will be rising.
> The most gay and yet not so gay as it was.

"My parents," Herta says, "might have been Jews. Their bodies were consumed by flames. So not in one place, but another."

"Don't," Saul Lederman says.

Herta is rising in bright red. "Your life is hard," Herta says. "You need comforting."

"Yes."

"You and I are wearing too much clothes."

She lies with her legs out straight. "This way," she says, "I can feel all of your body." She opens her legs and thrusts his penis into her. "Ah," Herta says. "Pump, pump, pump."

He hears her voice close to his ear. "Ah," Herta calls, "you are pleasing me. Ah, ah, ah!"

He thrusts wildly and her breath storms past his ear and she begins to keen.

The cry reminds him. He remembers. The word assaults him as she screams in passion.

*Auschwitz.*

Dead children and the future cold in infant ashes.

*Auschwitz.*

Old rabbis, naked, and corpses of poets, shoveled like peat.

*Ausch-*
> *witz.*

*Ausch-*
> *witz.*

*Ausch-*
> *witz.*

Her keening rises. He sees her head, under the violent hair, rocking from side to side.

He makes himself lie still. Screaming, she thrusts. Saul does not move. He will not help the German.

"Oh, Jesus!" Herta cries. "Sweet Christ. Do something.

Goddamnit, something!" She surges under him. He shrivels. He will not.

"Oh," Herta calls, begging. "Oh!"

Saul lies as still as death, dead as a victim.

At four o'clock in the morning of April 29, 1945, Adolf Hitler signed his political testament, underneath the burning city of Berlin. Josef Goebbels, Martin Bormann and two military aides served as witnesses. Thirty-five-and-a-half-hours later Hitler placed a loaded pistol into his mouth and fired.

The testament proclaims the man. He did not desire war, Hitler wrote; World War II was plotted solely by "statesmen of Jewish descent." As blank, final sands ran through his glass, Hitler was comforted to believe that "out of the ruins of our towns and monuments," anti-Semitism would continue to grow for centuries. In his final words to Germany, Hitler demanded, above everything else, "merciless opposition to the universal poisoner of all peoples, international Jewry." Auschwitz and Treblinka had left him unappeased.

During World War II, the Nazis overran all, or part, of nineteen European countries. According to indictments prepared for the Nuremberg Trials, 5,700,000 Jews, out of a total Jewish population of 9,600,000, "disappeared from the rolls" of occupied nations. They disappeared because they were slaughtered. In addition, the Nazis killed almost every Jew who did not escape from Germany. The total continental European figure of six million Jewish victims is true. Under Hitler, the Germans murdered one-and-a-quarter million European Jewish children. It is no coincidence that American anti-Semitism has declined since such facts have been disclosed.

The evidence suggests an astonishing turnabout. During the years before World War II, anti-Semitism mounted inexorably in the United States; it may well have reached a peak while the War raged. "The Jews' War," people called World War II, echoing and anticipating Hitler. "The Jews got us into it," some said.

In June of 1944, the Opinion Research Corporation surveyed a sampling of 2,296 Americans, asking what "religious and national groups" constituted the greatest threat to the country (which was, of course, fighting Germany and Japan). Six per cent of those responding mentioned Germans. Nine per cent mentioned Japanese. Twenty-four per cent—almost a quarter—insisted that the greatest threat to America was the Jews. Eighteen years later, in June of 1962, George Gallup's American Institute of Public Opinion conducted a similar investigation. The difference was remarkable. By 1962, only one per cent of·a Christian sample of 1,471 felt that Jews were any sort of menace at all.

One need not simply accept the evidence of polls. On the basis of a variety of studies, all the responsible Jewish organizations in the United States agree, in rare consensus, that anti-Semitism is at a modern low. Despite the Aryan country clubs and the *Judenrein* directorates, Jews move more freely in American society than at any time in the last seventy-five years. They are a greater part of American life than they have ever been.

Theoreticians propose various postulates. As more Christian Americans meet more Jews, the irrationality of anti-Semitism is exposed. Nothing defeats a monstrous conception of Jews more surely than meeting Jewish individuals. *Damnit, Teresa,* says the old Coughlinite in integrated Long Island, *they ain't all so bad.* Jews have done a remarkable public relations job for themselves, and in a harsh way, the Negro revolt has helped them too. The Klansman worried about keeping his sister safe from the lusting of Dr. Ralph Bunche has little time to fume at Jewish plots. Negroes driving for freedom attract psychotic hatreds away from Jews.

But all of these considerations are supervened by the impact of Adolf Hitler. It is embarrassing in a comfortable American home to find oneself close to a tyrant's camp. Once it was acceptable—indeed almost fashionable—to speak of the "damned Jews." It is not, not after Hitler cursed *verdammt Juden.* Once it was socially acceptable to suggest that Jews be put in their place. It is not, not after Hitler put Jews into death camps.

By his success, Hitler exposed anti-Semitism. He ripped from it philosophy, theology, rationale, dignity and all the other layers of disguise. It stands now as a bestiality, nothing more. "Hitler," one American journalist remarks with careful irony, "gave anti-Semitism a bad name."

The impact diffuses through society. An Episcopalian lady, who once described her tailor as a dirty little Jew, now holds her tongue. A Methodist lawyer will not say, "He Jewed me down." Neither of these people deserves acclaim, but each restraint and each reaction is important. Multiply them by several million and that is several million people who have stopped saying "dirty Jew" and stopped using the title of a religion as a verb.

The old hates fed themselves in petty ways. Perhaps the fact that in this generation a boy can grow to manhood without once hearing "Jew bastard" is important to more than just the boy. Perhaps it is the signal of an end. And perhaps not. But in the wake of Hitler, vast change has come to America.

"If a Hitler arose here," one Protestant lady who is married to a Jew has found herself musing aloud, "then I would die."

"No," the husband said. "*I* would die. You'd be able to pass."

"The children," the lady said, "they would kill my boys and I would defend them and I would die."

Touched, the husband offered a soft look. "Now," he said, after a pause, "you understand a little of what it is to see the world as a Jew."

## DAVID NAZARETSKY OF KRASNOWICZ, AUSCHWITZ AND CALIFORNIA

The couple, the Jewish man and the Protestant wife who have considered Hitler, are visiting in the afternoon sunlight. A survivor has invited them to swim. The survivor suffers from loneliness and uneasiness in America, and these young people, Arnold and Julie Gimpel, seemed interested when he met them at the Dollars-For-Israel Party at the Sunset Club last week. Besides Arnold is a writer. He has sold scripts to television. The survivor is always looking for someone to write his biography.

He is a small man, unpretentious, overdressed and obsessed with bearing drinks to people beside his pool. He does not swim himself, or sunbathe. Acid burns have scarred his body. He has been in Auschwitz and his story may not be different from the stories of several million others, except that he is alive.

David Nazaretsky is alive and vastly wealthy in California. He has made his fortune by borrowing money, buying land, building and selling homes. He has intensity beyond most men's and it is a point of his virility that not one of the eight thousand homes that he sold has been foreclosed. When an owner falls too far behind in the mortgage payments, David himself buys back the house. His credit rating is impeccable and he finds construction money when few other builders can. He is a man of calculation and ferocious pride.

The sun of the California autumn is warm and the American couple, the Gimpels, have put on bathing suits. The man sits sunning, sipping a Scotch. Julie Gimpel, in a bikini, lies prone and decorous on David's diving board. The pool is lined with mosaic tile. As sunlight strikes the water, the tiles show rippling patterns. Julie, who paints, leans forward and sketches on the water with one finger.

"My dear sir, my dear madam," David says. "Is everything all right? Can I get you anything?" David is wearing a black suit and a dark tie, with a diamond stickpin. He holds himself erect. "My view from here," he says, "is second largest in compass degrees of all views in the city of Beverly Hills. I found that out before I bought this house."

"I can darn near see Phoenix," says Arnold Gimpel.

"Sunrise," Julie says, "must be so soft."

"The house cost six-hundred-thirty-four-thousand dollars to build," David says. "I did not pay that myself, but that was what it cost the man who built it." David Nazaretsky has a fighter's face, flat nose, broad brow, and he is horseshoe bald. He looks a decade older than his forty-three years. David hopes vaguely that Arnold Gimpel will suddenly plead to write the story of his life. And he hopes vaguely that Arnold will not. To David Nazaretsky, the survivor, his own life is vastly too private. At times it is even obscene.

"Anything you want," David says. "You want to work a little, sometime. Do your writing. Rest. You can have a lovely study with such a view, and a stereo."

"Thank you," Arnold says.

"This house is yours, my friends," David announces.

Embarrassed, Julie resumes drawing on the water.

David extends both arms. "My dear sir," he says, "my dear friends." He is not comfortable with this couple, although he likes them. Christian and Jew, still they are native to each other. David is native to no one.

He would like to tell the Gimpels how it was to be a young man in Krasnowicz, Poland, before the Germans came, and how Krasnowicz was home even though the Poles called him Christ killer, and *Zhid* and spat at him. In Krasnowicz, there were Jewish doctors, Rubinstein and Himmelman, and Jewish lawyers and merchants and skilled workers. Jews were not al-lowed to bear arms; at least no Krasnowicz Jew had ever been granted a permit. A Jew with a beard wandering into *goyische* streets could be beaten. But Krasnowicz was home, where David had grown up and where he would have a clothing store, bigger than his father's. He was proud of Krasnowicz, where even without guns, the Jews had their *Militz,* a sturdy, unarmed militia. When the Poles went too far and beat one Jew too many, the *Militz,* the biggest and burliest Jewish boys, went out and beat up Krasnowicz Poles. David did not think the balance unfair.

On September 18, 1939, a German Panzer division cap-tured Krasnowicz. Three days later, Yakov Kurlander and Lasar Kronsky of the *Militz* were shot dead in front of a to-bacco shop on Cracow Boulevard. Their crime was that they had been walking in the street. Kronsky, big and stronger than any Pole, was shot in the stomach and cried before he died. The Poles who heard him did not answer the rhythmic, rolling howls for water.

So it was clear, David's mother told him. She was a strong woman, the leader of the family. Jews were not to wander in the streets. They would have to stay within their neighbor-hoods. But, his mother, Fanya, told him with a quick reassur-ing smile, in their own neighborhoods, Jews would still be safe.

On September 23, a squad of German soldiers rode into each of the two Jewish quarters in Krasnowicz and burned the synagogues. A corporal shot Rabbi Mendel Brachman, but the other rabbi, old Chaimov, was not molested. A day later, as most of the nine hundred Jews of Krasnowicz re-mained behind locked doors, *Judische Verein,* a common council of Jews, was established to govern the ghettoes. Fanya Nazaretsky said at least that would mean peace. She did not know that the *Judische Verein* of Krasnowicz was created by the Gestapo.

Three weeks later, at David's house, 23 Kilinski Street, Itzko Zaidel of the *Militz* delivered a notice from the *Ju-dische Verein.* It was an order for David Nazaretsky to ap-pear, at 9:15 A.M. October 13, 1939, in Pilsudski Square, on the border of the Jewish neighborhood. He was to bring with him supplies for three days. Although the Jews of Krasno-wicz were hungry, the council would provide for his family, provided that he obeyed. David was the first-born son. If

David did not appear, the order stated, the entire Nazaretsky family, both parents and his younger sister, would be killed.

The first-born sons of all the Jewish families of Krasnowicz arose at dawn on October 13. By 9:15, they stood assembled, three hundred strong in the square. Some of them wept. The parents, kept at a distance by German soldiers, wept more loudly.

A German officer roared up, chauffeured in the side car of a motorcycle. He climbed a little platform in the center of Pilsudski Square and began to shout through a bullhorn.

*"Geh,"* he said. *"Geh. Geh, nach hause. Geh, Juden. Geh!"* Go home, the German was telling them. *Go home.* David never forgot the next sound that he heard filling the Square. It was a vast rhapsodic Judaic sob.

The first-born ran through the streets of Krasnowicz screaming for joy. They would not have to go. The parents followed, praying, thanking God.

When the German officer returned to headquarters he began to make out his report. He had been instructed to test the theory of the closeness of the Jewish family unit.

The test had been a complete success.

In the sunlight, David means to talk earnestly with his guests and put them at their ease. The dark-haired girl is lovely and to his taste. But he cannot chat. No small graces remain within him.

"Israel interests you?" Arnold Gimpel, the writer, asks.

"So much," David says. "If there had been Israel when I was young, everything would have been different."

Julie Gimpel sits up on the diving board. The dark hair flows lightly down her back. Her skin is a pale tan. "Would it have mattered," she asks, "to somebody like Hitler?"

David smiles over clenched teeth. "It would have helped us to make our fight."

"I don't know what I would have done," Arnold says, waving his small glass. "Certainly not as well as you. But I like to think that if they came around, I'd have taken one of the bastards with me."

"But it would not be like that at all," David says. Julie has climbed down from the board and is walking toward them. "You see, if you fought, they would kill *her*." David's strong gesture sweeps toward the dark-haired girl, moving lightly in the white bikini.

"Now, how am I going to risk my family for my own life?" David says. "I cannot do that."

"But what choice was there?" Arnold says.

"Do you think we believed that the terrible things that went on, the killings and the beatings, could continue? We never thought the outside world would let it. We believed that time was with us. We fought for time. The Germans knew how we thought. They had studied us as though we were animals. And unfortunately, too, they knew the outside world. It was the Germans, not the Jews, who understood that the outside world didn't care, and that time was not the Jews' ally and that for Jews the only certainty was death."

Four weeks after the first test in Krasnowicz, with winter heavy upon Poland, the Germans again ordered Jews to Pilsudski Square. The pattern was as before. Someone from the *Militz* appeared carrying a notice from the *Judische Verein*: There was the threat: You can save your family only by doing as you are told. But the group this time was smaller, only seventeen young men and women. The seventeen went to the Square and not one was sent back. The Germans had mastered the leverage of Jewish family loyalty.

Other groups followed. The Germans were making Krasnowicz *Judenrein*, clean of Jews, a little at a time. On the evening of January 11, 1940, when Itzok Zaidel, the *Militz*, knocked at the Nazaretsky's door, David seized the notice. He could barely believe what he read. Not he, but Fanya Nazaretsky, was ordered to report at the Square by eight o'clock the following morning. Mama was to be the first.

The family sat up late. "Mama, do not go," David said. "Make them come here to get you. I will not let them."

Aaron, David's father, could not understand. "What does this mean?" he said. "It has no meaning."

"Mama," David said. "I exercise my authority and I positively forbid you to go."

Mama said David's name twice and stood above him and held his head in her arms. He began to cry and she said over and over, "It will be all right." But very late that night, while he lay wide-awake, David heard his own mother crying like a child.

"My dear friends," David says at poolside. "Your drinks are empty. I must get you fresh ones."

Julie Gimpel returns to the diving board and plunges into the water. "She never takes more than one before dinner," Arnold says. The bald man with the fighter's face scuttles over the terrace, but stops halfway across. "I want you to see my fountain, sir," he calls. "I will push a button and you will."

A series of concealed nozzles throws a thick luminous spray, centering at the spot where Julie Gimpel is floating on her back. She gives a little cry and submerges. Immediately the fountain is extinguished.

When Julie reappears, David Nazaretsky rushes to the poolside and squats. "My dear lady, my dear lady. I am sorry."

Julie smiles warmly. "Oh, David," she says. "There is nothing to apologize for. I loved the fountain. I love the rain."

David looks at her and returns her smile with a little cracked grin and hurries off to make her husband's drink.

The wind comes up suddenly and when David returns, Julie has left the pool. A gray sweatshirt reaches to just below her thighs.

"Was there much religion in the camps?" Julie says. "Did they allow you to worship God in Auschwitz?"

"Block thirty," David says, "was where they had the gas chambers and the crematorium. I went to block thirty in August, 1944. The High Holidays—Rosh Hashanah and Yom Kippur—came in October. For Yom Kippur, we decided we would pray.

"After the sundown we got together. We had no *tallises*, but we had a few blankets. For six men, one blanket was a prayer shawl. As we were sitting on the floor of the barracks, praying, Bauman, the *blockmeister*, came in. He said he was a poet, but Bauman was as much a killer as any SS man. Because we were caught praying we were given a beating that is beyond human imagination. After that, there was no worshipping, except what you had in your mind or heart."

Julie is shuddering. "Frightful," she says. There are tears in her eyes.

"Not at all," David Nazaretsky says.

"I don't understand," Arnold Gimpel says.

"You see, for me," David says, "God had died many years before."

Julie blinks.

"It was, dear friends, beyond tears."

Mama was not sent far. The Germans had built an intern-ment barracks seven miles beyond town across a bleak wood and Mama was sent there along with others for whom there was no immediate use or place.

David was able to find out where his mother was. The in-ternment camp guards were bored and easily bribed. Someone procured a list which circulated through the ghetto and David saw the name of Fanya Nazaretsky.

He knew that Mama must be hungry. He obtained several large soup kettles from a Jewish restaurant and drew the ket-tles by wagon all the way to the entrance of the camp. The guards, two men, were older than he had thought.

"Food," David said in gruff German. "I have brought food. Soup."

"For the inmates?"

"And for you, my dear friends."

"The little Jew," one German said, "has some respect."

"Good soup. From black beans. It may be something you yourself do not get often."

"The little Jew," the other German said, "presumes."

"My dear friends, my dear friends," David said. "I am sorry."

"The little Jew can bring one kettle in, if he leaves the other three with us."

Inside, David found Mama in the second of the three build-ings. She wore the clothes in which she had left, the long gray skirt and coarse white blouse. Her eyes were hollow. She was not really changed. Children were around her. They called her Mama.

Mama cried when she saw David, but the children there, the little ones, were watching, and she stopped. "The soup will warm them, David, my good David, my brave boy."

After the first trips, the guards demanded more than soup and at length David had to steal a chicken. The fifth time he entered the internment camp, Mama told him what to do. "This little boy," she said, "this Mendele. You can save little Mendele, my David."

Mendele was five. He was small for his age and fair for a Polish Jew and his face had not a single line. Between the golden hair, cut close, and the long, slender nose, Mendele Abramovitz had enormous eyes, all dark and deep. He had seen David before, playing soccer. "Hello, Mr. David," Mendele said.

David led Mendele to an empty soup kettle. He lifted the boy into it and told him, "Crouch."

"I'm too big," Mendele said, proudly.

"Crouch," David ordered. "And you must be very quiet."

"I will not be very quiet," Mendele said.

Under the lid of the soup kettle, David smuggled Mendele Abramovitz past the barbed wire of the Krasnowicz Internment Station, while one of the guards waved genially. But he could not take Mendele into the city. All the Abramovitz family was gone. Perhaps they were dead. The ghettos were smaller now and the *Militz* men were vigilant. Because of the vigilant *Militz*, there was no place to hide a child.

Beyond sight of the German guards, two miles past the barbed wire, in a small, obscure hollow under pin oaks, David stopped pulling his little wagon.

"Mendele," he said, gently. "Mendele."

"Yes," the five-year-old whispered. "Yes."

"You can come out, Mendele."

The boy lifted the lid of the kettle and stood up. His young body was at once straight. He said, "What, David?"

"You are free."

"What, David?"

"Eat bark, Mendele, and roots."

"Where is Mama, David?"

"And drink only clear water."

"I want Mama."

"Listen to me, Mendele. When you are afraid, say *Sh'ma Yisroel, Adonai Elohenu, Adonai Echad.*" Hear, O Israel, the Lord our God, the Lord is One.

But in that place and in that time, no one heard. Not Israel and not God. On his next trip, three days later, David came upon the body of Mendele, white and frozen under barren oaks.

In California, the wind has stopped and the sun beats warmly on the poolside. "I don't want to presume," Arnold Gimpel says, "but I just can't imagine a circumstance where I wouldn't try to save my mother."

"I could not try," David Nazaretsky says, his dark eyes

going blank, "because my mother was six-and-one-half inches too tall to fit into a soup kettle."

Immigration quotas, adopted by the American Congress in 1924 and sustained through all the Hitler years, helped make Europe a sepulchre for Jews. Some filtered through while Hitler ruled, 120,894 immigrants from Germany were legally admitted into the United States. The overwhelming majority were Jewish. Max Reinhardt was among them and Kurt Weill and Albert Einstein. Refugees improved the strain of American theater and wrote "September Song" and helped to build the nuclear bomb. In accepting those few refugees it did, the United States received more than it gave.

A quarter-century later, history bears witness. Not once did the United States cross swords with Germany on the issue of anti-Semitism. The U.S. did not even break diplomatic relations or limit trade. President Franklin Roosevelt himself was mute. Stripped of euphemism and verbiage, the official foreign policy of the United States during the Hitler years was to tolerate Nazi persecution of Jews.

Now one finds hundreds, perhaps thousands, of such men as David Nazaretsky, who testify to the result. American national pride fades in the presence of survivors, the men and women whose lives are peopled by ghosts. One cringes before the unasked question: *Why were we abandoned to savages?*

On their own testimony, people were able to survive in Auschwitz only because they were tough; or able to corrupt their captors; or capable, while in a nightmare, of believing in reality; or, above all other things, fortunate. Nathan Shapell of Los Angeles classifies himself and others like him as "miracle Jews."

"I am here by coincidence," Mr. Shapell says. "I was many times in groups of 'selectees' when Dr. Mengele came. I escaped just by the way his finger pointed."

Josef Mengele, M.D., a tall, stygian figure given to wearing jackboots, was the so-called Medical Director of Auschwitz. It pleased him to put on a black uniform and then to select which inmates, having been beaten and starved past usefulness, were clinically ready for extermination. Ont of Mengele's rules provided for the murder of anyone he found in the Auschwitz infirmary on successive weeks. Tuesday was the day he made his rounds.

Wracked by a high fever, Nathan Shapell lay in bed for longer than a week. As Mengele approached on the second Tuesday, Shapell waited, too weak to move but strong enough to be afraid to die. Mengele examined him briefly. "I like this case," he said. "The fever interests me." By the margin of that interest, Shapell lives. (Mengele himself is alive and free in South America.)

A Hungarian-born Jew who now sells insurance in New York City, recalls a bloody, forced march from the Nazi camp at Oranienburg in 1945. "The Germans had given orders for us to go for thirty or forty kilometers," he says. "They knew that we were weak from lack of food. A guard walked right behind me with a submachine gun. He was Dutch, and not such a bad fellow."

While the men marched, the Dutch guard said, "Please don't fall. If you fall, I will have to shoot you."

"Why?" the Hungarian said.

"Because if I do not," the guard said, "the Germans will shoot me."

"That Dutchman and I became good friends," the Hungarian survivor insists. "And why not? We walked side by side for a very long time."

Few people who endured death camps are entirely normal, within the general American understanding of the term. One survivor, a cellist, tells odd jokes. "Some of my best friends," he says, "are lampshades." A woman who runs a small shop with penury and petty lies wears dresses with short sleeves. When caught lying, she rotates one arm until the tatooed numbers are visible. They are her justification to the world.

Survivors are seldom what everyone else would like. Saved from martyrdom, they still fall short of sainthood. A term at Auschwitz did not beatify. We can, perhaps, be thankful that those who were there and who live among us are not more bitter than they are.

The old synagogues in Berlin and Warsaw and Alsace and Vilna are burned. Suddenly, without real warning or extended preparation, the Jews of America have become the most important Jewish community on earth. The Russian Jews are silent. The Jews of Israel struggle to exist. The heartland of Europe is gone. Upon Jews in America rests final responsibility for survival. If *they* do not survive as Jews, who will?

The question presses with the weight of centuries. It shapes men's lives. To survive as Jews after Hitler, American Jews join temples which their fathers abandoned and spout Yiddish phrases which their fathers forgot and fight over anti-Semitic remarks which their fathers ignored. To be a Jew is anger and remorse and guilt and pride.

It has been a long journey, long and fruitful. The America to which Jacob Linderman and Chaim Vrotchnik came almost a century ago was slowly moving toward separatism. American anti-Semitism scarred both their lives. When Samson Wilson was trying to enter medical school in New York, admission deans boasted and joked about their quotas. As a girl, Harriet Cohen learned the word "sheeney." Saul Farberman and Mort Applebaum grew up as "kikes."

Such things have changed. Jews are regarded with tolerance and sometimes even with favor in the world's most favored land. Neither Stuyvesant nor Mather would be happy with the reigning egalitarianism. University quotas have been outlawed in New York State. Almost everywhere, Jewish children mature without the influences of epithets. For all the bigotry that endures, the movement of this era is toward an end of anti-Semitism. Jefferson and Adams would approve. Such currents change, but for Jews in America now, the time is free.

And yet among the freedoms, Jews remember. Two of Harry Wolf's uncles "disappeared" from Austria during the Holocaust. Sixteen of Bernard Rogovin's East European relatives were killed. Even Harry Goldenrammer lost cousins. It is a strange and troubling thing to live in the warmth of freedom and to remember that the unlined face of five-year-old Mendele Abramovitz was frozen into the rictus of death not so many winters ago. How old would Mendele be now? Thirty-two or thirty-five. Perhaps he would have come to America, a fair and gentle Jew. A *mensch*.

The Jewish American who studies recent history and who thinks, at once wins agony. American Jews are studiers whose thinking does them proud; their agony shows all about us. Perhaps an American Jew pours out his heart too indiscriminately, or extends his compassion too carelessly, or trumpets his success too loudly or punishes a sniveling anti-Semite more fiercely than the creature deserves. Perhaps his laugh is raucous and too often he yields to tears.

American Jews are not placid in their comfort. How could

they be? As Jews they are not yet a full generation distant from slaughter. But almost precisely in proportion to the freedom that the United States extends them, the Jews of America, these passionate people, do honor to themselves and to mankind.

# An Acknowledgment

I am grateful to Hillel Black of William Morrow for the care and devotion he lavished on my manuscript. His attentions were flattering and invaluable.

A number of people in the editorial offices of the *Saturday Evening Post* were particularly kind. I am grateful to William A. Emerson, Jr., the editor, who was generous in his confidence, and to the Curtis Editorial Library staff directed by Mrs. Lia Smits, which was generous with research assistance.

Richard Salutin, a remarkable young scholar, variously provided encouragement, the case for *Yahveh* and research into religious matters. I look forward eventually to reading books of his own.

Sterling Lord, my agent, established contractual arrangements for the book which freed me from the need to hurry my work. No single consideration was more important.

I compiled lists of people to see from a number of sources. Major Jewish organizations made hundreds of names available. Newspaper editors helped me find unorganized, unaffiliated Jews. In each of the forty-one communities that I considered, people led on to people and way led on to way.

I thank the following individuals for their assistance:

Morris B. Abram, Mrs. Samuel Adelman for the late Rabbi Samuel Adelman, Mrs. Ita K. Adelstein, Harry Alderman, Frank Angelo, Colonel Jacob Arvey, the Honorable Walton Bachrach, Dr. Max W. Bay, Rabbi Leonard I. Beerman, Dr. Samuel Belkin, Nathan C. Belth, Mandel Berenbaum, Rabbi Elmer Berger, Mr. and Mrs. Philip I. Berman, Philip Bernstein, Theodore Bikel, Professor Joseph Blav, Sam Bloom, Mr. and Mrs. Aaron Bohrod, John Bugas, Mr. and Mrs. Milton Carey, Professor Stanley F. Chyet, Richard Cohen, David S. Collins, Robert Cromie, Aaron Cushman, Norman Davis, Rabbi Maurice N. Eisendrath, Jack Eisner, Milton Ellerin, C.

V. Ellwell, Benjamin Epstein, Professor Leonard J. Fein, Benjy Feldman, Mr. and Mrs. Cy Feldman, Dr. Louis Finkelstein, Max M. Fisher, George Friede, Andrew Gaynor, Dr. Nelson Glueck, Rabbi Aaron S. Gold, Judge Harry D. Goldman, Dr. Jacob E. Goldman, Joe H. Golman, Henry Goodman, Jerry Goodman, Dr. Samuel Goodside, Shecky Greene, Hank M. Greenspun, Robert D. Gries, Norman Hahn, Rabbi Abraham Joshua Heschel, Rabbi Eugene Hibshman, Palmer Hoyt, Charles Hubbs, Louis R. Hurwitz, Rabbi Leo Jung, Rabbi Joseph Kaminetsky, Mr. and Mrs. Marvin Kastenbaum, Rabbi and Mrs. C. E. H. Kauvar, Richard Korn, Rabbi Yehuda Krinsky, Rabbi Norman Lamm, Dr. Harry Levinson, Ambassador Sol M. Linowitz, Stanley H. Lowell, Mr. and Mrs. Will Maslow, Mrs. Anna Walling Matson, Miles McMillin, Garson Meyer, Rabbi Israel Miller, Miss Betty Millman, Mrs. Norma Moss, Emanuel Muravchik, Dr. Isidore S. Meyer, Dr. Alfred Neuman, Gabe Paul, Steven Prystowsky, Herbert Rand, Dr. Lawrence Ritter, Albert Ropfogel, Leonard Ropfogel, Zeke Rose, Al Rosen, Judge Charles Rosenbaum, Mrs. John Rosenfield for the late John Rosenfield, August Rothschild, Manheim S. Shapiro, Dr. John Slawson, Richard D. Smyser, Neil Sandberg, Rabbi Edward T. Sandrow, Julius Schatz, Dr. John Scheinen, Harvey Schechter, Murray Seasongood, Rabbi Bernard Segal, Dr. Ralph Segalman, Nathan Shapell, Julius Sheppes, Robert E. Sinton, Howard Squadron, Sheldon Steinhauser, Phillip Stollman, Robert Sunshine, Rabbi Manfred Swarzensky, Benjamin H. Swig, Rabbi Marc H. Tanenbaum, Charles Tobias, Jr., Bill Veeck, Sidney Vincent, Albert Vorspan, Rabbi Jacob J. Weinstein, Larry Weiss, Mr. and Mrs. William L. White, Rabbi Arnold Jacob Wolf, Rabbi Daniel Wolk, Morton Yarmon, Anson Yeager, Professor Irving Younger, Dr. Walter P. Zand, Al Zipser and Tony Zoppi. My apologies to anyone whose name I have overlooked.

Although many of these people provided source material, none is responsible for the accuracy of the book. That responsibility, like the viewpoint, is mine.

Misses Margaret Beall and Beverly Cummings typed the manuscript. Miss Eva Zucker transcribed many of the tape recordings I made. Mrs. Miriam Black compiled the index. Mrs. Olga R. Kahn contributed historical data.

My sons, Gordon J. and Roger L., endured varying degrees of abandonment while I worked and traveled. They bore up well, as the good sports they are. However, I am grateful to Mrs. Joan Brackbill, who assumed command of one obstreperous young man at a critical point when his mother and I were forced to leave him.

I have no words to thank my wife, Alice Russell Kahn. While raising children, keeping house, balancing checkbooks and cooking, she found time and heart to devote herself to my work as if it were her own. In my want, perhaps another's words suffice:

*Sweet lady,*
    *Here have I read for certain that my ships*
*Are safely come to road.*

ROGER KAHN
New York, New York
1968

# Index